image® COMICS PRESENTS

PvP PLAYER VS. PLAYER goes BANANAS!

BY SCOTT R. KURTZ

Collecting issues 19-24 of PvP, Vol. 2
Originally published by Image Comics

FOR IMAGE COMICS

Erik Larsen - Publisher
Todd McFarlane - President
Marc Silvestri - CEO
Jim Valentino - Vice-President

Eric Stephenson - Executive Director
Mark Haven Britt - Director of Marketing
Thao Le - Accounts Manager
Traci Hui - Administrative Assistant
Joe Keatinge - Traffic Manager
Allen Hui - Production Manager
Jonathan Chan - Production Artist
Drew Gill - Production Artist
Chris Giarrusso - Production Artist

www.imagecomics.com

For Kirby.

CHOOSE YOUR PLAYER

1P PRESS A TO SELECT

COLE RICHARDS
Editor in Chief

SPECIAL MOVE:
Assign Overtime.

The glue that holds PvP together, Cole tries to retain a small semblance of sanity amidst the chaos of his employees. This makes him an obvious target. Confused and disturbed by the latest computer game releases, Cole is happiest playing classic 80's arcade game emulators on his computer.

BRENT SIENNA
Creative Director

SPECIAL MOVE:
Caffeine Rage

Brent has little time to play computer games, however he always finds time to mock those who do. Pretentious and pompous, Brent is the master of the inappropriate comment. Despite his rough exterior, he's managed to show Jade his softer side and the two have become romantically involved.

JADE FONTAINE
Lead Staff Writer

SPECIAL MOVE:
"The Stare"

"Women play games too." That's what Jade Fontaine wants to tell the world. Jade can compete with the best of the boys but prefers the escape of a good online RPG and is hopelessly addicted to chat and email. Despite herself, Jade has fallen for Brent Sienna, the Magazine's Creative Director.

FRANCIS OTTOMAN
Tech Support

SPECIAL MOVE:
Spinning Cobra Clutch

If you have ever wanted to kill someone you've met online, then you know Francis Ray Ottoman. That's not to say that Francis is all bad, he does call in sick every once in a while. Francis knows everything there is to know about gaming, mostly because his life revolves around it.

CHOOSE YOUR PLAYER

PREPARE FOR HUMOR BATTLE!

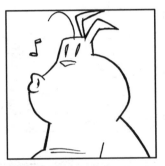

SKULL
The Troll

SPECIAL MOVE:
Stand Dumbfounded

▣

The heart of PvP Magazine lies deep within the chest of this gentle giant. Skull was living in the janitor's closet when the staff moved in. Being a creature of Myth, Skull's only need is attention; something the staff is more than willing to provide. Skull holds the position of intern, a title he's quite proud of.

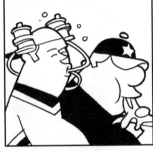

ROBBIE & JASE
Charity Cases.

SPECIAL MOVE:
Convert beer to pee

▣ ▣ ▣ P

Their asses firmly attached to their old couch, these two ex-jocks spend all day playing sports games, drinking beer and eating junk food. Despite his better judgment, Cole can't bring himself to fire Robbie and Jase, who he used to dorm with back in college. The two serve no practical function whatsoever.

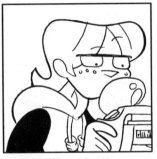

Marcy Wisniewsky
World's top ranked cyber-athlete

SPECIAL MOVE:
Invincibility.

↓ → ▣

Little is known about this fifteen year old spitfire who goes by the online name DEVILFISH. Not only did she steal Francis' title, but she seems to have stolen his heart. Whether this is simply friendly competition or the start of something more remains to be seen.

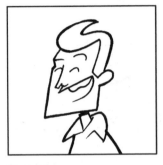

Max Powers
The Jerk

SPECIAL MOVE:
Passive Aggressive attack

↙ ↙ L ⊗

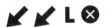

Years ago, something happened between Cole and Max that turned Cole sour. Years later, Max has popped up again to be a thorn in Cole's side. He started a rival video-game review magazine and set up his own offices in the same building, just one floor above the PvP offices.

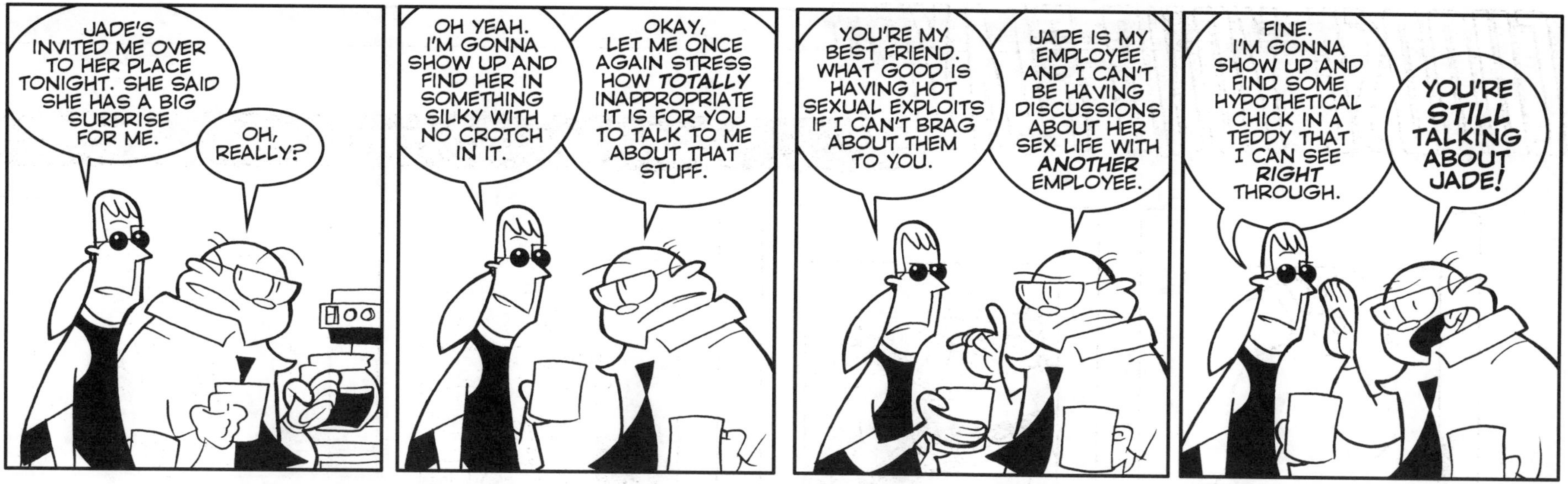
JADE'S INVITED ME OVER TO HER PLACE TONIGHT. SHE SAID SHE HAS A BIG SURPRISE FOR ME.
OH, REALLY?
OH YEAH. I'M GONNA SHOW UP AND FIND HER IN SOMETHING SILKY WITH NO CROTCH IN IT.
OKAY, LET ME ONCE AGAIN STRESS HOW *TOTALLY* INAPPROPRIATE IT IS FOR YOU TO TALK TO ME ABOUT THAT STUFF.
YOU'RE MY BEST FRIEND. WHAT GOOD IS HAVING HOT SEXUAL EXPLOITS IF I CAN'T BRAG ABOUT THEM TO YOU.
JADE IS MY EMPLOYEE AND I CAN'T BE HAVING DISCUSSIONS ABOUT HER SEX LIFE WITH *ANOTHER* EMPLOYEE.
FINE. I'M GONNA SHOW UP AND FIND SOME HYPOTHETICAL CHICK IN A TEDDY THAT I CAN SEE *RIGHT* THROUGH.
YOU'RE *STILL* TALKING ABOUT JADE!

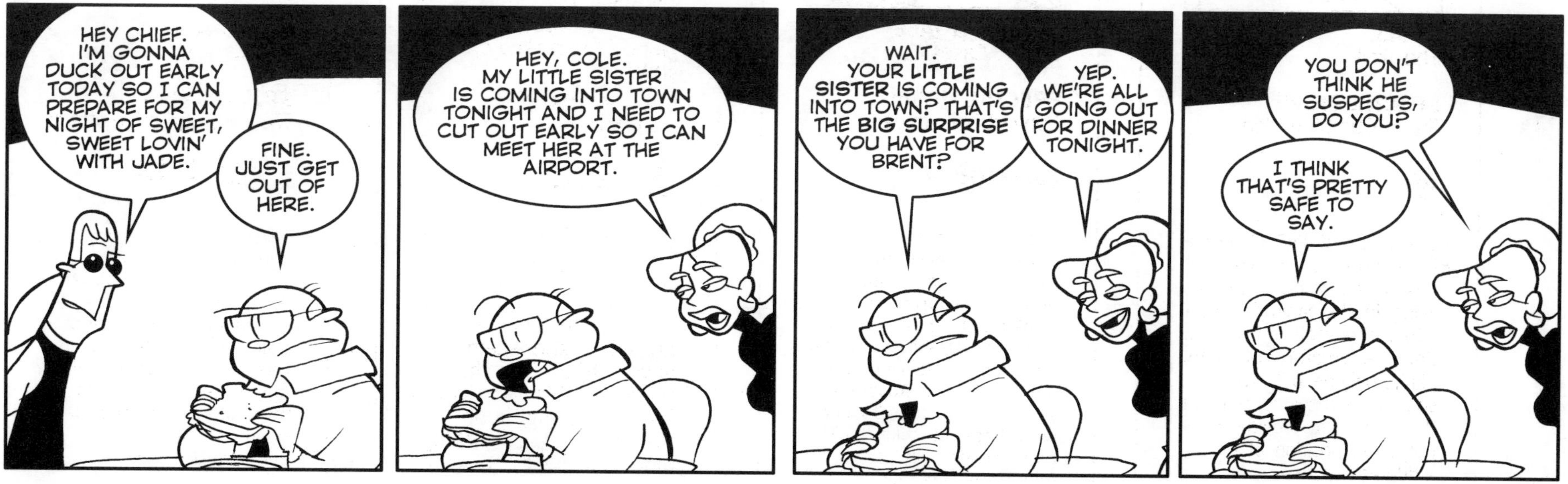
HEY CHIEF. I'M GONNA DUCK OUT EARLY TODAY SO I CAN PREPARE FOR MY NIGHT OF SWEET, SWEET LOVIN' WITH JADE.
FINE. JUST GET OUT OF HERE.
HEY, COLE. MY LITTLE SISTER IS COMING INTO TOWN TONIGHT AND I NEED TO CUT OUT EARLY SO I CAN MEET HER AT THE AIRPORT.
WAIT. YOUR **LITTLE SISTER** IS COMING INTO TOWN? THAT'S THE **BIG SURPRISE** YOU HAVE FOR BRENT?
YEP. WE'RE ALL GOING OUT FOR DINNER TONIGHT.
YOU DON'T THINK HE SUSPECTS, DO YOU?
I THINK THAT'S PRETTY SAFE TO SAY.

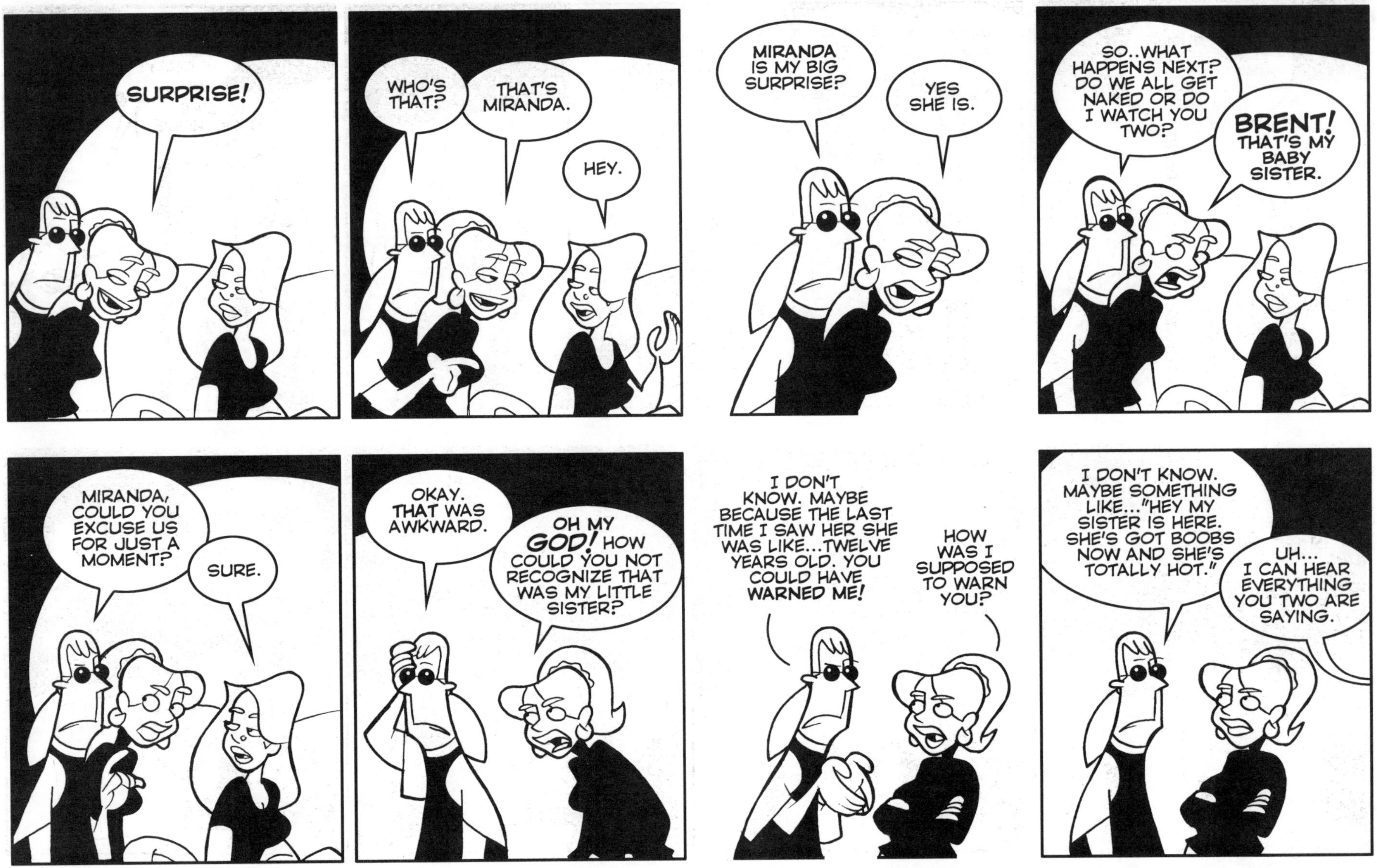
SURPRISE!
WHO'S THAT?
THAT'S MIRANDA.
HEY.
MIRANDA IS MY BIG SURPRISE?
YES SHE IS.
SO..WHAT HAPPENS NEXT? DO WE ALL GET NAKED OR DO I WATCH YOU TWO?
BRENT! THAT'S MY BABY SISTER.
MIRANDA, COULD YOU EXCUSE US FOR JUST A MOMENT?
SURE.
OKAY. THAT WAS AWKWARD.
OH MY GOD! HOW COULD YOU NOT RECOGNIZE THAT WAS MY LITTLE SISTER?
I DON'T KNOW. MAYBE BECAUSE THE LAST TIME I SAW HER SHE WAS LIKE...TWELVE YEARS OLD. YOU COULD HAVE WARNED ME!
HOW WAS I SUPPOSED TO WARN YOU?
I DON'T KNOW. MAYBE SOMETHING LIKE..."HEY MY SISTER IS HERE. SHE'S GOT BOOBS NOW AND SHE'S TOTALLY HOT."
UH... I CAN HEAR EVERYTHING YOU TWO ARE SAYING.

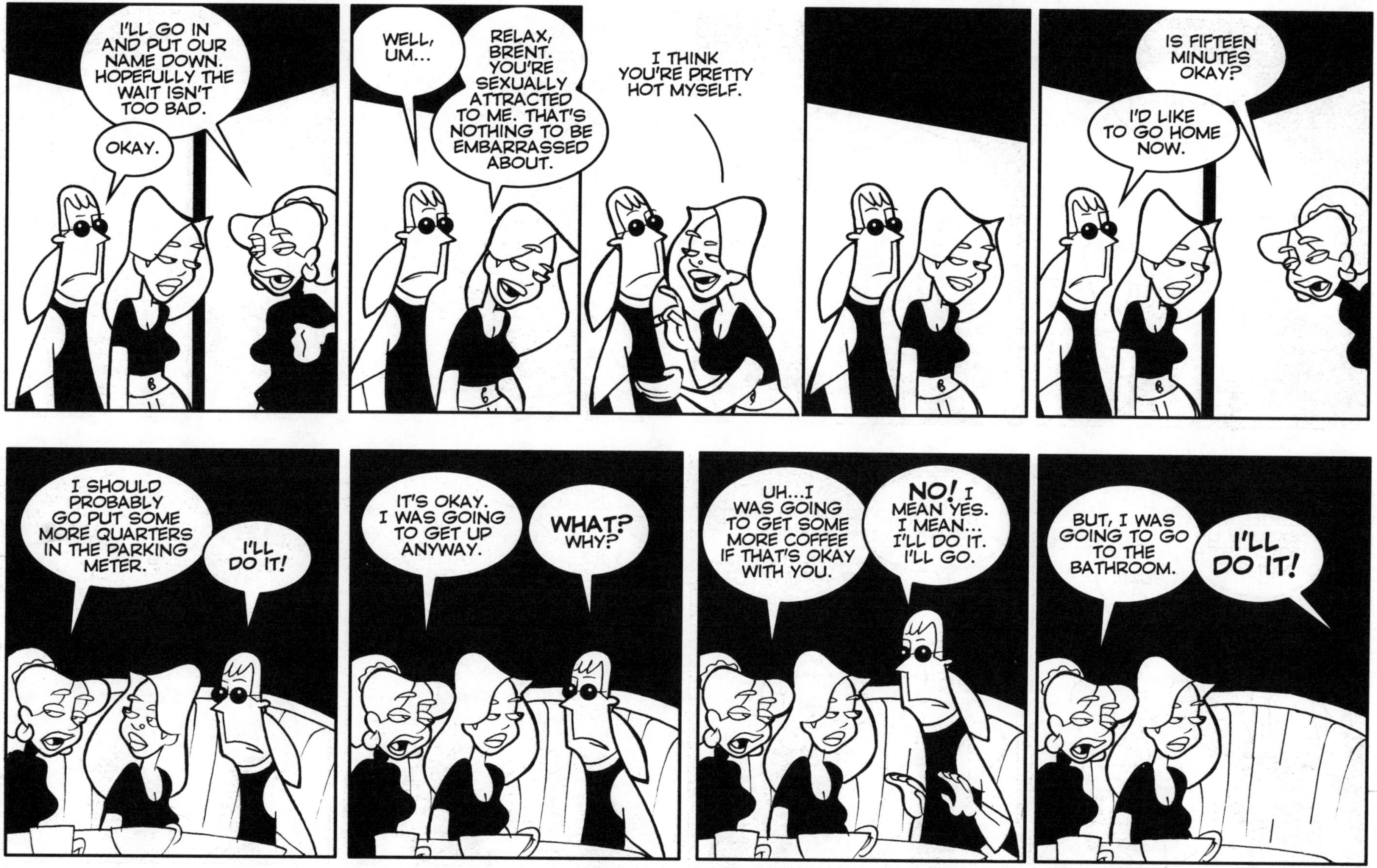
I'LL GO IN AND PUT OUR NAME DOWN. HOPEFULLY THE WAIT ISN'T TOO BAD.
OKAY.
WELL, UM...
RELAX, BRENT. YOU'RE SEXUALLY ATTRACTED TO ME. THAT'S NOTHING TO BE EMBARRASSED ABOUT.
I THINK YOU'RE PRETTY HOT MYSELF.
IS FIFTEEN MINUTES OKAY?
I'D LIKE TO GO HOME NOW.
I SHOULD PROBABLY GO PUT SOME MORE QUARTERS IN THE PARKING METER.
I'LL DO IT!
IT'S OKAY. I WAS GOING TO GET UP ANYWAY.
WHAT? WHY?
UH...I WAS GOING TO GET SOME MORE COFFEE IF THAT'S OKAY WITH YOU.
NO! I MEAN YES. I MEAN... I'LL DO IT. I'LL GO.
BUT, I WAS GOING TO GO TO THE BATHROOM.
I'LL DO IT!

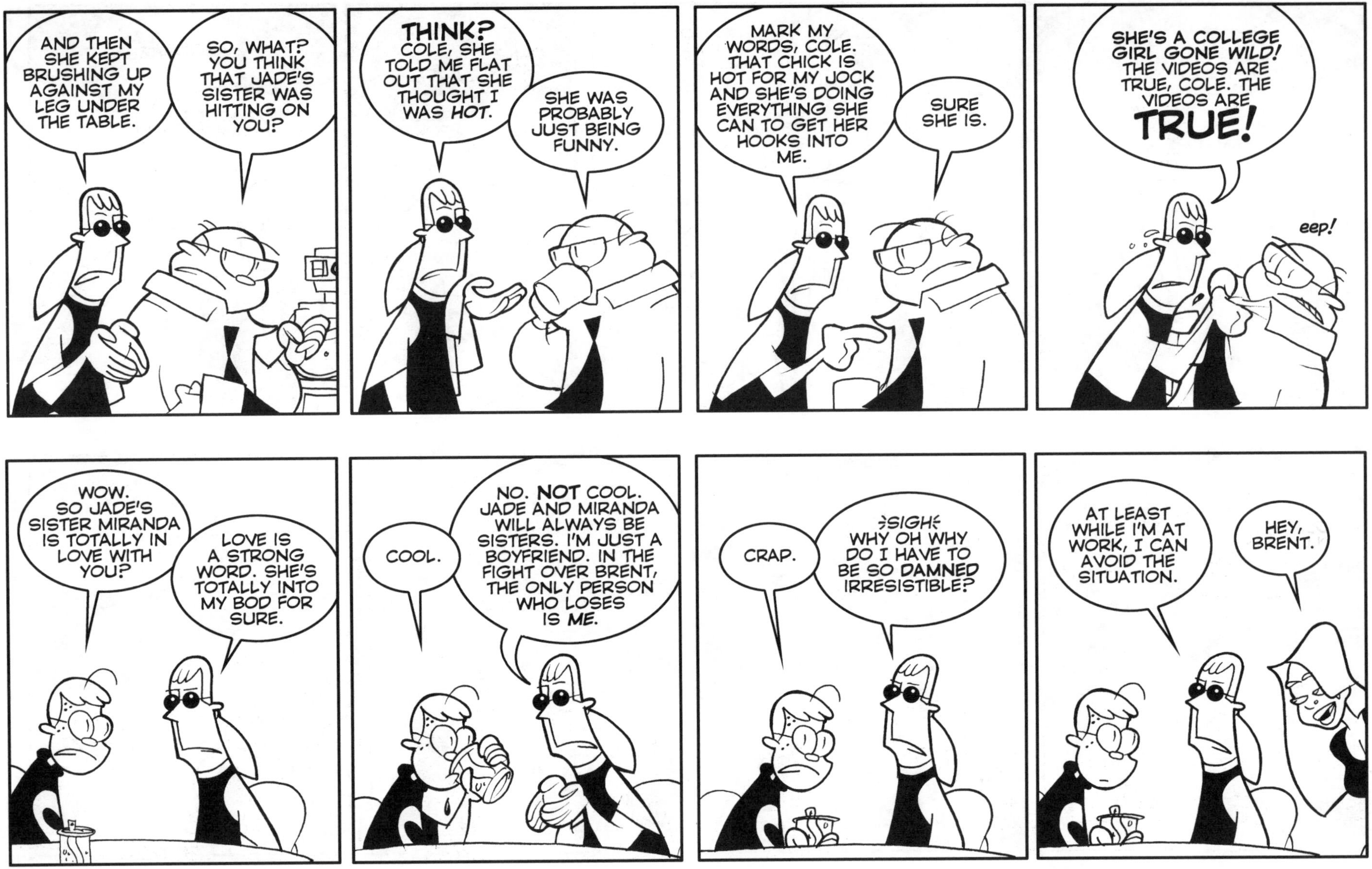
AND THEN SHE KEPT BRUSHING UP AGAINST MY LEG UNDER THE TABLE.
SO, WHAT? YOU THINK THAT JADE'S SISTER WAS HITTING ON YOU?
THINK? COLE, SHE TOLD ME FLAT OUT THAT SHE THOUGHT I WAS HOT.
SHE WAS PROBABLY JUST BEING FUNNY.
MARK MY WORDS, COLE. THAT CHICK IS HOT FOR MY JOCK AND SHE'S DOING EVERYTHING SHE CAN TO GET HER HOOKS INTO ME.
SURE SHE IS.
SHE'S A COLLEGE GIRL GONE WILD! THE VIDEOS ARE TRUE, COLE. THE VIDEOS ARE TRUE!
eep!
WOW. SO JADE'S SISTER MIRANDA IS TOTALLY IN LOVE WITH YOU?
LOVE IS A STRONG WORD. SHE'S TOTALLY INTO MY BOD FOR SURE.
COOL.
NO. NOT COOL. JADE AND MIRANDA WILL ALWAYS BE SISTERS. I'M JUST A BOYFRIEND. IN THE FIGHT OVER BRENT, THE ONLY PERSON WHO LOSES IS ME.
CRAP.
SIGH
WHY OH WHY DO I HAVE TO BE SO DAMNED IRRESISTIBLE?
AT LEAST WHILE I'M AT WORK, I CAN AVOID THE SITUATION.
HEY, BRENT.

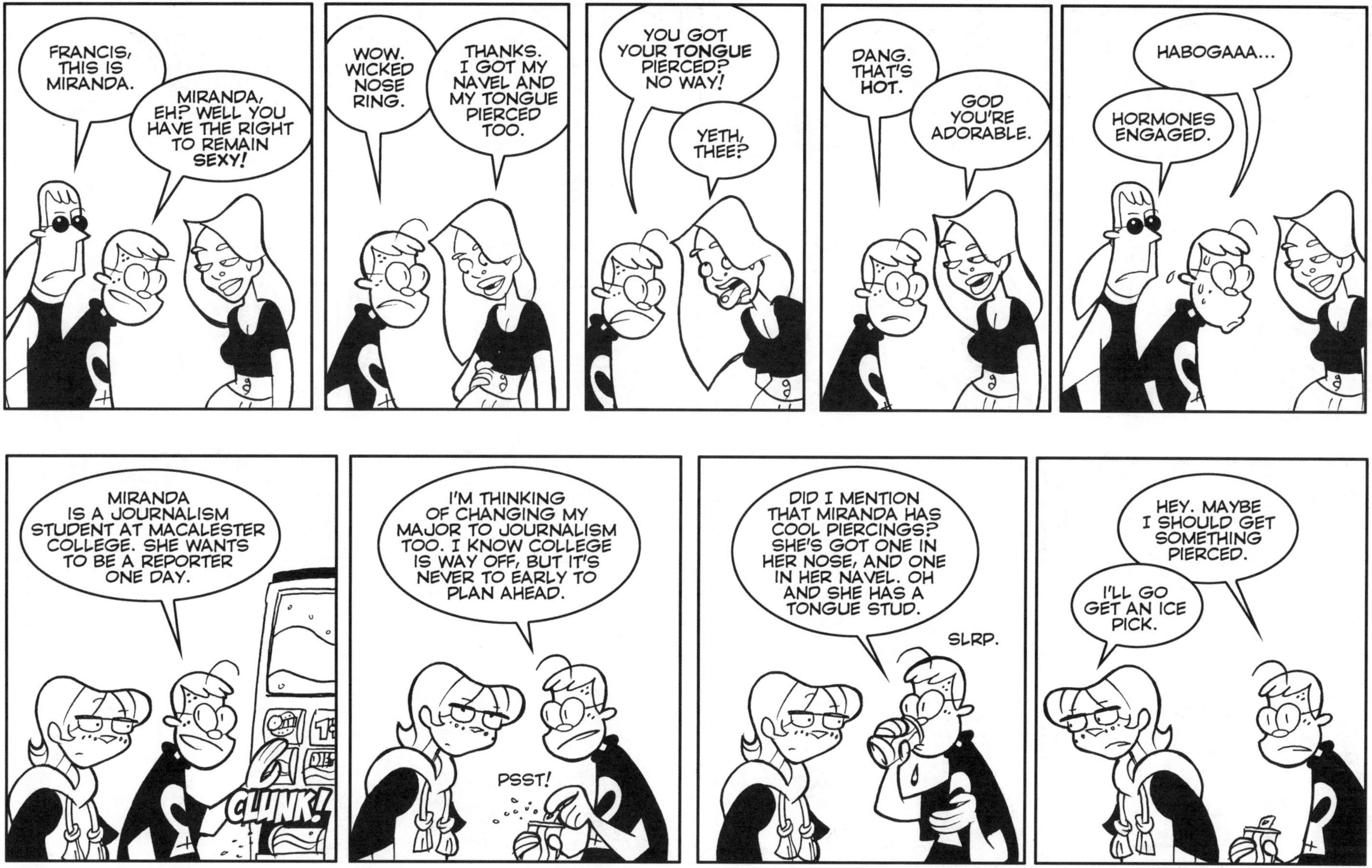
FRANCIS, THIS IS MIRANDA.
MIRANDA, EH? WELL YOU HAVE THE RIGHT TO REMAIN SEXY!
WOW. WICKED NOSE RING.
THANKS. I GOT MY NAVEL AND MY TONGUE PIERCED TOO.
YOU GOT YOUR TONGUE PIERCED? NO WAY!
YETH, THEE?
DANG. THAT'S HOT.
GOD YOU'RE ADORABLE.
HABOGAAA...
HORMONES ENGAGED.
MIRANDA IS A JOURNALISM STUDENT AT MACALESTER COLLEGE. SHE WANTS TO BE A REPORTER ONE DAY.
CLUNK!
I'M THINKING OF CHANGING MY MAJOR TO JOURNALISM TOO. I KNOW COLLEGE IS WAY OFF, BUT IT'S NEVER TO EARLY TO PLAN AHEAD.
PSST!
DID I MENTION THAT MIRANDA HAS COOL PIERCINGS? SHE'S GOT ONE IN HER NOSE, AND ONE IN HER NAVEL. OH AND SHE HAS A TONGUE STUD.
SLRP.
HEY. MAYBE I SHOULD GET SOMETHING PIERCED.
I'LL GO GET AN ICE PICK.

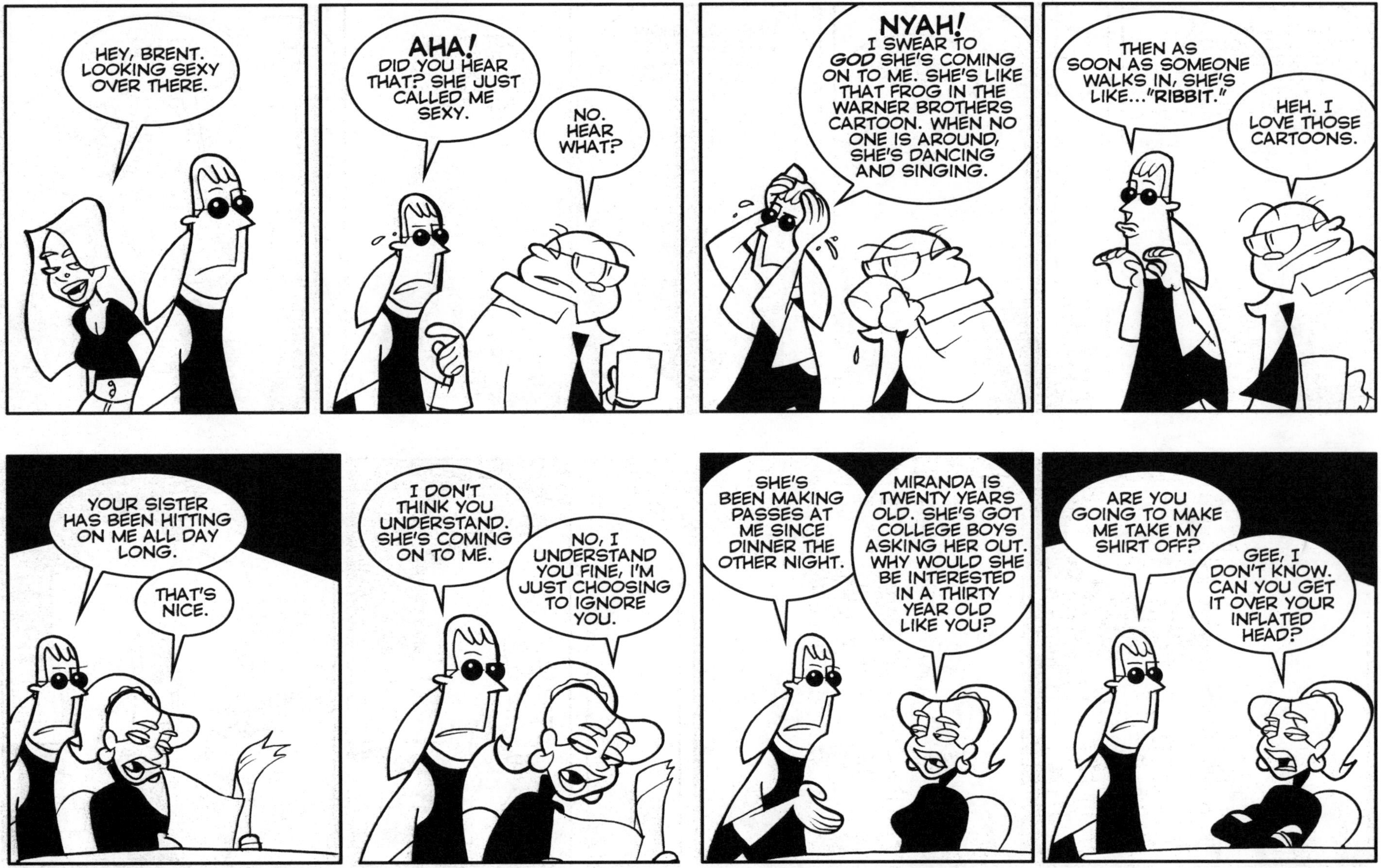
HEY, BRENT. LOOKING SEXY OVER THERE.
AHA! DID YOU HEAR THAT? SHE JUST CALLED ME SEXY.
NO. HEAR WHAT?
NYAH! I SWEAR TO GOD SHE'S COMING ON TO ME. SHE'S LIKE THAT FROG IN THE WARNER BROTHERS CARTOON. WHEN NO ONE IS AROUND, SHE'S DANCING AND SINGING.
THEN AS SOON AS SOMEONE WALKS IN, SHE'S LIKE..."RIBBIT."
HEH. I LOVE THOSE CARTOONS.
YOUR SISTER HAS BEEN HITTING ON ME ALL DAY LONG.
THAT'S NICE.
I DON'T THINK YOU UNDERSTAND. SHE'S COMING ON TO ME.
NO, I UNDERSTAND YOU FINE, I'M JUST CHOOSING TO IGNORE YOU.
SHE'S BEEN MAKING PASSES AT ME SINCE DINNER THE OTHER NIGHT.
MIRANDA IS TWENTY YEARS OLD. SHE'S GOT COLLEGE BOYS ASKING HER OUT. WHY WOULD SHE BE INTERESTED IN A THIRTY YEAR OLD LIKE YOU?
ARE YOU GOING TO MAKE ME TAKE MY SHIRT OFF?
GEE, I DON'T KNOW. CAN YOU GET IT OVER YOUR INFLATED HEAD?

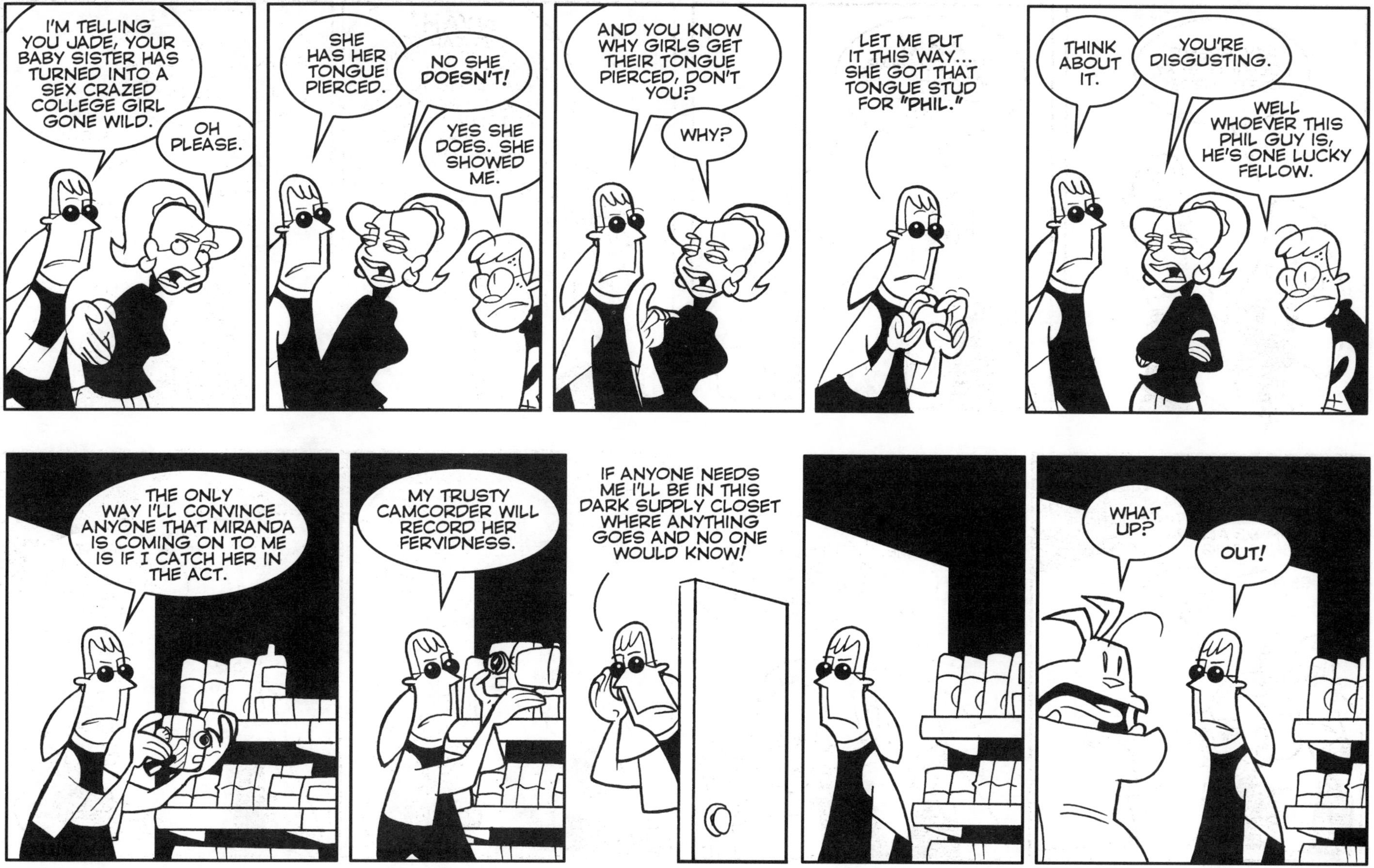
I'M TELLING YOU JADE, YOUR BABY SISTER HAS TURNED INTO A SEX CRAZED COLLEGE GIRL GONE WILD.
OH PLEASE.
SHE HAS HER TONGUE PIERCED.
NO SHE DOESN'T!
YES SHE DOES. SHE SHOWED ME.
AND YOU KNOW WHY GIRLS GET THEIR TONGUE PIERCED, DON'T YOU?
WHY?
LET ME PUT IT THIS WAY... SHE GOT THAT TONGUE STUD FOR "PHIL."
THINK ABOUT IT.
YOU'RE DISGUSTING.
WELL WHOEVER THIS PHIL GUY IS, HE'S ONE LUCKY FELLOW.
THE ONLY WAY I'LL CONVINCE ANYONE THAT MIRANDA IS COMING ON TO ME IS IF I CATCH HER IN THE ACT.
MY TRUSTY CAMCORDER WILL RECORD HER FERVIDNESS.
IF ANYONE NEEDS ME I'LL BE IN THIS DARK SUPPLY CLOSET WHERE ANYTHING GOES AND NO ONE WOULD KNOW!
WHAT UP?
OUT!

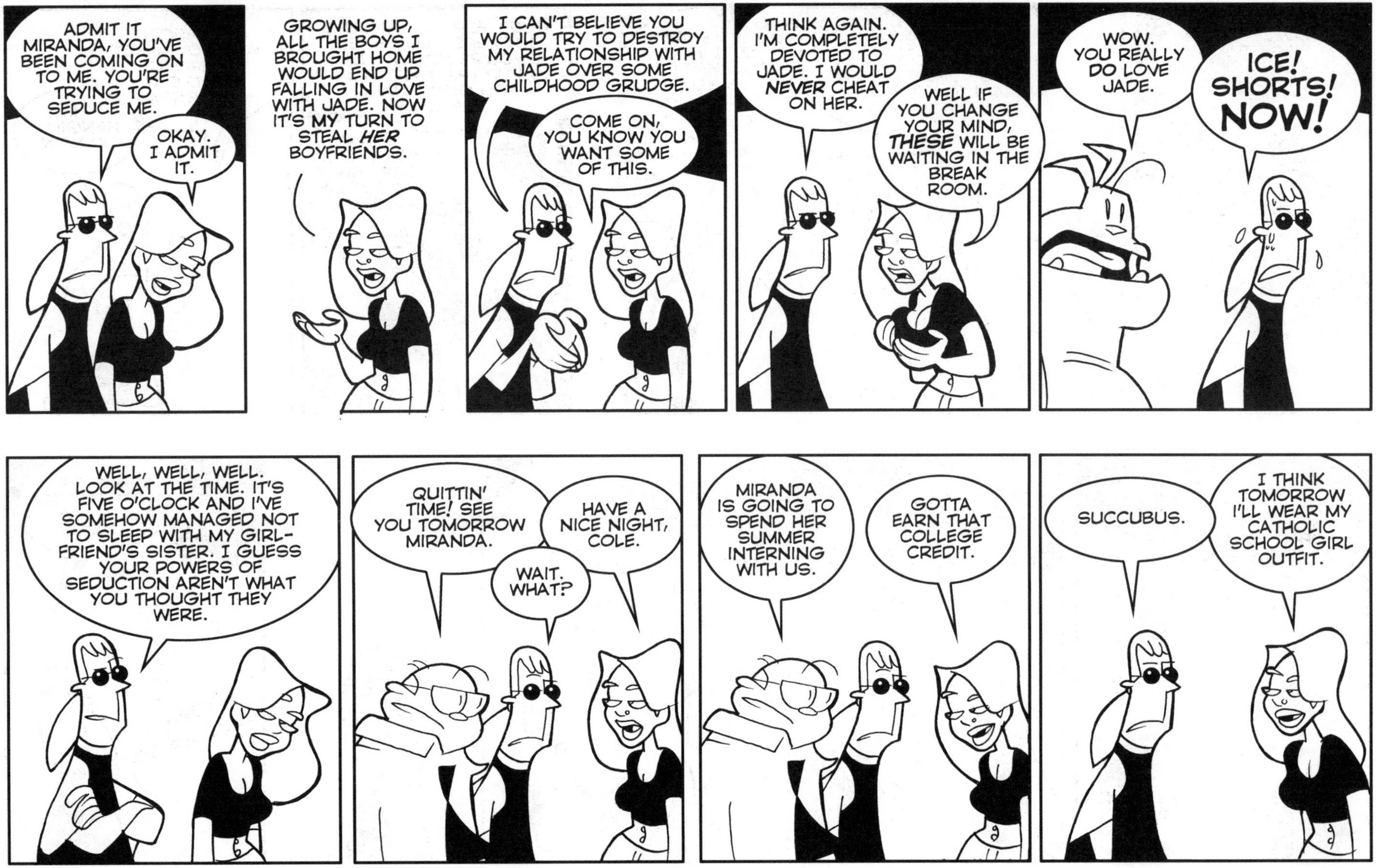
ADMIT IT MIRANDA, YOU'VE BEEN COMING ON TO ME. YOU'RE TRYING TO SEDUCE ME.
OKAY. I ADMIT IT.
GROWING UP, ALL THE BOYS I BROUGHT HOME WOULD END UP FALLING IN LOVE WITH JADE. NOW IT'S MY TURN TO STEAL *HER* BOYFRIENDS.
I CAN'T BELIEVE YOU WOULD TRY TO DESTROY MY RELATIONSHIP WITH JADE OVER SOME CHILDHOOD GRUDGE.
COME ON, YOU KNOW YOU WANT SOME OF THIS.
THINK AGAIN. I'M COMPLETELY DEVOTED TO JADE. I WOULD *NEVER* CHEAT ON HER.
WELL IF YOU CHANGE YOUR MIND, *THESE* WILL BE WAITING IN THE BREAK ROOM.
WOW. YOU REALLY DO LOVE JADE.
ICE! SHORTS! NOW!
WELL, WELL, WELL. LOOK AT THE TIME. IT'S FIVE O'CLOCK AND I'VE SOMEHOW MANAGED NOT TO SLEEP WITH MY GIRL-FRIEND'S SISTER. I GUESS YOUR POWERS OF SEDUCTION AREN'T WHAT YOU THOUGHT THEY WERE.
QUITTIN' TIME! SEE YOU TOMORROW MIRANDA.
HAVE A NICE NIGHT, COLE.
WAIT. WHAT?
MIRANDA IS GOING TO SPEND HER SUMMER INTERNING WITH US.
GOTTA EARN THAT COLLEGE CREDIT.
SUCCUBUS.
I THINK TOMORROW I'LL WEAR MY CATHOLIC SCHOOL GIRL OUTFIT.

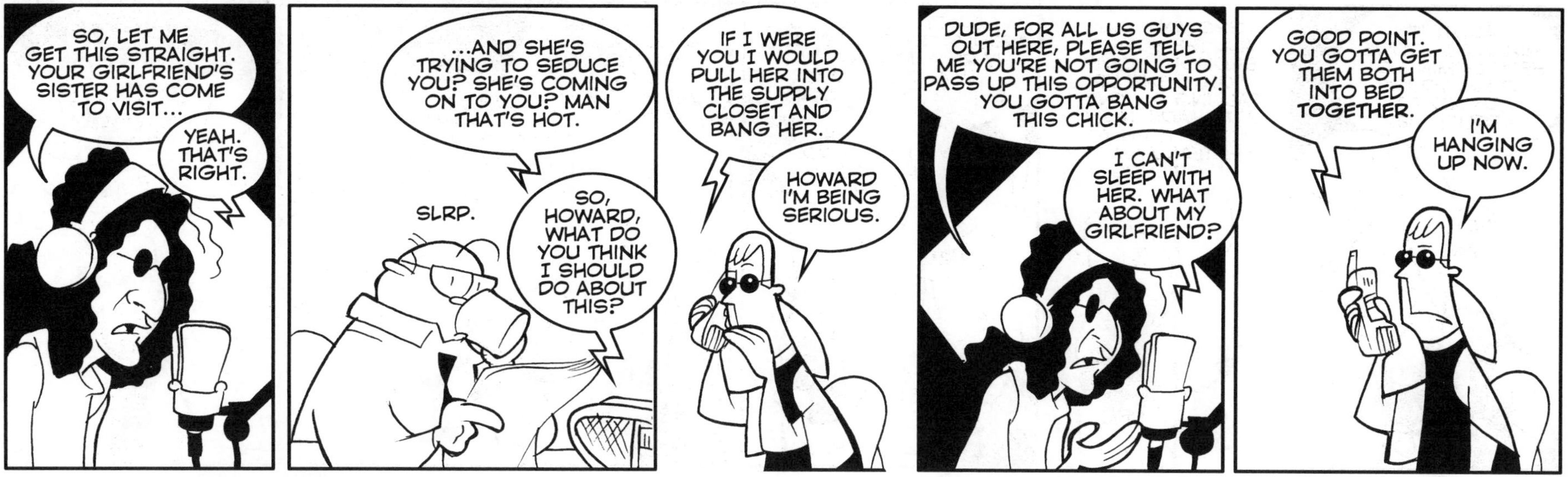
SO, LET ME GET THIS STRAIGHT. YOUR GIRLFRIEND'S SISTER HAS COME TO VISIT...
YEAH. THAT'S RIGHT.
...AND SHE'S TRYING TO SEDUCE YOU? SHE'S COMING ON TO YOU? MAN THAT'S HOT.
SLRP.
SO, HOWARD, WHAT DO YOU THINK I SHOULD DO ABOUT THIS?
IF I WERE YOU I WOULD PULL HER INTO THE SUPPLY CLOSET AND BANG HER.
HOWARD I'M BEING SERIOUS.
DUDE, FOR ALL US GUYS OUT HERE, PLEASE TELL ME YOU'RE NOT GOING TO PASS UP THIS OPPORTUNITY. YOU GOTTA BANG THIS CHICK.
I CAN'T SLEEP WITH HER. WHAT ABOUT MY GIRLFRIEND?
GOOD POINT. YOU GOTTA GET THEM BOTH INTO BED **TOGETHER**.
I'M HANGING UP NOW.

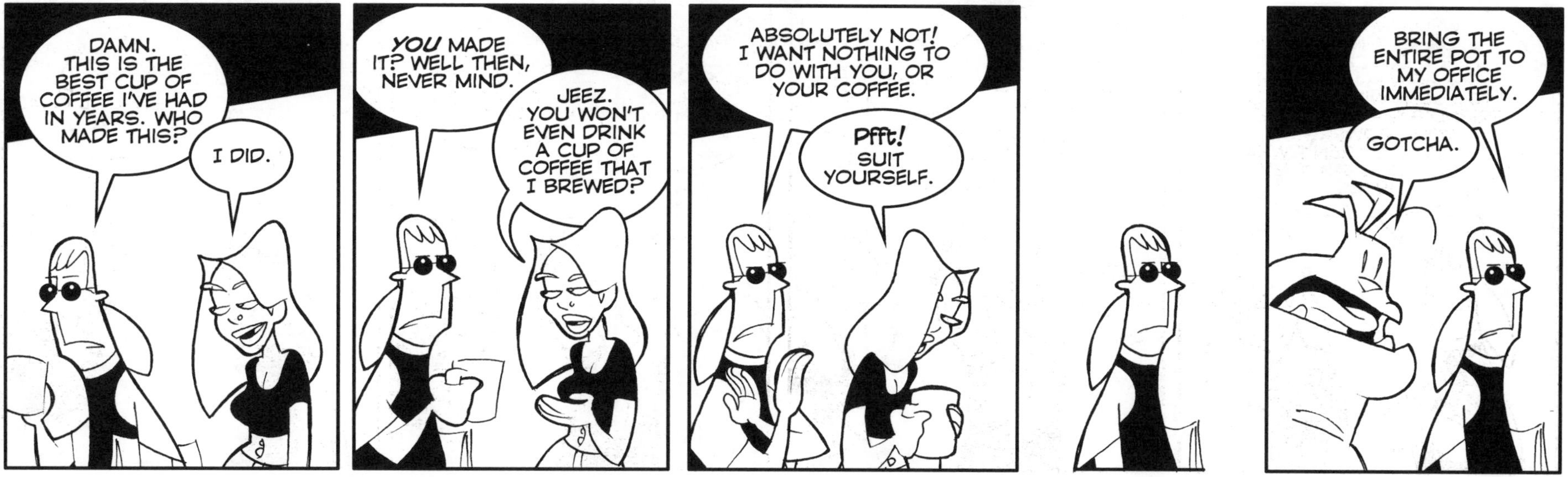
DAMN. THIS IS THE BEST CUP OF COFFEE I'VE HAD IN YEARS. WHO MADE THIS?
I DID.
YOU MADE IT? WELL THEN, NEVER MIND.
JEEZ. YOU WON'T EVEN DRINK A CUP OF COFFEE THAT I BREWED?
ABSOLUTELY NOT! I WANT NOTHING TO DO WITH YOU, OR YOUR COFFEE.
Pfft! SUIT YOURSELF.
BRING THE ENTIRE POT TO MY OFFICE IMMEDIATELY.
GOTCHA.

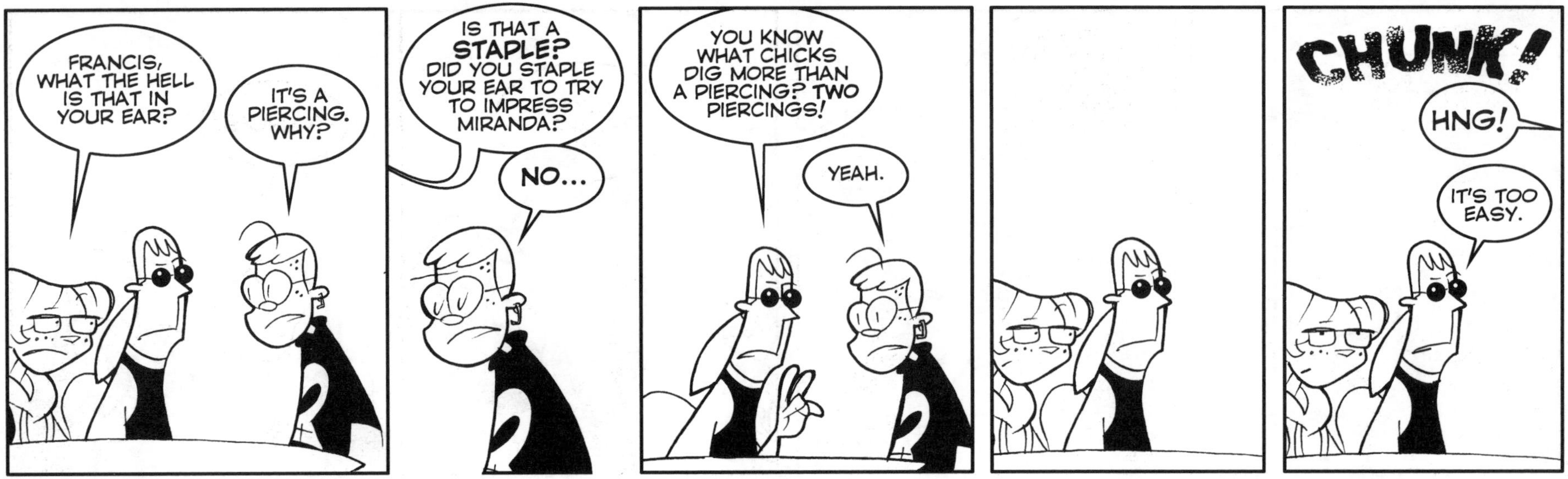
FRANCIS, WHAT THE HELL IS THAT IN YOUR EAR?
IT'S A PIERCING. WHY?
IS THAT A STAPLE? DID YOU STAPLE YOUR EAR TO TRY TO IMPRESS MIRANDA?
NO...
YOU KNOW WHAT CHICKS DIG MORE THAN A PIERCING? TWO PIERCINGS!
YEAH.
CHUNK!
HNG!
IT'S TOO EASY.

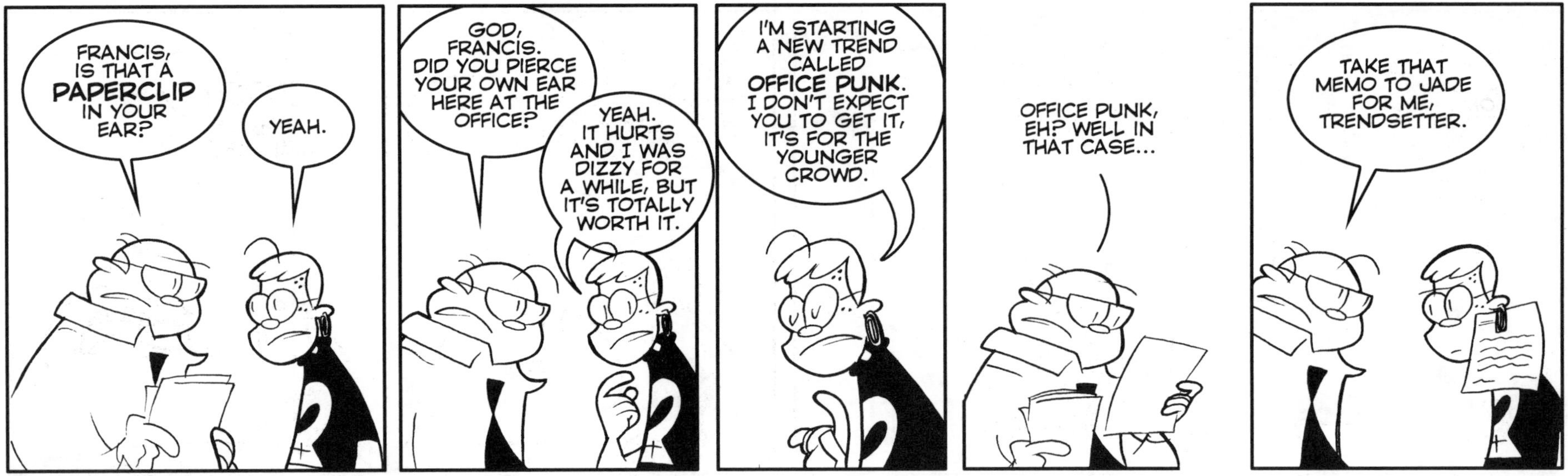
FRANCIS, IS THAT A PAPERCLIP IN YOUR EAR?
YEAH.
GOD, FRANCIS. DID YOU PIERCE YOUR OWN EAR HERE AT THE OFFICE?
YEAH. IT HURTS AND I WAS DIZZY FOR A WHILE, BUT IT'S TOTALLY WORTH IT.
I'M STARTING A NEW TREND CALLED OFFICE PUNK. I DON'T EXPECT YOU TO GET IT, IT'S FOR THE YOUNGER CROWD.
OFFICE PUNK, EH? WELL IN THAT CASE...
TAKE THAT MEMO TO JADE FOR ME, TRENDSETTER.

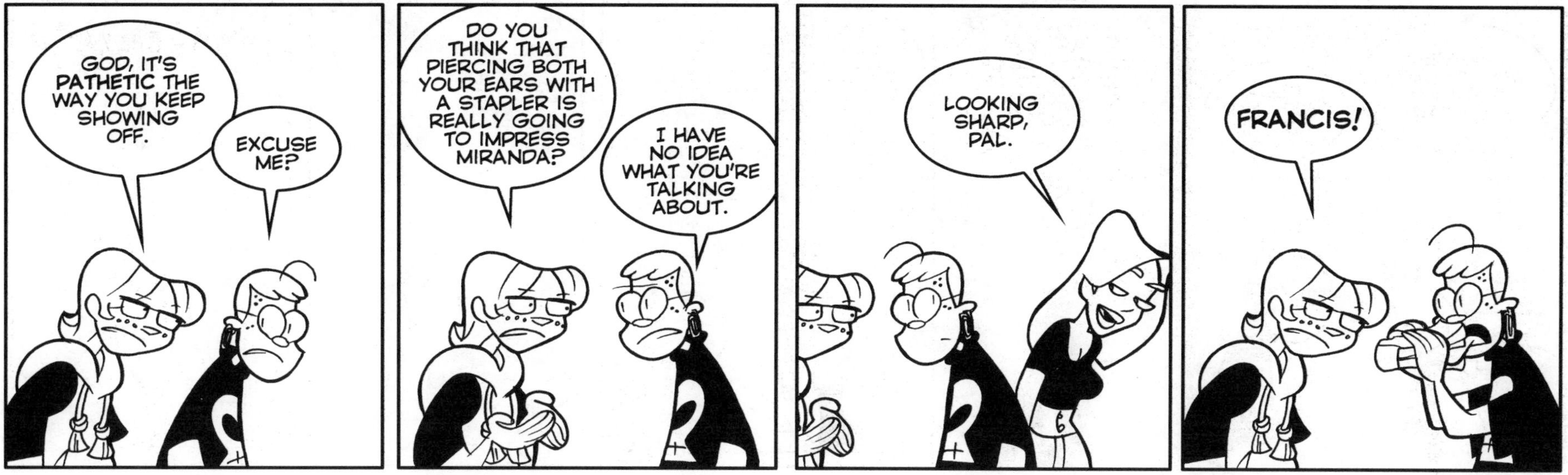

GOD, IT'S PATHETIC THE WAY YOU KEEP SHOWING OFF.
EXCUSE ME?
DO YOU THINK THAT PIERCING BOTH YOUR EARS WITH A STAPLER IS REALLY GOING TO IMPRESS MIRANDA?
I HAVE NO IDEA WHAT YOU'RE TALKING ABOUT.
LOOKING SHARP, PAL.
FRANCIS!

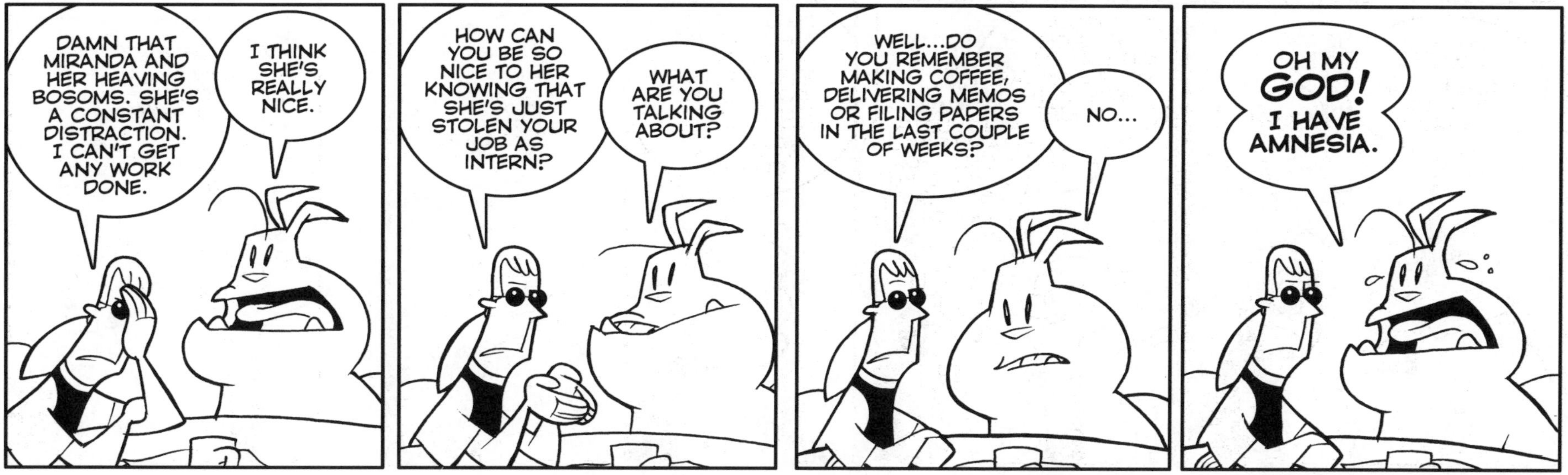

DAMN THAT MIRANDA AND HER HEAVING BOSOMS. SHE'S A CONSTANT DISTRACTION. I CAN'T GET ANY WORK DONE.
I THINK SHE'S REALLY NICE.
HOW CAN YOU BE SO NICE TO HER KNOWING THAT SHE'S JUST STOLEN YOUR JOB AS INTERN?
WHAT ARE YOU TALKING ABOUT?
WELL...DO YOU REMEMBER MAKING COFFEE, DELIVERING MEMOS OR FILING PAPERS IN THE LAST COUPLE OF WEEKS?
NO...
OH MY GOD! I HAVE AMNESIA.

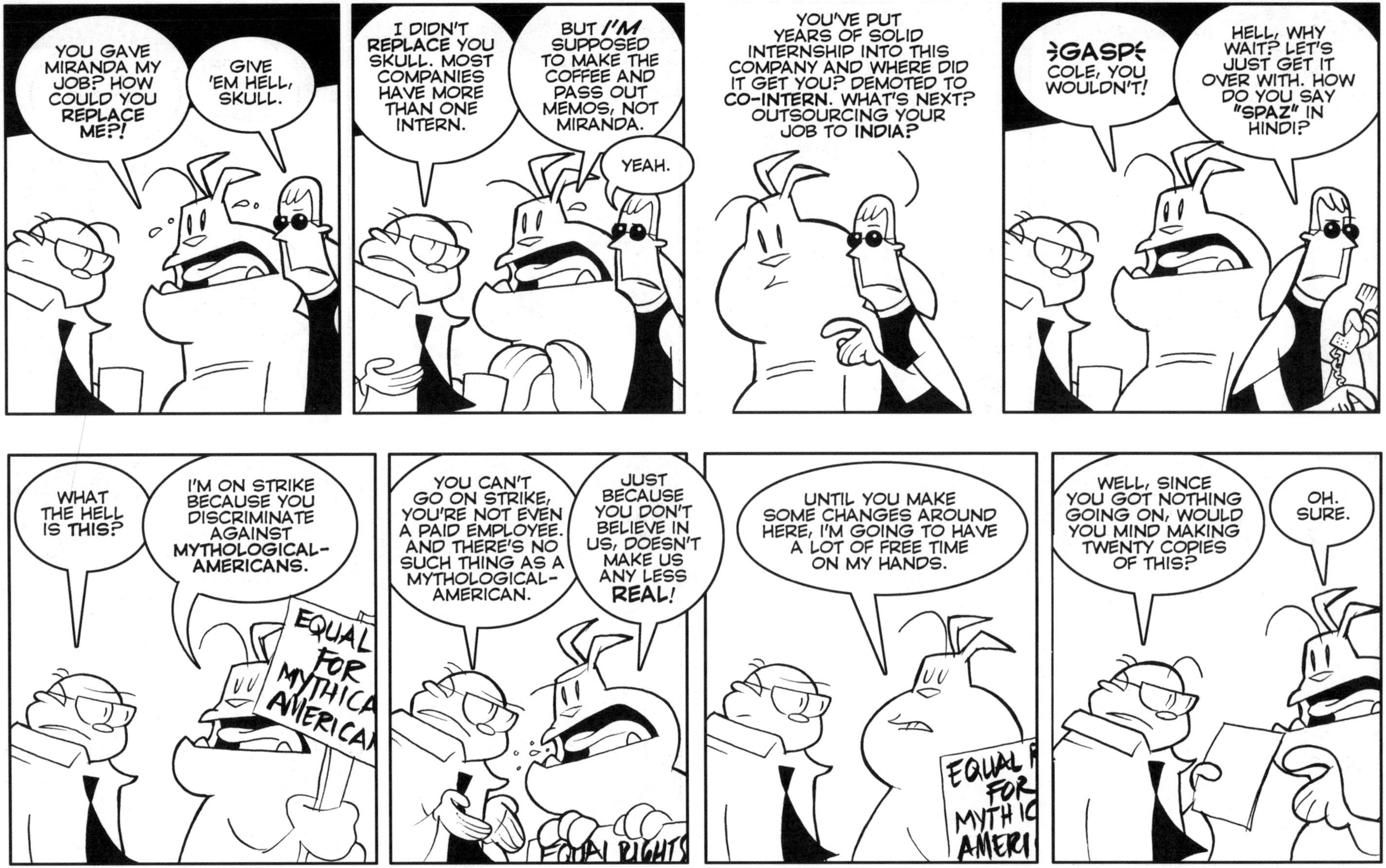

YOU GAVE MIRANDA MY JOB? HOW COULD YOU **REPLACE** ME?!
GIVE 'EM HELL, SKULL.
I DIDN'T **REPLACE** YOU SKULL. MOST COMPANIES HAVE MORE THAN ONE INTERN.
BUT ***I'M*** SUPPOSED TO MAKE THE COFFEE AND PASS OUT MEMOS, NOT MIRANDA.
YEAH.
YOU'VE PUT YEARS OF SOLID INTERNSHIP INTO THIS COMPANY AND WHERE DID IT GET YOU? DEMOTED TO **CO-INTERN**. WHAT'S NEXT? OUTSOURCING YOUR JOB TO **INDIA**?
GASP COLE, YOU WOULDN'T!
HELL, WHY WAIT? LET'S JUST GET IT OVER WITH. HOW DO YOU SAY ***"SPAZ"*** IN HINDI?
WHAT THE HELL IS **THIS**?
I'M ON STRIKE BECAUSE YOU DISCRIMINATE AGAINST **MYTHOLOGICAL-AMERICANS.**
EQUAL FOR MYTHICA AMERICAN
YOU CAN'T GO ON STRIKE, YOU'RE NOT EVEN A PAID EMPLOYEE. AND THERE'S NO SUCH THING AS A MYTHOLOGICAL-AMERICAN.
JUST BECAUSE YOU DON'T BELIEVE IN US, DOESN'T MAKE US ANY LESS **REAL**!
EQUAL RIGHTS
UNTIL YOU MAKE SOME CHANGES AROUND HERE, I'M GOING TO HAVE A LOT OF FREE TIME ON MY HANDS.
EQUAL FOR MYTHIC AMERI
WELL, SINCE YOU GOT NOTHING GOING ON, WOULD YOU MIND MAKING TWENTY COPIES OF THIS?
OH. SURE.

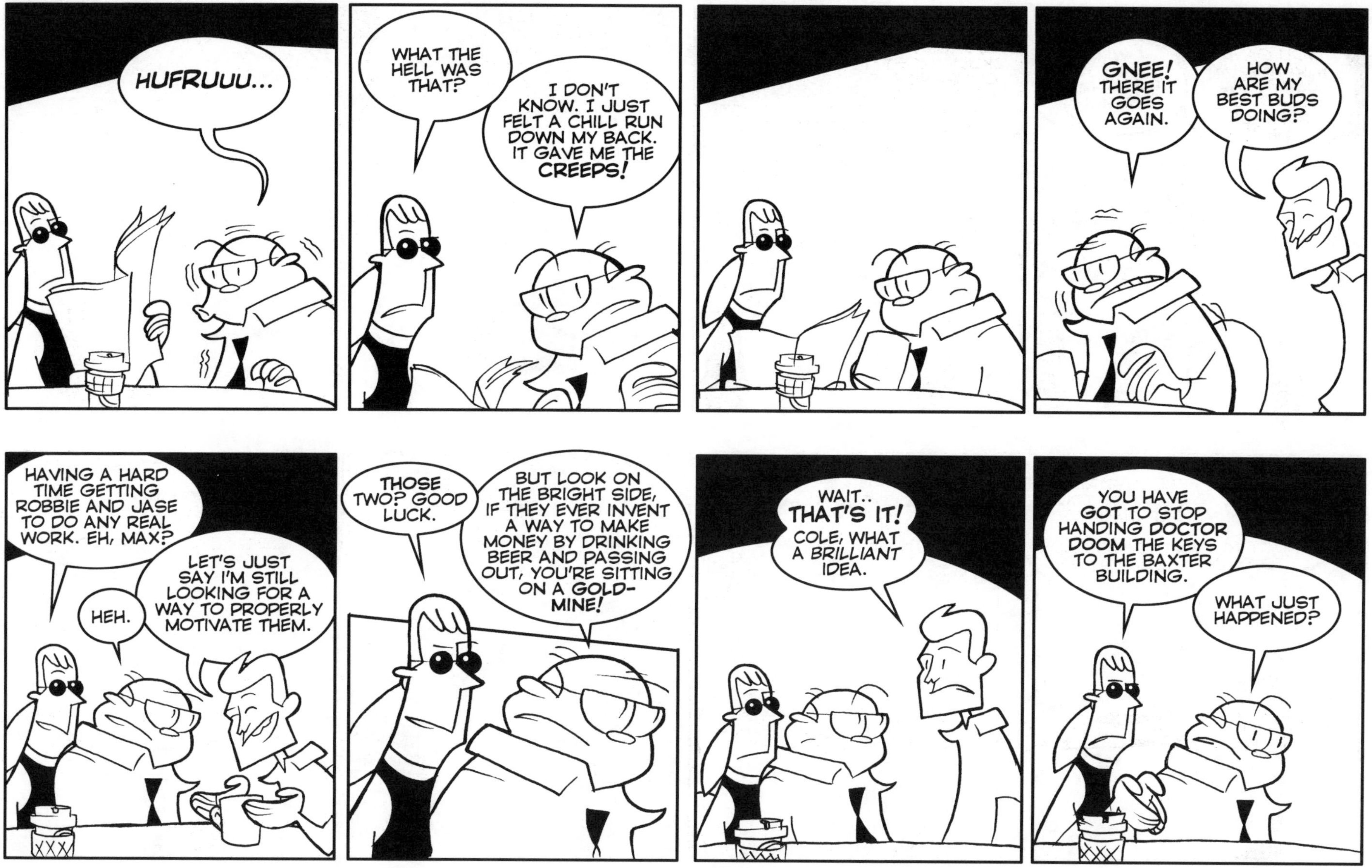

HUFRUUU...
WHAT THE HELL WAS THAT?
I DON'T KNOW. I JUST FELT A CHILL RUN DOWN MY BACK. IT GAVE ME THE CREEPS!
GNEE! THERE IT GOES AGAIN.
HOW ARE MY BEST BUDS DOING?
HAVING A HARD TIME GETTING ROBBIE AND JASE TO DO ANY REAL WORK. EH, MAX?
HEH.
LET'S JUST SAY I'M STILL LOOKING FOR A WAY TO PROPERLY MOTIVATE THEM.
THOSE TWO? GOOD LUCK.
BUT LOOK ON THE BRIGHT SIDE, IF THEY EVER INVENT A WAY TO MAKE MONEY BY DRINKING BEER AND PASSING OUT, YOU'RE SITTING ON A GOLD-MINE!
WAIT.. THAT'S IT!
COLE, WHAT A BRILLIANT IDEA.
YOU HAVE GOT TO STOP HANDING DOCTOR DOOM THE KEYS TO THE BAXTER BUILDING.
WHAT JUST HAPPENED?

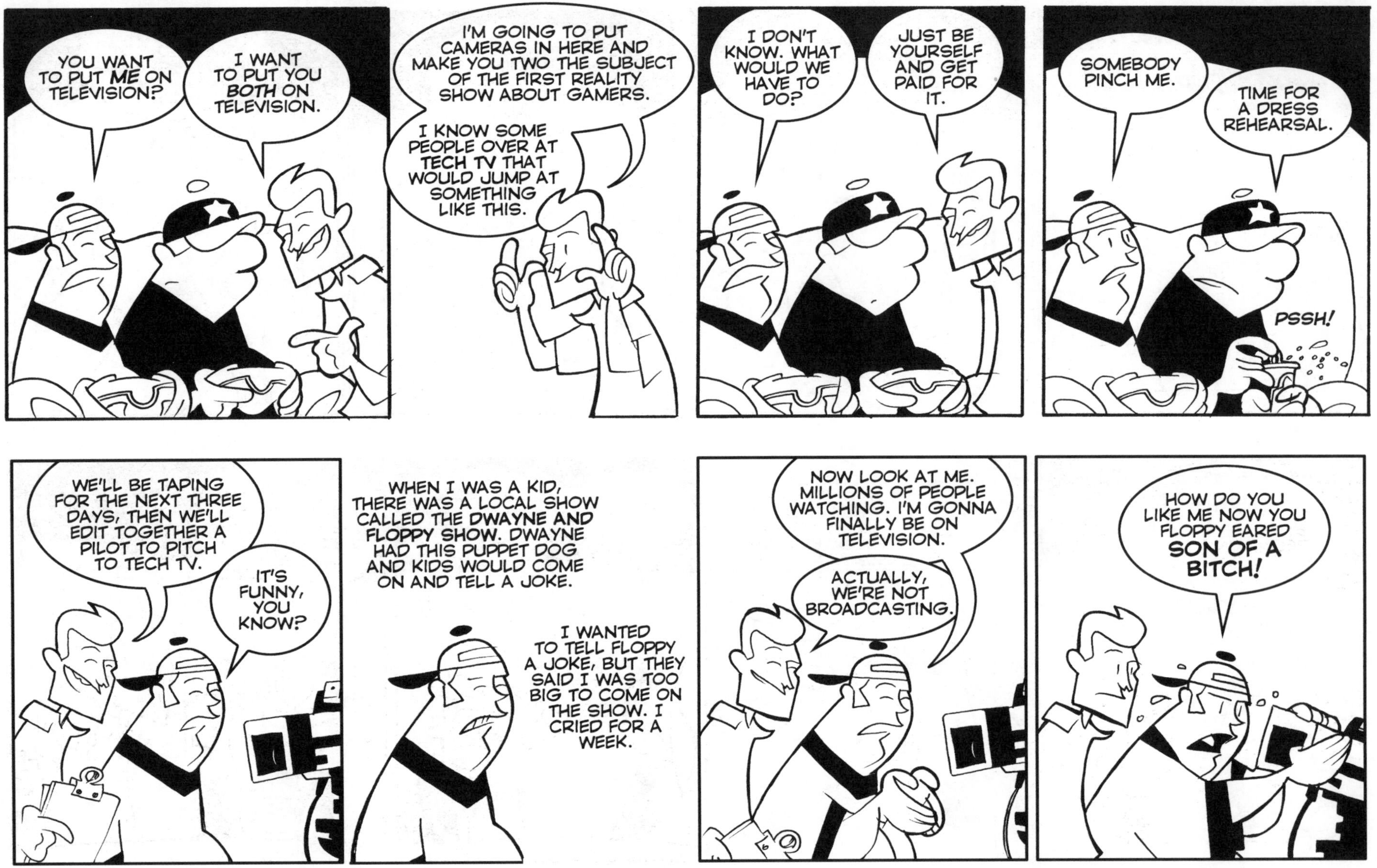
YOU WANT TO PUT ME ON TELEVISION?
I WANT TO PUT YOU BOTH ON TELEVISION.
I'M GOING TO PUT CAMERAS IN HERE AND MAKE YOU TWO THE SUBJECT OF THE FIRST REALITY SHOW ABOUT GAMERS.
I KNOW SOME PEOPLE OVER AT TECH TV THAT WOULD JUMP AT SOMETHING LIKE THIS.
I DON'T KNOW. WHAT WOULD WE HAVE TO DO?
JUST BE YOURSELF AND GET PAID FOR IT.
SOMEBODY PINCH ME.
TIME FOR A DRESS REHEARSAL.
PSSH!
WE'LL BE TAPING FOR THE NEXT THREE DAYS, THEN WE'LL EDIT TOGETHER A PILOT TO PITCH TO TECH TV.
IT'S FUNNY, YOU KNOW?
WHEN I WAS A KID, THERE WAS A LOCAL SHOW CALLED THE DWAYNE AND FLOPPY SHOW. DWAYNE HAD THIS PUPPET DOG AND KIDS WOULD COME ON AND TELL A JOKE.
I WANTED TO TELL FLOPPY A JOKE, BUT THEY SAID I WAS TOO BIG TO COME ON THE SHOW. I CRIED FOR A WEEK.
NOW LOOK AT ME. MILLIONS OF PEOPLE WATCHING. I'M GONNA FINALLY BE ON TELEVISION.
ACTUALLY, WE'RE NOT BROADCASTING.
HOW DO YOU LIKE ME NOW YOU FLOPPY EARED SON OF A BITCH!

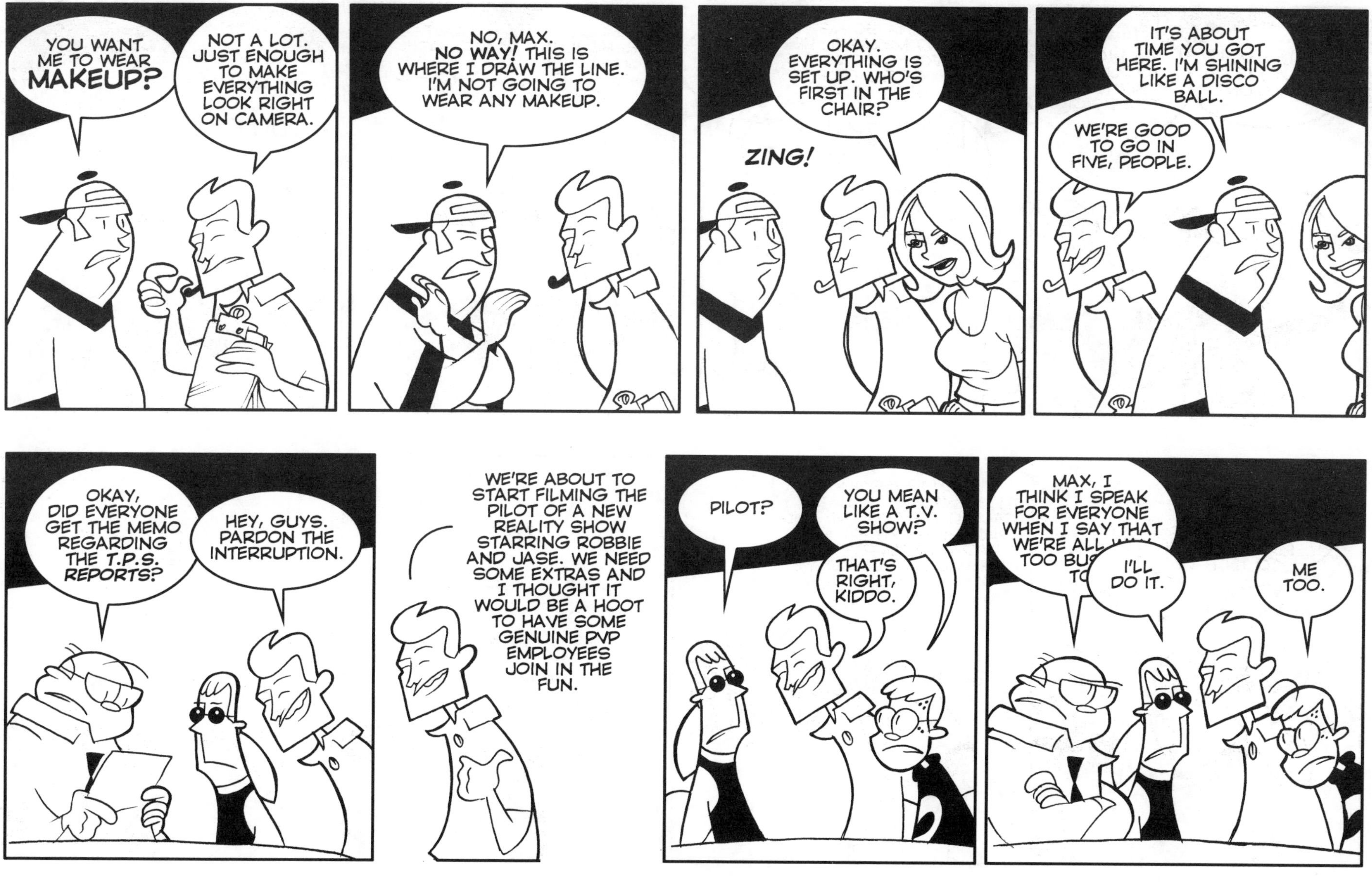
YOU WANT ME TO WEAR **MAKEUP?**
NOT A LOT. JUST ENOUGH TO MAKE EVERYTHING LOOK RIGHT ON CAMERA.
NO, MAX. **NO WAY!** THIS IS WHERE I DRAW THE LINE. I'M NOT GOING TO WEAR ANY MAKEUP.
ZING!
OKAY. EVERYTHING IS SET UP. WHO'S FIRST IN THE CHAIR?
IT'S ABOUT TIME YOU GOT HERE. I'M SHINING LIKE A DISCO BALL.
WE'RE GOOD TO GO IN FIVE, PEOPLE.
OKAY, DID EVERYONE GET THE MEMO REGARDING THE *T.P.S. REPORTS?*
HEY, GUYS. PARDON THE INTERRUPTION.
WE'RE ABOUT TO START FILMING THE PILOT OF A NEW REALITY SHOW STARRING ROBBIE AND JASE. WE NEED SOME EXTRAS AND I THOUGHT IT WOULD BE A HOOT TO HAVE SOME GENUINE PVP EMPLOYEES JOIN IN THE FUN.
PILOT?
YOU MEAN LIKE A T.V. SHOW?
THAT'S RIGHT, KIDDO.
MAX, I THINK I SPEAK FOR EVERYONE WHEN I SAY THAT WE'RE ALL
I'LL DO IT.
ME TOO.

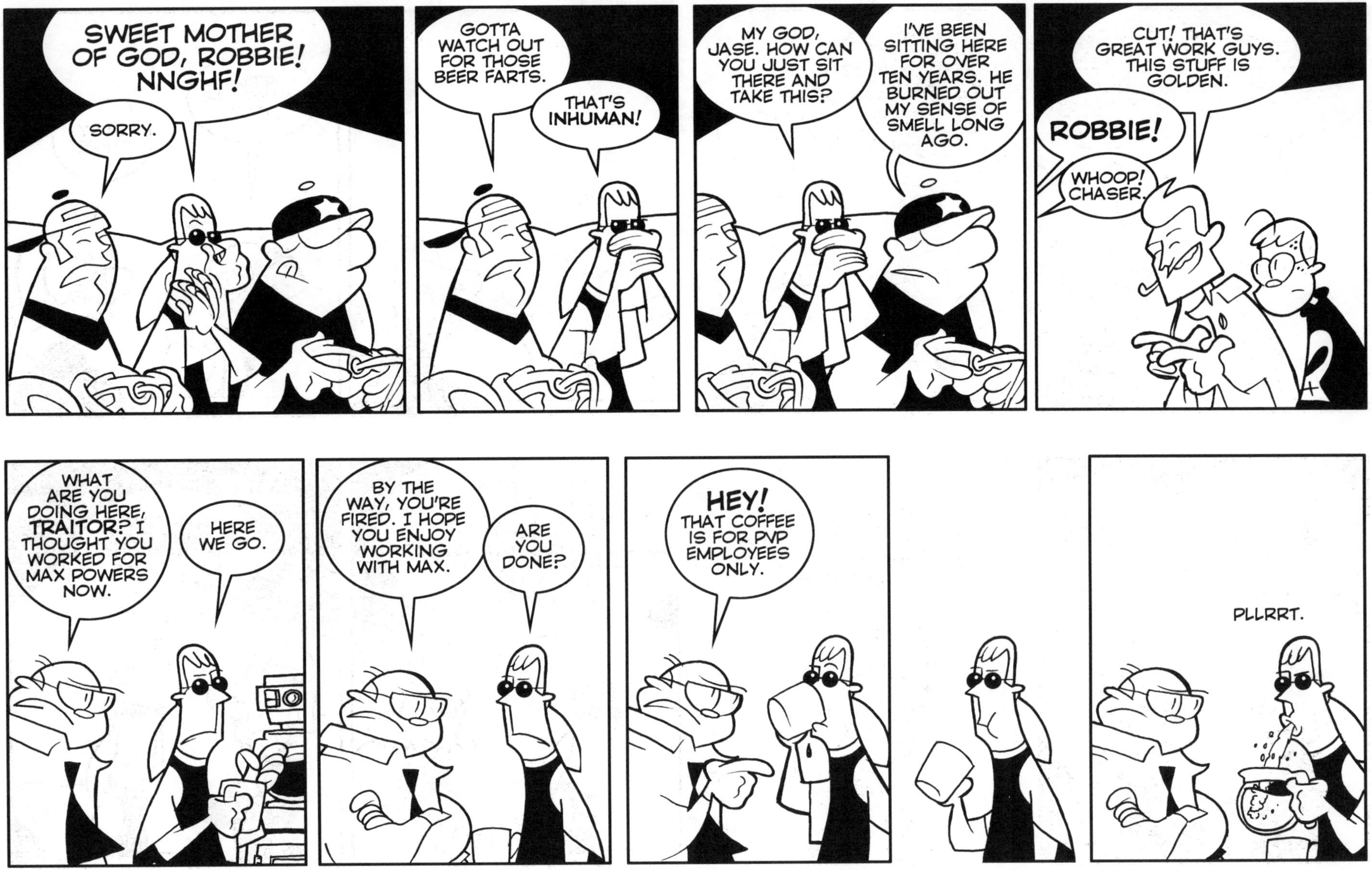
SWEET MOTHER OF GOD, ROBBIE! NNGHF!
SORRY.
GOTTA WATCH OUT FOR THOSE BEER FARTS.
THAT'S INHUMAN!
MY GOD, JASE. HOW CAN YOU JUST SIT THERE AND TAKE THIS?
I'VE BEEN SITTING HERE FOR OVER TEN YEARS. HE BURNED OUT MY SENSE OF SMELL LONG AGO.
CUT! THAT'S GREAT WORK GUYS. THIS STUFF IS GOLDEN.
ROBBIE!
WHOOP! CHASER.
WHAT ARE YOU DOING HERE, TRAITOR? I THOUGHT YOU WORKED FOR MAX POWERS NOW.
HERE WE GO.
BY THE WAY, YOU'RE FIRED. I HOPE YOU ENJOY WORKING WITH MAX.
ARE YOU DONE?
HEY! THAT COFFEE IS FOR PVP EMPLOYEES ONLY.
PLLRRT.

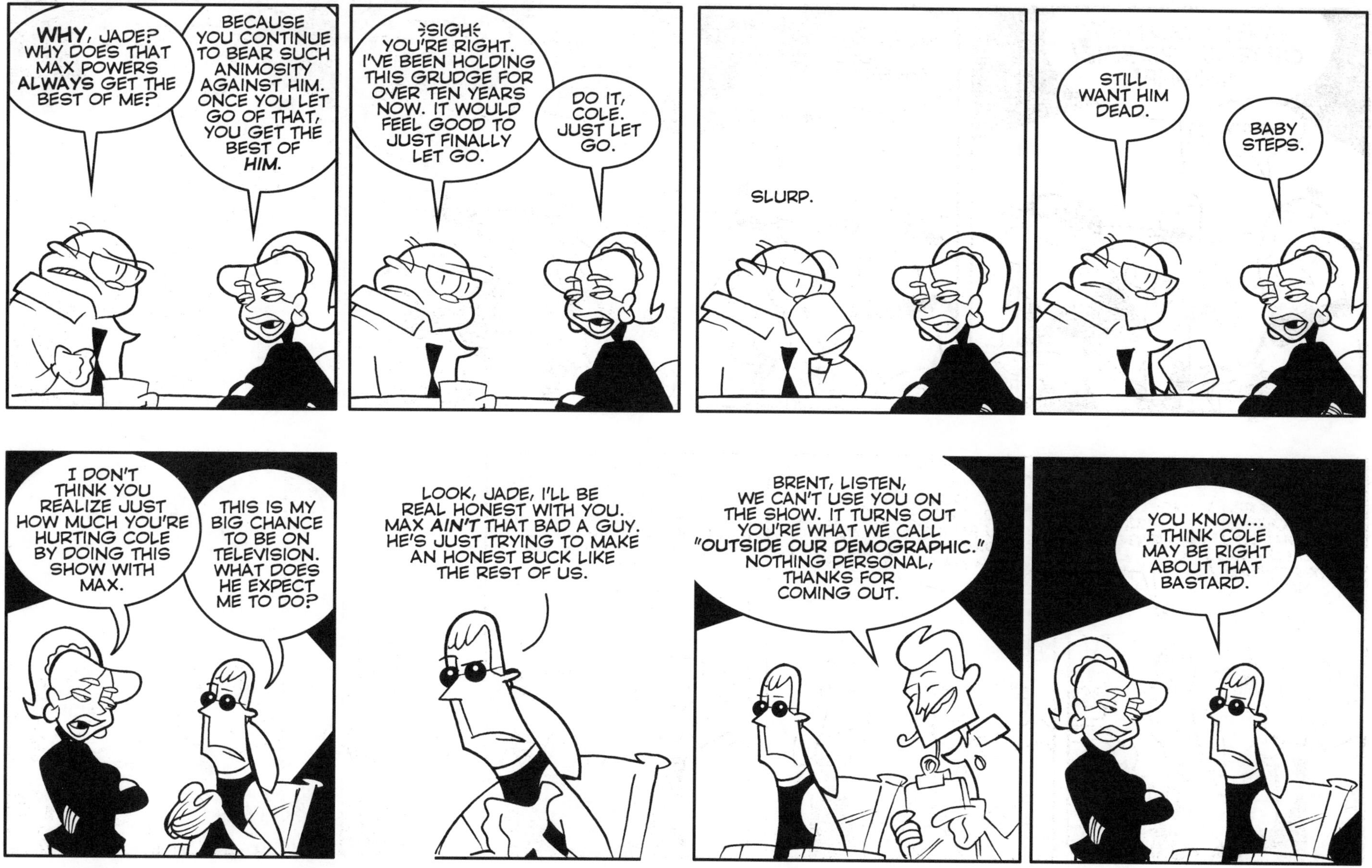

WHY, JADE? WHY DOES THAT MAX POWERS ALWAYS GET THE BEST OF ME?
BECAUSE YOU CONTINUE TO BEAR SUCH ANIMOSITY AGAINST HIM. ONCE YOU LET GO OF THAT, YOU GET THE BEST OF HIM.
SIGH YOU'RE RIGHT. I'VE BEEN HOLDING THIS GRUDGE FOR OVER TEN YEARS NOW. IT WOULD FEEL GOOD TO JUST FINALLY LET GO.
DO IT, COLE. JUST LET GO.
SLURP.
STILL WANT HIM DEAD.
BABY STEPS.
I DON'T THINK YOU REALIZE JUST HOW MUCH YOU'RE HURTING COLE BY DOING THIS SHOW WITH MAX.
THIS IS MY BIG CHANCE TO BE ON TELEVISION. WHAT DOES HE EXPECT ME TO DO?
LOOK, JADE, I'LL BE REAL HONEST WITH YOU. MAX AIN'T THAT BAD A GUY. HE'S JUST TRYING TO MAKE AN HONEST BUCK LIKE THE REST OF US.
BRENT, LISTEN, WE CAN'T USE YOU ON THE SHOW. IT TURNS OUT YOU'RE WHAT WE CALL "OUTSIDE OUR DEMOGRAPHIC." NOTHING PERSONAL, THANKS FOR COMING OUT.
YOU KNOW... I THINK COLE MAY BE RIGHT ABOUT THAT BASTARD.

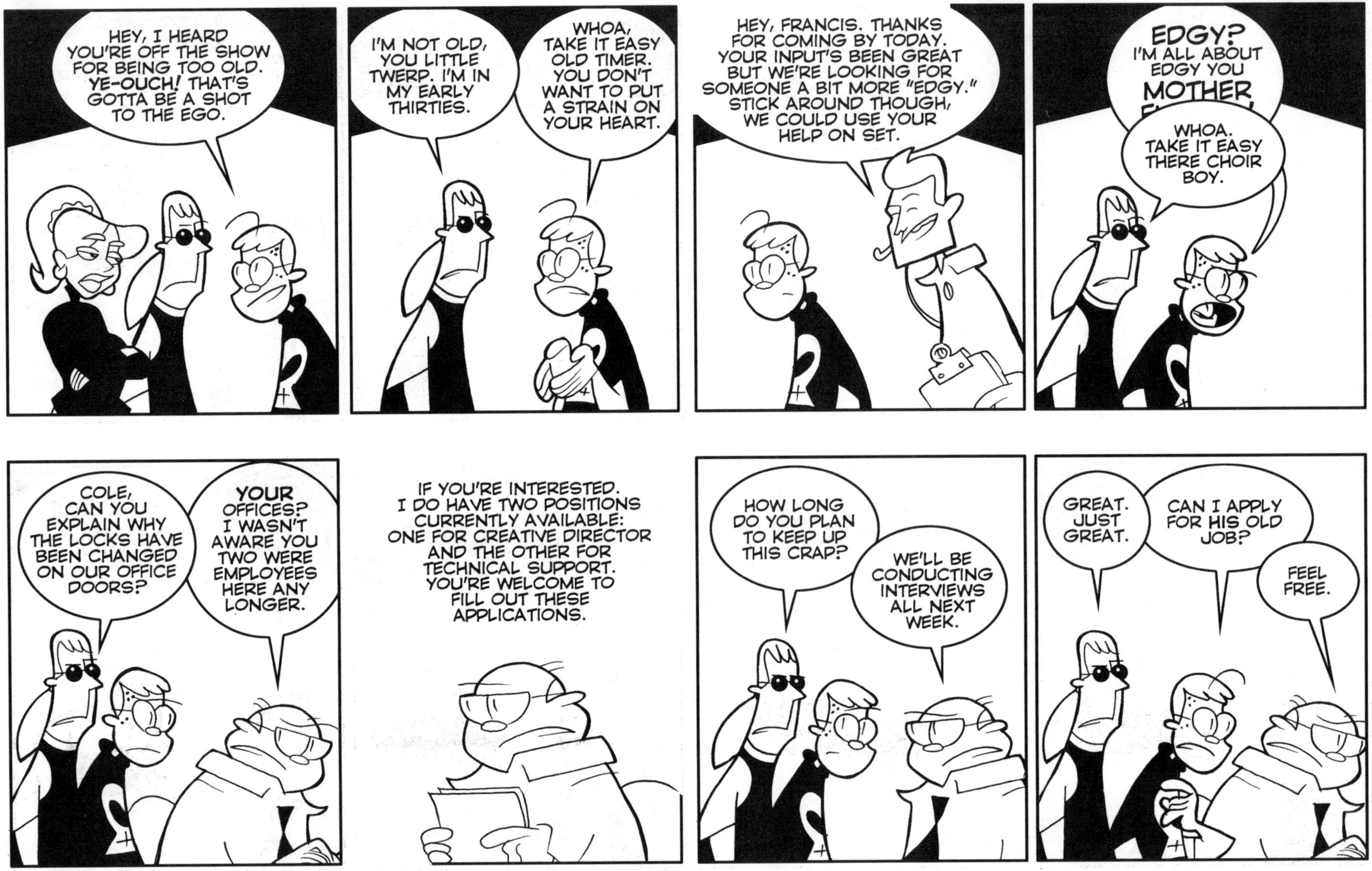
HEY, I HEARD YOU'RE OFF THE SHOW FOR BEING TOO OLD. YE-OUCH! THAT'S GOTTA BE A SHOT TO THE EGO.
I'M NOT OLD, YOU LITTLE TWERP. I'M IN MY EARLY THIRTIES.
WHOA, TAKE IT EASY OLD TIMER. YOU DON'T WANT TO PUT A STRAIN ON YOUR HEART.
HEY, FRANCIS. THANKS FOR COMING BY TODAY. YOUR INPUT'S BEEN GREAT BUT WE'RE LOOKING FOR SOMEONE A BIT MORE "EDGY." STICK AROUND THOUGH, WE COULD USE YOUR HELP ON SET.
EDGY? I'M ALL ABOUT EDGY YOU MOTHER
WHOA. TAKE IT EASY THERE CHOIR BOY.
COLE, CAN YOU EXPLAIN WHY THE LOCKS HAVE BEEN CHANGED ON OUR OFFICE DOORS?
YOUR OFFICES? I WASN'T AWARE YOU TWO WERE EMPLOYEES HERE ANY LONGER.
IF YOU'RE INTERESTED. I DO HAVE TWO POSITIONS CURRENTLY AVAILABLE: ONE FOR CREATIVE DIRECTOR AND THE OTHER FOR TECHNICAL SUPPORT. YOU'RE WELCOME TO FILL OUT THESE APPLICATIONS.
HOW LONG DO YOU PLAN TO KEEP UP THIS CRAP?
WE'LL BE CONDUCTING INTERVIEWS ALL NEXT WEEK.
GREAT. JUST GREAT.
CAN I APPLY FOR HIS OLD JOB?
FEEL FREE.

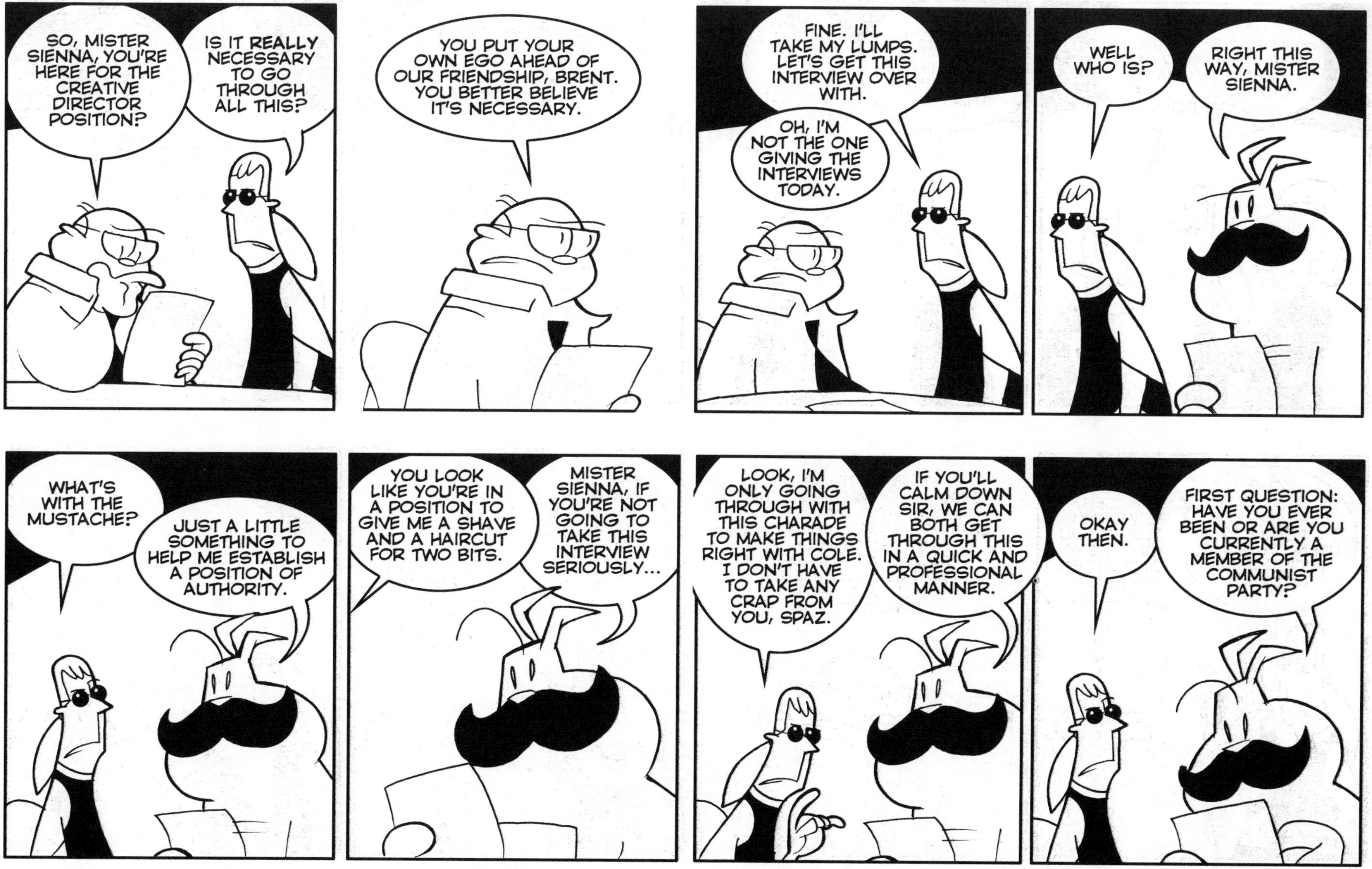
SO, MISTER SIENNA, YOU'RE HERE FOR THE CREATIVE DIRECTOR POSITION?
IS IT REALLY NECESSARY TO GO THROUGH ALL THIS?
YOU PUT YOUR OWN EGO AHEAD OF OUR FRIENDSHIP, BRENT. YOU BETTER BELIEVE IT'S NECESSARY.
FINE. I'LL TAKE MY LUMPS. LET'S GET THIS INTERVIEW OVER WITH.
OH, I'M NOT THE ONE GIVING THE INTERVIEWS TODAY.
WELL WHO IS?
RIGHT THIS WAY, MISTER SIENNA.
WHAT'S WITH THE MUSTACHE?
JUST A LITTLE SOMETHING TO HELP ME ESTABLISH A POSITION OF AUTHORITY.
YOU LOOK LIKE YOU'RE IN A POSITION TO GIVE ME A SHAVE AND A HAIRCUT FOR TWO BITS.
MISTER SIENNA, IF YOU'RE NOT GOING TO TAKE THIS INTERVIEW SERIOUSLY...
LOOK, I'M ONLY GOING THROUGH WITH THIS CHARADE TO MAKE THINGS RIGHT WITH COLE. I DON'T HAVE TO TAKE ANY CRAP FROM YOU, SPAZ.
IF YOU'LL CALM DOWN SIR, WE CAN BOTH GET THROUGH THIS IN A QUICK AND PROFESSIONAL MANNER.
OKAY THEN.
FIRST QUESTION: HAVE YOU EVER BEEN OR ARE YOU CURRENTLY A MEMBER OF THE COMMUNIST PARTY?

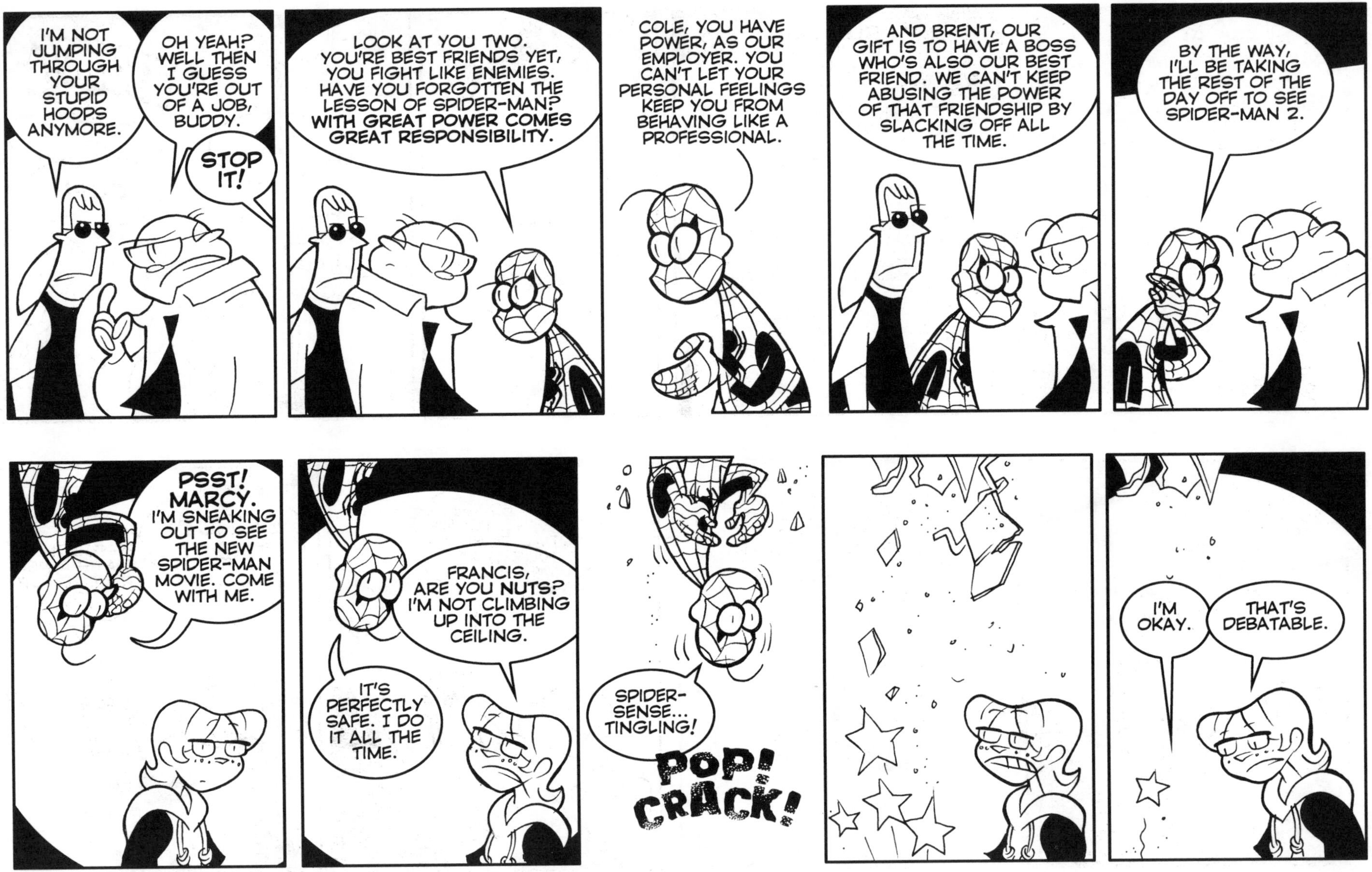
I'M NOT JUMPING THROUGH YOUR STUPID HOOPS ANYMORE.
OH YEAH? WELL THEN I GUESS YOU'RE OUT OF A JOB, BUDDY.
STOP IT!
LOOK AT YOU TWO. YOU'RE BEST FRIENDS YET, YOU FIGHT LIKE ENEMIES. HAVE YOU FORGOTTEN THE LESSON OF SPIDER-MAN? WITH GREAT POWER COMES GREAT RESPONSIBILITY.
COLE, YOU HAVE POWER, AS OUR EMPLOYER. YOU CAN'T LET YOUR PERSONAL FEELINGS KEEP YOU FROM BEHAVING LIKE A PROFESSIONAL.
AND BRENT, OUR GIFT IS TO HAVE A BOSS WHO'S ALSO OUR BEST FRIEND. WE CAN'T KEEP ABUSING THE POWER OF THAT FRIENDSHIP BY SLACKING OFF ALL THE TIME.
BY THE WAY, I'LL BE TAKING THE REST OF THE DAY OFF TO SEE SPIDER-MAN 2.
PSST! MARCY. I'M SNEAKING OUT TO SEE THE NEW SPIDER-MAN MOVIE. COME WITH ME.
FRANCIS, ARE YOU NUTS? I'M NOT CLIMBING UP INTO THE CEILING.
IT'S PERFECTLY SAFE. I DO IT ALL THE TIME.
SPIDER-SENSE... TINGLING!
POP! CRACK!
I'M OKAY.
THAT'S DEBATABLE.

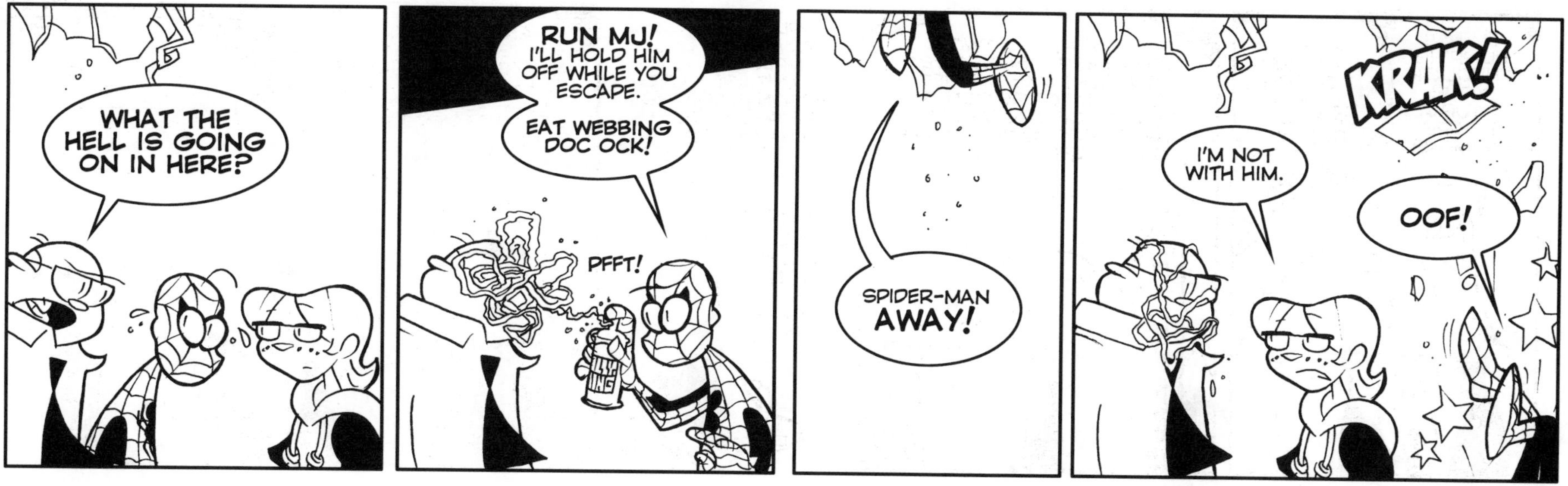
WHAT THE HELL IS GOING ON IN HERE?
RUN MJ! I'LL HOLD HIM OFF WHILE YOU ESCAPE.
EAT WEBBING DOC OCK!
PFFT!
SPIDER-MAN AWAY!
KRAK!
I'M NOT WITH HIM.
OOF!

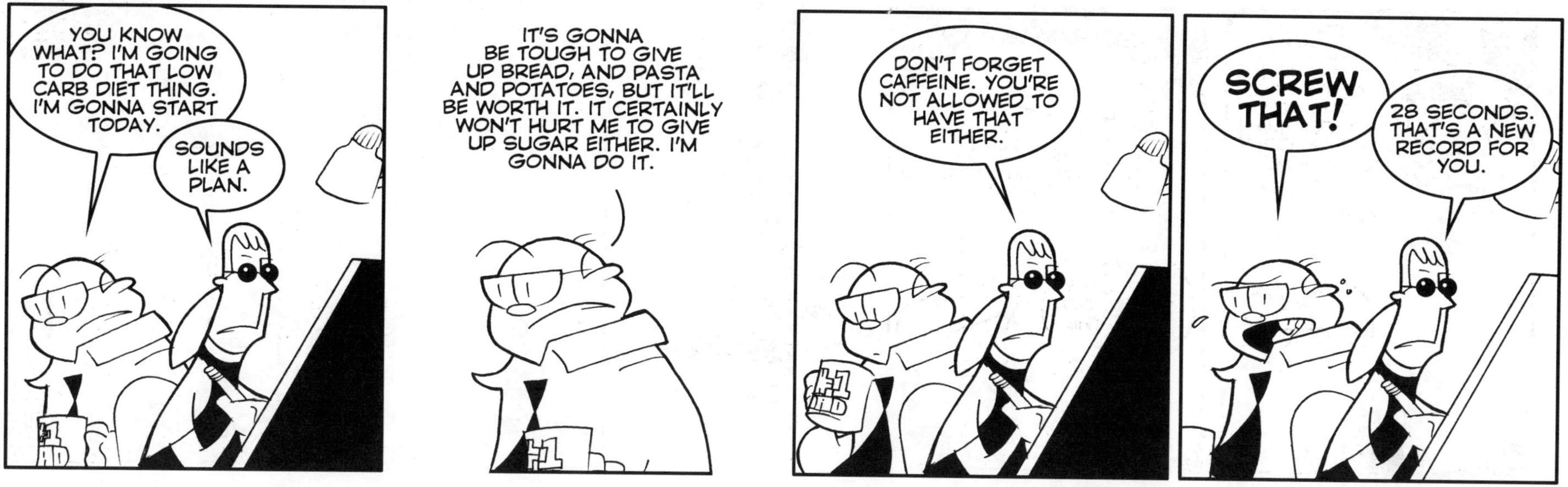
YOU KNOW WHAT? I'M GOING TO DO THAT LOW CARB DIET THING. I'M GONNA START TODAY.
SOUNDS LIKE A PLAN.
IT'S GONNA BE TOUGH TO GIVE UP BREAD, AND PASTA AND POTATOES, BUT IT'LL BE WORTH IT. IT CERTAINLY WON'T HURT ME TO GIVE UP SUGAR EITHER. I'M GONNA DO IT.
DON'T FORGET CAFFEINE. YOU'RE NOT ALLOWED TO HAVE THAT EITHER.
SCREW THAT!
28 SECONDS. THAT'S A NEW RECORD FOR YOU.

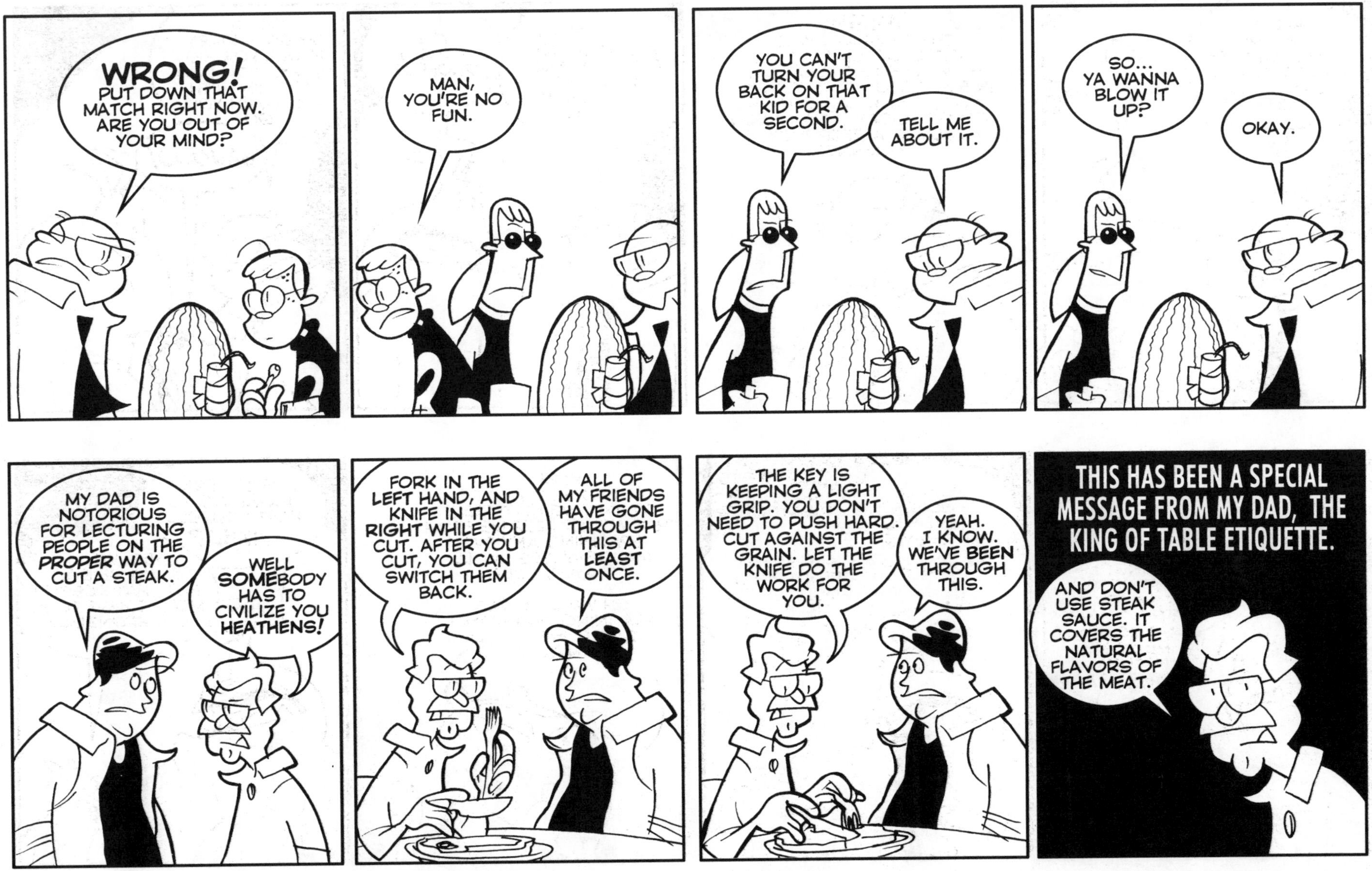
WRONG! PUT DOWN THAT MATCH RIGHT NOW. ARE YOU OUT OF YOUR MIND?
MAN, YOU'RE NO FUN.
YOU CAN'T TURN YOUR BACK ON THAT KID FOR A SECOND.
TELL ME ABOUT IT.
SO... YA WANNA BLOW IT UP?
OKAY.
MY DAD IS NOTORIOUS FOR LECTURING PEOPLE ON THE PROPER WAY TO CUT A STEAK.
WELL SOMEBODY HAS TO CIVILIZE YOU HEATHENS!
FORK IN THE LEFT HAND, AND KNIFE IN THE RIGHT WHILE YOU CUT. AFTER YOU CUT, YOU CAN SWITCH THEM BACK.
ALL OF MY FRIENDS HAVE GONE THROUGH THIS AT LEAST ONCE.
THE KEY IS KEEPING A LIGHT GRIP. YOU DON'T NEED TO PUSH HARD. CUT AGAINST THE GRAIN. LET THE KNIFE DO THE WORK FOR YOU.
YEAH. I KNOW. WE'VE BEEN THROUGH THIS.
THIS HAS BEEN A SPECIAL MESSAGE FROM MY DAD, THE KING OF TABLE ETIQUETTE.
AND DON'T USE STEAK SAUCE. IT COVERS THE NATURAL FLAVORS OF THE MEAT.

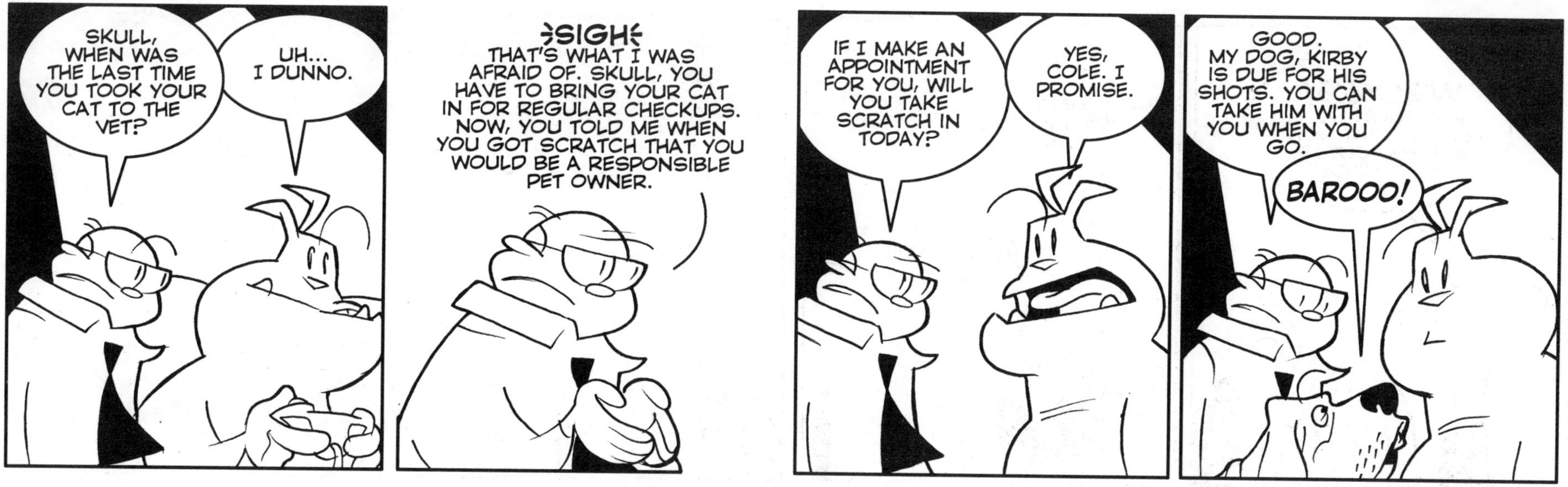
SKULL, WHEN WAS THE LAST TIME YOU TOOK YOUR CAT TO THE VET?
UH... I DUNNO.
SIGH
THAT'S WHAT I WAS AFRAID OF. SKULL, YOU HAVE TO BRING YOUR CAT IN FOR REGULAR CHECKUPS. NOW, YOU TOLD ME WHEN YOU GOT SCRATCH THAT YOU WOULD BE A RESPONSIBLE PET OWNER.
IF I MAKE AN APPOINTMENT FOR YOU, WILL YOU TAKE SCRATCH IN TODAY?
YES, COLE. I PROMISE.
GOOD. MY DOG, KIRBY IS DUE FOR HIS SHOTS. YOU CAN TAKE HIM WITH YOU WHEN YOU GO.
BAROOO!

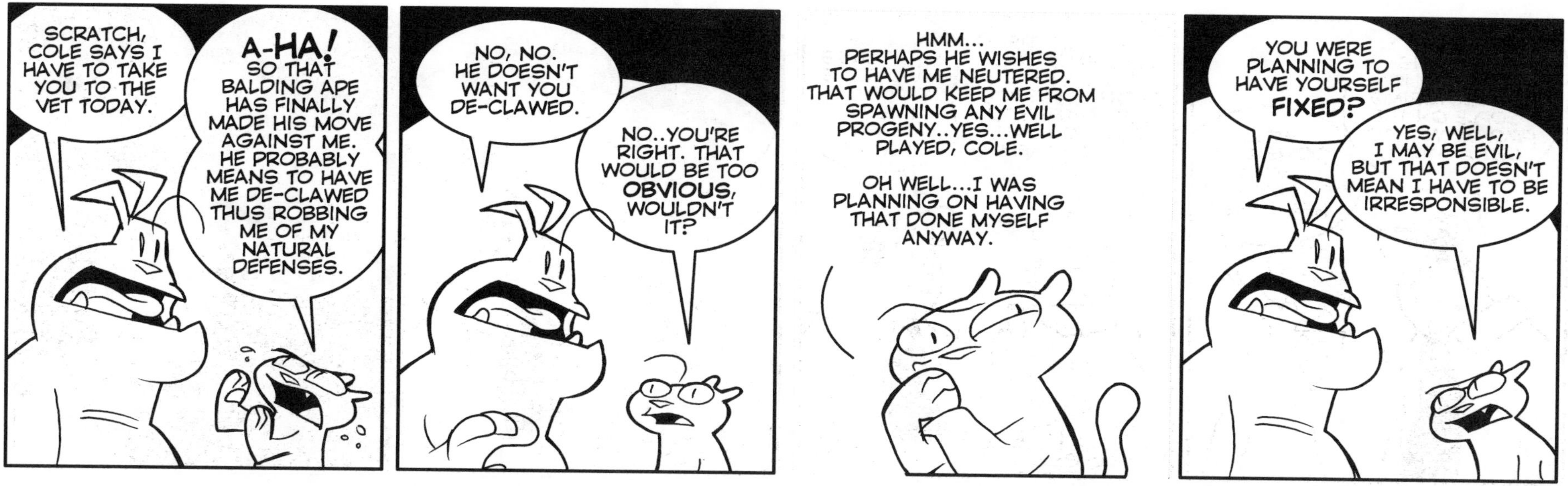
SCRATCH, COLE SAYS I HAVE TO TAKE YOU TO THE VET TODAY.
A-HA! SO THAT BALDING APE HAS FINALLY MADE HIS MOVE AGAINST ME. HE PROBABLY MEANS TO HAVE ME DE-CLAWED THUS ROBBING ME OF MY NATURAL DEFENSES.
NO, NO. HE DOESN'T WANT YOU DE-CLAWED.
NO..YOU'RE RIGHT. THAT WOULD BE TOO OBVIOUS, WOULDN'T IT?
HMM... PERHAPS HE WISHES TO HAVE ME NEUTERED. THAT WOULD KEEP ME FROM SPAWNING ANY EVIL PROGENY..YES...WELL PLAYED, COLE.
OH WELL...I WAS PLANNING ON HAVING THAT DONE MYSELF ANYWAY.
YOU WERE PLANNING TO HAVE YOURSELF FIXED?
YES, WELL, I MAY BE EVIL, BUT THAT DOESN'T MEAN I HAVE TO BE IRRESPONSIBLE.

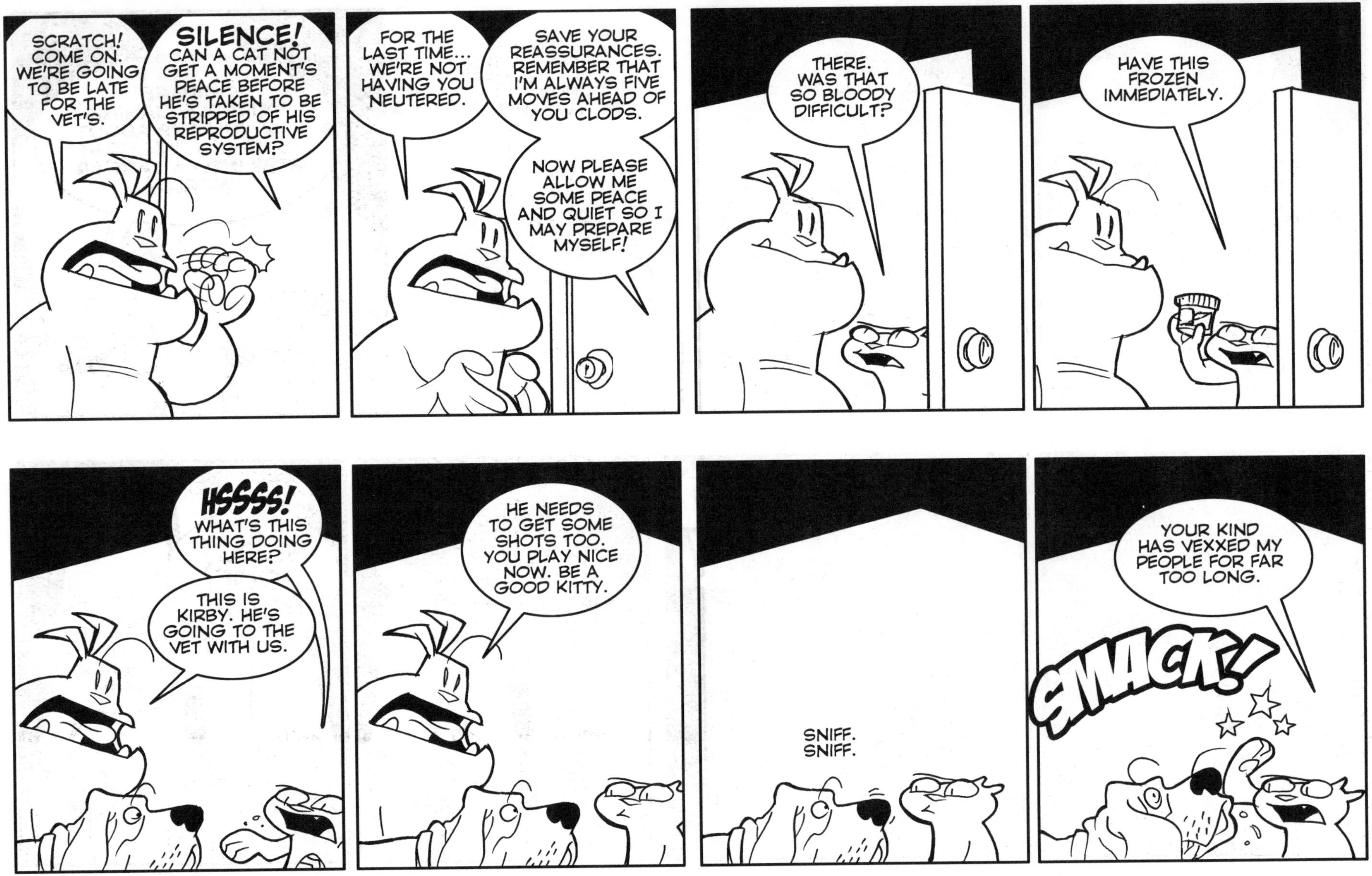
SCRATCH! COME ON. WE'RE GOING TO BE LATE FOR THE VET'S.
SILENCE! CAN A CAT NOT GET A MOMENT'S PEACE BEFORE HE'S TAKEN TO BE STRIPPED OF HIS REPRODUCTIVE SYSTEM?
FOR THE LAST TIME... WE'RE NOT HAVING YOU NEUTERED.
SAVE YOUR REASSURANCES. REMEMBER THAT I'M ALWAYS FIVE MOVES AHEAD OF YOU CLODS.
NOW PLEASE ALLOW ME SOME PEACE AND QUIET SO I MAY PREPARE MYSELF!
THERE. WAS THAT SO BLOODY DIFFICULT?
HAVE THIS FROZEN IMMEDIATELY.
HSSSS! WHAT'S THIS THING DOING HERE?
THIS IS KIRBY. HE'S GOING TO THE VET WITH US.
HE NEEDS TO GET SOME SHOTS TOO. YOU PLAY NICE NOW. BE A GOOD KITTY.
SNIFF. SNIFF.
YOUR KIND HAS VEXXED MY PEOPLE FOR FAR TOO LONG.
SMACK!

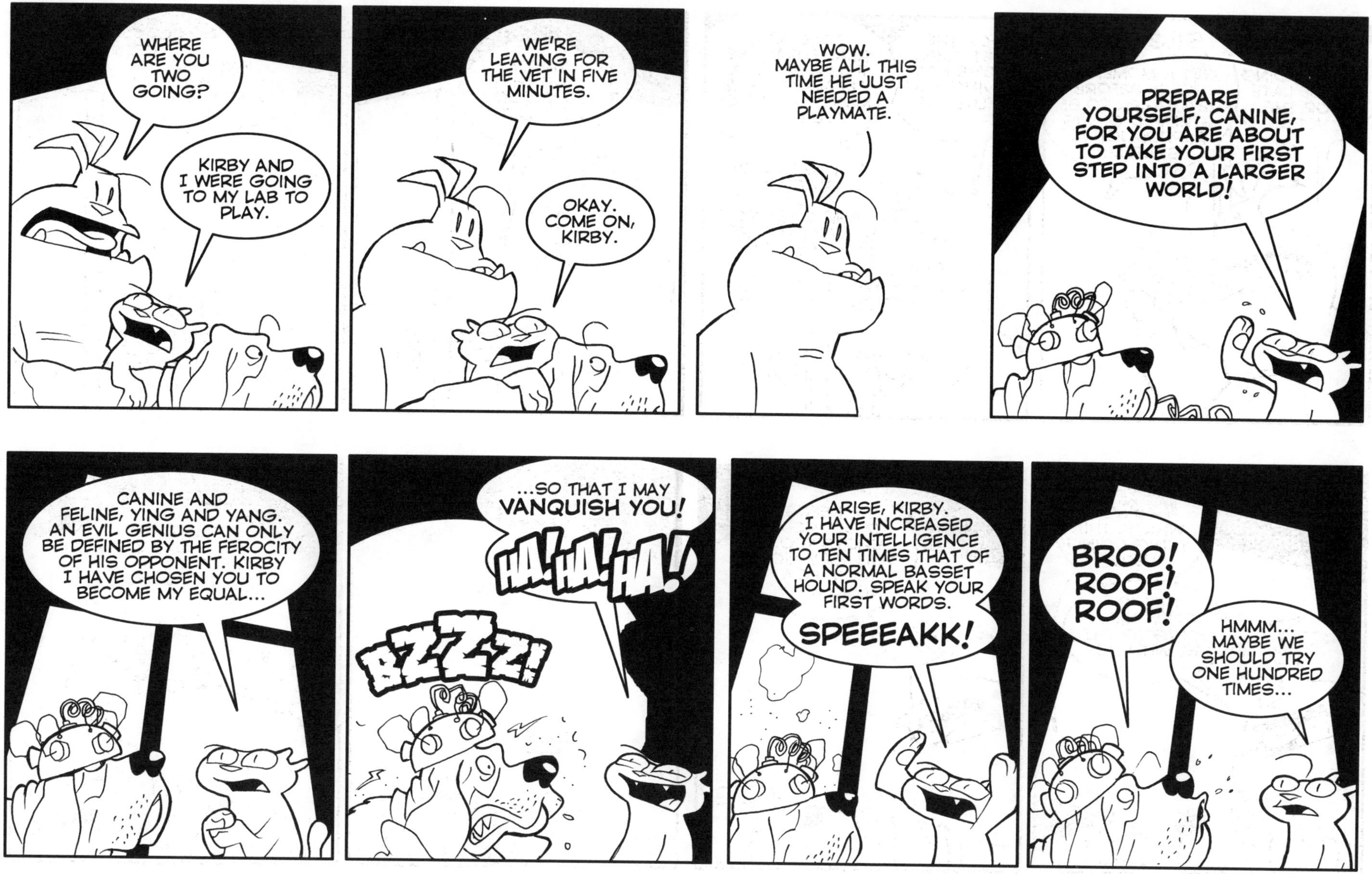
WHERE ARE YOU TWO GOING?
KIRBY AND I WERE GOING TO MY LAB TO PLAY.
WE'RE LEAVING FOR THE VET IN FIVE MINUTES.
OKAY. COME ON, KIRBY.
WOW. MAYBE ALL THIS TIME HE JUST NEEDED A PLAYMATE.
PREPARE YOURSELF, CANINE, FOR YOU ARE ABOUT TO TAKE YOUR FIRST STEP INTO A LARGER WORLD!
CANINE AND FELINE, YING AND YANG. AN EVIL GENIUS CAN ONLY BE DEFINED BY THE FEROCITY OF HIS OPPONENT. KIRBY I HAVE CHOSEN YOU TO BECOME MY EQUAL...
...SO THAT I MAY VANQUISH YOU!
HA! HA! HA!
BZZZZ!
ARISE, KIRBY. I HAVE INCREASED YOUR INTELLIGENCE TO TEN TIMES THAT OF A NORMAL BASSET HOUND. SPEAK YOUR FIRST WORDS.
SPEEEAKK!
BROO! ROOF! ROOF!
HMMM... MAYBE WE SHOULD TRY ONE HUNDRED TIMES...

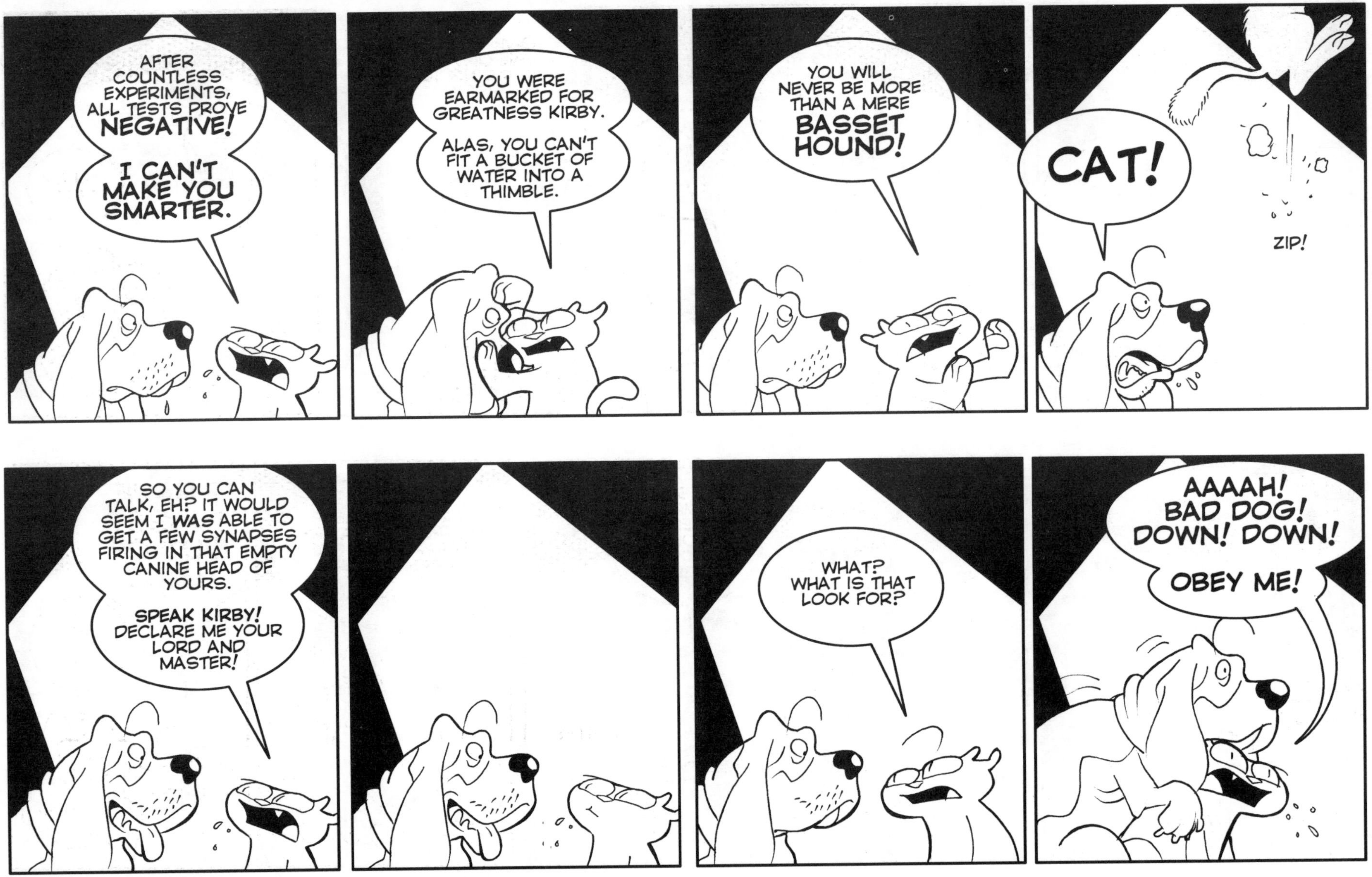
AFTER COUNTLESS EXPERIMENTS, ALL TESTS PROVE NEGATIVE!
I CAN'T MAKE YOU SMARTER.
YOU WERE EARMARKED FOR GREATNESS KIRBY.
ALAS, YOU CAN'T FIT A BUCKET OF WATER INTO A THIMBLE.
YOU WILL NEVER BE MORE THAN A MERE BASSET HOUND!
CAT!
ZIP!
SO YOU CAN TALK, EH? IT WOULD SEEM I WAS ABLE TO GET A FEW SYNAPSES FIRING IN THAT EMPTY CANINE HEAD OF YOURS.
SPEAK KIRBY! DECLARE ME YOUR LORD AND MASTER!
WHAT? WHAT IS THAT LOOK FOR?
AAAAH! BAD DOG! DOWN! DOWN!
OBEY ME!

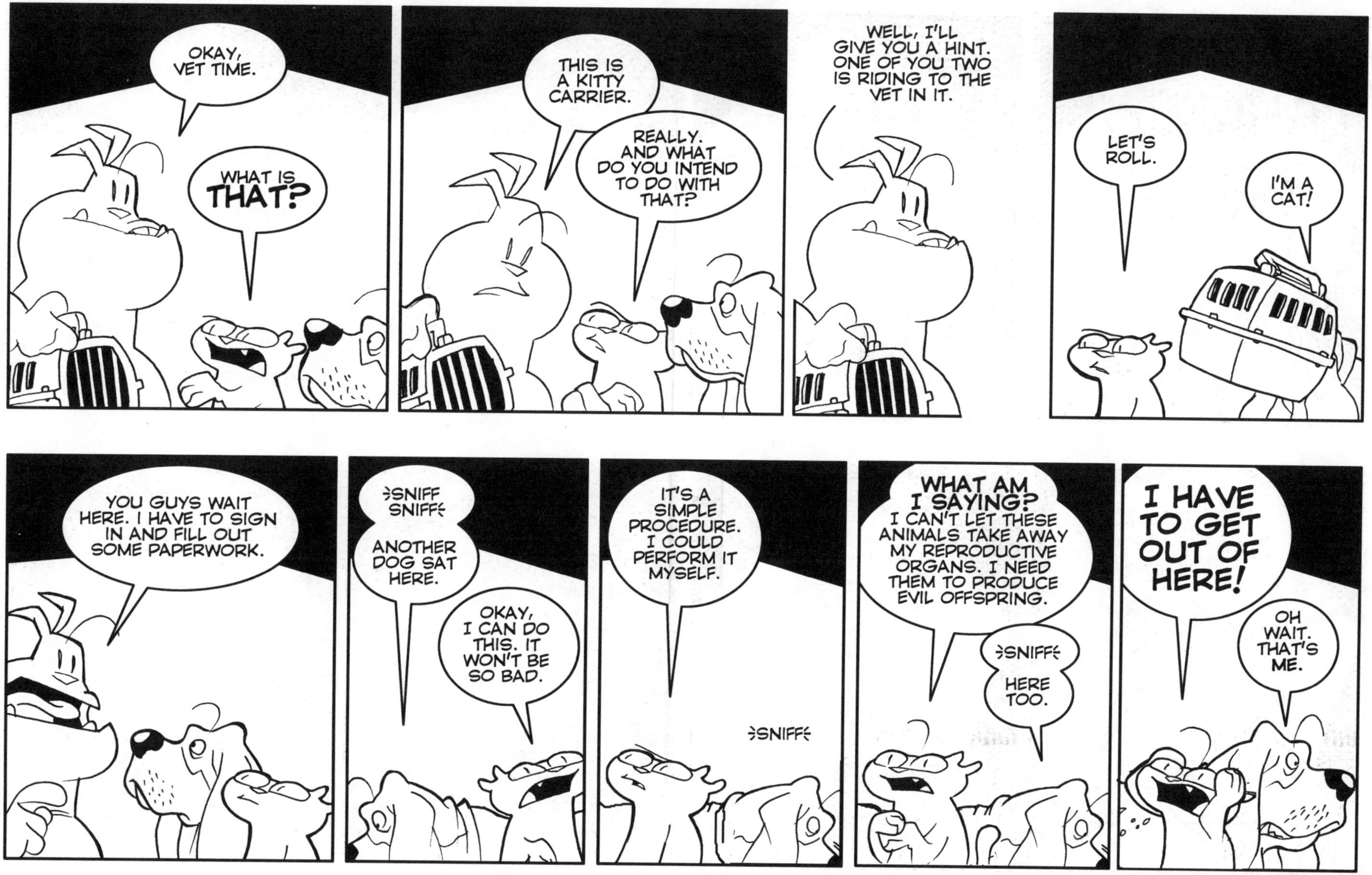
OKAY, VET TIME.
WHAT IS THAT?
THIS IS A KITTY CARRIER.
REALLY. AND WHAT DO YOU INTEND TO DO WITH THAT?
WELL, I'LL GIVE YOU A HINT. ONE OF YOU TWO IS RIDING TO THE VET IN IT.
LET'S ROLL.
I'M A CAT!
YOU GUYS WAIT HERE. I HAVE TO SIGN IN AND FILL OUT SOME PAPERWORK.
SNIFF SNIFF
ANOTHER DOG SAT HERE.
OKAY, I CAN DO THIS. IT WON'T BE SO BAD.
IT'S A SIMPLE PROCEDURE. I COULD PERFORM IT MYSELF.
SNIFF
WHAT AM I SAYING? I CAN'T LET THESE ANIMALS TAKE AWAY MY REPRODUCTIVE ORGANS. I NEED THEM TO PRODUCE EVIL OFFSPRING.
SNIFF
HERE TOO.
I HAVE TO GET OUT OF HERE!
OH WAIT. THAT'S ME.

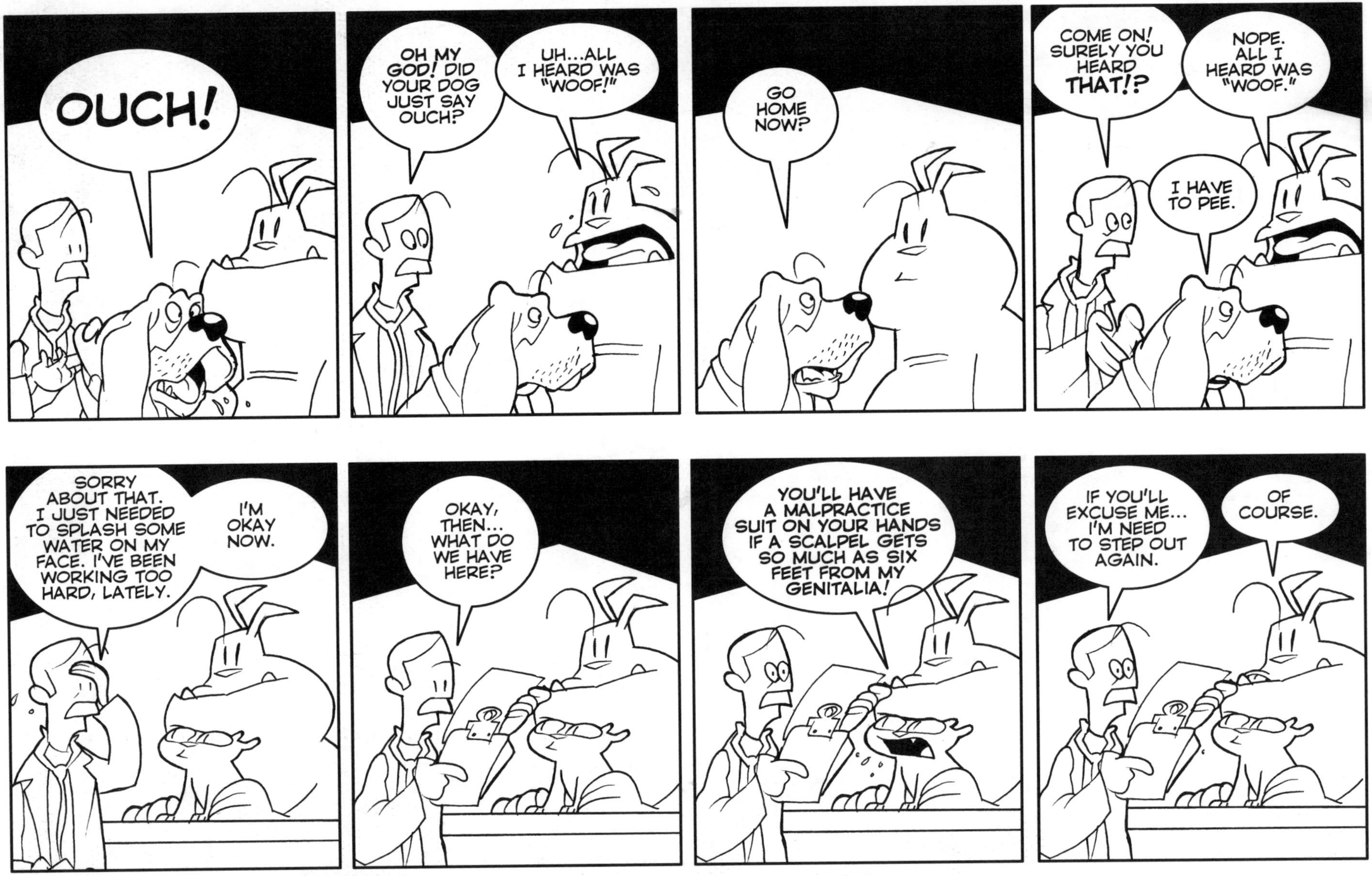
OUCH!
OH MY GOD! DID YOUR DOG JUST SAY OUCH?
UH...ALL I HEARD WAS "WOOF!"
GO HOME NOW?
COME ON! SURELY YOU HEARD THAT!?
NOPE. ALL I HEARD WAS "WOOF."
I HAVE TO PEE.
SORRY ABOUT THAT. I JUST NEEDED TO SPLASH SOME WATER ON MY FACE. I'VE BEEN WORKING TOO HARD, LATELY.
I'M OKAY NOW.
OKAY, THEN... WHAT DO WE HAVE HERE?
YOU'LL HAVE A MALPRACTICE SUIT ON YOUR HANDS IF A SCALPEL GETS SO MUCH AS SIX FEET FROM MY GENITALIA!
IF YOU'LL EXCUSE ME... I'M NEED TO STEP OUT AGAIN.
OF COURSE.

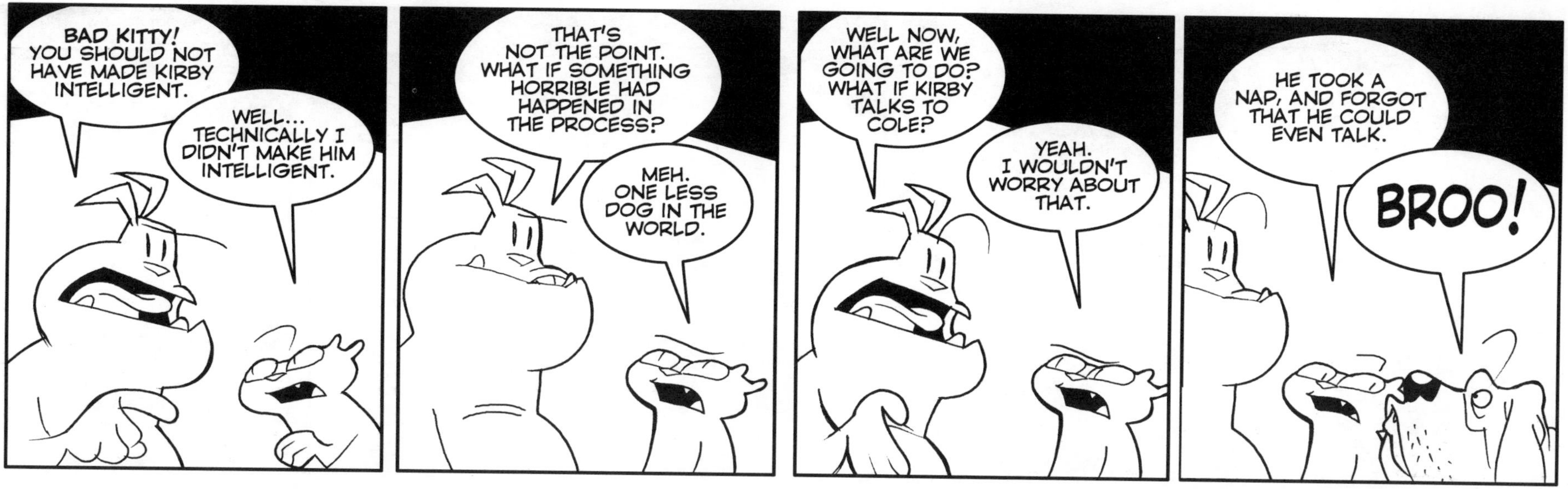
BAD KITTY! YOU SHOULD NOT HAVE MADE KIRBY INTELLIGENT.
WELL... TECHNICALLY I DIDN'T MAKE HIM INTELLIGENT.
THAT'S NOT THE POINT. WHAT IF SOMETHING HORRIBLE HAD HAPPENED IN THE PROCESS?
MEH. ONE LESS DOG IN THE WORLD.
WELL NOW, WHAT ARE WE GOING TO DO? WHAT IF KIRBY TALKS TO COLE?
YEAH. I WOULDN'T WORRY ABOUT THAT.
HE TOOK A NAP, AND FORGOT THAT HE COULD EVEN TALK.
BROO!

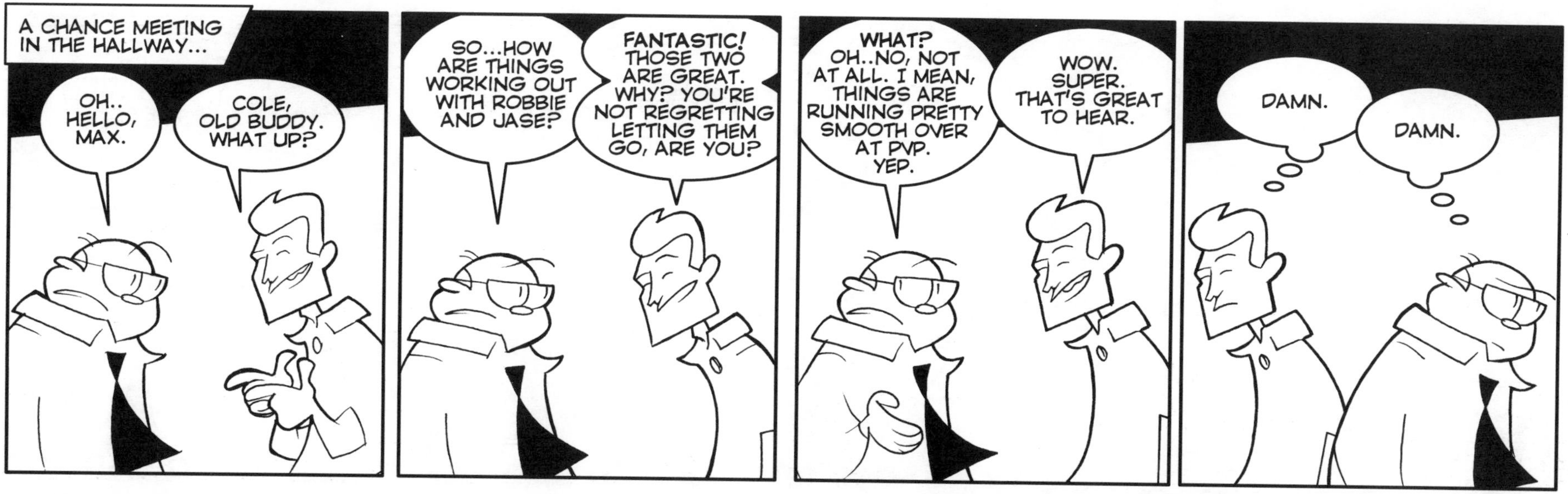
A CHANCE MEETING IN THE HALLWAY...
OH.. HELLO, MAX.
COLE, OLD BUDDY. WHAT UP?
SO...HOW ARE THINGS WORKING OUT WITH ROBBIE AND JASE?
FANTASTIC! THOSE TWO ARE GREAT. WHY? YOU'RE NOT REGRETTING LETTING THEM GO, ARE YOU?
WHAT? OH..NO, NOT AT ALL. I MEAN, THINGS ARE RUNNING PRETTY SMOOTH OVER AT PVP. YEP.
WOW. SUPER. THAT'S GREAT TO HEAR.
DAMN.
DAMN.

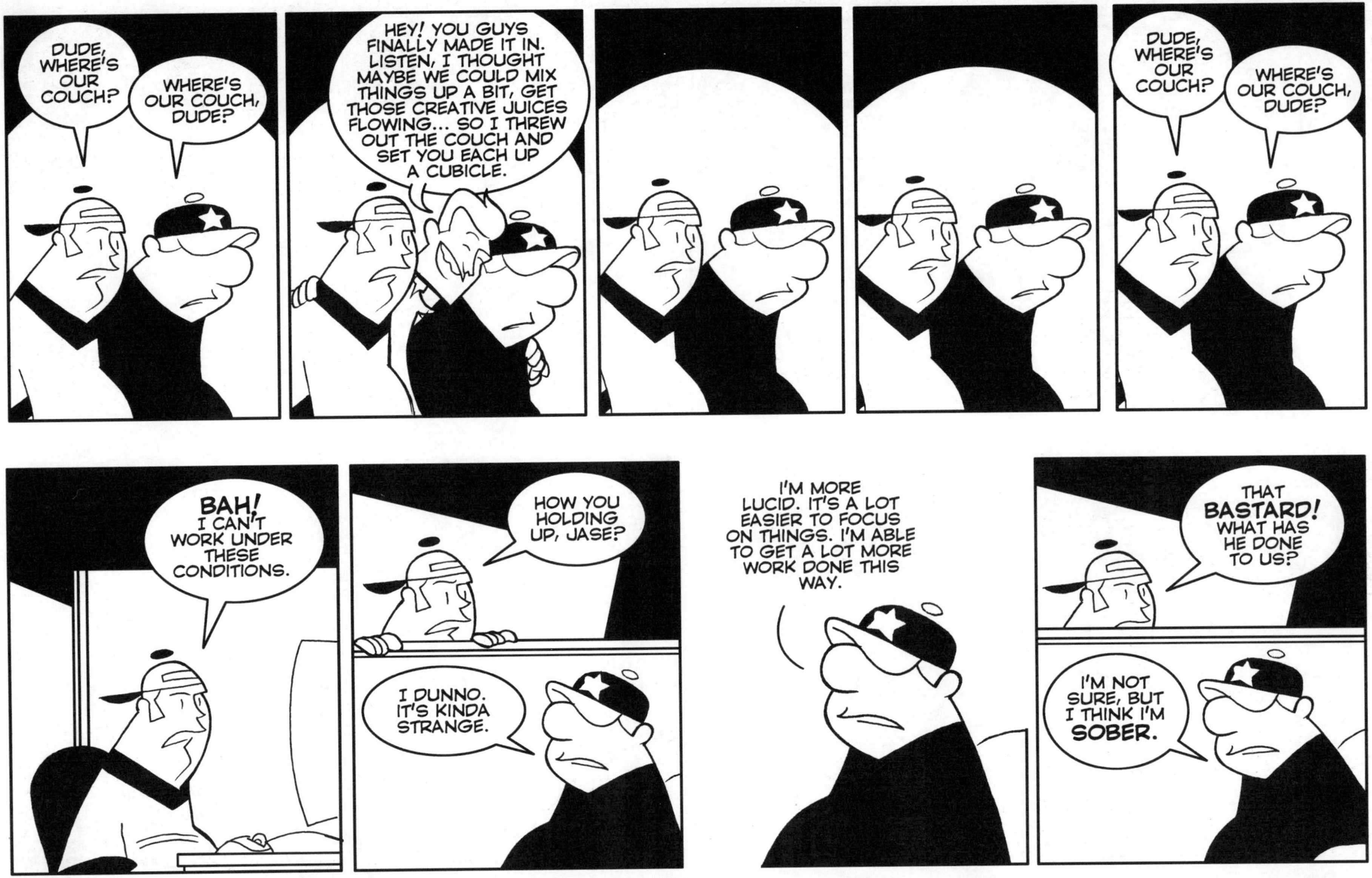
DUDE, WHERE'S OUR COUCH?
WHERE'S OUR COUCH, DUDE?
HEY! YOU GUYS FINALLY MADE IT IN. LISTEN, I THOUGHT MAYBE WE COULD MIX THINGS UP A BIT, GET THOSE CREATIVE JUICES FLOWING... SO I THREW OUT THE COUCH AND SET YOU EACH UP A CUBICLE.
DUDE, WHERE'S OUR COUCH?
WHERE'S OUR COUCH, DUDE?
BAH! I CAN'T WORK UNDER THESE CONDITIONS.
HOW YOU HOLDING UP, JASE?
I DUNNO. IT'S KINDA STRANGE.
I'M MORE LUCID. IT'S A LOT EASIER TO FOCUS ON THINGS. I'M ABLE TO GET A LOT MORE WORK DONE THIS WAY.
THAT BASTARD! WHAT HAS HE DONE TO US?
I'M NOT SURE, BUT I THINK I'M SOBER.

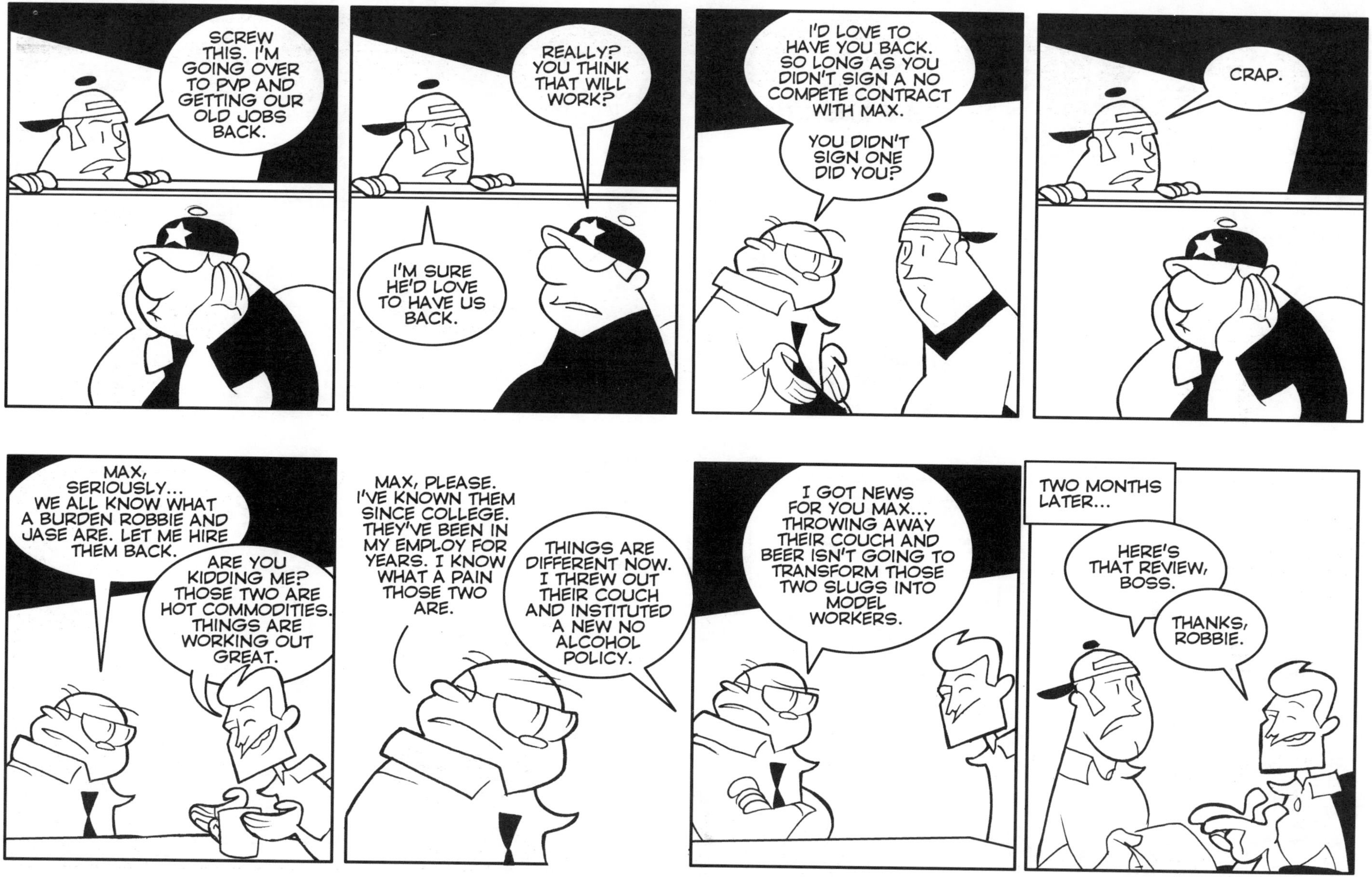
SCREW THIS. I'M GOING OVER TO PVP AND GETTING OUR OLD JOBS BACK.
REALLY? YOU THINK THAT WILL WORK?
I'M SURE HE'D LOVE TO HAVE US BACK.
I'D LOVE TO HAVE YOU BACK. SO LONG AS YOU DIDN'T SIGN A NO COMPETE CONTRACT WITH MAX.
YOU DIDN'T SIGN ONE DID YOU?
CRAP.
MAX, SERIOUSLY... WE ALL KNOW WHAT A BURDEN ROBBIE AND JASE ARE. LET ME HIRE THEM BACK.
ARE YOU KIDDING ME? THOSE TWO ARE HOT COMMODITIES. THINGS ARE WORKING OUT GREAT.
MAX, PLEASE. I'VE KNOWN THEM SINCE COLLEGE. THEY'VE BEEN IN MY EMPLOY FOR YEARS. I KNOW WHAT A PAIN THOSE TWO ARE.
THINGS ARE DIFFERENT NOW. I THREW OUT THEIR COUCH AND INSTITUTED A NEW NO ALCOHOL POLICY.
I GOT NEWS FOR YOU MAX... THROWING AWAY THEIR COUCH AND BEER ISN'T GOING TO TRANSFORM THOSE TWO SLUGS INTO MODEL WORKERS.
TWO MONTHS LATER...
HERE'S THAT REVIEW, BOSS.
THANKS, ROBBIE.

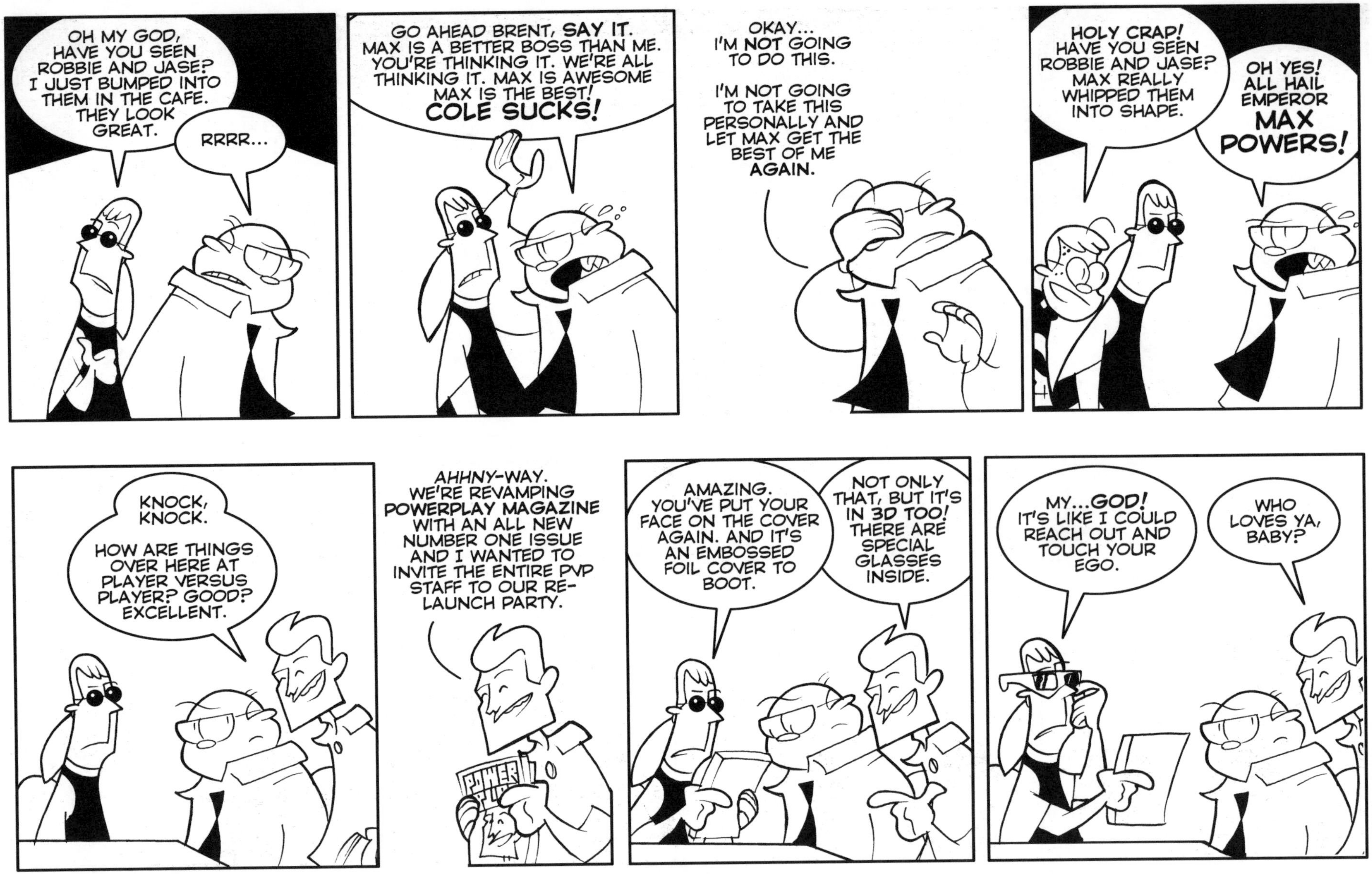
OH MY GOD, HAVE YOU SEEN ROBBIE AND JASE? I JUST BUMPED INTO THEM IN THE CAFE. THEY LOOK GREAT.
RRRR...
GO AHEAD BRENT, **SAY IT.** MAX IS A BETTER BOSS THAN ME. YOU'RE THINKING IT. WE'RE ALL THINKING IT. MAX IS AWESOME MAX IS THE BEST! **COLE SUCKS!**
OKAY... I'M **NOT** GOING TO DO THIS.
I'M NOT GOING TO TAKE THIS PERSONALLY AND LET MAX GET THE BEST OF ME **AGAIN.**
HOLY CRAP! HAVE YOU SEEN ROBBIE AND JASE? MAX REALLY WHIPPED THEM INTO SHAPE.
OH YES! ALL HAIL EMPEROR **MAX POWERS!**
KNOCK, KNOCK.
HOW ARE THINGS OVER HERE AT PLAYER VERSUS PLAYER? GOOD? EXCELLENT.
AHHNY-WAY. WE'RE REVAMPING **POWERPLAY MAGAZINE** WITH AN ALL NEW NUMBER ONE ISSUE AND I WANTED TO INVITE THE ENTIRE PVP STAFF TO OUR RE-LAUNCH PARTY.
AMAZING. YOU'VE PUT YOUR FACE ON THE COVER AGAIN. AND IT'S AN EMBOSSED FOIL COVER TO BOOT.
NOT ONLY THAT, BUT IT'S IN **3D TOO!** THERE ARE SPECIAL GLASSES INSIDE.
MY...**GOD!** IT'S LIKE I COULD REACH OUT AND TOUCH YOUR EGO.
WHO LOVES YA, BABY?

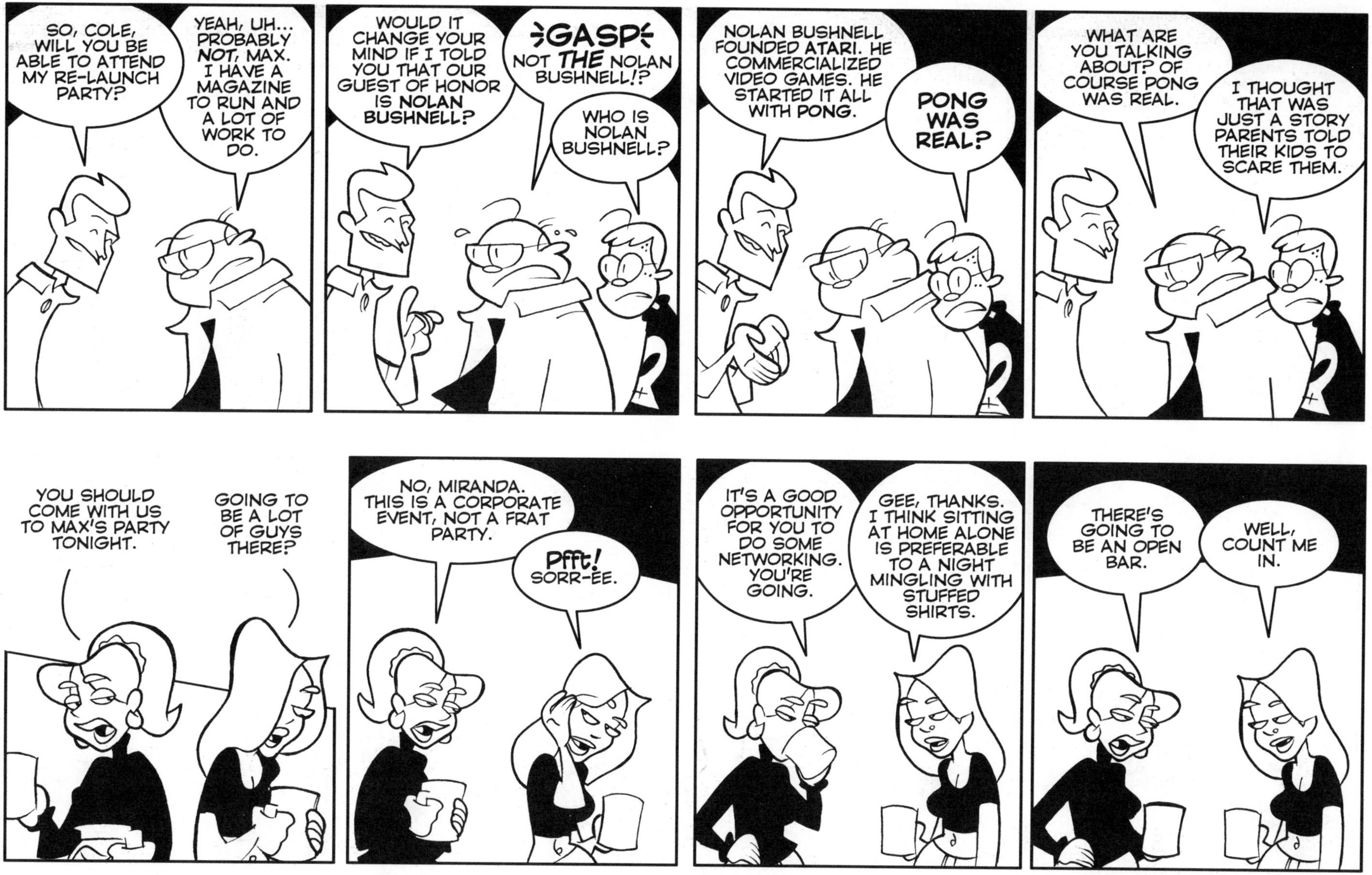
SO, COLE, WILL YOU BE ABLE TO ATTEND MY RE-LAUNCH PARTY?
YEAH, UH... PROBABLY NOT, MAX. I HAVE A MAGAZINE TO RUN AND A LOT OF WORK TO DO.
WOULD IT CHANGE YOUR MIND IF I TOLD YOU THAT OUR GUEST OF HONOR IS NOLAN BUSHNELL?
GASP NOT THE NOLAN BUSHNELL!?
WHO IS NOLAN BUSHNELL?
NOLAN BUSHNELL FOUNDED ATARI. HE COMMERCIALIZED VIDEO GAMES. HE STARTED IT ALL WITH PONG.
PONG WAS REAL?
WHAT ARE YOU TALKING ABOUT? OF COURSE PONG WAS REAL.
I THOUGHT THAT WAS JUST A STORY PARENTS TOLD THEIR KIDS TO SCARE THEM.
YOU SHOULD COME WITH US TO MAX'S PARTY TONIGHT.
GOING TO BE A LOT OF GUYS THERE?
NO, MIRANDA. THIS IS A CORPORATE EVENT, NOT A FRAT PARTY.
Pfft! SORR-EE.
IT'S A GOOD OPPORTUNITY FOR YOU TO DO SOME NETWORKING. YOU'RE GOING.
GEE, THANKS. I THINK SITTING AT HOME ALONE IS PREFERABLE TO A NIGHT MINGLING WITH STUFFED SHIRTS.
THERE'S GOING TO BE AN OPEN BAR.
WELL, COUNT ME IN.

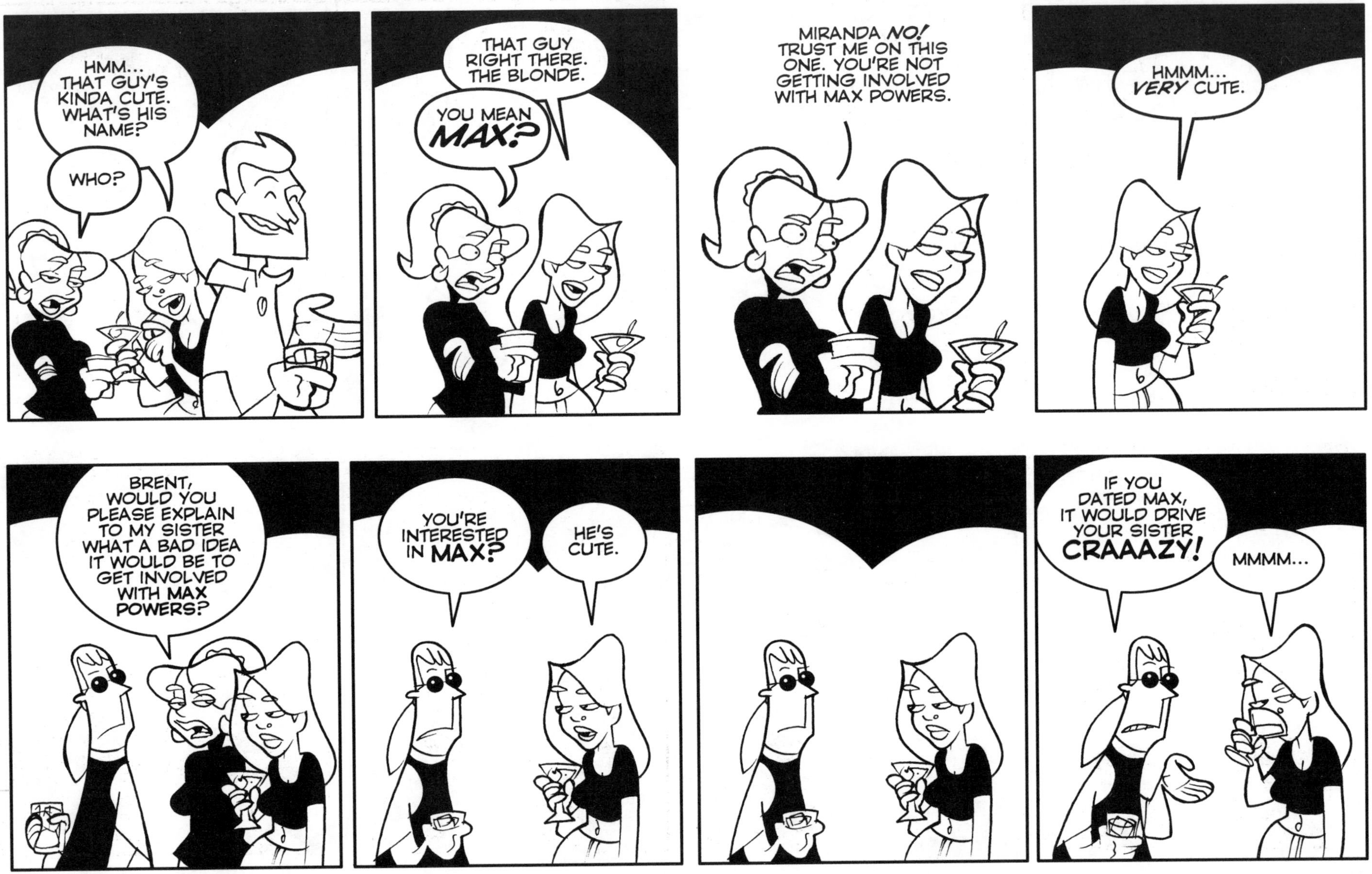
HMM... THAT GUY'S KINDA CUTE. WHAT'S HIS NAME?
WHO?
THAT GUY RIGHT THERE. THE BLONDE.
YOU MEAN MAX?
MIRANDA NO! TRUST ME ON THIS ONE. YOU'RE NOT GETTING INVOLVED WITH MAX POWERS.
HMMM... VERY CUTE.
BRENT, WOULD YOU PLEASE EXPLAIN TO MY SISTER WHAT A BAD IDEA IT WOULD BE TO GET INVOLVED WITH MAX POWERS?
YOU'RE INTERESTED IN MAX?
HE'S CUTE.
IF YOU DATED MAX, IT WOULD DRIVE YOUR SISTER CRAAAZY!
MMMM...

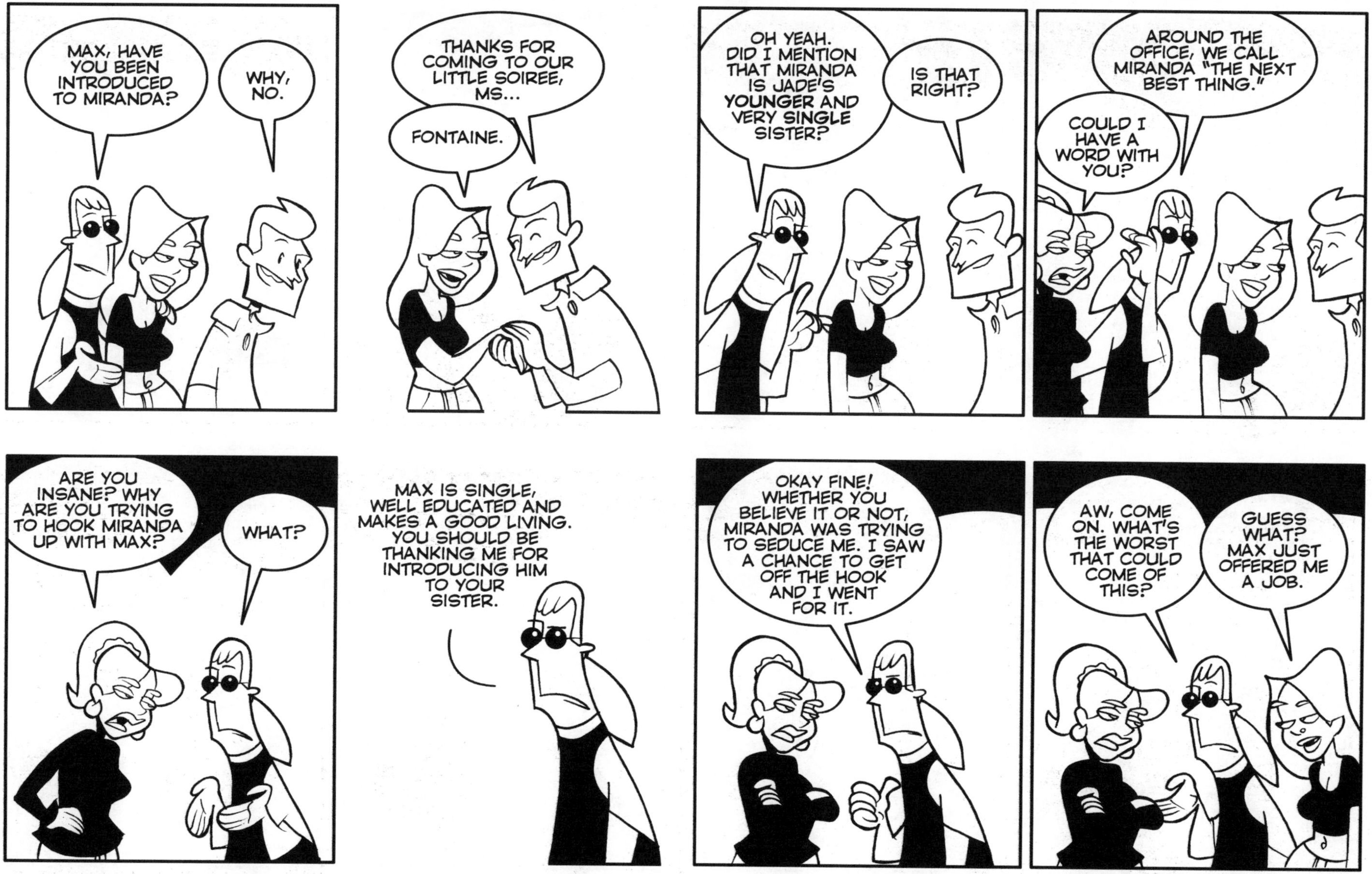
MAX, HAVE YOU BEEN INTRODUCED TO MIRANDA?
WHY, NO.
THANKS FOR COMING TO OUR LITTLE SOIREE, MS...
FONTAINE.
OH YEAH. DID I MENTION THAT MIRANDA IS JADE'S YOUNGER AND VERY SINGLE SISTER?
IS THAT RIGHT?
AROUND THE OFFICE, WE CALL MIRANDA "THE NEXT BEST THING."
COULD I HAVE A WORD WITH YOU?
ARE YOU INSANE? WHY ARE YOU TRYING TO HOOK MIRANDA UP WITH MAX?
WHAT?
MAX IS SINGLE, WELL EDUCATED AND MAKES A GOOD LIVING. YOU SHOULD BE THANKING ME FOR INTRODUCING HIM TO YOUR SISTER.
OKAY FINE! WHETHER YOU BELIEVE IT OR NOT, MIRANDA WAS TRYING TO SEDUCE ME. I SAW A CHANCE TO GET OFF THE HOOK AND I WENT FOR IT.
AW, COME ON. WHAT'S THE WORST THAT COULD COME OF THIS?
GUESS WHAT? MAX JUST OFFERED ME A JOB.

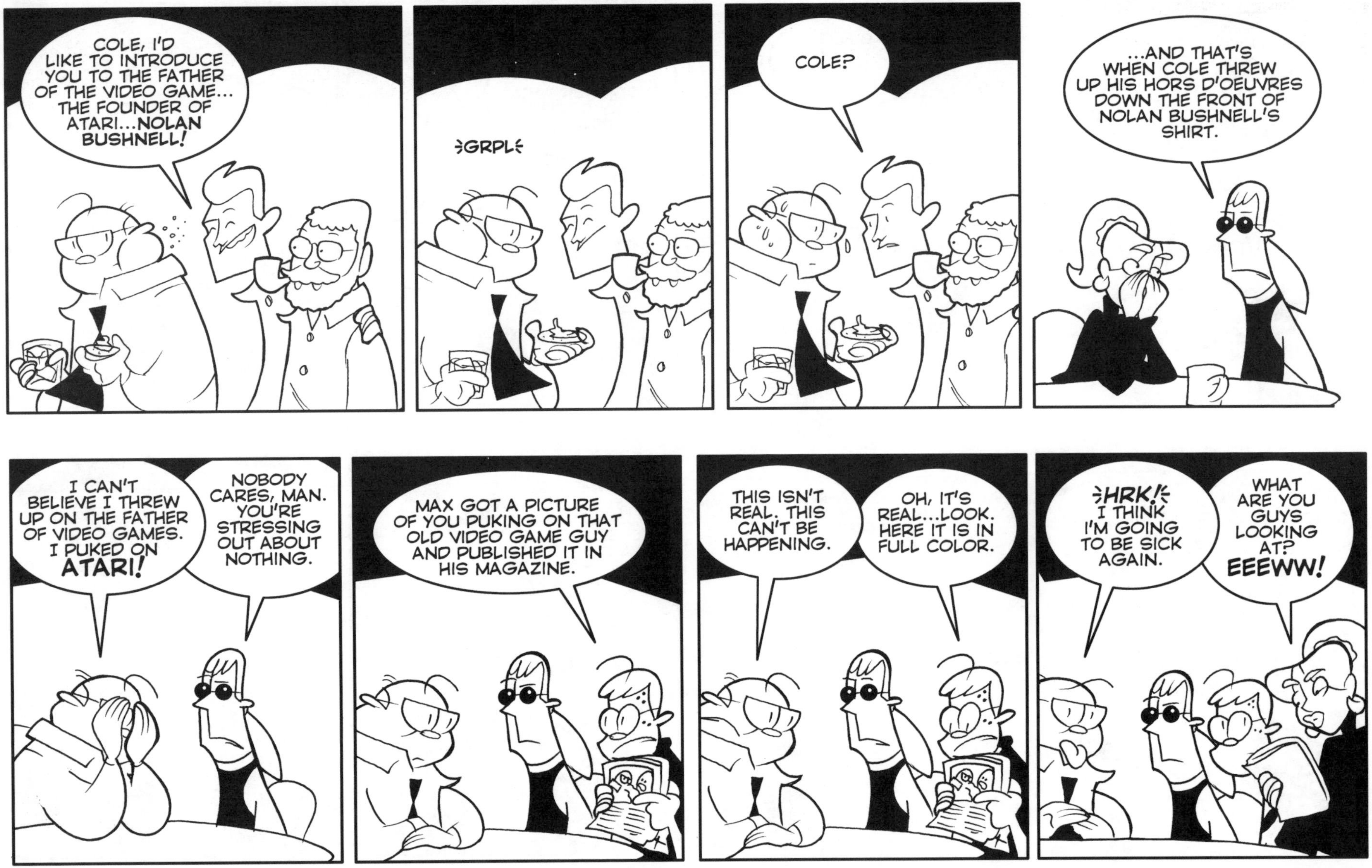

COLE, I'D LIKE TO INTRODUCE YOU TO THE FATHER OF THE VIDEO GAME... THE FOUNDER OF ATARI...NOLAN BUSHNELL!
GRPL
COLE?
...AND THAT'S WHEN COLE THREW UP HIS HORS D'OEUVRES DOWN THE FRONT OF NOLAN BUSHNELL'S SHIRT.
I CAN'T BELIEVE I THREW UP ON THE FATHER OF VIDEO GAMES. I PUKED ON ATARI!
NOBODY CARES, MAN. YOU'RE STRESSING OUT ABOUT NOTHING.
MAX GOT A PICTURE OF YOU PUKING ON THAT OLD VIDEO GAME GUY AND PUBLISHED IT IN HIS MAGAZINE.
THIS ISN'T REAL. THIS CAN'T BE HAPPENING.
OH, IT'S REAL...LOOK. HERE IT IS IN FULL COLOR.
HRK! I THINK I'M GOING TO BE SICK AGAIN.
WHAT ARE YOU GUYS LOOKING AT? EEEWW!

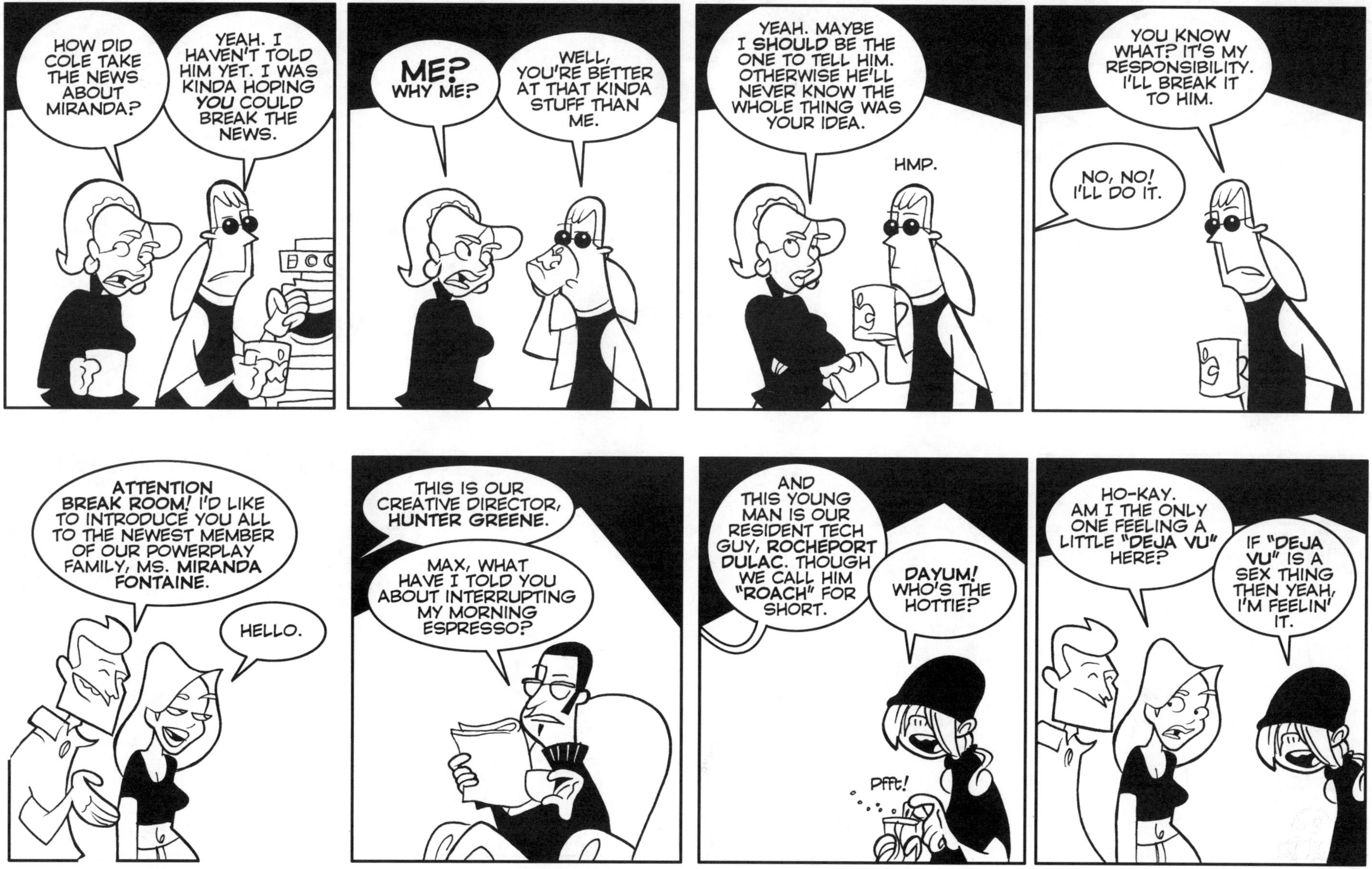
HOW DID COLE TAKE THE NEWS ABOUT MIRANDA?
YEAH. I HAVEN'T TOLD HIM YET. I WAS KINDA HOPING YOU COULD BREAK THE NEWS.
ME? WHY ME?
WELL, YOU'RE BETTER AT THAT KINDA STUFF THAN ME.
YEAH. MAYBE I SHOULD BE THE ONE TO TELL HIM. OTHERWISE HE'LL NEVER KNOW THE WHOLE THING WAS YOUR IDEA.
HMP.
YOU KNOW WHAT? IT'S MY RESPONSIBILITY. I'LL BREAK IT TO HIM.
NO, NO! I'LL DO IT.
ATTENTION BREAK ROOM! I'D LIKE TO INTRODUCE YOU ALL TO THE NEWEST MEMBER OF OUR POWERPLAY FAMILY, MS. MIRANDA FONTAINE.
HELLO.
THIS IS OUR CREATIVE DIRECTOR, HUNTER GREENE.
MAX, WHAT HAVE I TOLD YOU ABOUT INTERRUPTING MY MORNING ESPRESSO?
AND THIS YOUNG MAN IS OUR RESIDENT TECH GUY, ROCHEPORT DULAC. THOUGH WE CALL HIM "ROACH" FOR SHORT.
DAYUM! WHO'S THE HOTTIE?
Pfft!
HO-KAY. AM I THE ONLY ONE FEELING A LITTLE "DEJA VU" HERE?
IF "DEJA VU" IS A SEX THING THEN YEAH, I'M FEELIN' IT.

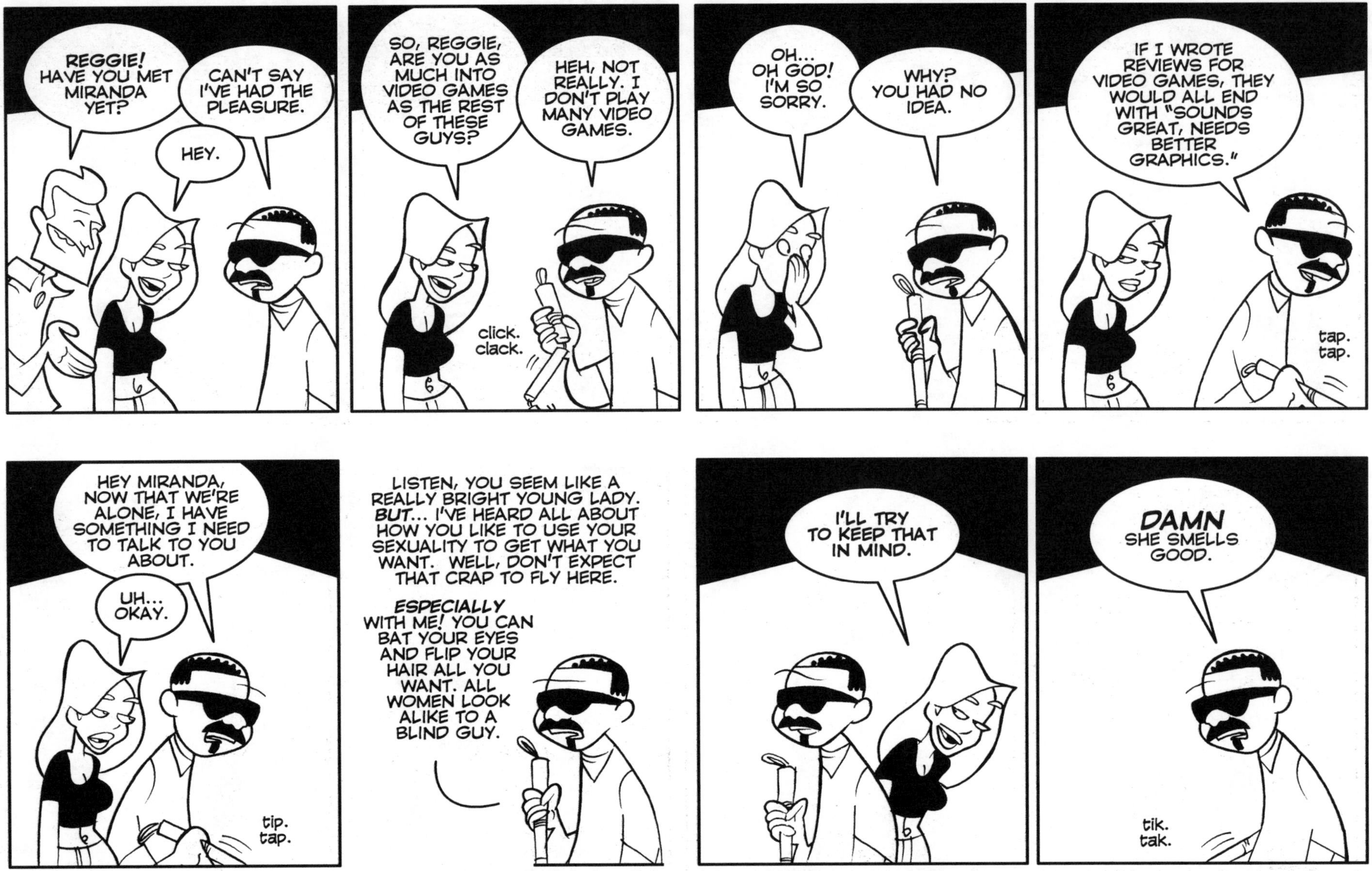
REGGIE! HAVE YOU MET MIRANDA YET?
CAN'T SAY I'VE HAD THE PLEASURE.
HEY.
SO, REGGIE, ARE YOU AS MUCH INTO VIDEO GAMES AS THE REST OF THESE GUYS?
HEH, NOT REALLY. I DON'T PLAY MANY VIDEO GAMES.
click. clack.
OH... OH GOD! I'M SO SORRY.
WHY? YOU HAD NO IDEA.
IF I WROTE REVIEWS FOR VIDEO GAMES, THEY WOULD ALL END WITH "SOUNDS GREAT, NEEDS BETTER GRAPHICS."
tap. tap.
HEY MIRANDA, NOW THAT WE'RE ALONE, I HAVE SOMETHING I NEED TO TALK TO YOU ABOUT.
UH... OKAY.
tip. tap.
LISTEN, YOU SEEM LIKE A REALLY BRIGHT YOUNG LADY. *BUT*... I'VE HEARD ALL ABOUT HOW YOU LIKE TO USE YOUR SEXUALITY TO GET WHAT YOU WANT. WELL, DON'T EXPECT THAT CRAP TO FLY HERE.
ESPECIALLY WITH ME! YOU CAN BAT YOUR EYES AND FLIP YOUR HAIR ALL YOU WANT. ALL WOMEN LOOK ALIKE TO A BLIND GUY.
I'LL TRY TO KEEP THAT IN MIND.
DAMN SHE SMELLS GOOD.
tik. tak.

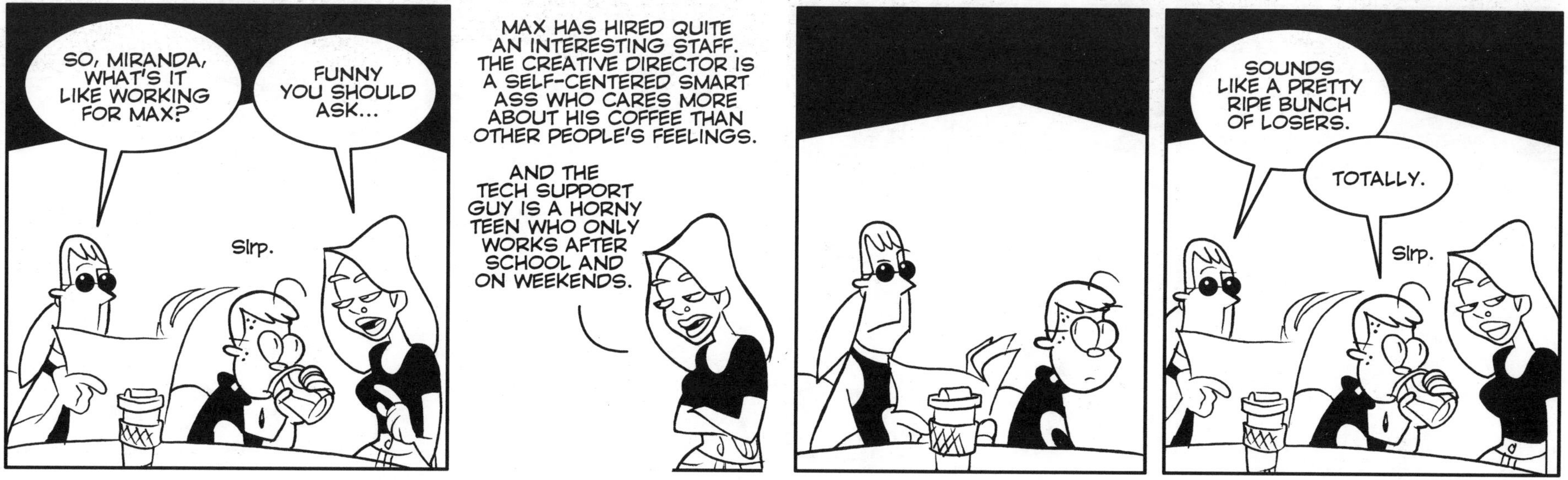
SO, MIRANDA, WHAT'S IT LIKE WORKING FOR MAX?
FUNNY YOU SHOULD ASK...
Slrp.
MAX HAS HIRED QUITE AN INTERESTING STAFF. THE CREATIVE DIRECTOR IS A SELF-CENTERED SMART ASS WHO CARES MORE ABOUT HIS COFFEE THAN OTHER PEOPLE'S FEELINGS.
AND THE TECH SUPPORT GUY IS A HORNY TEEN WHO ONLY WORKS AFTER SCHOOL AND ON WEEKENDS.
SOUNDS LIKE A PRETTY RIPE BUNCH OF LOSERS.
TOTALLY.
Slrp.

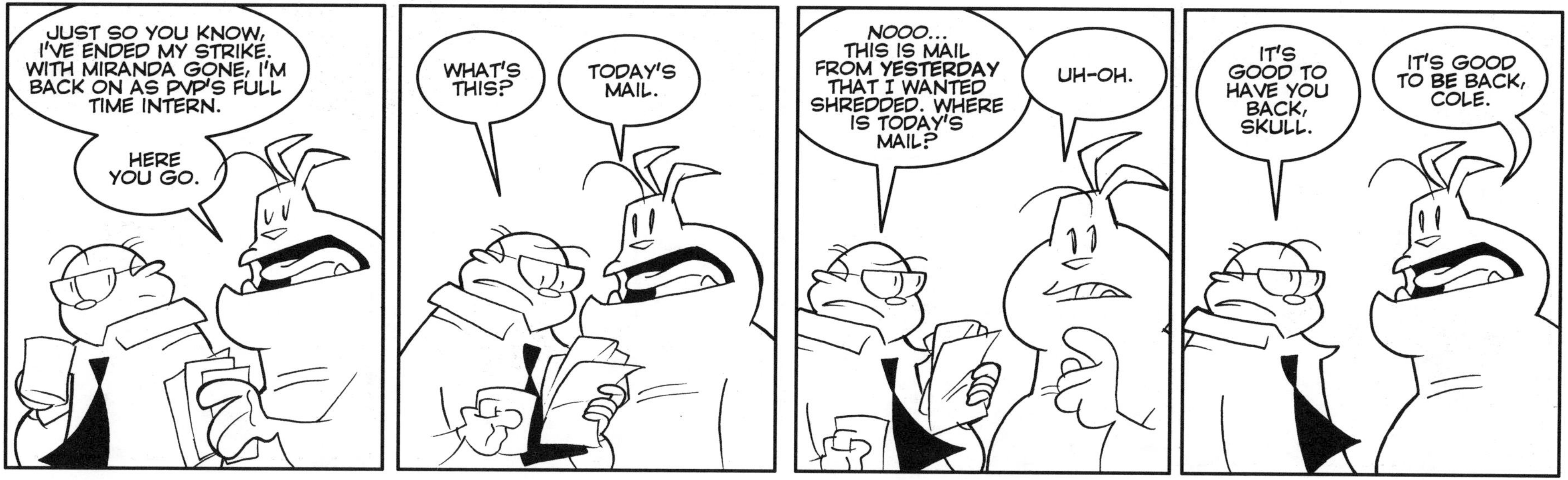
JUST SO YOU KNOW, I'VE ENDED MY STRIKE. WITH MIRANDA GONE, I'M BACK ON AS PVP'S FULL TIME INTERN.
HERE YOU GO.
WHAT'S THIS?
TODAY'S MAIL.
NOOO... THIS IS MAIL FROM YESTERDAY THAT I WANTED SHREDDED. WHERE IS TODAY'S MAIL?
UH-OH.
IT'S GOOD TO HAVE YOU BACK, SKULL.
IT'S GOOD TO BE BACK, COLE.

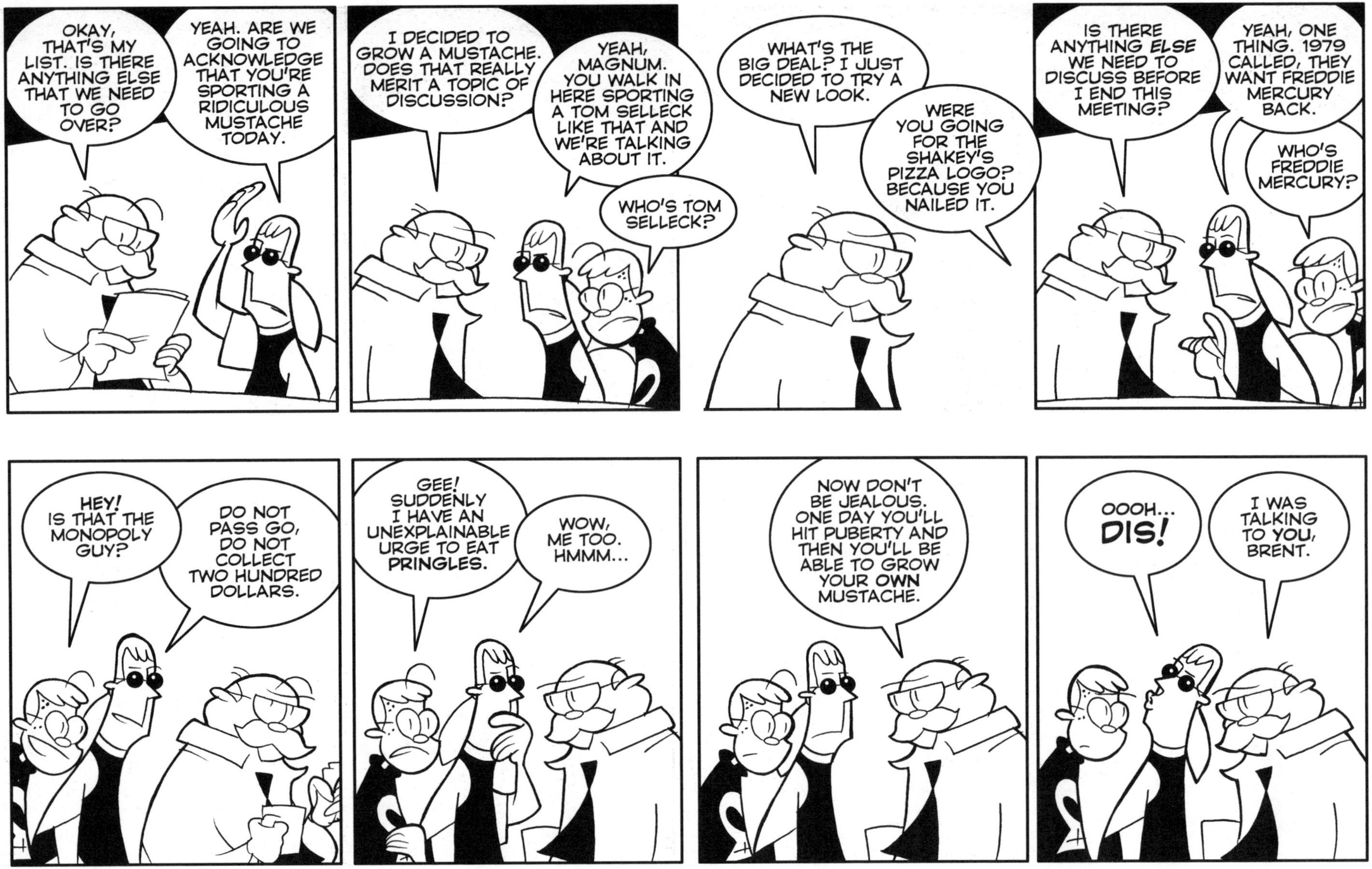
OKAY, THAT'S MY LIST. IS THERE ANYTHING ELSE THAT WE NEED TO GO OVER?
YEAH. ARE WE GOING TO ACKNOWLEDGE THAT YOU'RE SPORTING A RIDICULOUS MUSTACHE TODAY.
I DECIDED TO GROW A MUSTACHE. DOES THAT REALLY MERIT A TOPIC OF DISCUSSION?
YEAH, MAGNUM. YOU WALK IN HERE SPORTING A TOM SELLECK LIKE THAT AND WE'RE TALKING ABOUT IT.
WHO'S TOM SELLECK?
WHAT'S THE BIG DEAL? I JUST DECIDED TO TRY A NEW LOOK.
WERE YOU GOING FOR THE SHAKEY'S PIZZA LOGO? BECAUSE YOU NAILED IT.
IS THERE ANYTHING ELSE WE NEED TO DISCUSS BEFORE I END THIS MEETING?
YEAH, ONE THING. 1979 CALLED, THEY WANT FREDDIE MERCURY BACK.
WHO'S FREDDIE MERCURY?
HEY! IS THAT THE MONOPOLY GUY?
DO NOT PASS GO, DO NOT COLLECT TWO HUNDRED DOLLARS.
GEE! SUDDENLY I HAVE AN UNEXPLAINABLE URGE TO EAT PRINGLES.
WOW, ME TOO. HMMM...
NOW DON'T BE JEALOUS. ONE DAY YOU'LL HIT PUBERTY AND THEN YOU'LL BE ABLE TO GROW YOUR OWN MUSTACHE.
OOOH... DIS!
I WAS TALKING TO YOU, BRENT.

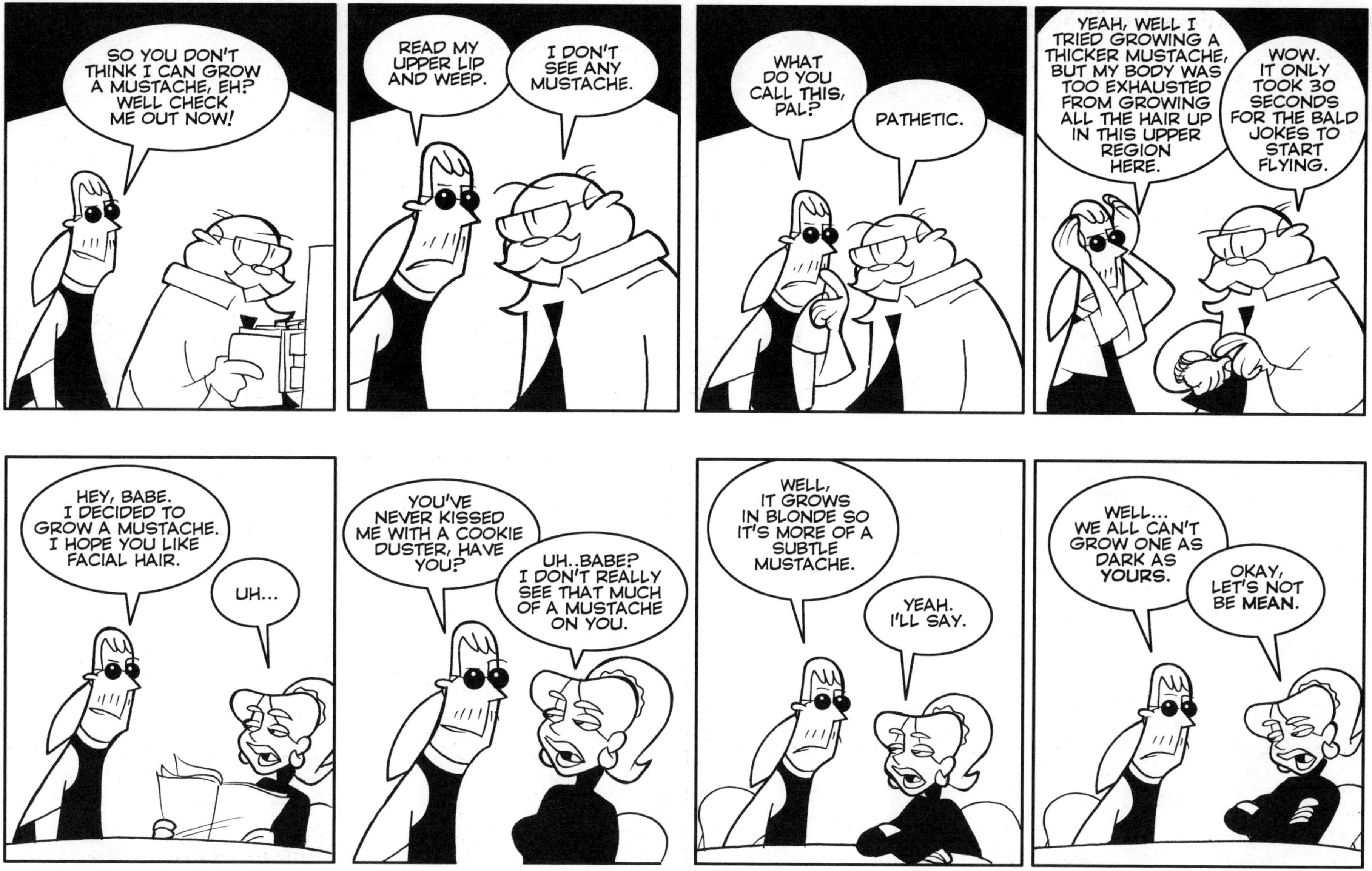
SO YOU DON'T THINK I CAN GROW A MUSTACHE, EH? WELL CHECK ME OUT NOW!
READ MY UPPER LIP AND WEEP.
I DON'T SEE ANY MUSTACHE.
WHAT DO YOU CALL THIS, PAL?
PATHETIC.
YEAH, WELL I TRIED GROWING A THICKER MUSTACHE, BUT MY BODY WAS TOO EXHAUSTED FROM GROWING ALL THE HAIR UP IN THIS UPPER REGION HERE.
WOW. IT ONLY TOOK 30 SECONDS FOR THE BALD JOKES TO START FLYING.
HEY, BABE. I DECIDED TO GROW A MUSTACHE. I HOPE YOU LIKE FACIAL HAIR.
UH...
YOU'VE NEVER KISSED ME WITH A COOKIE DUSTER, HAVE YOU?
UH..BABE? I DON'T REALLY SEE THAT MUCH OF A MUSTACHE ON YOU.
WELL, IT GROWS IN BLONDE SO IT'S MORE OF A SUBTLE MUSTACHE.
YEAH. I'LL SAY.
WELL... WE ALL CAN'T GROW ONE AS DARK AS YOURS.
OKAY, LET'S NOT BE MEAN.

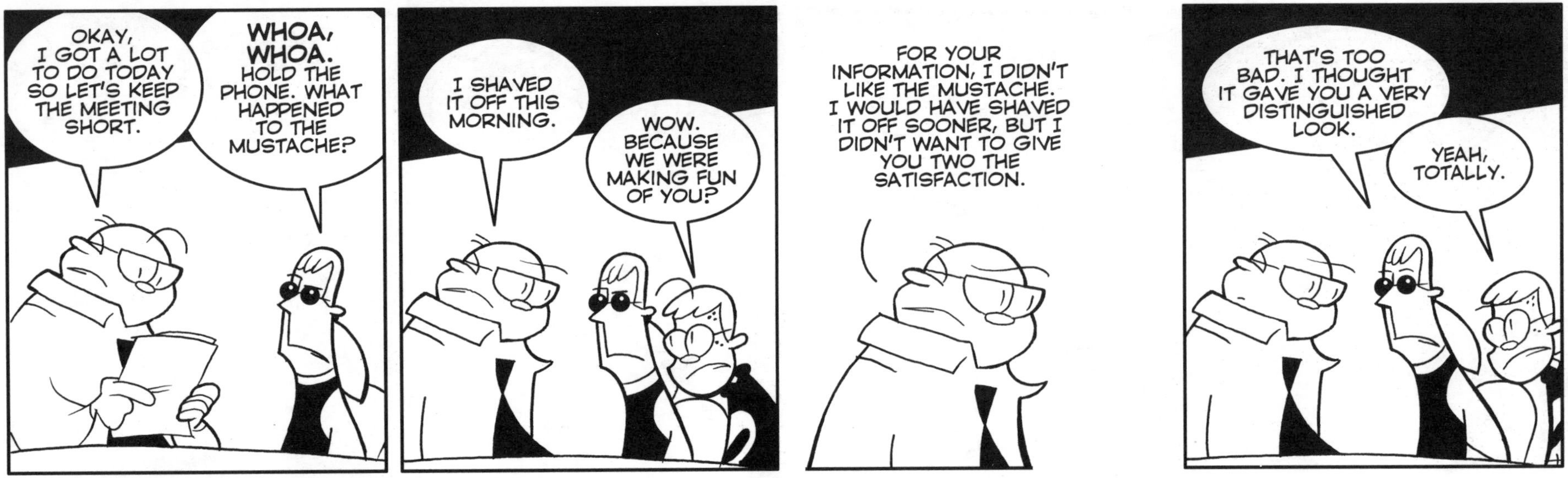
OKAY, I GOT A LOT TO DO TODAY SO LET'S KEEP THE MEETING SHORT.
WHOA, WHOA. HOLD THE PHONE. WHAT HAPPENED TO THE MUSTACHE?
I SHAVED IT OFF THIS MORNING.
WOW. BECAUSE WE WERE MAKING FUN OF YOU?
FOR YOUR INFORMATION, I DIDN'T LIKE THE MUSTACHE. I WOULD HAVE SHAVED IT OFF SOONER, BUT I DIDN'T WANT TO GIVE YOU TWO THE SATISFACTION.
THAT'S TOO BAD. I THOUGHT IT GAVE YOU A VERY DISTINGUISHED LOOK.
YEAH, TOTALLY.

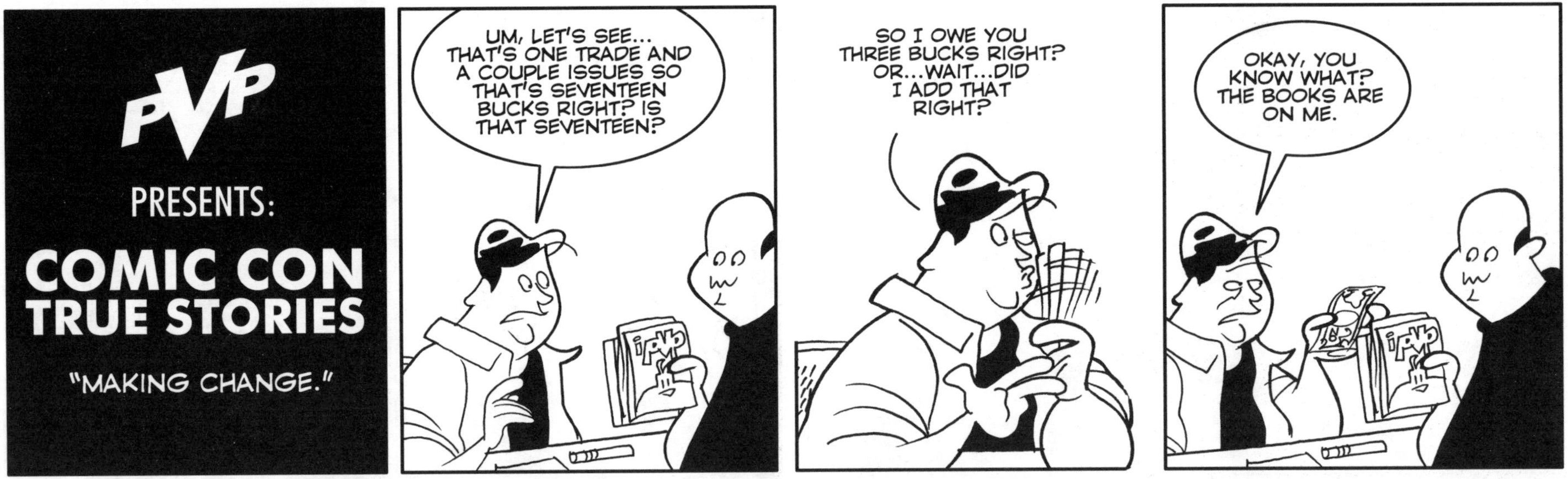
PVP
PRESENTS:
COMIC CON TRUE STORIES
"MAKING CHANGE."
UM, LET'S SEE... THAT'S ONE TRADE AND A COUPLE ISSUES SO THAT'S SEVENTEEN BUCKS RIGHT? IS THAT SEVENTEEN?
SO I OWE YOU THREE BUCKS RIGHT? OR...WAIT...DID I ADD THAT RIGHT?
OKAY, YOU KNOW WHAT? THE BOOKS ARE ON ME.

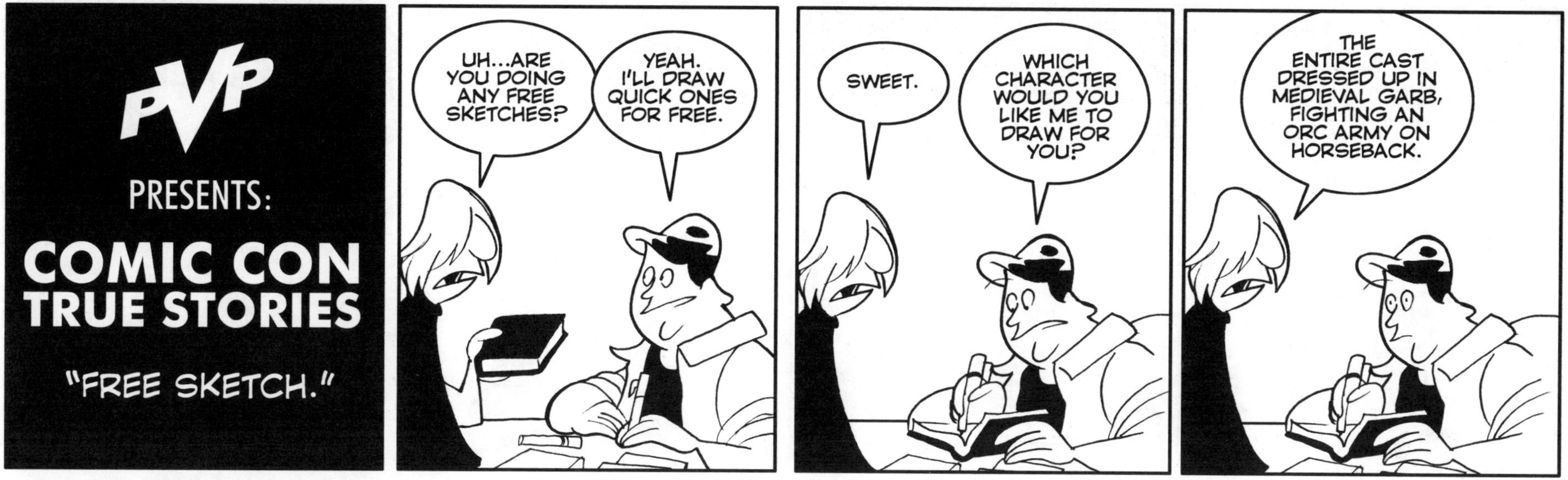
PVP
PRESENTS:
COMIC CON TRUE STORIES
"FREE SKETCH."
UH...ARE YOU DOING ANY FREE SKETCHES?
YEAH. I'LL DRAW QUICK ONES FOR FREE.
SWEET.
WHICH CHARACTER WOULD YOU LIKE ME TO DRAW FOR YOU?
THE ENTIRE CAST DRESSED UP IN MEDIEVAL GARB, FIGHTING AN ORC ARMY ON HORSEBACK.

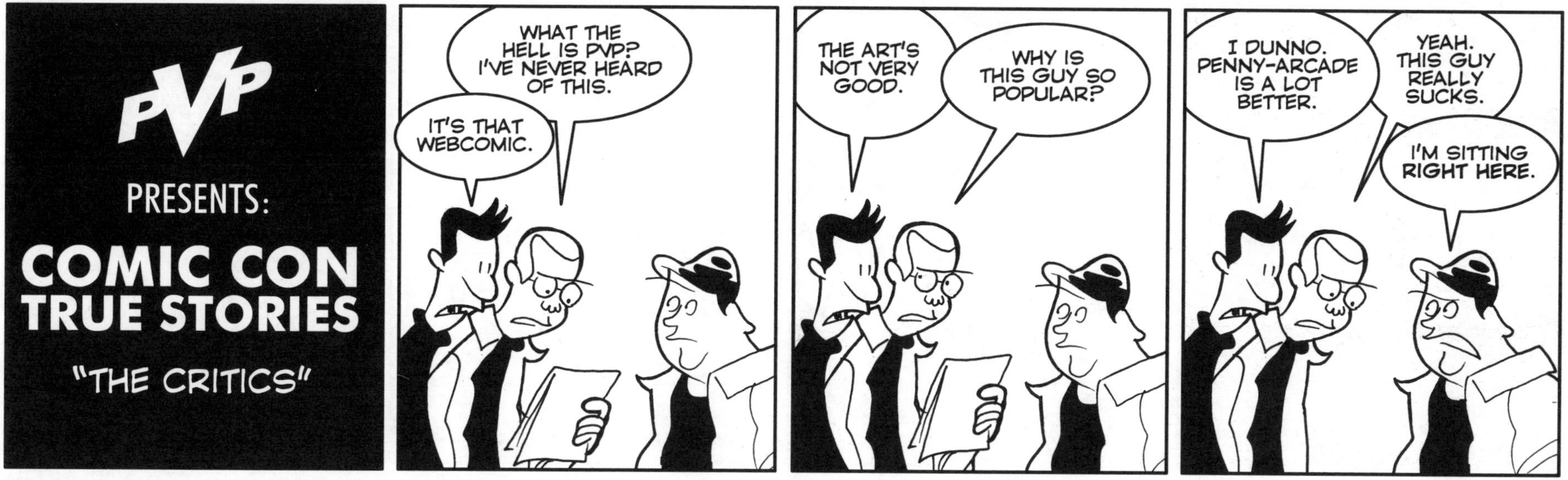
PVP
PRESENTS:
COMIC CON TRUE STORIES
"THE CRITICS"
WHAT THE HELL IS PVP? I'VE NEVER HEARD OF THIS.
IT'S THAT WEBCOMIC.
THE ART'S NOT VERY GOOD.
WHY IS THIS GUY SO POPULAR?
I DUNNO. PENNY-ARCADE IS A LOT BETTER.
YEAH. THIS GUY REALLY SUCKS.
I'M SITTING RIGHT HERE.

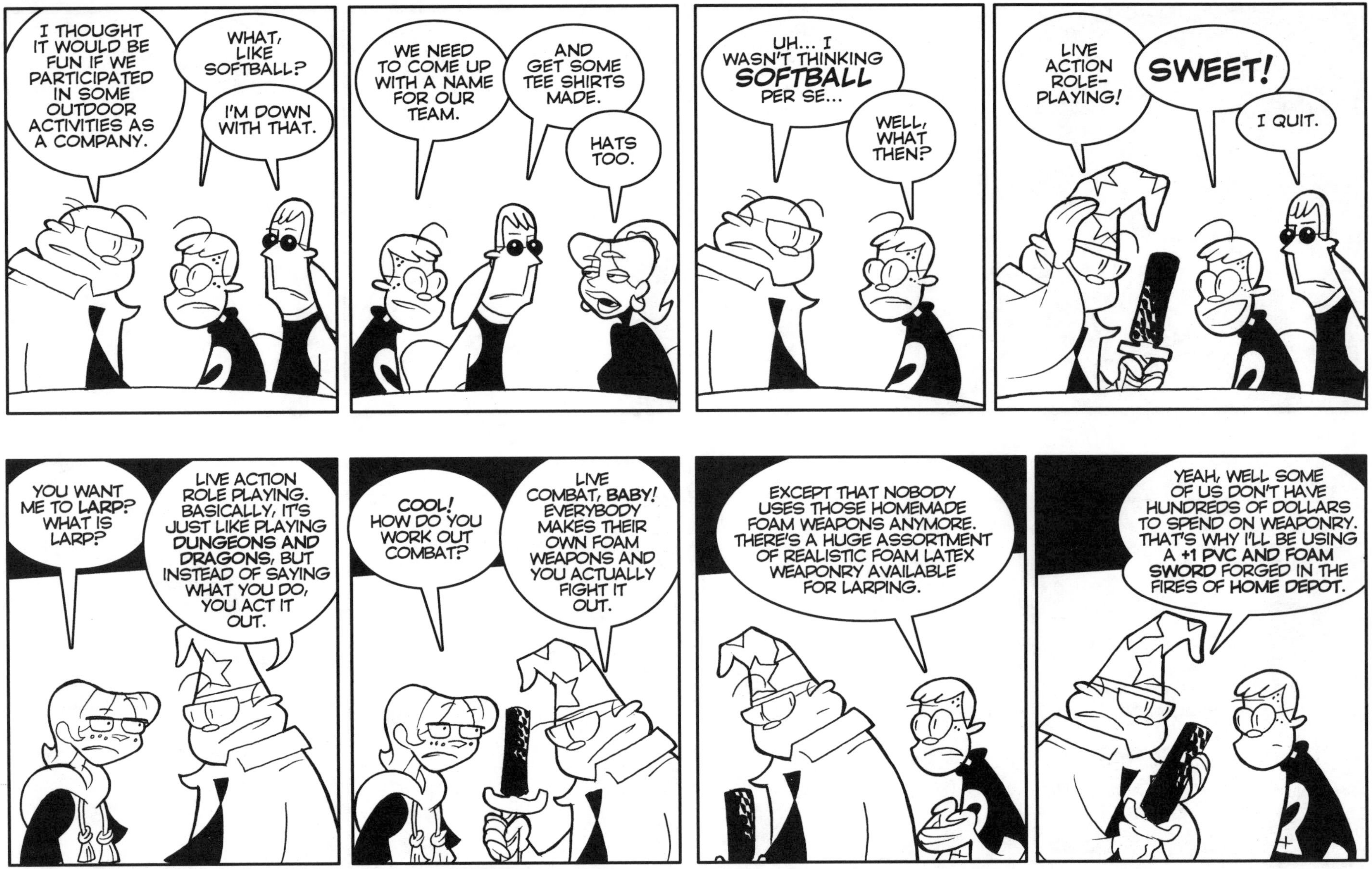
I THOUGHT IT WOULD BE FUN IF WE PARTICIPATED IN SOME OUTDOOR ACTIVITIES AS A COMPANY.
WHAT, LIKE SOFTBALL?
I'M DOWN WITH THAT.
WE NEED TO COME UP WITH A NAME FOR OUR TEAM.
AND GET SOME TEE SHIRTS MADE.
HATS TOO.
UH... I WASN'T THINKING **SOFTBALL** PER SE...
WELL, WHAT THEN?
LIVE ACTION ROLE-PLAYING!
SWEET!
I QUIT.
YOU WANT ME TO **LARP**? WHAT IS LARP?
LIVE ACTION ROLE PLAYING. BASICALLY, IT'S JUST LIKE PLAYING **DUNGEONS AND DRAGONS**, BUT INSTEAD OF SAYING WHAT YOU DO, YOU ACT IT OUT.
COOL! HOW DO YOU WORK OUT COMBAT?
LIVE COMBAT, **BABY!** EVERYBODY MAKES THEIR OWN FOAM WEAPONS AND YOU ACTUALLY FIGHT IT OUT.
EXCEPT THAT NOBODY USES THOSE HOMEMADE FOAM WEAPONS ANYMORE. THERE'S A HUGE ASSORTMENT OF REALISTIC FOAM LATEX WEAPONRY AVAILABLE FOR LARPING.
YEAH, WELL SOME OF US DON'T HAVE HUNDREDS OF DOLLARS TO SPEND ON WEAPONRY. THAT'S WHY I'LL BE USING A **+1 PVC AND FOAM SWORD** FORGED IN THE FIRES OF **HOME DEPOT**.

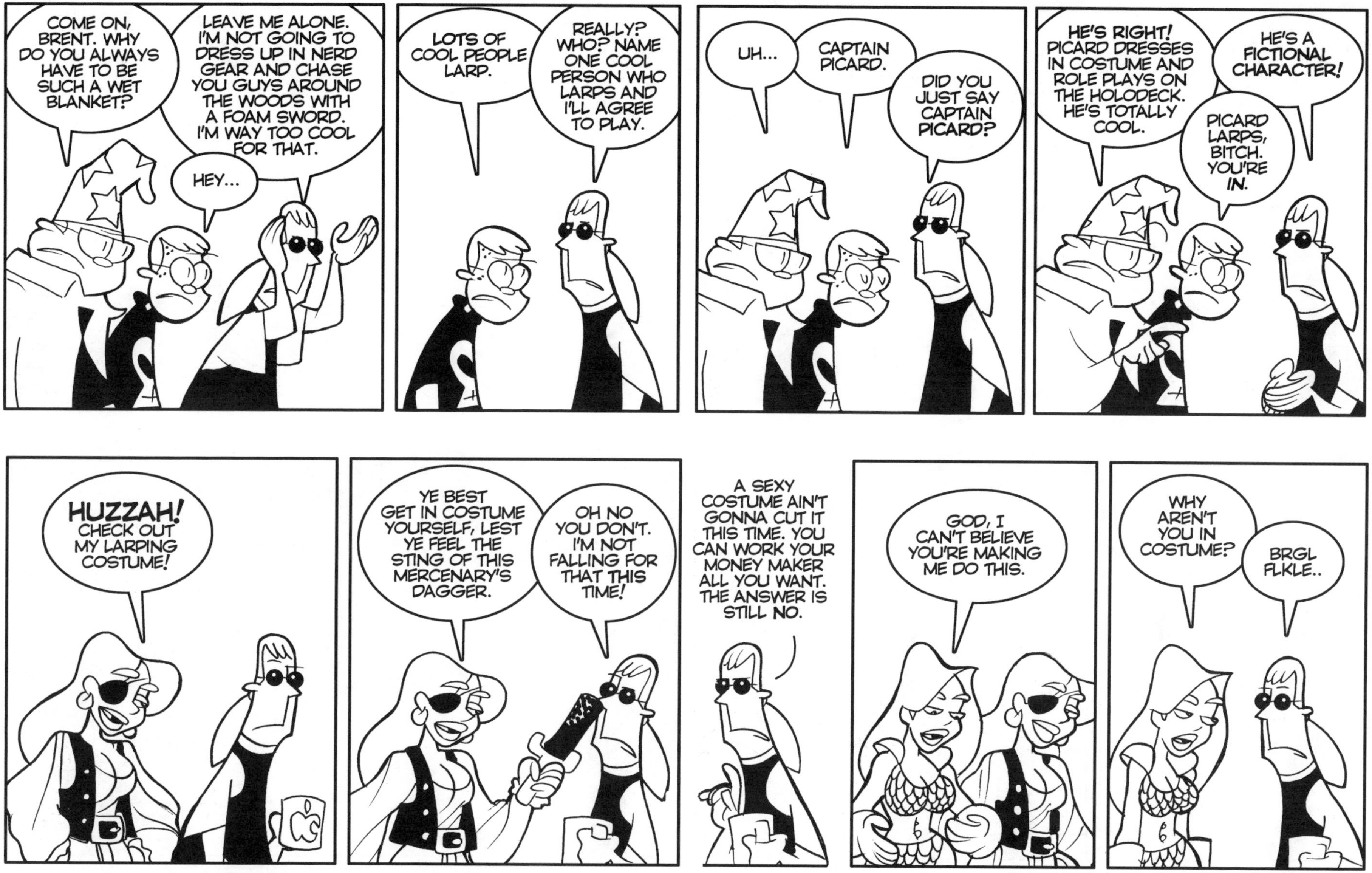
COME ON, BRENT. WHY DO YOU ALWAYS HAVE TO BE SUCH A WET BLANKET?
LEAVE ME ALONE. I'M NOT GOING TO DRESS UP IN NERD GEAR AND CHASE YOU GUYS AROUND THE WOODS WITH A FOAM SWORD. I'M WAY TOO COOL FOR THAT.
HEY...
LOTS OF COOL PEOPLE LARP.
REALLY? WHO? NAME ONE COOL PERSON WHO LARPS AND I'LL AGREE TO PLAY.
UH...
CAPTAIN PICARD.
DID YOU JUST SAY CAPTAIN PICARD?
HE'S RIGHT! PICARD DRESSES IN COSTUME AND ROLE PLAYS ON THE HOLODECK. HE'S TOTALLY COOL.
HE'S A FICTIONAL CHARACTER!
PICARD LARPS, BITCH. YOU'RE IN.
HUZZAH! CHECK OUT MY LARPING COSTUME!
YE BEST GET IN COSTUME YOURSELF, LEST YE FEEL THE STING OF THIS MERCENARY'S DAGGER.
OH NO YOU DON'T. I'M NOT FALLING FOR THAT THIS TIME!
A SEXY COSTUME AIN'T GONNA CUT IT THIS TIME. YOU CAN WORK YOUR MONEY MAKER ALL YOU WANT. THE ANSWER IS STILL NO.
GOD, I CAN'T BELIEVE YOU'RE MAKING ME DO THIS.
WHY AREN'T YOU IN COSTUME?
BRGL FLKLE..

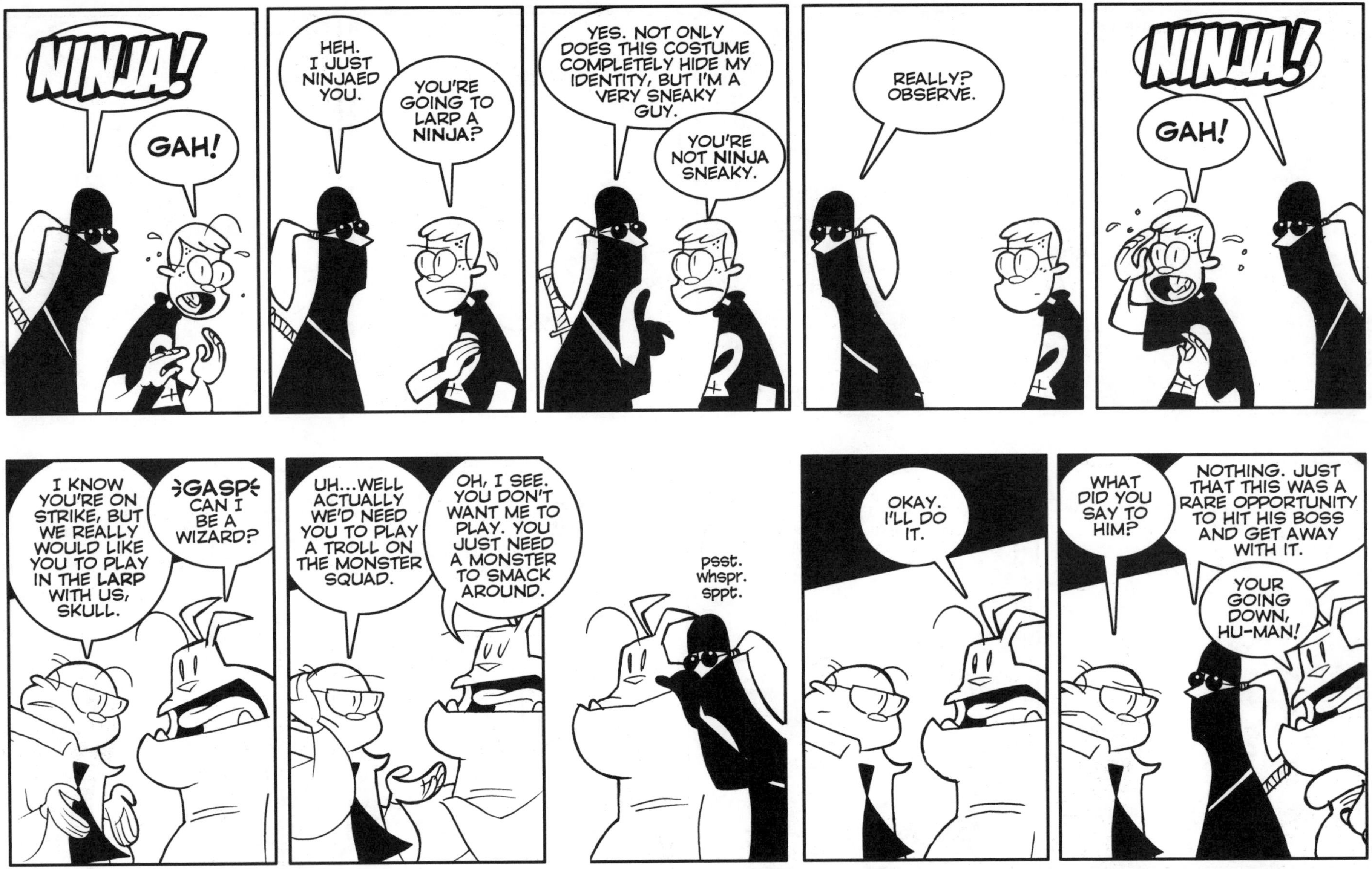
NINJA!
GAH!
HEH. I JUST NINJAED YOU.
YOU'RE GOING TO LARP A NINJA?
YES. NOT ONLY DOES THIS COSTUME COMPLETELY HIDE MY IDENTITY, BUT I'M A VERY SNEAKY GUY.
YOU'RE NOT NINJA SNEAKY.
REALLY? OBSERVE.
NINJA!
GAH!
I KNOW YOU'RE ON STRIKE, BUT WE REALLY WOULD LIKE YOU TO PLAY IN THE LARP WITH US, SKULL.
GASP CAN I BE A WIZARD?
UH...WELL ACTUALLY WE'D NEED YOU TO PLAY A TROLL ON THE MONSTER SQUAD.
OH, I SEE. YOU DON'T WANT ME TO PLAY. YOU JUST NEED A MONSTER TO SMACK AROUND.
psst. whspr. sppt.
OKAY. I'LL DO IT.
WHAT DID YOU SAY TO HIM?
NOTHING. JUST THAT THIS WAS A RARE OPPORTUNITY TO HIT HIS BOSS AND GET AWAY WITH IT.
YOUR GOING DOWN, HU-MAN!

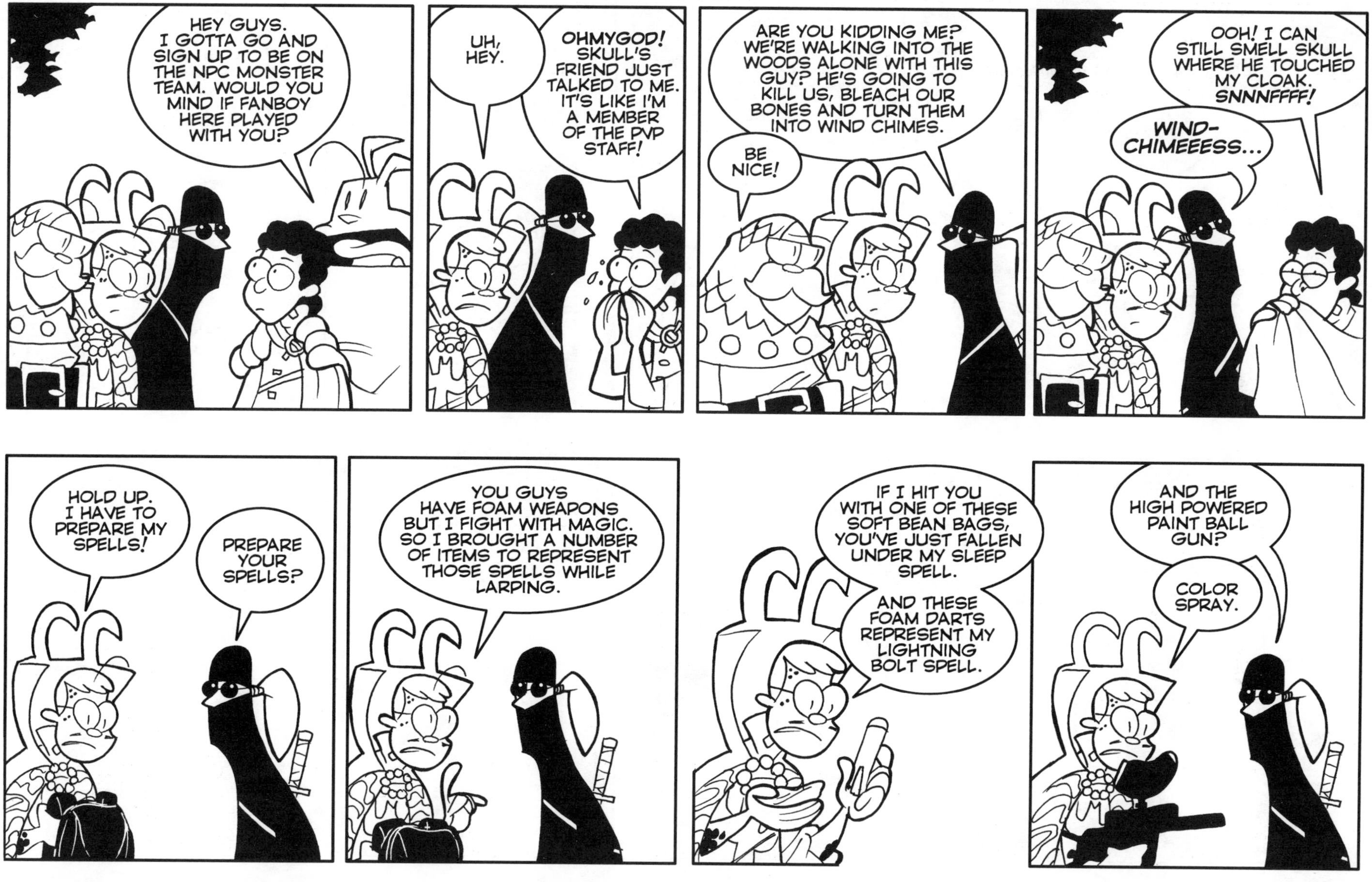
HEY GUYS. I GOTTA GO AND SIGN UP TO BE ON THE NPC MONSTER TEAM. WOULD YOU MIND IF FANBOY HERE PLAYED WITH YOU?
UH, HEY.
OHMYGOD! SKULL'S FRIEND JUST TALKED TO ME. IT'S LIKE I'M A MEMBER OF THE PVP STAFF!
ARE YOU KIDDING ME? WE'RE WALKING INTO THE WOODS ALONE WITH THIS GUY? HE'S GOING TO KILL US, BLEACH OUR BONES AND TURN THEM INTO WIND CHIMES.
BE NICE!
OOH! I CAN STILL SMELL SKULL WHERE HE TOUCHED MY CLOAK. SNNNFFFF!
WIND-CHIMEEESS...
HOLD UP. I HAVE TO PREPARE MY SPELLS!
PREPARE YOUR SPELLS?
YOU GUYS HAVE FOAM WEAPONS BUT I FIGHT WITH MAGIC. SO I BROUGHT A NUMBER OF ITEMS TO REPRESENT THOSE SPELLS WHILE LARPING.
IF I HIT YOU WITH ONE OF THESE SOFT BEAN BAGS, YOU'VE JUST FALLEN UNDER MY SLEEP SPELL.
AND THESE FOAM DARTS REPRESENT MY LIGHTNING BOLT SPELL.
AND THE HIGH POWERED PAINT BALL GUN?
COLOR SPRAY.

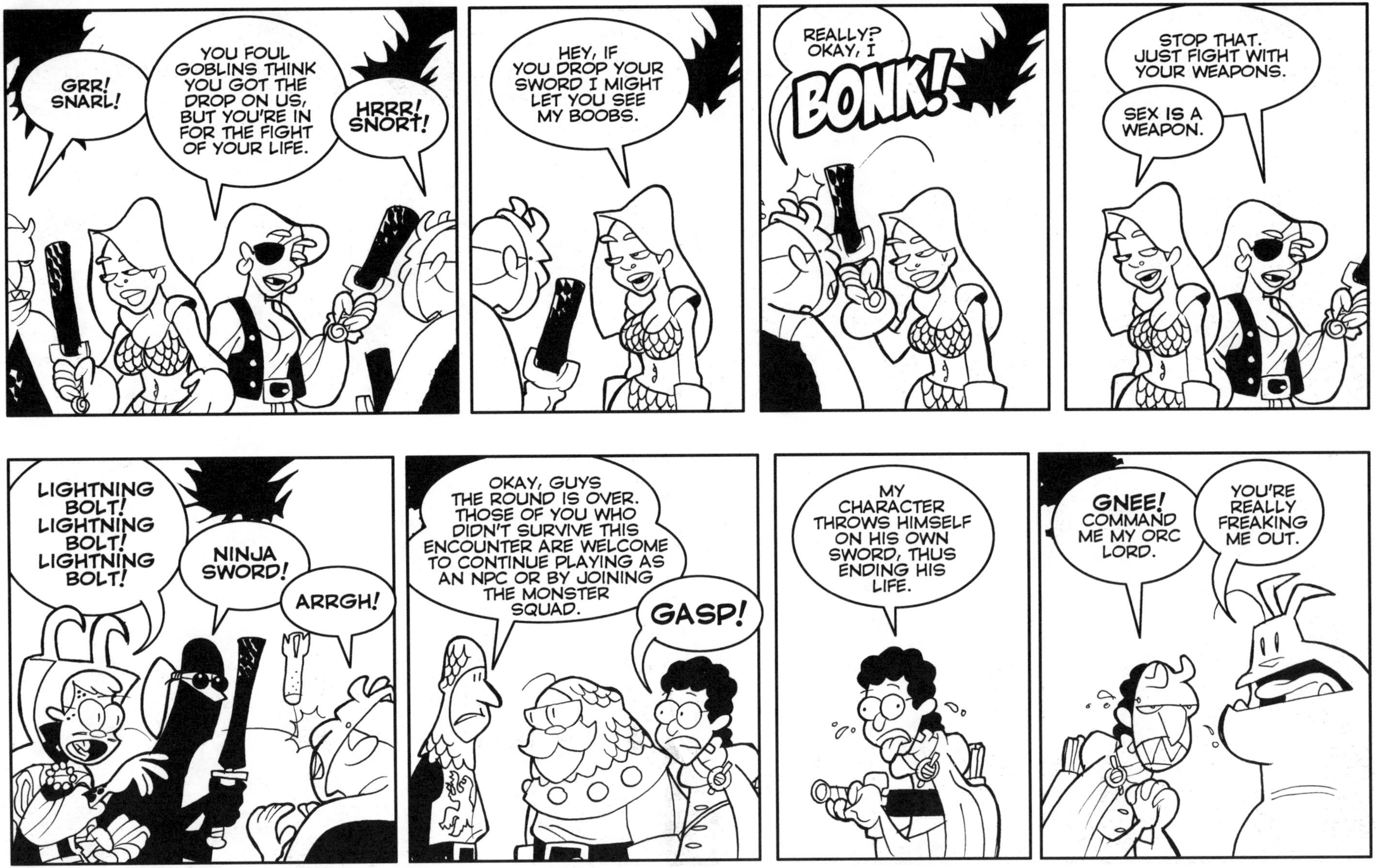
GRR! SNARL!
YOU FOUL GOBLINS THINK YOU GOT THE DROP ON US, BUT YOU'RE IN FOR THE FIGHT OF YOUR LIFE.
HRRR! SNORT!
HEY, IF YOU DROP YOUR SWORD I MIGHT LET YOU SEE MY BOOBS.
REALLY? OKAY, I
BONK!
STOP THAT. JUST FIGHT WITH YOUR WEAPONS.
SEX IS A WEAPON.
LIGHTNING BOLT! LIGHTNING BOLT! LIGHTNING BOLT!
NINJA SWORD!
ARRGH!
OKAY, GUYS THE ROUND IS OVER. THOSE OF YOU WHO DIDN'T SURVIVE THIS ENCOUNTER ARE WELCOME TO CONTINUE PLAYING AS AN NPC OR BY JOINING THE MONSTER SQUAD.
GASP!
MY CHARACTER THROWS HIMSELF ON HIS OWN SWORD, THUS ENDING HIS LIFE.
GNEE! COMMAND ME MY ORC LORD.
YOU'RE REALLY FREAKING ME OUT.

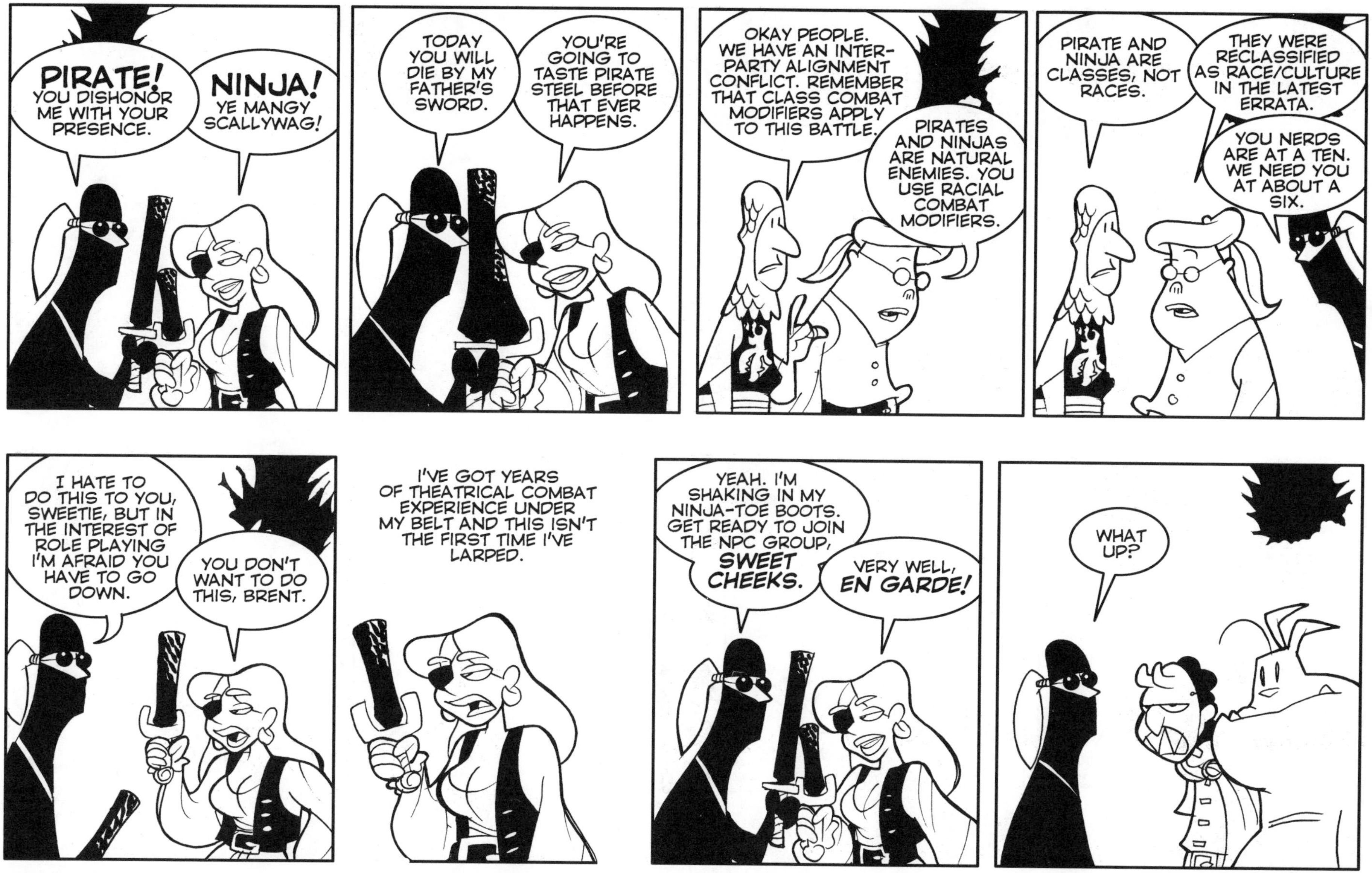
PIRATE! YOU DISHONOR ME WITH YOUR PRESENCE.
NINJA! YE MANGY SCALLYWAG!
TODAY YOU WILL DIE BY MY FATHER'S SWORD.
YOU'RE GOING TO TASTE PIRATE STEEL BEFORE THAT EVER HAPPENS.
OKAY PEOPLE. WE HAVE AN INTER-PARTY ALIGNMENT CONFLICT. REMEMBER THAT CLASS COMBAT MODIFIERS APPLY TO THIS BATTLE.
PIRATES AND NINJAS ARE NATURAL ENEMIES. YOU USE RACIAL COMBAT MODIFIERS.
PIRATE AND NINJA ARE CLASSES, NOT RACES.
THEY WERE RECLASSIFIED AS RACE/CULTURE IN THE LATEST ERRATA.
YOU NERDS ARE AT A TEN. WE NEED YOU AT ABOUT A SIX.
I HATE TO DO THIS TO YOU, SWEETIE, BUT IN THE INTEREST OF ROLE PLAYING I'M AFRAID YOU HAVE TO GO DOWN.
YOU DON'T WANT TO DO THIS, BRENT.
I'VE GOT YEARS OF THEATRICAL COMBAT EXPERIENCE UNDER MY BELT AND THIS ISN'T THE FIRST TIME I'VE LARPED.
YEAH. I'M SHAKING IN MY NINJA-TOE BOOTS. GET READY TO JOIN THE NPC GROUP, SWEET CHEEKS.
VERY WELL, EN GARDE!
WHAT UP?

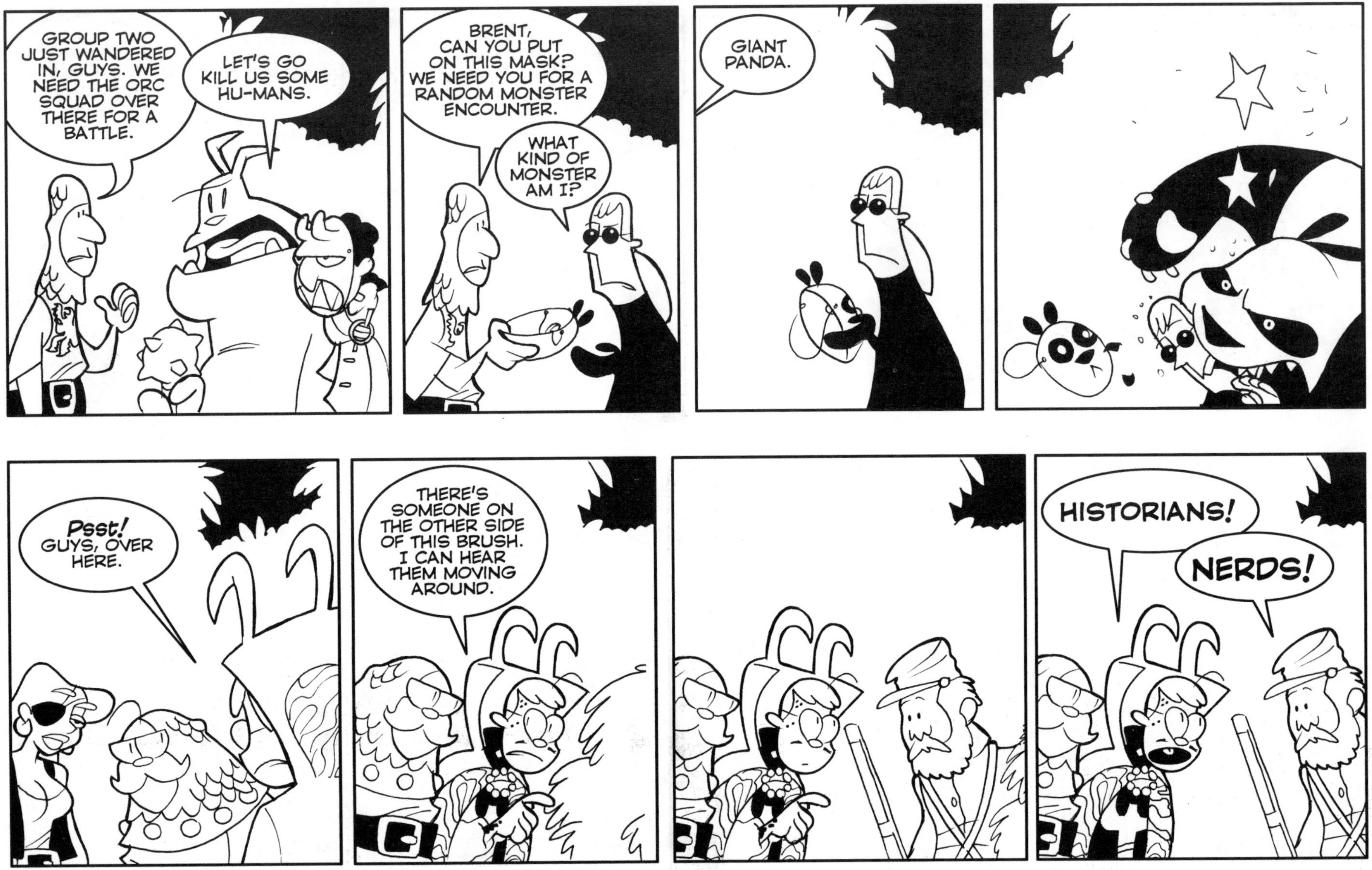
GROUP TWO JUST WANDERED IN, GUYS. WE NEED THE ORC SQUAD OVER THERE FOR A BATTLE.
LET'S GO KILL US SOME HU-MANS.
BRENT, CAN YOU PUT ON THIS MASK? WE NEED YOU FOR A RANDOM MONSTER ENCOUNTER.
WHAT KIND OF MONSTER AM I?
GIANT PANDA.
Psst! GUYS, OVER HERE.
THERE'S SOMEONE ON THE OTHER SIDE OF THIS BRUSH. I CAN HEAR THEM MOVING AROUND.
HISTORIANS!
NERDS!

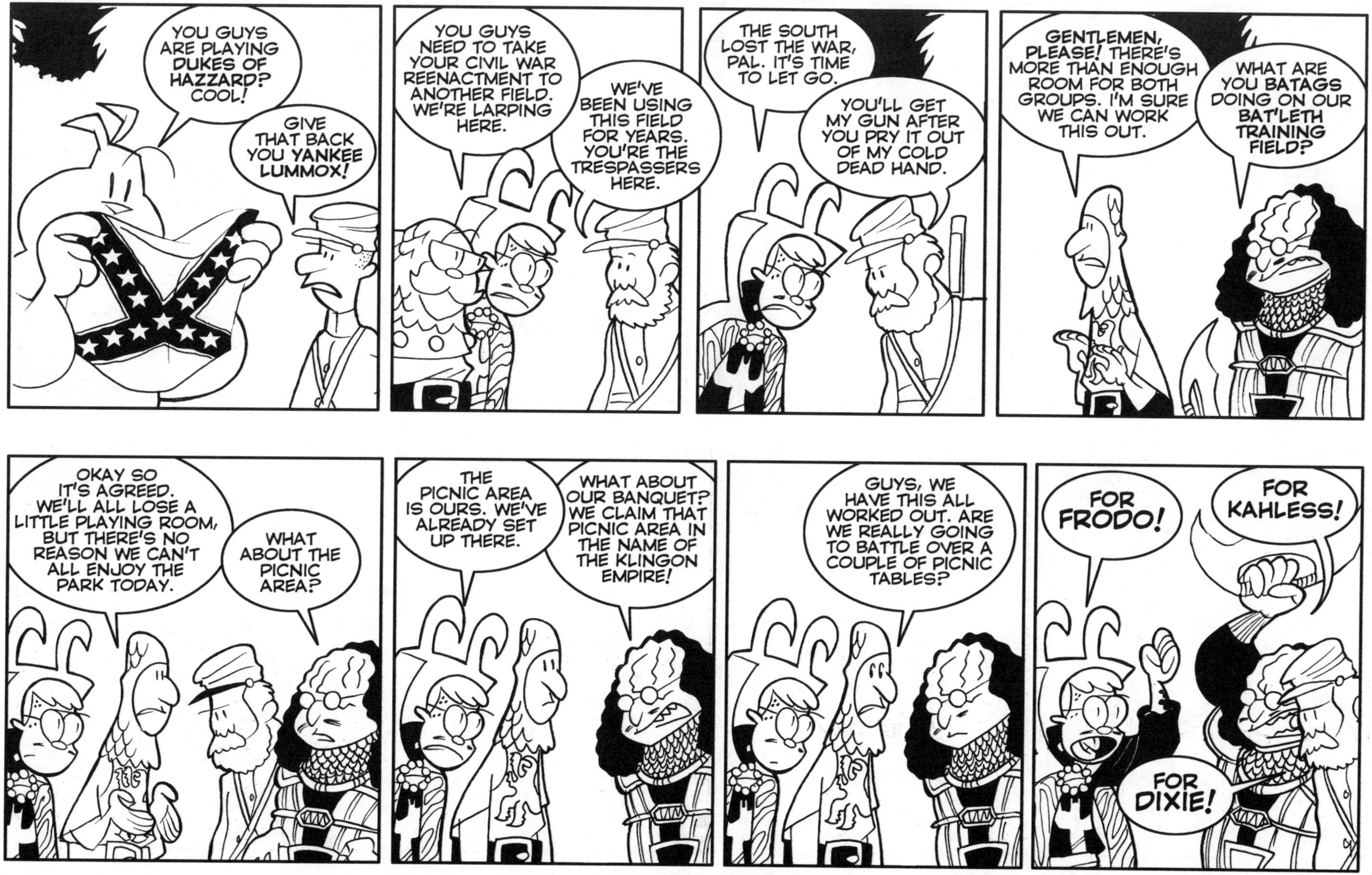
YOU GUYS ARE PLAYING DUKES OF HAZZARD? COOL!
GIVE THAT BACK YOU YANKEE LUMMOX!
YOU GUYS NEED TO TAKE YOUR CIVIL WAR REENACTMENT TO ANOTHER FIELD. WE'RE LARPING HERE.
WE'VE BEEN USING THIS FIELD FOR YEARS. YOU'RE THE TRESPASSERS HERE.
THE SOUTH LOST THE WAR, PAL. IT'S TIME TO LET GO.
YOU'LL GET MY GUN AFTER YOU PRY IT OUT OF MY COLD DEAD HAND.
GENTLEMEN, PLEASE! THERE'S MORE THAN ENOUGH ROOM FOR BOTH GROUPS. I'M SURE WE CAN WORK THIS OUT.
WHAT ARE YOU BATAGS DOING ON OUR BAT'LETH TRAINING FIELD?
OKAY SO IT'S AGREED. WE'LL ALL LOSE A LITTLE PLAYING ROOM, BUT THERE'S NO REASON WE CAN'T ALL ENJOY THE PARK TODAY.
WHAT ABOUT THE PICNIC AREA?
THE PICNIC AREA IS OURS. WE'VE ALREADY SET UP THERE.
WHAT ABOUT OUR BANQUET? WE CLAIM THAT PICNIC AREA IN THE NAME OF THE KLINGON EMPIRE!
GUYS, WE HAVE THIS ALL WORKED OUT. ARE WE REALLY GOING TO BATTLE OVER A COUPLE OF PICNIC TABLES?
FOR FRODO!
FOR KAHLESS!
FOR DIXIE!

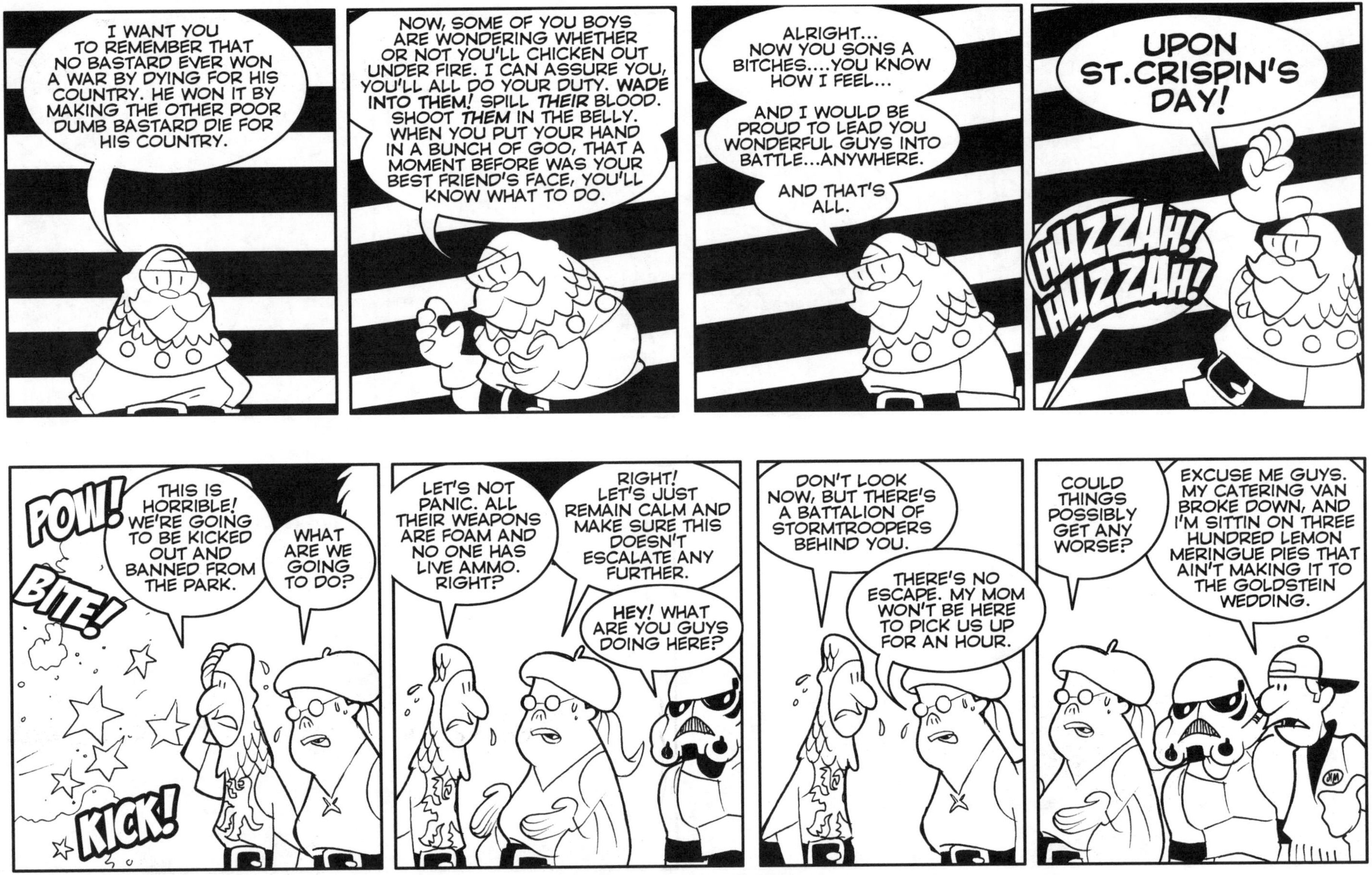
I WANT YOU TO REMEMBER THAT NO BASTARD EVER WON A WAR BY DYING FOR HIS COUNTRY. HE WON IT BY MAKING THE OTHER POOR DUMB BASTARD DIE FOR HIS COUNTRY.
NOW, SOME OF YOU BOYS ARE WONDERING WHETHER OR NOT YOU'LL CHICKEN OUT UNDER FIRE. I CAN ASSURE YOU, YOU'LL ALL DO YOUR DUTY. WADE INTO THEM! SPILL THEIR BLOOD. SHOOT THEM IN THE BELLY. WHEN YOU PUT YOUR HAND IN A BUNCH OF GOO, THAT A MOMENT BEFORE WAS YOUR BEST FRIEND'S FACE, YOU'LL KNOW WHAT TO DO.
ALRIGHT... NOW YOU SONS A BITCHES....YOU KNOW HOW I FEEL...
AND I WOULD BE PROUD TO LEAD YOU WONDERFUL GUYS INTO BATTLE...ANYWHERE.
AND THAT'S ALL.
UPON ST.CRISPIN'S DAY!
HUZZAH! HUZZAH!
POW!
BITE!
KICK!
THIS IS HORRIBLE! WE'RE GOING TO BE KICKED OUT AND BANNED FROM THE PARK.
WHAT ARE WE GOING TO DO?
LET'S NOT PANIC. ALL THEIR WEAPONS ARE FOAM AND NO ONE HAS LIVE AMMO. RIGHT?
RIGHT! LET'S JUST REMAIN CALM AND MAKE SURE THIS DOESN'T ESCALATE ANY FURTHER.
HEY! WHAT ARE YOU GUYS DOING HERE?
DON'T LOOK NOW, BUT THERE'S A BATTALION OF STORMTROOPERS BEHIND YOU.
THERE'S NO ESCAPE. MY MOM WON'T BE HERE TO PICK US UP FOR AN HOUR.
COULD THINGS POSSIBLY GET ANY WORSE?
EXCUSE ME GUYS. MY CATERING VAN BROKE DOWN, AND I'M SITTIN ON THREE HUNDRED LEMON MERINGUE PIES THAT AIN'T MAKING IT TO THE GOLDSTEIN WEDDING.

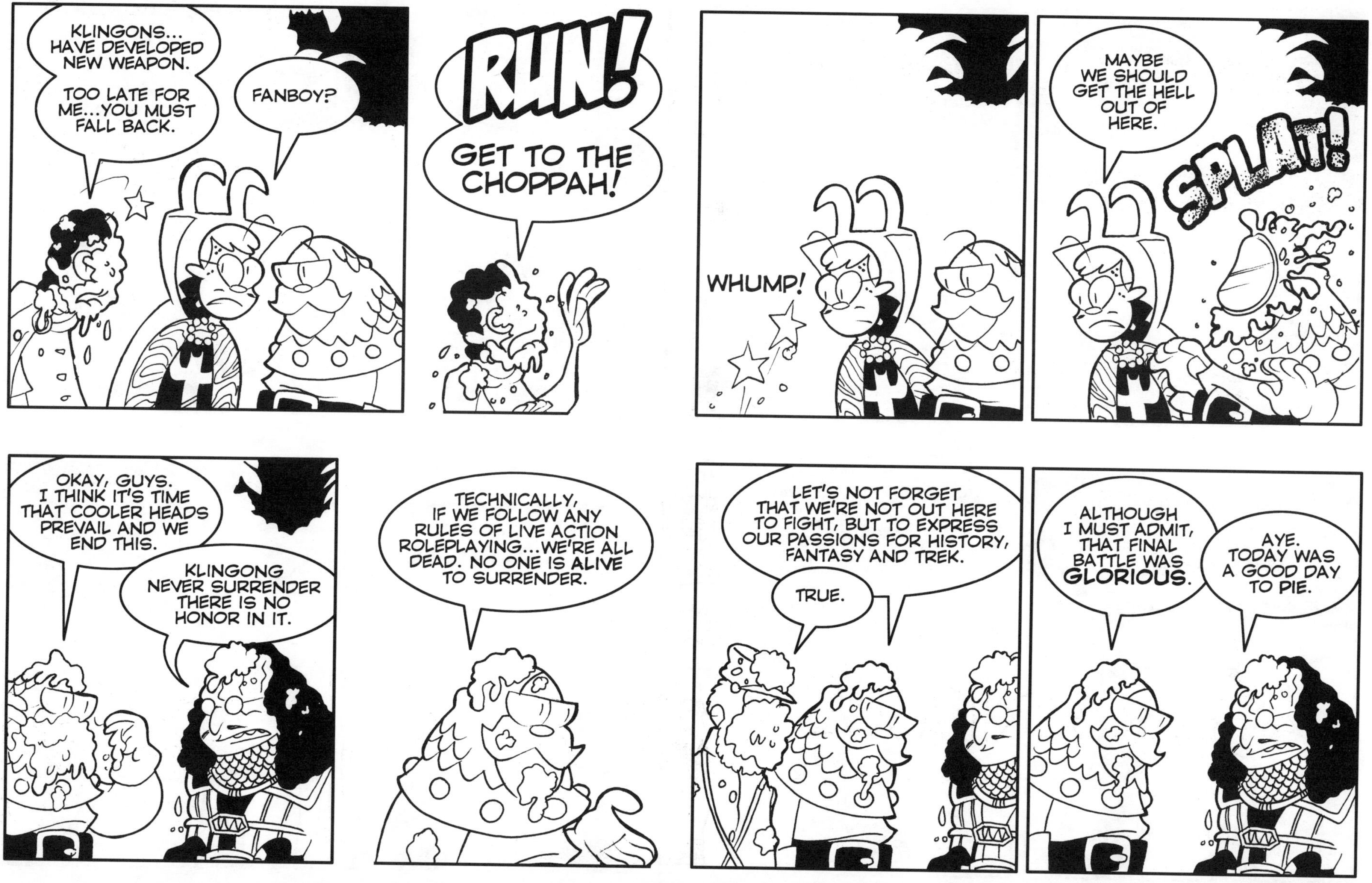
KLINGONS... HAVE DEVELOPED NEW WEAPON.
TOO LATE FOR ME...YOU MUST FALL BACK.
FANBOY?
RUN!
GET TO THE CHOPPAH!
WHUMP!
MAYBE WE SHOULD GET THE HELL OUT OF HERE.
SPLAT!
OKAY, GUYS. I THINK IT'S TIME THAT COOLER HEADS PREVAIL AND WE END THIS.
KLINGONG NEVER SURRENDER THERE IS NO HONOR IN IT.
TECHNICALLY, IF WE FOLLOW ANY RULES OF LIVE ACTION ROLEPLAYING...WE'RE ALL DEAD. NO ONE IS ALIVE TO SURRENDER.
LET'S NOT FORGET THAT WE'RE NOT OUT HERE TO FIGHT, BUT TO EXPRESS OUR PASSIONS FOR HISTORY, FANTASY AND TREK.
TRUE.
ALTHOUGH I MUST ADMIT, THAT FINAL BATTLE WAS GLORIOUS.
AYE. TODAY WAS A GOOD DAY TO PIE.

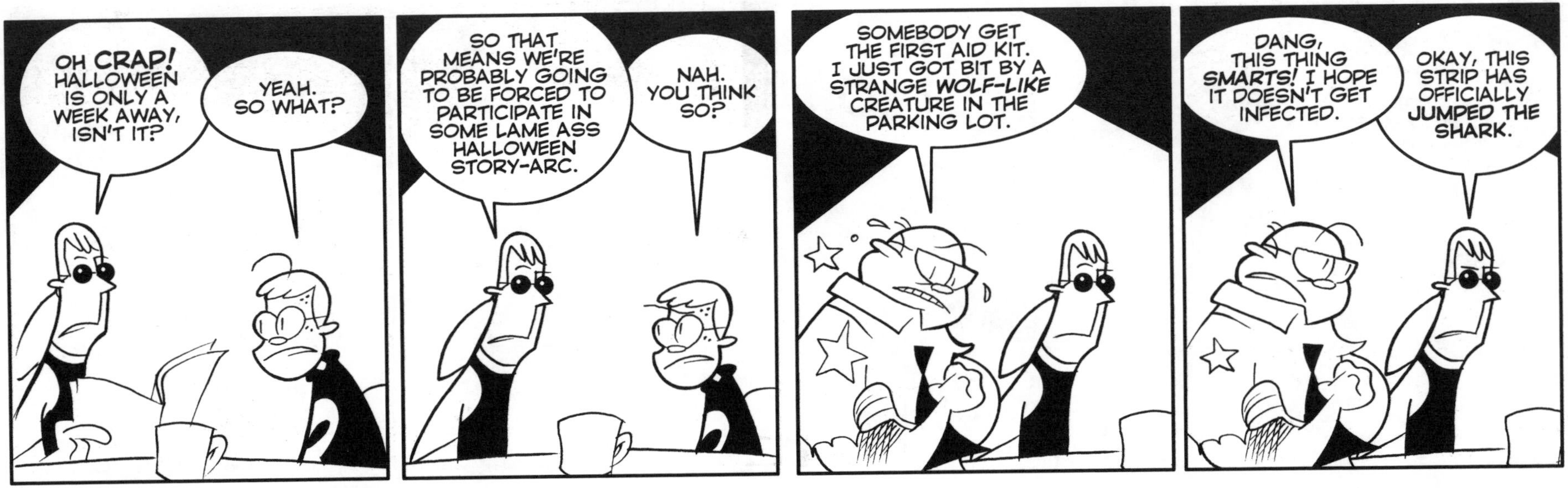
OH CRAP! HALLOWEEN IS ONLY A WEEK AWAY, ISN'T IT?
YEAH. SO WHAT?
SO THAT MEANS WE'RE PROBABLY GOING TO BE FORCED TO PARTICIPATE IN SOME LAME ASS HALLOWEEN STORY-ARC.
NAH. YOU THINK SO?
SOMEBODY GET THE FIRST AID KIT. I JUST GOT BIT BY A STRANGE WOLF-LIKE CREATURE IN THE PARKING LOT.
DANG, THIS THING SMARTS! I HOPE IT DOESN'T GET INFECTED.
OKAY, THIS STRIP HAS OFFICIALLY JUMPED THE SHARK.

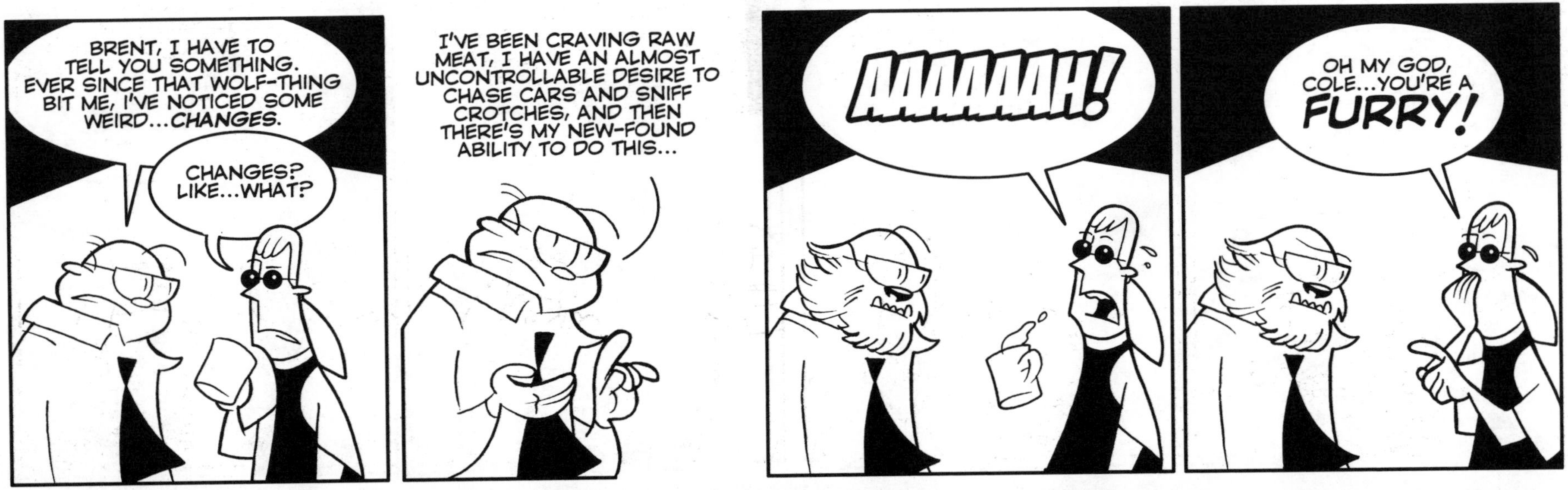
BRENT, I HAVE TO TELL YOU SOMETHING. EVER SINCE THAT WOLF-THING BIT ME, I'VE NOTICED SOME WEIRD...CHANGES.
CHANGES? LIKE...WHAT?
I'VE BEEN CRAVING RAW MEAT, I HAVE AN ALMOST UNCONTROLLABLE DESIRE TO CHASE CARS AND SNIFF CROTCHES, AND THEN THERE'S MY NEW-FOUND ABILITY TO DO THIS...
AAAAAAAH!
OH MY GOD, COLE...YOU'RE A FURRY!

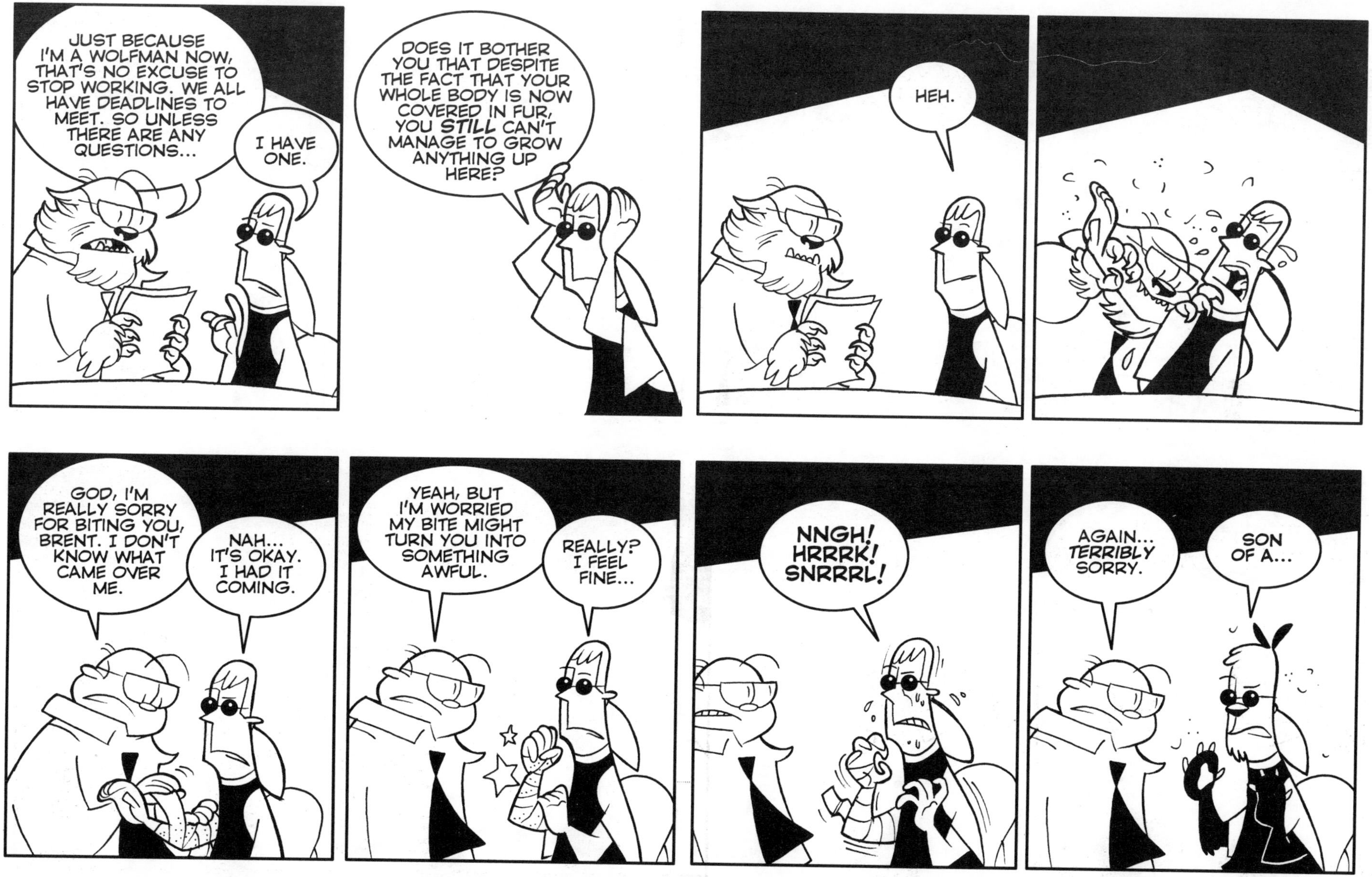
JUST BECAUSE I'M A WOLFMAN NOW, THAT'S NO EXCUSE TO STOP WORKING. WE ALL HAVE DEADLINES TO MEET. SO UNLESS THERE ARE ANY QUESTIONS...
I HAVE ONE.
DOES IT BOTHER YOU THAT DESPITE THE FACT THAT YOUR WHOLE BODY IS NOW COVERED IN FUR, YOU **STILL** CAN'T MANAGE TO GROW ANYTHING UP HERE?
HEH.
GOD, I'M REALLY SORRY FOR BITING YOU, BRENT. I DON'T KNOW WHAT CAME OVER ME.
NAH... IT'S OKAY. I HAD IT COMING.
YEAH, BUT I'M WORRIED MY BITE MIGHT TURN YOU INTO SOMETHING AWFUL.
REALLY? I FEEL FINE...
NNGH! HRRRK! SNRRRL!
AGAIN... *TERRIBLY* SORRY.
SON OF A...

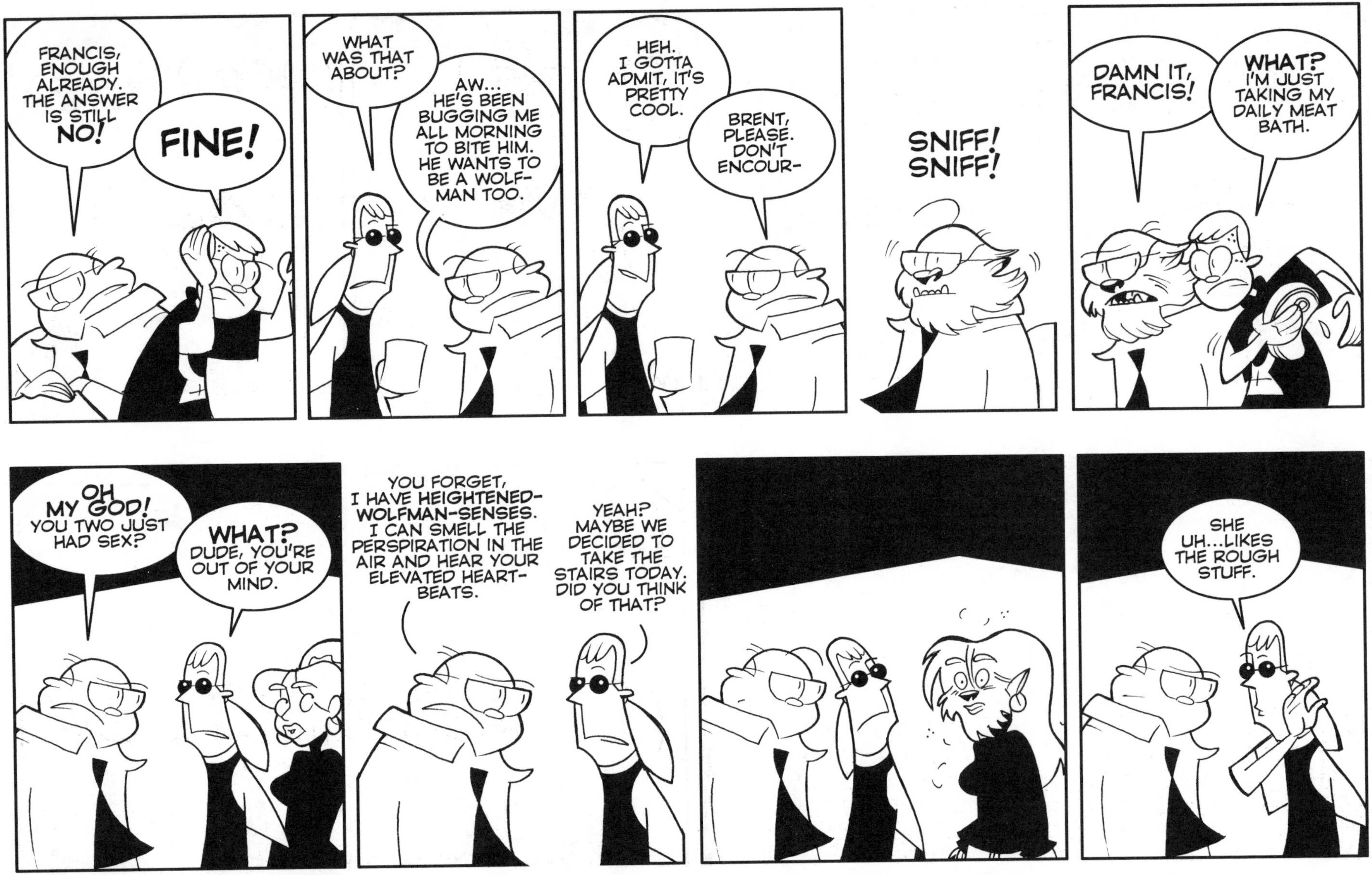

FRANCIS, ENOUGH ALREADY. THE ANSWER IS STILL NO!
FINE!
WHAT WAS THAT ABOUT?
AW... HE'S BEEN BUGGING ME ALL MORNING TO BITE HIM. HE WANTS TO BE A WOLF-MAN TOO.
HEH. I GOTTA ADMIT, IT'S PRETTY COOL.
BRENT, PLEASE. DON'T ENCOUR-
SNIFF! SNIFF!
DAMN IT, FRANCIS!
WHAT? I'M JUST TAKING MY DAILY MEAT BATH.
OH MY GOD! YOU TWO JUST HAD SEX?
WHAT? DUDE, YOU'RE OUT OF YOUR MIND.
YOU FORGET, I HAVE HEIGHTENED-WOLFMAN-SENSES. I CAN SMELL THE PERSPIRATION IN THE AIR AND HEAR YOUR ELEVATED HEART-BEATS.
YEAH? MAYBE WE DECIDED TO TAKE THE STAIRS TODAY. DID YOU THINK OF THAT?
SHE UH...LIKES THE ROUGH STUFF.

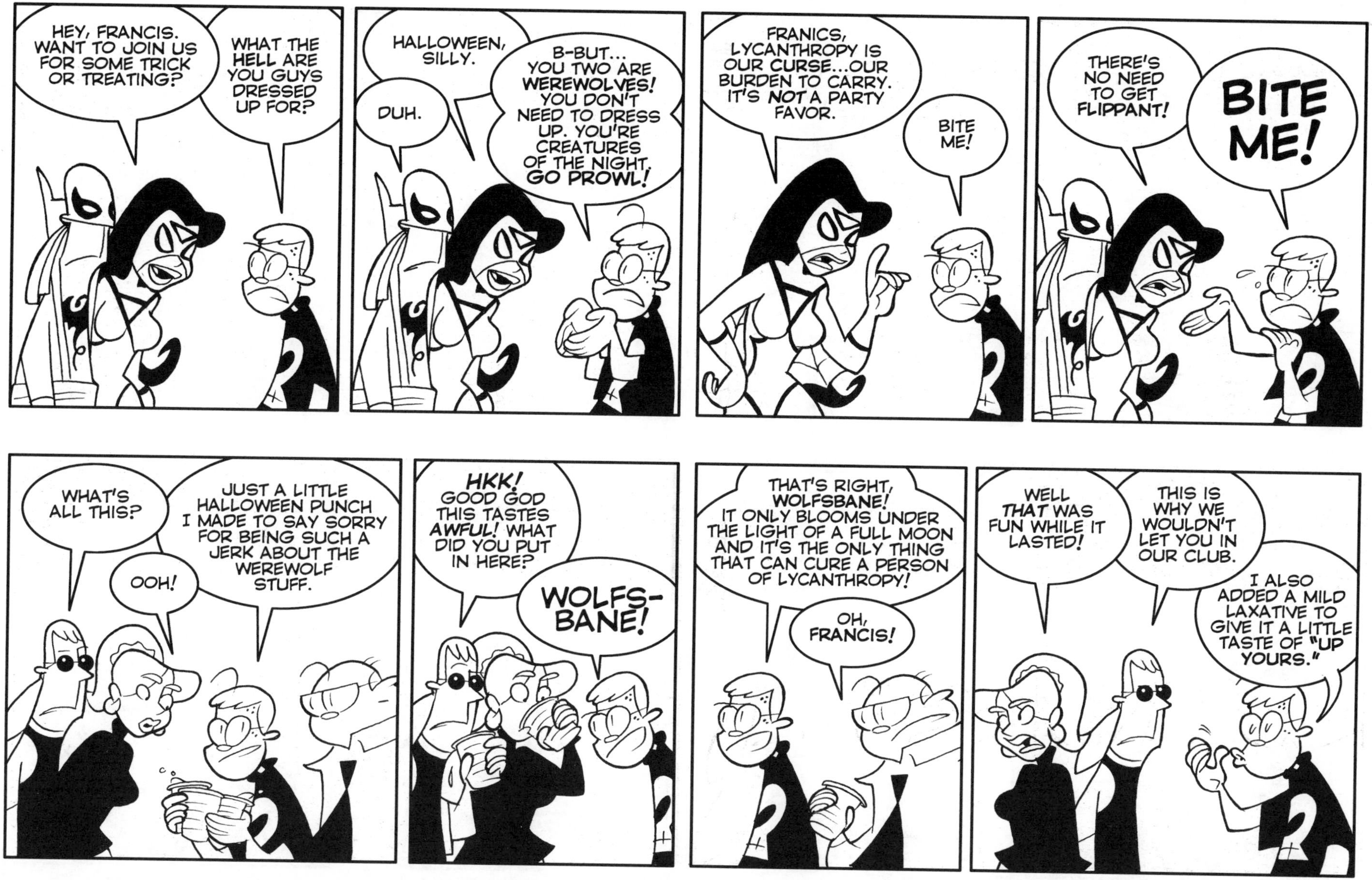
HEY, FRANCIS. WANT TO JOIN US FOR SOME TRICK OR TREATING?
WHAT THE **HELL** ARE YOU GUYS DRESSED UP FOR?
HALLOWEEN, SILLY.
DUH.
B-BUT... YOU TWO ARE **WEREWOLVES!** YOU DON'T NEED TO DRESS UP. YOU'RE CREATURES OF THE NIGHT. **GO PROWL!**
FRANICS, LYCANTHROPY IS OUR **CURSE**...OUR BURDEN TO CARRY. IT'S ***NOT*** A PARTY FAVOR.
BITE ME!
THERE'S NO NEED TO GET **FLIPPANT!**
BITE ME!
WHAT'S ALL THIS?
JUST A LITTLE HALLOWEEN PUNCH I MADE TO SAY SORRY FOR BEING SUCH A JERK ABOUT THE WEREWOLF STUFF.
OOH!
HKK! GOOD GOD THIS TASTES ***AWFUL!*** WHAT DID YOU PUT IN HERE?
WOLFS-BANE!
THAT'S RIGHT, **WOLFSBANE!** IT ONLY BLOOMS UNDER THE LIGHT OF A FULL MOON AND IT'S THE ONLY THING THAT CAN CURE A PERSON OF LYCANTHROPY!
OH, **FRANCIS!**
WELL ***THAT*** WAS FUN WHILE IT LASTED!
THIS IS WHY WE WOULDN'T LET YOU IN OUR CLUB.
I ALSO ADDED A MILD LAXATIVE TO GIVE IT A LITTLE TASTE OF **"UP YOURS."**

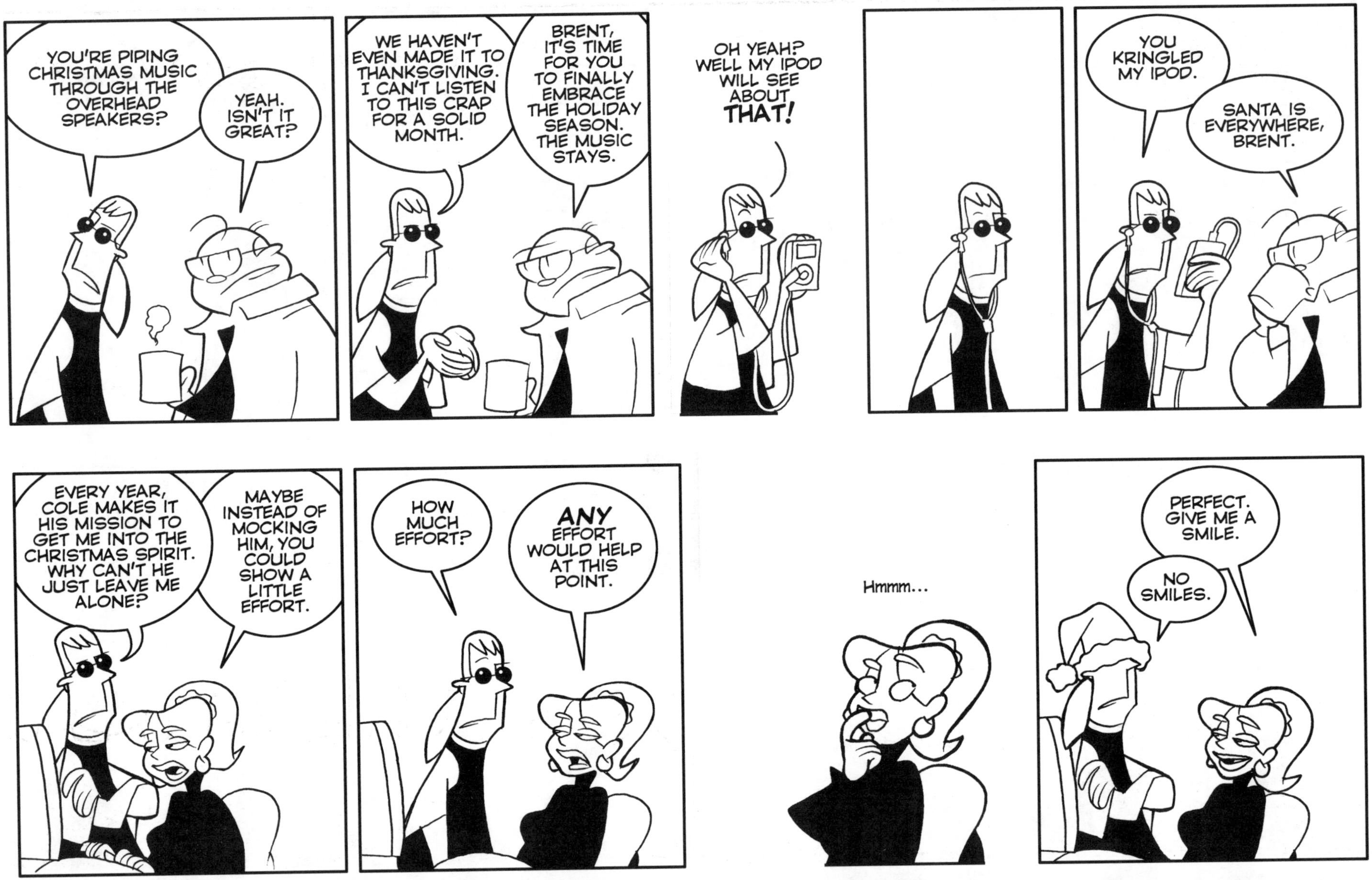

YOU'RE PIPING CHRISTMAS MUSIC THROUGH THE OVERHEAD SPEAKERS?
YEAH. ISN'T IT GREAT?
WE HAVEN'T EVEN MADE IT TO THANKSGIVING. I CAN'T LISTEN TO THIS CRAP FOR A SOLID MONTH.
BRENT, IT'S TIME FOR YOU TO FINALLY EMBRACE THE HOLIDAY SEASON. THE MUSIC STAYS.
OH YEAH? WELL MY IPOD WILL SEE ABOUT THAT!
YOU KRINGLED MY IPOD.
SANTA IS EVERYWHERE, BRENT.
EVERY YEAR, COLE MAKES IT HIS MISSION TO GET ME INTO THE CHRISTMAS SPIRIT. WHY CAN'T HE JUST LEAVE ME ALONE?
MAYBE INSTEAD OF MOCKING HIM, YOU COULD SHOW A LITTLE EFFORT.
HOW MUCH EFFORT?
ANY EFFORT WOULD HELP AT THIS POINT.
Hmmm...
PERFECT. GIVE ME A SMILE.
NO SMILES.

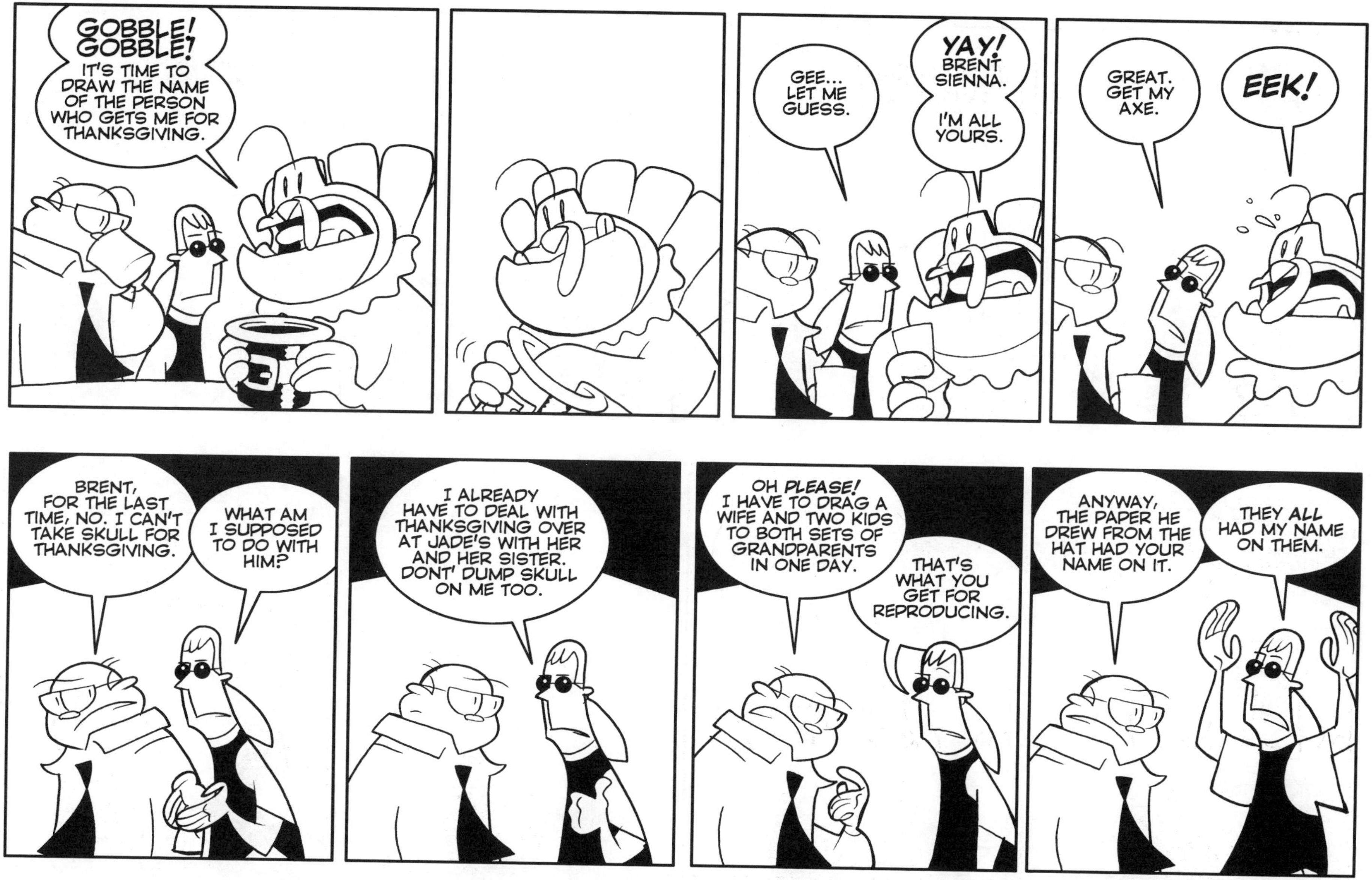

GOBBLE! GOBBLE! IT'S TIME TO DRAW THE NAME OF THE PERSON WHO GETS ME FOR THANKSGIVING.
GEE... LET ME GUESS.
YAY! BRENT SIENNA.
I'M ALL YOURS.
GREAT. GET MY AXE.
EEK!
BRENT, FOR THE LAST TIME, NO. I CAN'T TAKE SKULL FOR THANKSGIVING.
WHAT AM I SUPPOSED TO DO WITH HIM?
I ALREADY HAVE TO DEAL WITH THANKSGIVING OVER AT JADE'S WITH HER AND HER SISTER. DONT' DUMP SKULL ON ME TOO.
OH PLEASE! I HAVE TO DRAG A WIFE AND TWO KIDS TO BOTH SETS OF GRANDPARENTS IN ONE DAY.
THAT'S WHAT YOU GET FOR REPRODUCING.
ANYWAY, THE PAPER HE DREW FROM THE HAT HAD YOUR NAME ON IT.
THEY ALL HAD MY NAME ON THEM.

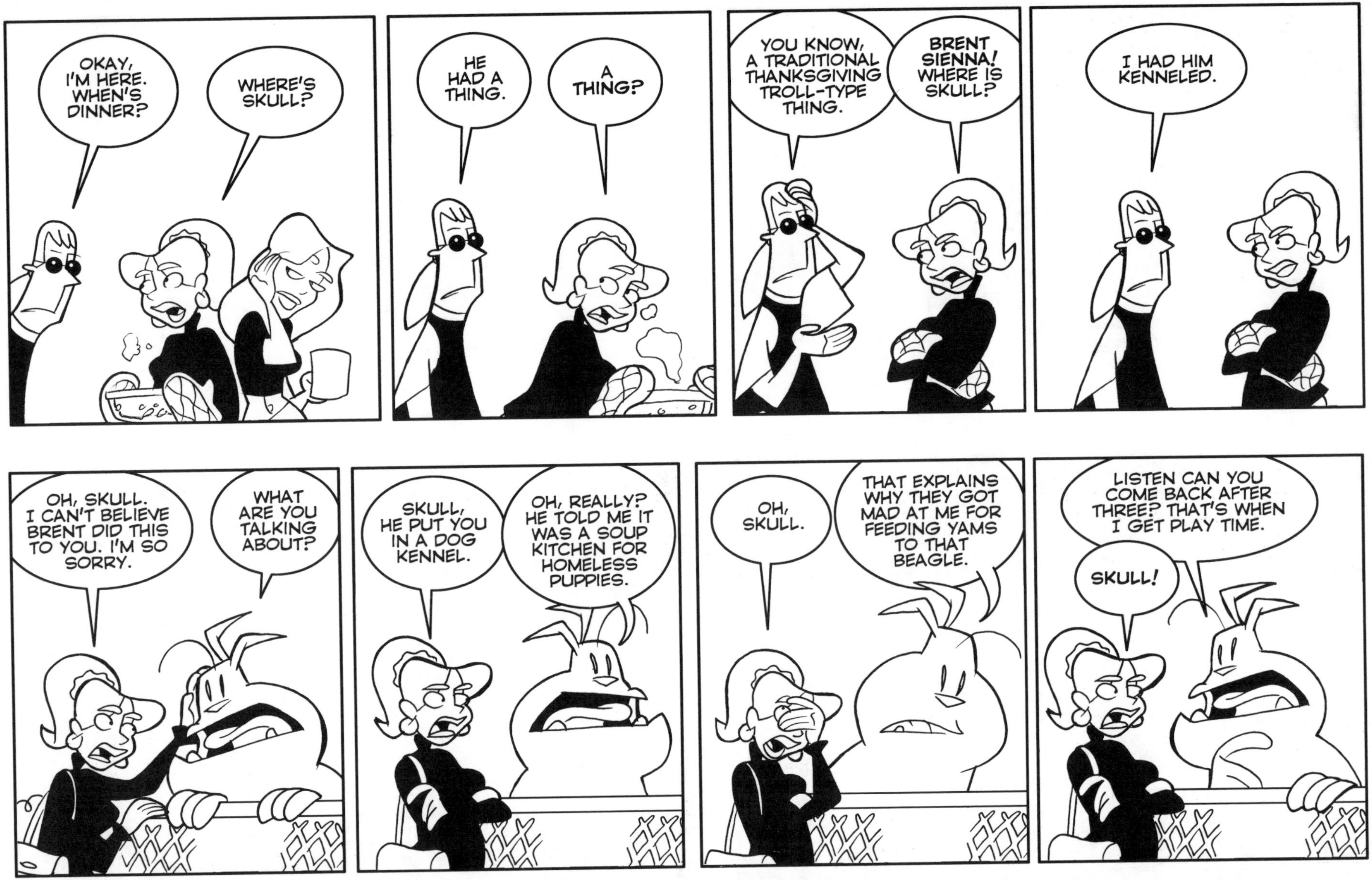
OKAY, I'M HERE. WHEN'S DINNER?
WHERE'S SKULL?
HE HAD A THING.
A THING?
YOU KNOW, A TRADITIONAL THANKSGIVING TROLL-TYPE THING.
BRENT SIENNA! WHERE IS SKULL?
I HAD HIM KENNELED.
OH, SKULL. I CAN'T BELIEVE BRENT DID THIS TO YOU. I'M SO SORRY.
WHAT ARE YOU TALKING ABOUT?
SKULL, HE PUT YOU IN A DOG KENNEL.
OH, REALLY? HE TOLD ME IT WAS A SOUP KITCHEN FOR HOMELESS PUPPIES.
OH, SKULL.
THAT EXPLAINS WHY THEY GOT MAD AT ME FOR FEEDING YAMS TO THAT BEAGLE.
LISTEN CAN YOU COME BACK AFTER THREE? THAT'S WHEN I GET PLAY TIME.
SKULL!

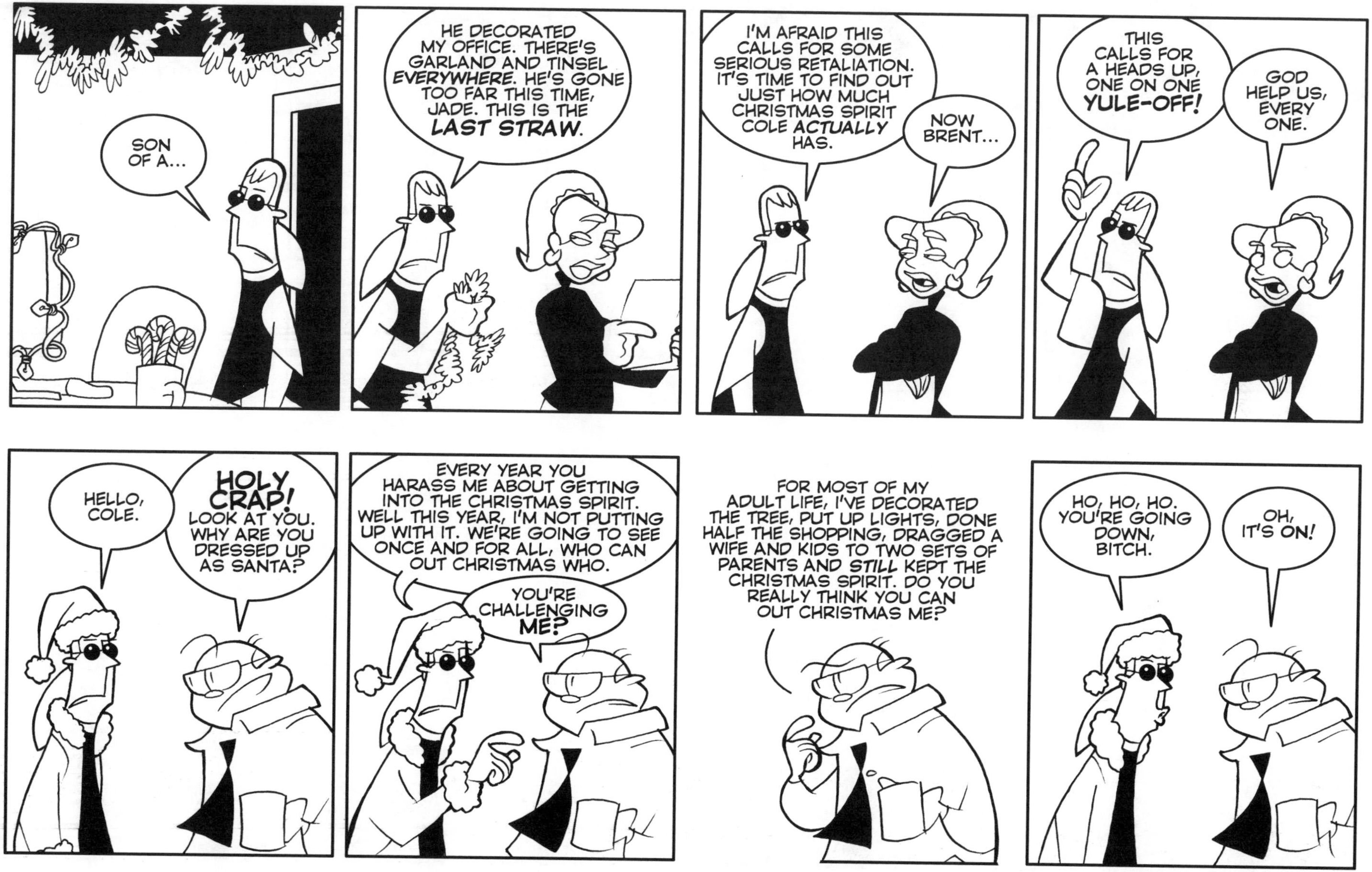
SON OF A...
HE DECORATED MY OFFICE. THERE'S GARLAND AND TINSEL EVERYWHERE. HE'S GONE TOO FAR THIS TIME, JADE. THIS IS THE LAST STRAW.
I'M AFRAID THIS CALLS FOR SOME SERIOUS RETALIATION. IT'S TIME TO FIND OUT JUST HOW MUCH CHRISTMAS SPIRIT COLE ACTUALLY HAS.
NOW BRENT...
THIS CALLS FOR A HEADS UP, ONE ON ONE YULE-OFF!
GOD HELP US, EVERY ONE.
HELLO, COLE.
HOLY CRAP! LOOK AT YOU. WHY ARE YOU DRESSED UP AS SANTA?
EVERY YEAR YOU HARASS ME ABOUT GETTING INTO THE CHRISTMAS SPIRIT. WELL THIS YEAR, I'M NOT PUTTING UP WITH IT. WE'RE GOING TO SEE ONCE AND FOR ALL, WHO CAN OUT CHRISTMAS WHO.
YOU'RE CHALLENGING ME?
FOR MOST OF MY ADULT LIFE, I'VE DECORATED THE TREE, PUT UP LIGHTS, DONE HALF THE SHOPPING, DRAGGED A WIFE AND KIDS TO TWO SETS OF PARENTS AND STILL KEPT THE CHRISTMAS SPIRIT. DO YOU REALLY THINK YOU CAN OUT CHRISTMAS ME?
HO, HO, HO. YOU'RE GOING DOWN, BITCH.
OH, IT'S ON!

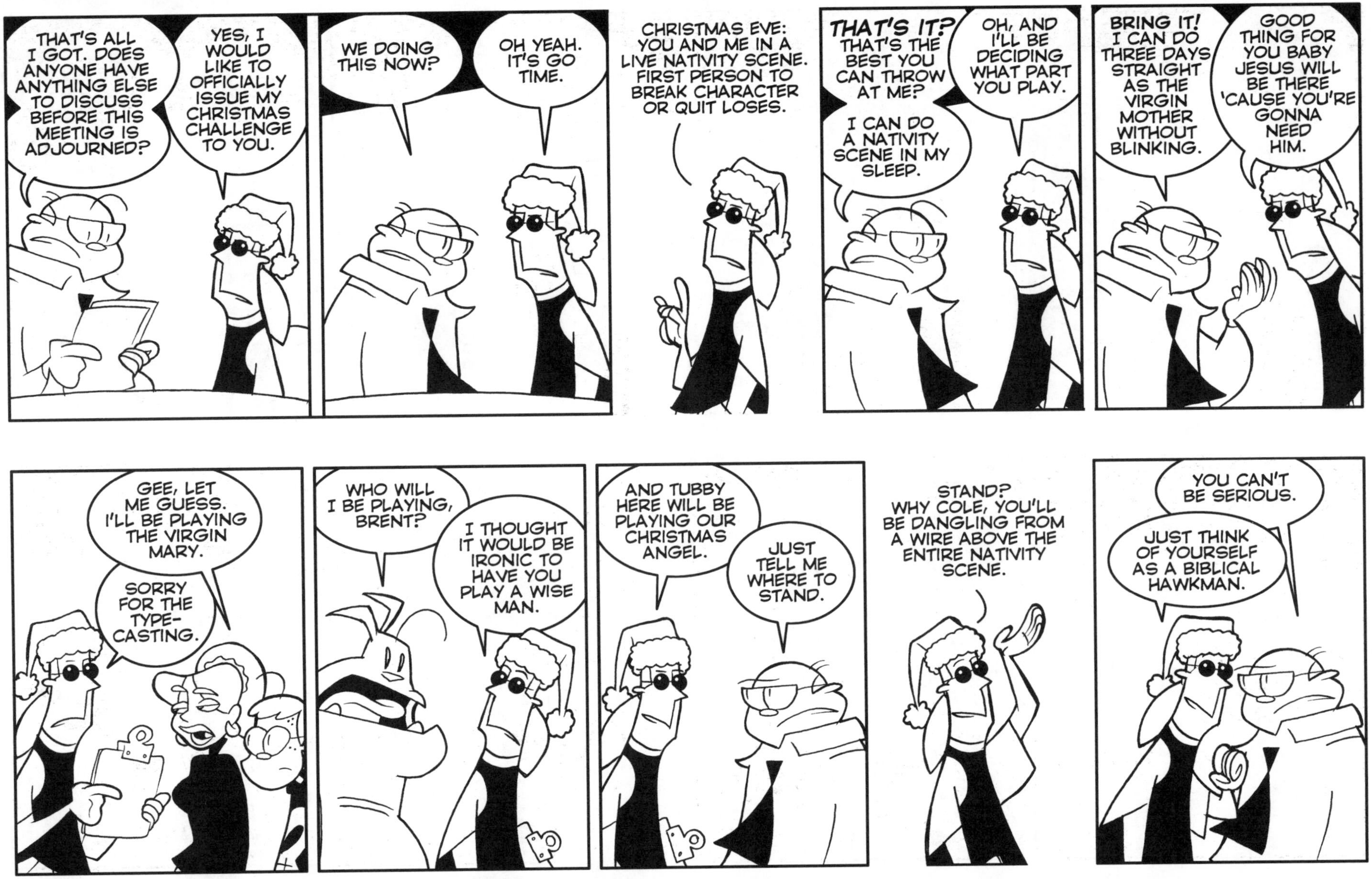
THAT'S ALL I GOT. DOES ANYONE HAVE ANYTHING ELSE TO DISCUSS BEFORE THIS MEETING IS ADJOURNED?
YES, I WOULD LIKE TO OFFICIALLY ISSUE MY CHRISTMAS CHALLENGE TO YOU.
WE DOING THIS NOW?
OH YEAH. IT'S GO TIME.
CHRISTMAS EVE: YOU AND ME IN A LIVE NATIVITY SCENE. FIRST PERSON TO BREAK CHARACTER OR QUIT LOSES.
THAT'S IT? THAT'S THE BEST YOU CAN THROW AT ME?
I CAN DO A NATIVITY SCENE IN MY SLEEP.
OH, AND I'LL BE DECIDING WHAT PART YOU PLAY.
BRING IT! I CAN DO THREE DAYS STRAIGHT AS THE VIRGIN MOTHER WITHOUT BLINKING.
GOOD THING FOR YOU BABY JESUS WILL BE THERE 'CAUSE YOU'RE GONNA NEED HIM.
GEE, LET ME GUESS. I'LL BE PLAYING THE VIRGIN MARY.
SORRY FOR THE TYPE-CASTING.
WHO WILL I BE PLAYING, BRENT?
I THOUGHT IT WOULD BE IRONIC TO HAVE YOU PLAY A WISE MAN.
AND TUBBY HERE WILL BE PLAYING OUR CHRISTMAS ANGEL.
JUST TELL ME WHERE TO STAND.
STAND? WHY COLE, YOU'LL BE DANGLING FROM A WIRE ABOVE THE ENTIRE NATIVITY SCENE.
YOU CAN'T BE SERIOUS.
JUST THINK OF YOURSELF AS A BIBLICAL HAWKMAN.

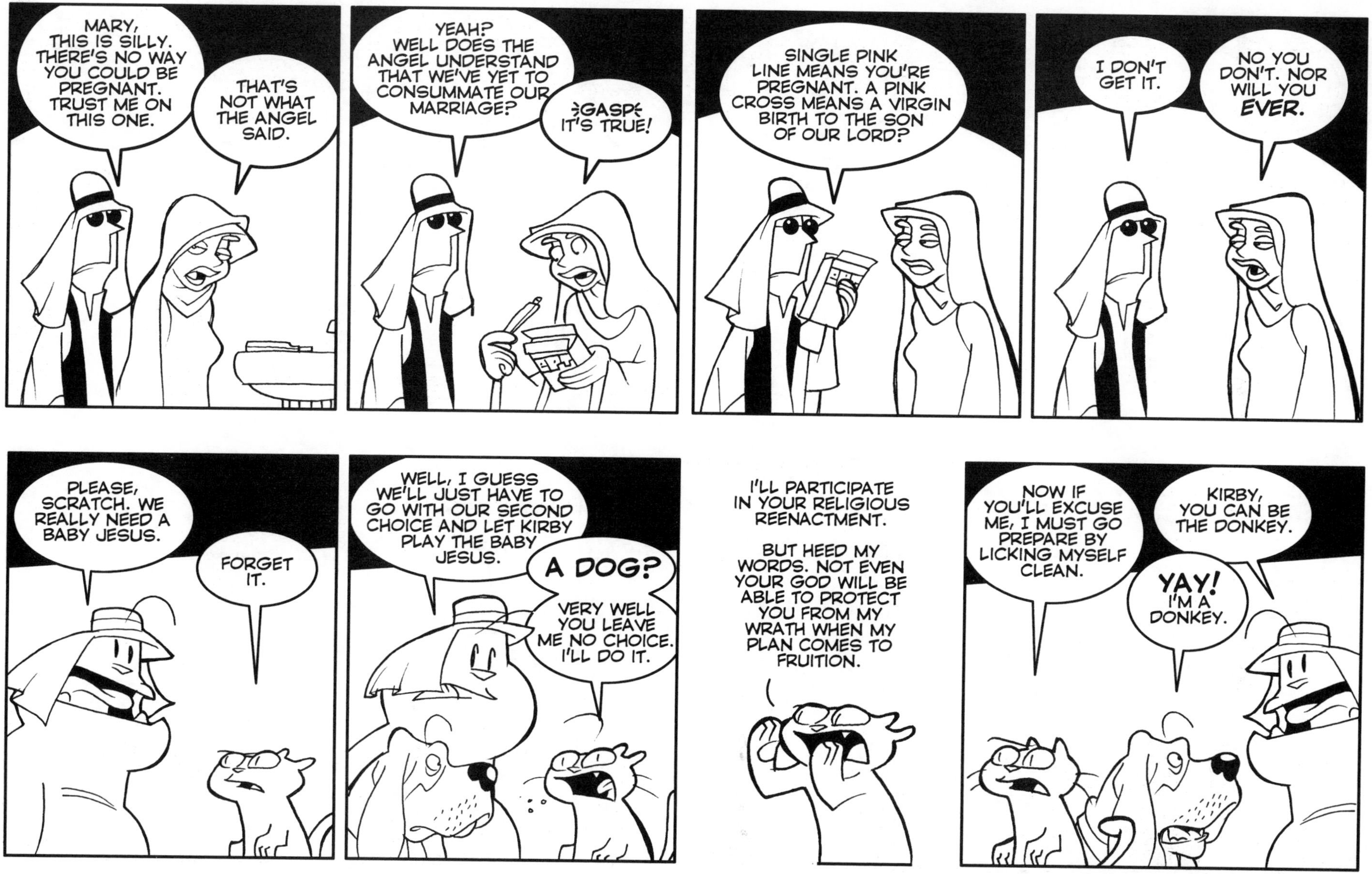
MARY, THIS IS SILLY. THERE'S NO WAY YOU COULD BE PREGNANT. TRUST ME ON THIS ONE.
THAT'S NOT WHAT THE ANGEL SAID.
YEAH? WELL DOES THE ANGEL UNDERSTAND THAT WE'VE YET TO CONSUMMATE OUR MARRIAGE?
GASP IT'S TRUE!
SINGLE PINK LINE MEANS YOU'RE PREGNANT. A PINK CROSS MEANS A VIRGIN BIRTH TO THE SON OF OUR LORD?
I DON'T GET IT.
NO YOU DON'T. NOR WILL YOU **EVER.**
PLEASE, SCRATCH. WE REALLY NEED A BABY JESUS.
FORGET IT.
WELL, I GUESS WE'LL JUST HAVE TO GO WITH OUR SECOND CHOICE AND LET KIRBY PLAY THE BABY JESUS.
A DOG?
VERY WELL YOU LEAVE ME NO CHOICE. I'LL DO IT.
I'LL PARTICIPATE IN YOUR RELIGIOUS REENACTMENT.
BUT HEED MY WORDS. NOT EVEN YOUR GOD WILL BE ABLE TO PROTECT YOU FROM MY WRATH WHEN MY PLAN COMES TO FRUITION.
NOW IF YOU'LL EXCUSE ME, I MUST GO PREPARE BY LICKING MYSELF CLEAN.
KIRBY, YOU CAN BE THE DONKEY.
YAY! I'M A DONKEY.

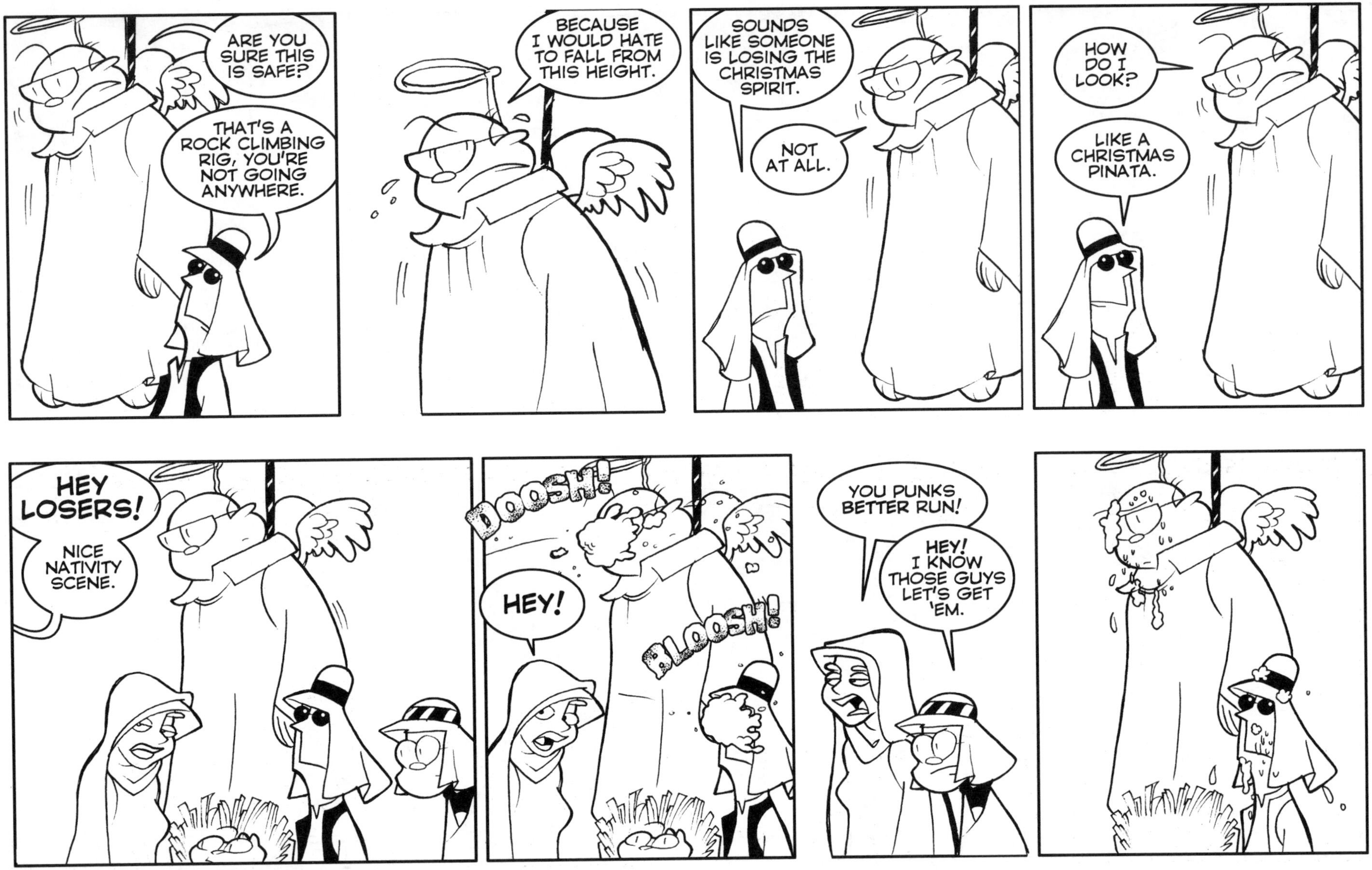
ARE YOU SURE THIS IS SAFE?
THAT'S A ROCK CLIMBING RIG, YOU'RE NOT GOING ANYWHERE.
BECAUSE I WOULD HATE TO FALL FROM THIS HEIGHT.
SOUNDS LIKE SOMEONE IS LOSING THE CHRISTMAS SPIRIT.
NOT AT ALL.
HOW DO I LOOK?
LIKE A CHRISTMAS PINATA.
HEY LOSERS!
NICE NATIVITY SCENE.
DOOSH!
HEY!
BLOOSH!
YOU PUNKS BETTER RUN!
HEY! I KNOW THOSE GUYS LET'S GET 'EM.

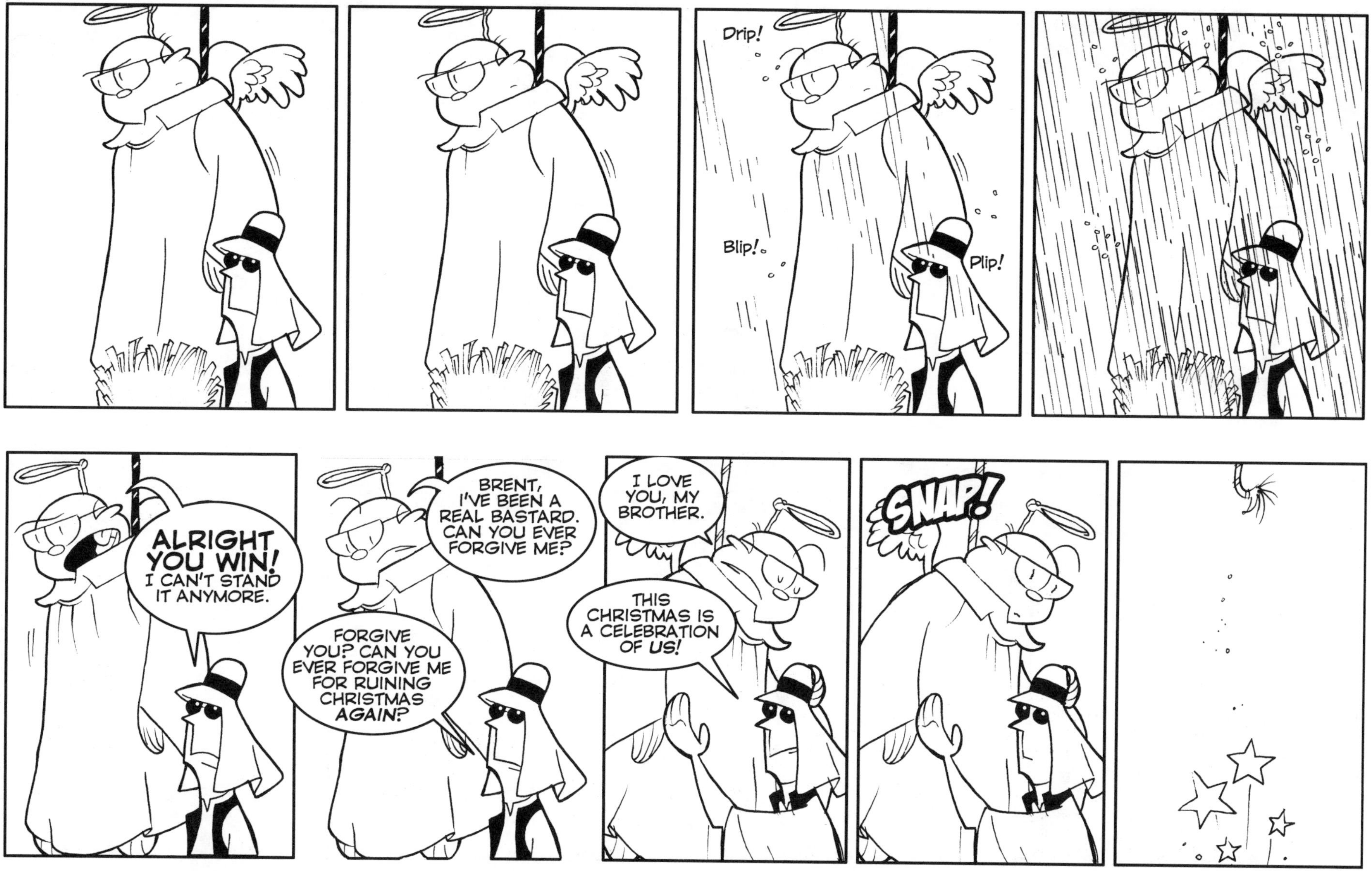
Drip!
Blip!
Plip!
ALRIGHT YOU WIN! I CAN'T STAND IT ANYMORE.
BRENT, I'VE BEEN A REAL BASTARD. CAN YOU EVER FORGIVE ME?
FORGIVE YOU? CAN YOU EVER FORGIVE ME FOR RUINING CHRISTMAS AGAIN?
I LOVE YOU, MY BROTHER.
THIS CHRISTMAS IS A CELEBRATION OF US!
SNAP!

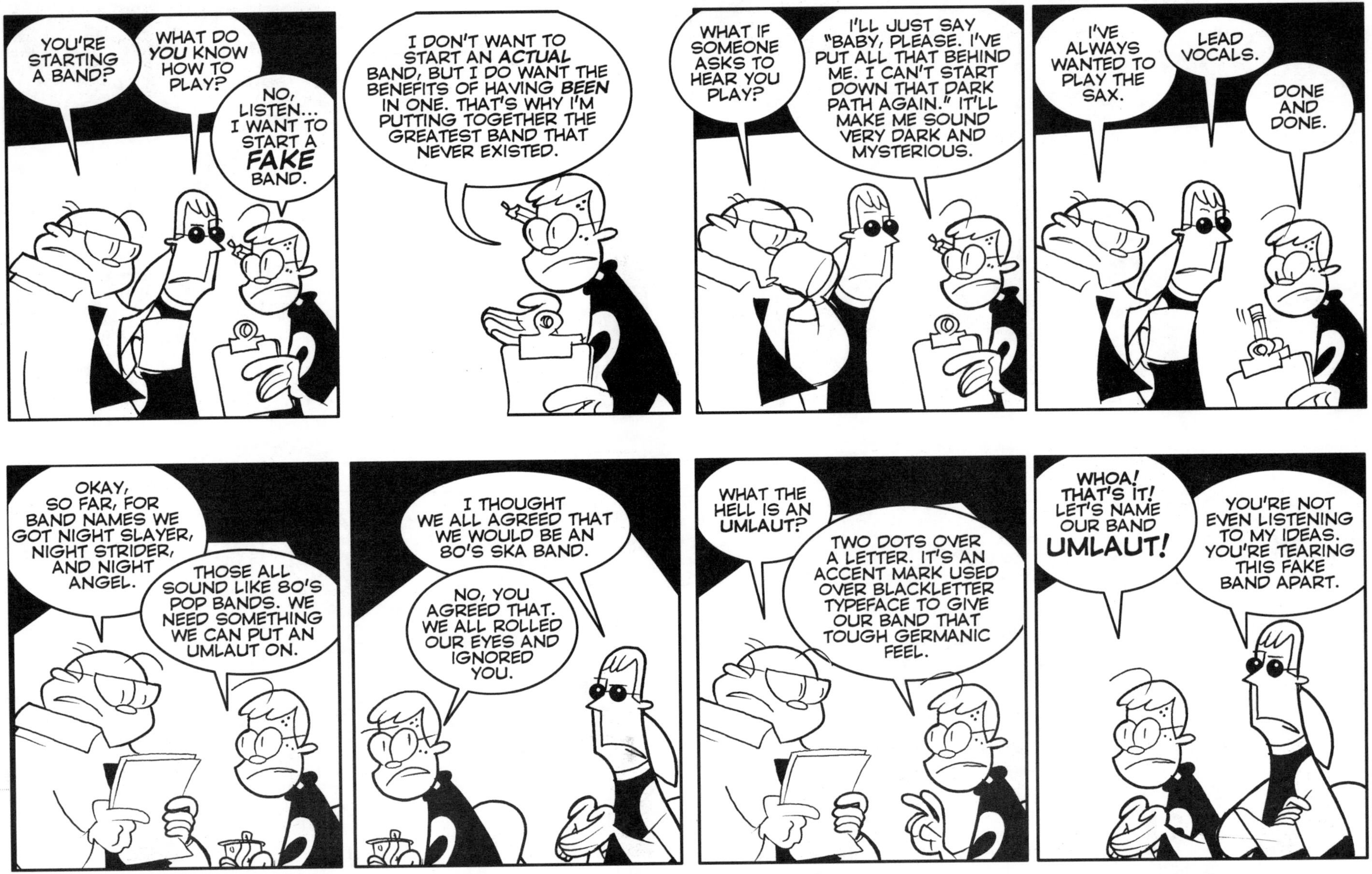
YOU'RE STARTING A BAND?
WHAT DO YOU KNOW HOW TO PLAY?
NO, LISTEN... I WANT TO START A FAKE BAND.
I DON'T WANT TO START AN ACTUAL BAND, BUT I DO WANT THE BENEFITS OF HAVING BEEN IN ONE. THAT'S WHY I'M PUTTING TOGETHER THE GREATEST BAND THAT NEVER EXISTED.
WHAT IF SOMEONE ASKS TO HEAR YOU PLAY?
I'LL JUST SAY "BABY, PLEASE. I'VE PUT ALL THAT BEHIND ME. I CAN'T START DOWN THAT DARK PATH AGAIN." IT'LL MAKE ME SOUND VERY DARK AND MYSTERIOUS.
I'VE ALWAYS WANTED TO PLAY THE SAX.
LEAD VOCALS.
DONE AND DONE.
OKAY, SO FAR, FOR BAND NAMES WE GOT NIGHT SLAYER, NIGHT STRIDER, AND NIGHT ANGEL.
THOSE ALL SOUND LIKE 80'S POP BANDS. WE NEED SOMETHING WE CAN PUT AN UMLAUT ON.
I THOUGHT WE ALL AGREED THAT WE WOULD BE AN 80'S SKA BAND.
NO, YOU AGREED THAT. WE ALL ROLLED OUR EYES AND IGNORED YOU.
WHAT THE HELL IS AN UMLAUT?
TWO DOTS OVER A LETTER. IT'S AN ACCENT MARK USED OVER BLACKLETTER TYPEFACE TO GIVE OUR BAND THAT TOUGH GERMANIC FEEL.
WHOA! THAT'S IT! LET'S NAME OUR BAND UMLAUT!
YOU'RE NOT EVEN LISTENING TO MY IDEAS. YOU'RE TEARING THIS FAKE BAND APART.

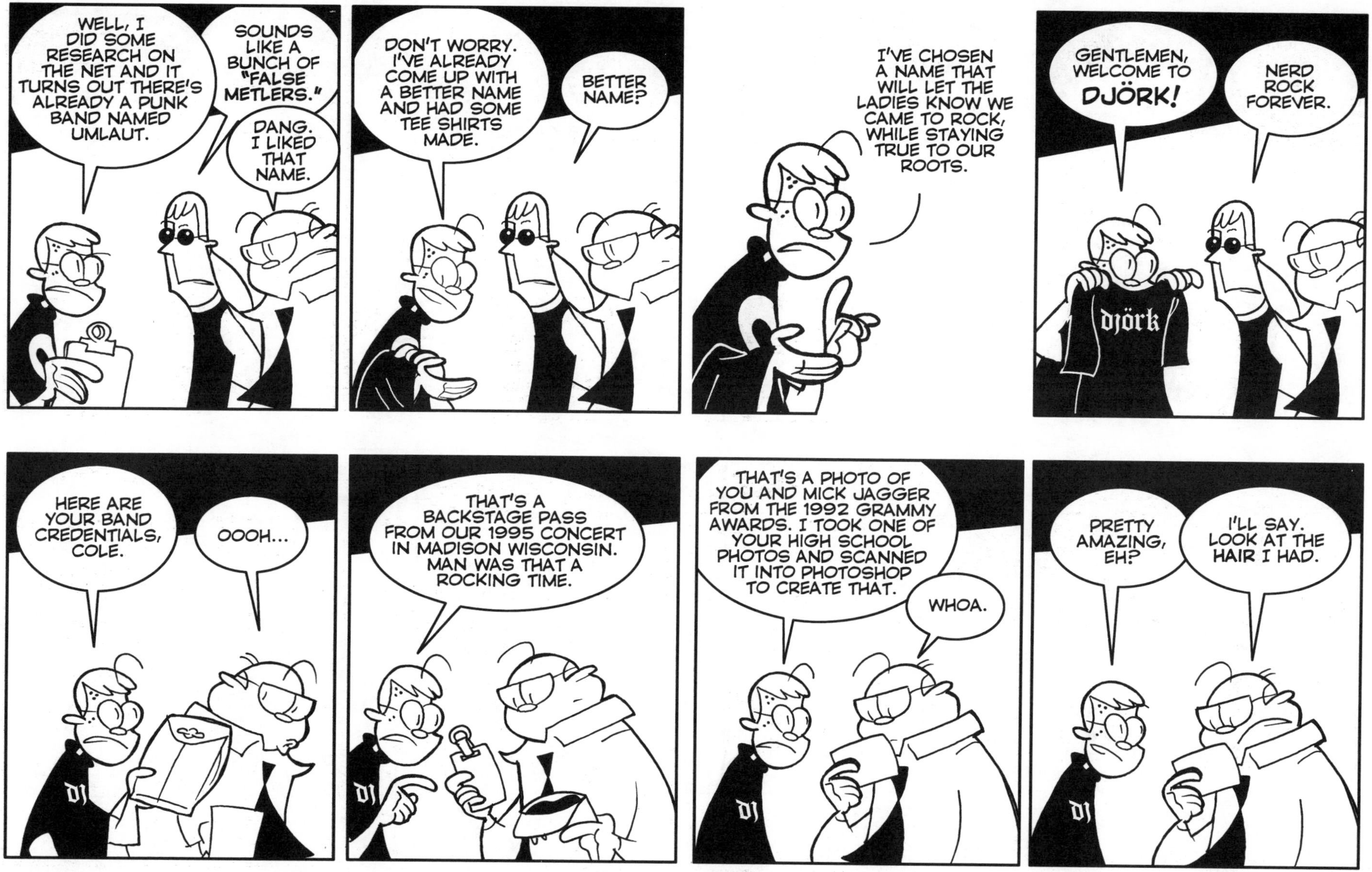
WELL, I DID SOME RESEARCH ON THE NET AND IT TURNS OUT THERE'S ALREADY A PUNK BAND NAMED UMLAUT.
SOUNDS LIKE A BUNCH OF "FALSE METLERS."
DANG. I LIKED THAT NAME.
DON'T WORRY. I'VE ALREADY COME UP WITH A BETTER NAME AND HAD SOME TEE SHIRTS MADE.
BETTER NAME?
I'VE CHOSEN A NAME THAT WILL LET THE LADIES KNOW WE CAME TO ROCK, WHILE STAYING TRUE TO OUR ROOTS.
GENTLEMEN, WELCOME TO DJÖRK!
NERD ROCK FOREVER.
djörk
HERE ARE YOUR BAND CREDENTIALS, COLE.
OOOH...
THAT'S A BACKSTAGE PASS FROM OUR 1995 CONCERT IN MADISON WISCONSIN. MAN WAS THAT A ROCKING TIME.
THAT'S A PHOTO OF YOU AND MICK JAGGER FROM THE 1992 GRAMMY AWARDS. I TOOK ONE OF YOUR HIGH SCHOOL PHOTOS AND SCANNED IT INTO PHOTOSHOP TO CREATE THAT.
WHOA.
PRETTY AMAZING, EH?
I'LL SAY. LOOK AT THE HAIR I HAD.

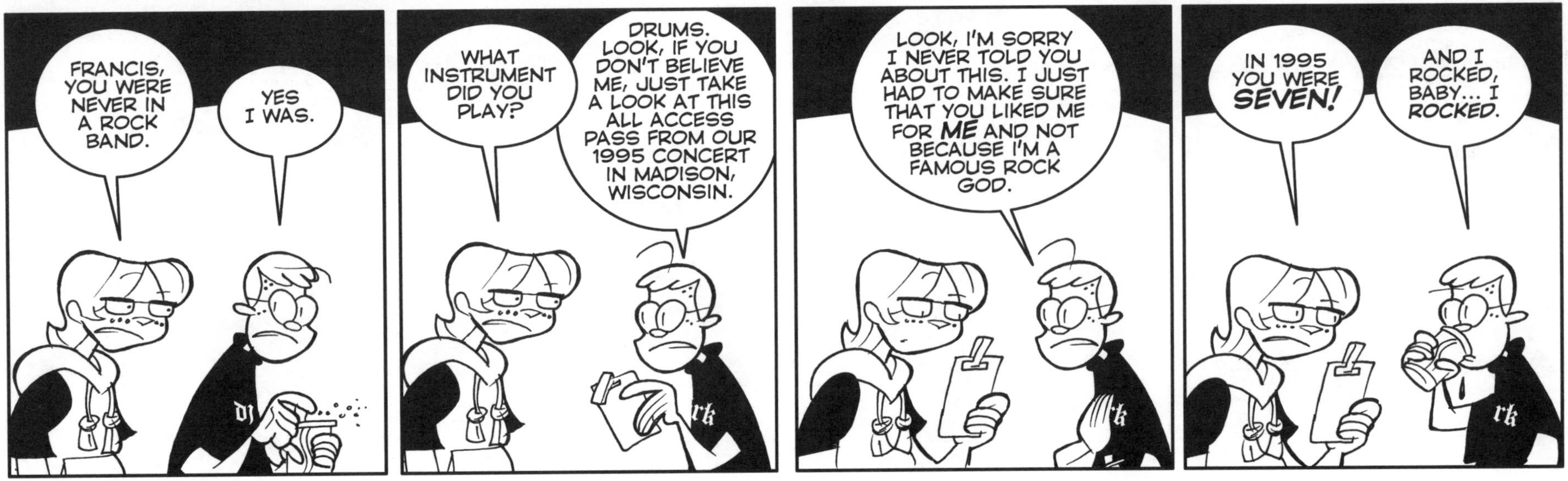
FRANCIS, YOU WERE NEVER IN A ROCK BAND.
YES I WAS.
WHAT INSTRUMENT DID YOU PLAY?
DRUMS. LOOK, IF YOU DON'T BELIEVE ME, JUST TAKE A LOOK AT THIS ALL ACCESS PASS FROM OUR 1995 CONCERT IN MADISON, WISCONSIN.
LOOK, I'M SORRY I NEVER TOLD YOU ABOUT THIS. I JUST HAD TO MAKE SURE THAT YOU LIKED ME FOR **ME** AND NOT BECAUSE I'M A FAMOUS ROCK GOD.
IN 1995 YOU WERE **SEVEN!**
AND I ROCKED, BABY... I *ROCKED*.

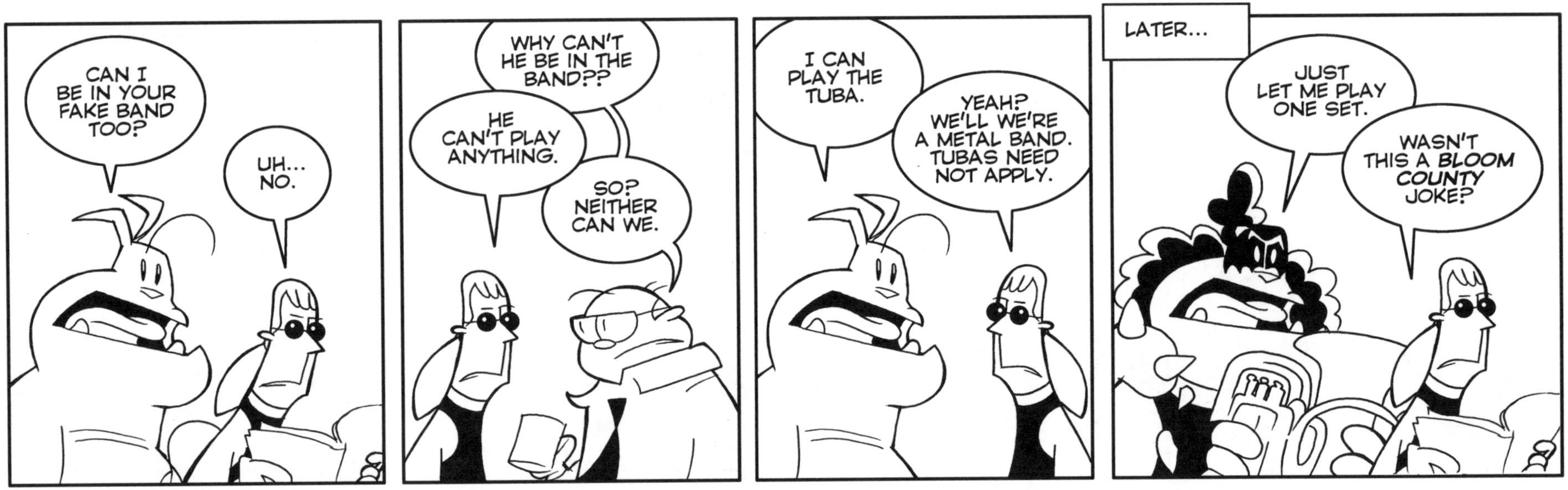
CAN I BE IN YOUR FAKE BAND TOO?
UH... NO.
WHY CAN'T HE BE IN THE BAND??
HE CAN'T PLAY ANYTHING.
SO? NEITHER CAN WE.
I CAN PLAY THE TUBA.
YEAH? WE'LL WE'RE A METAL BAND. TUBAS NEED NOT APPLY.
LATER...
JUST LET ME PLAY ONE SET.
WASN'T THIS A ***BLOOM COUNTY*** JOKE?

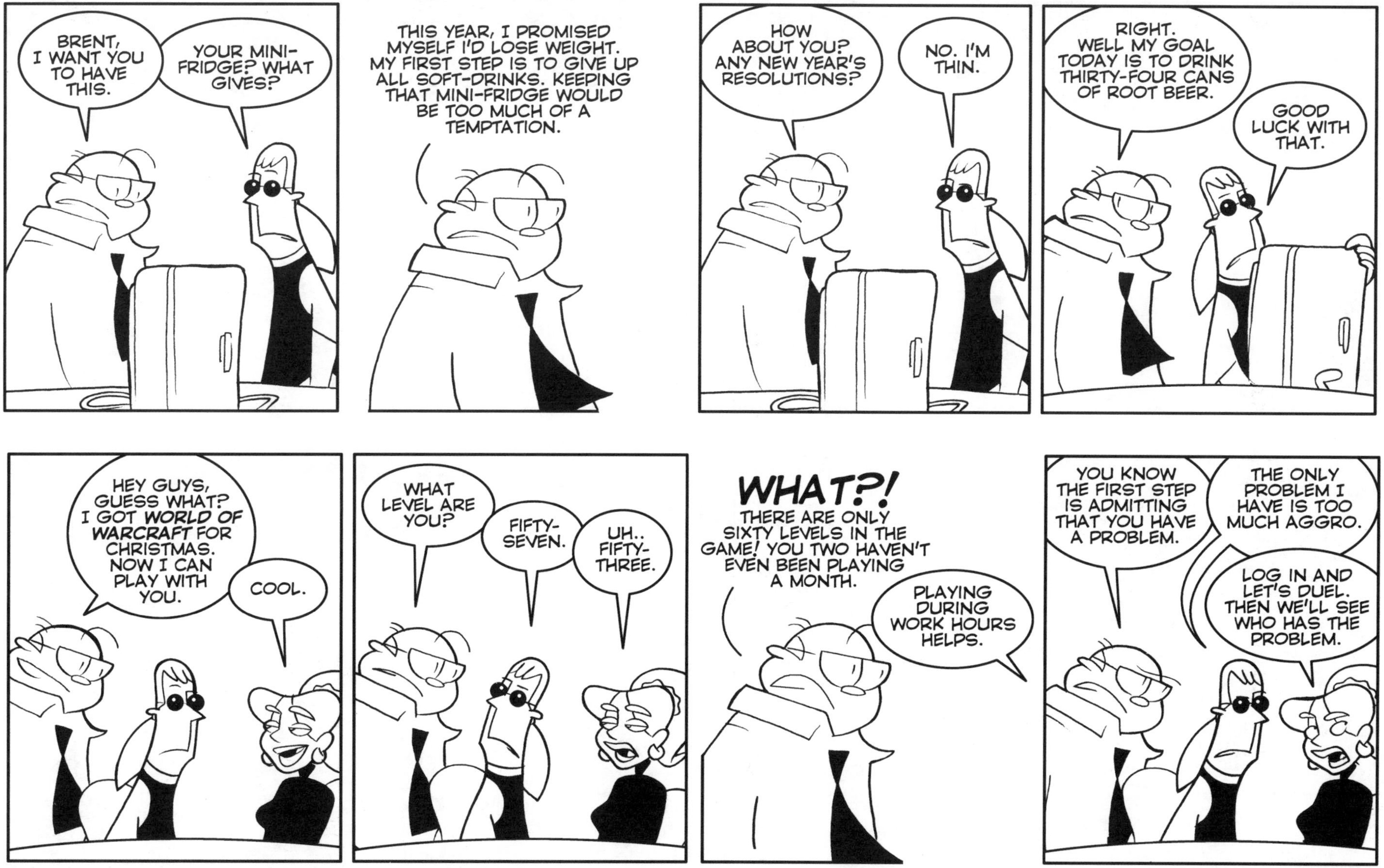
BRENT, I WANT YOU TO HAVE THIS.
YOUR MINI-FRIDGE? WHAT GIVES?
THIS YEAR, I PROMISED MYSELF I'D LOSE WEIGHT. MY FIRST STEP IS TO GIVE UP ALL SOFT-DRINKS. KEEPING THAT MINI-FRIDGE WOULD BE TOO MUCH OF A TEMPTATION.
HOW ABOUT YOU? ANY NEW YEAR'S RESOLUTIONS?
NO. I'M THIN.
RIGHT. WELL MY GOAL TODAY IS TO DRINK THIRTY-FOUR CANS OF ROOT BEER.
GOOD LUCK WITH THAT.
HEY GUYS, GUESS WHAT? I GOT *WORLD OF WARCRAFT* FOR CHRISTMAS. NOW I CAN PLAY WITH YOU.
COOL.
WHAT LEVEL ARE YOU?
FIFTY-SEVEN.
UH.. FIFTY-THREE.
WHAT?!
THERE ARE ONLY SIXTY LEVELS IN THE GAME! YOU TWO HAVEN'T EVEN BEEN PLAYING A MONTH.
PLAYING DURING WORK HOURS HELPS.
YOU KNOW THE FIRST STEP IS ADMITTING THAT YOU HAVE A PROBLEM.
THE ONLY PROBLEM I HAVE IS TOO MUCH AGGRO.
LOG IN AND LET'S DUEL. THEN WE'LL SEE WHO HAS THE PROBLEM.

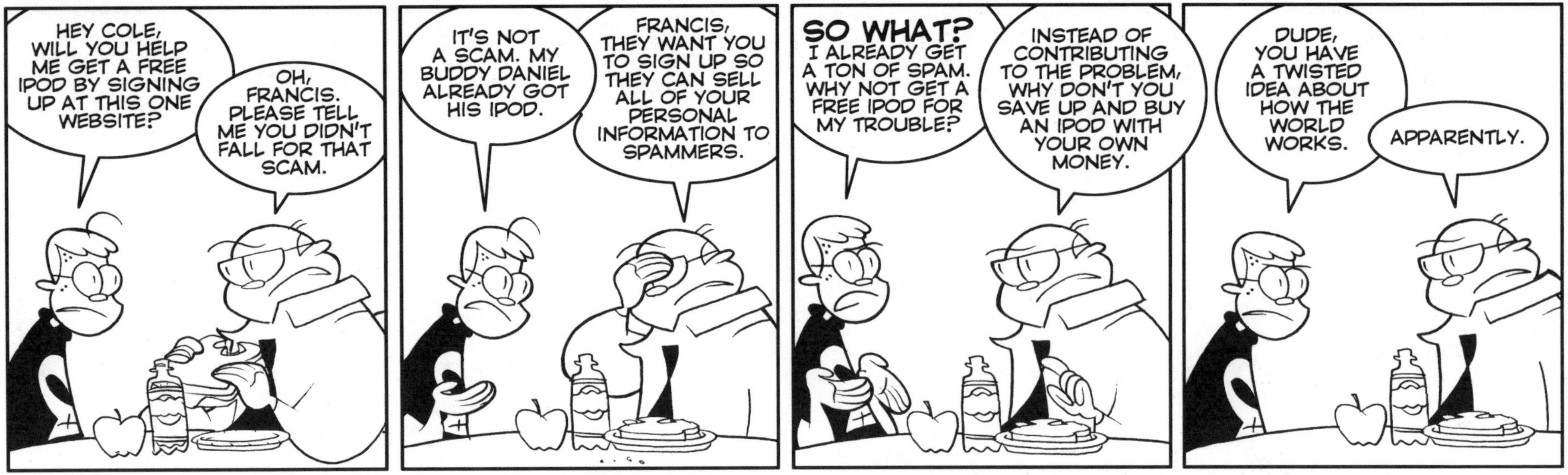
HEY COLE, WILL YOU HELP ME GET A FREE IPOD BY SIGNING UP AT THIS ONE WEBSITE?
OH, FRANCIS. PLEASE TELL ME YOU DIDN'T FALL FOR THAT SCAM.
IT'S NOT A SCAM. MY BUDDY DANIEL ALREADY GOT HIS IPOD.
FRANCIS, THEY WANT YOU TO SIGN UP SO THEY CAN SELL ALL OF YOUR PERSONAL INFORMATION TO SPAMMERS.
SO WHAT? I ALREADY GET A TON OF SPAM. WHY NOT GET A FREE IPOD FOR MY TROUBLE?
INSTEAD OF CONTRIBUTING TO THE PROBLEM, WHY DON'T YOU SAVE UP AND BUY AN IPOD WITH YOUR OWN MONEY.
DUDE, YOU HAVE A TWISTED IDEA ABOUT HOW THE WORLD WORKS.
APPARENTLY.

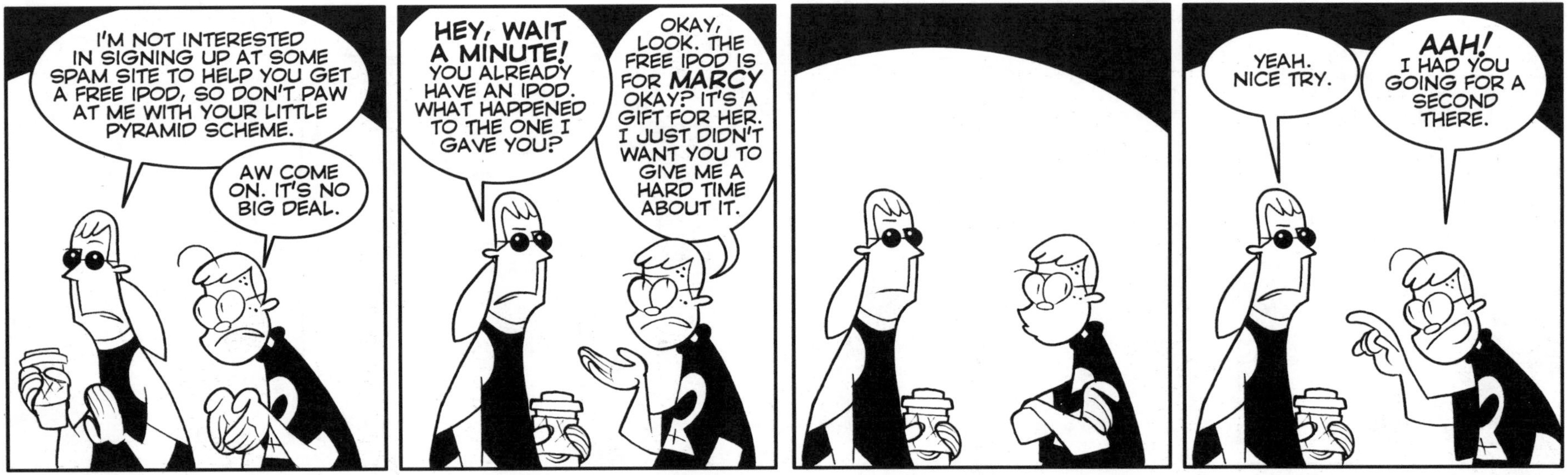
I'M NOT INTERESTED IN SIGNING UP AT SOME SPAM SITE TO HELP YOU GET A FREE IPOD, SO DON'T PAW AT ME WITH YOUR LITTLE PYRAMID SCHEME.
AW COME ON. IT'S NO BIG DEAL.
HEY, WAIT A MINUTE! YOU ALREADY HAVE AN IPOD. WHAT HAPPENED TO THE ONE I GAVE YOU?
OKAY, LOOK. THE FREE IPOD IS FOR MARCY OKAY? IT'S A GIFT FOR HER. I JUST DIDN'T WANT YOU TO GIVE ME A HARD TIME ABOUT IT.
YEAH. NICE TRY.
AAH! I HAD YOU GOING FOR A SECOND THERE.

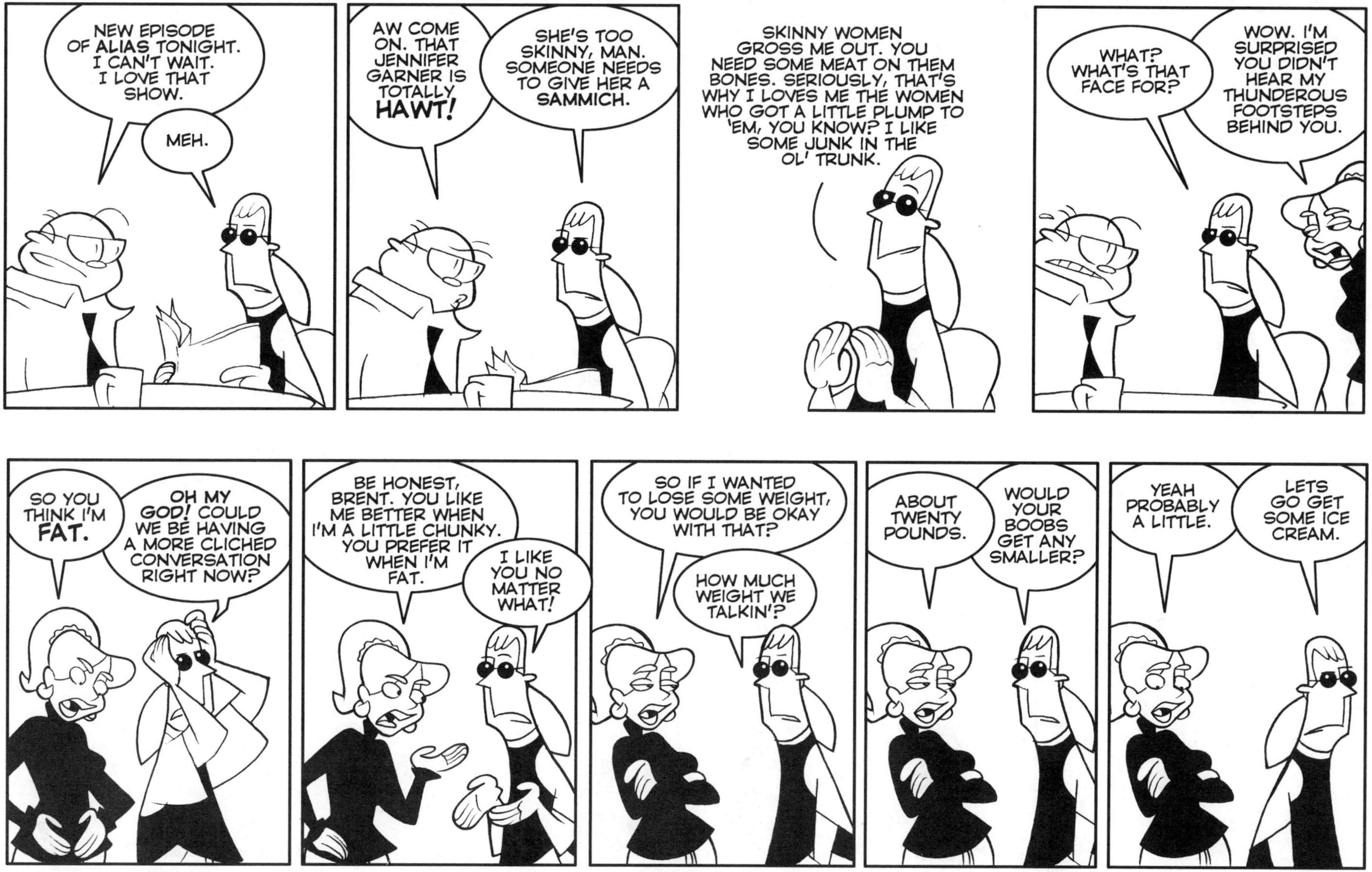
NEW EPISODE OF ALIAS TONIGHT. I CAN'T WAIT. I LOVE THAT SHOW.
MEH.
AW COME ON. THAT JENNIFER GARNER IS TOTALLY HAWT!
SHE'S TOO SKINNY, MAN. SOMEONE NEEDS TO GIVE HER A SAMMICH.
SKINNY WOMEN GROSS ME OUT. YOU NEED SOME MEAT ON THEM BONES. SERIOUSLY, THAT'S WHY I LOVES ME THE WOMEN WHO GOT A LITTLE PLUMP TO 'EM, YOU KNOW? I LIKE SOME JUNK IN THE OL' TRUNK.
WHAT? WHAT'S THAT FACE FOR?
WOW. I'M SURPRISED YOU DIDN'T HEAR MY THUNDEROUS FOOTSTEPS BEHIND YOU.
SO YOU THINK I'M FAT.
OH MY GOD! COULD WE BE HAVING A MORE CLICHED CONVERSATION RIGHT NOW?
BE HONEST, BRENT. YOU LIKE ME BETTER WHEN I'M A LITTLE CHUNKY. YOU PREFER IT WHEN I'M FAT.
I LIKE YOU NO MATTER WHAT!
SO IF I WANTED TO LOSE SOME WEIGHT, YOU WOULD BE OKAY WITH THAT?
HOW MUCH WEIGHT WE TALKIN'?
ABOUT TWENTY POUNDS.
WOULD YOUR BOOBS GET ANY SMALLER?
YEAH PROBABLY A LITTLE.
LETS GO GET SOME ICE CREAM.

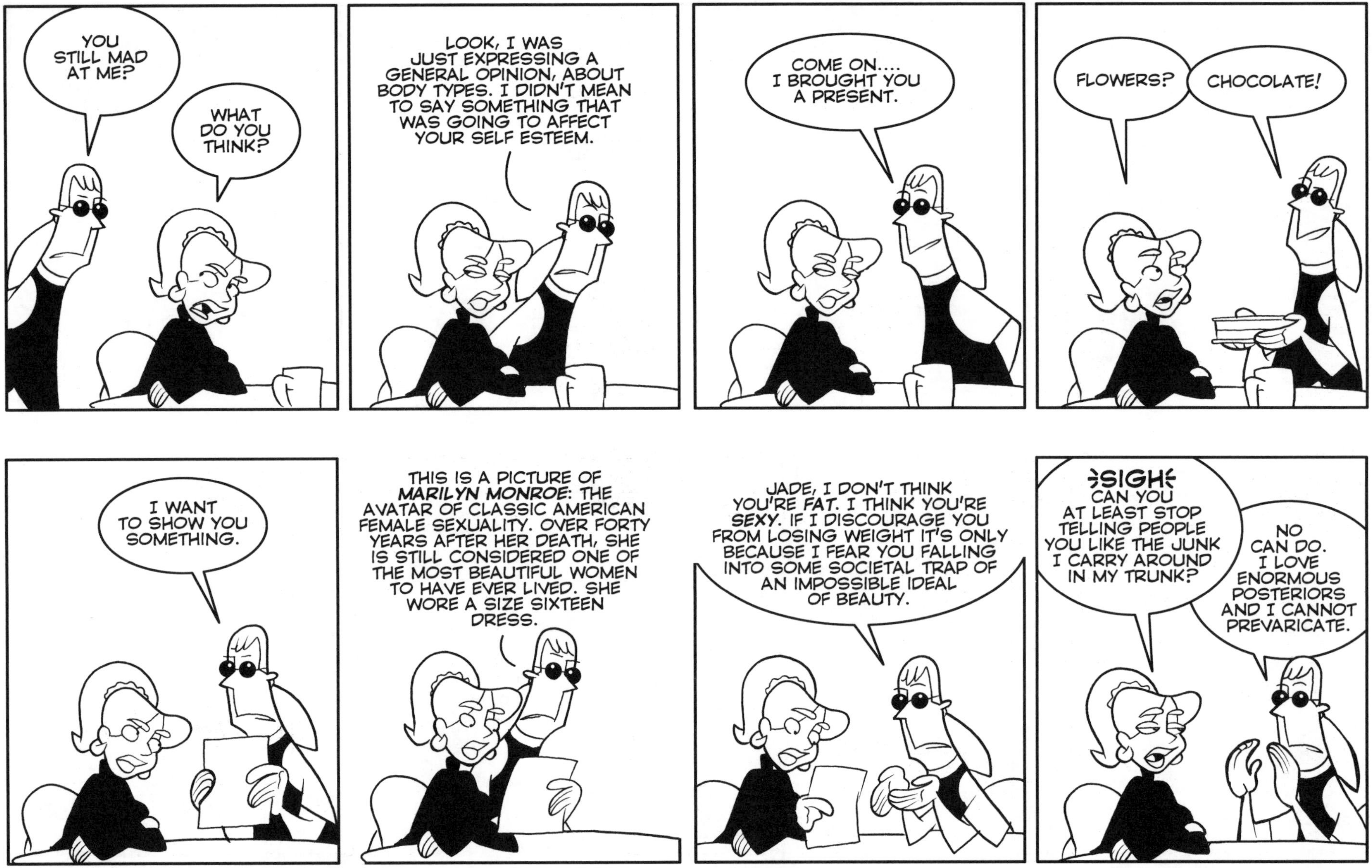
YOU STILL MAD AT ME?
WHAT DO YOU THINK?
LOOK, I WAS JUST EXPRESSING A GENERAL OPINION, ABOUT BODY TYPES. I DIDN'T MEAN TO SAY SOMETHING THAT WAS GOING TO AFFECT YOUR SELF ESTEEM.
COME ON.... I BROUGHT YOU A PRESENT.
FLOWERS?
CHOCOLATE!
I WANT TO SHOW YOU SOMETHING.
THIS IS A PICTURE OF ***MARILYN MONROE***: THE AVATAR OF CLASSIC AMERICAN FEMALE SEXUALITY. OVER FORTY YEARS AFTER HER DEATH, SHE IS STILL CONSIDERED ONE OF THE MOST BEAUTIFUL WOMEN TO HAVE EVER LIVED. SHE WORE A SIZE SIXTEEN DRESS.
JADE, I DON'T THINK YOU'RE ***FAT***. I THINK YOU'RE ***SEXY***. IF I DISCOURAGE YOU FROM LOSING WEIGHT IT'S ONLY BECAUSE I FEAR YOU FALLING INTO SOME SOCIETAL TRAP OF AN IMPOSSIBLE IDEAL OF BEAUTY.
SIGH
CAN YOU AT LEAST STOP TELLING PEOPLE YOU LIKE THE JUNK I CARRY AROUND IN MY TRUNK?
NO CAN DO. I LOVE ENORMOUS POSTERIORS AND I CANNOT PREVARICATE.

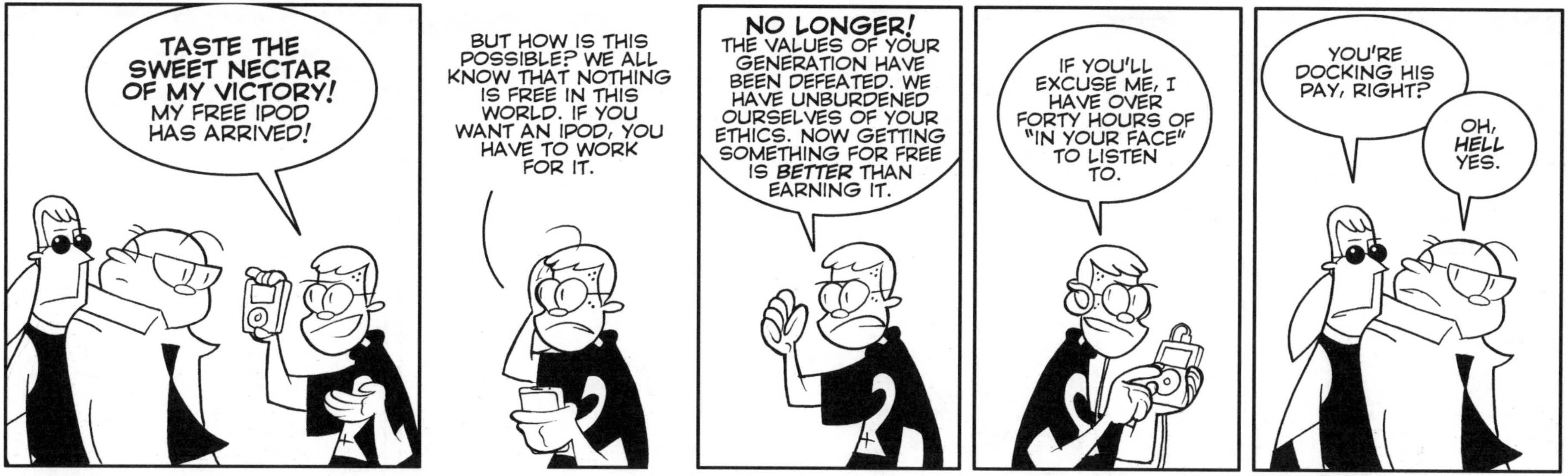
TASTE THE SWEET NECTAR OF MY VICTORY! MY FREE IPOD HAS ARRIVED!
BUT HOW IS THIS POSSIBLE? WE ALL KNOW THAT NOTHING IS FREE IN THIS WORLD. IF YOU WANT AN IPOD, YOU HAVE TO WORK FOR IT.
NO LONGER! THE VALUES OF YOUR GENERATION HAVE BEEN DEFEATED. WE HAVE UNBURDENED OURSELVES OF YOUR ETHICS. NOW GETTING SOMETHING FOR FREE IS BETTER THAN EARNING IT.
IF YOU'LL EXCUSE ME, I HAVE OVER FORTY HOURS OF "IN YOUR FACE" TO LISTEN TO.
YOU'RE DOCKING HIS PAY, RIGHT?
OH, HELL YES.

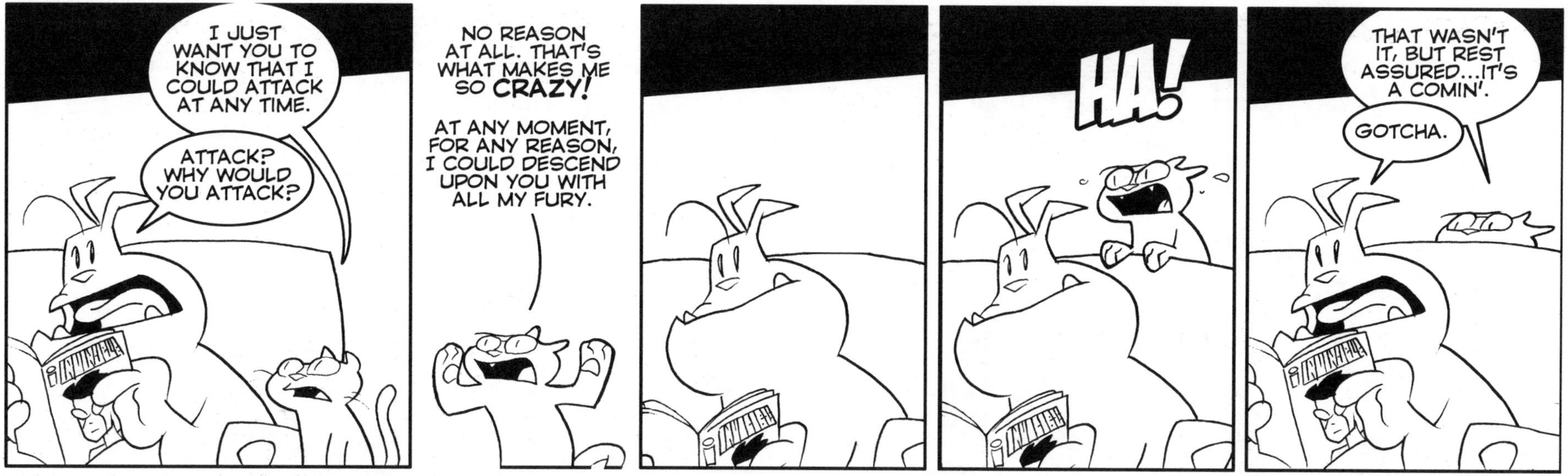
I JUST WANT YOU TO KNOW THAT I COULD ATTACK AT ANY TIME.
ATTACK? WHY WOULD YOU ATTACK?
NO REASON AT ALL. THAT'S WHAT MAKES ME SO CRAZY!
AT ANY MOMENT, FOR ANY REASON, I COULD DESCEND UPON YOU WITH ALL MY FURY.
HA!
THAT WASN'T IT, BUT REST ASSURED...IT'S A COMIN'.
GOTCHA.

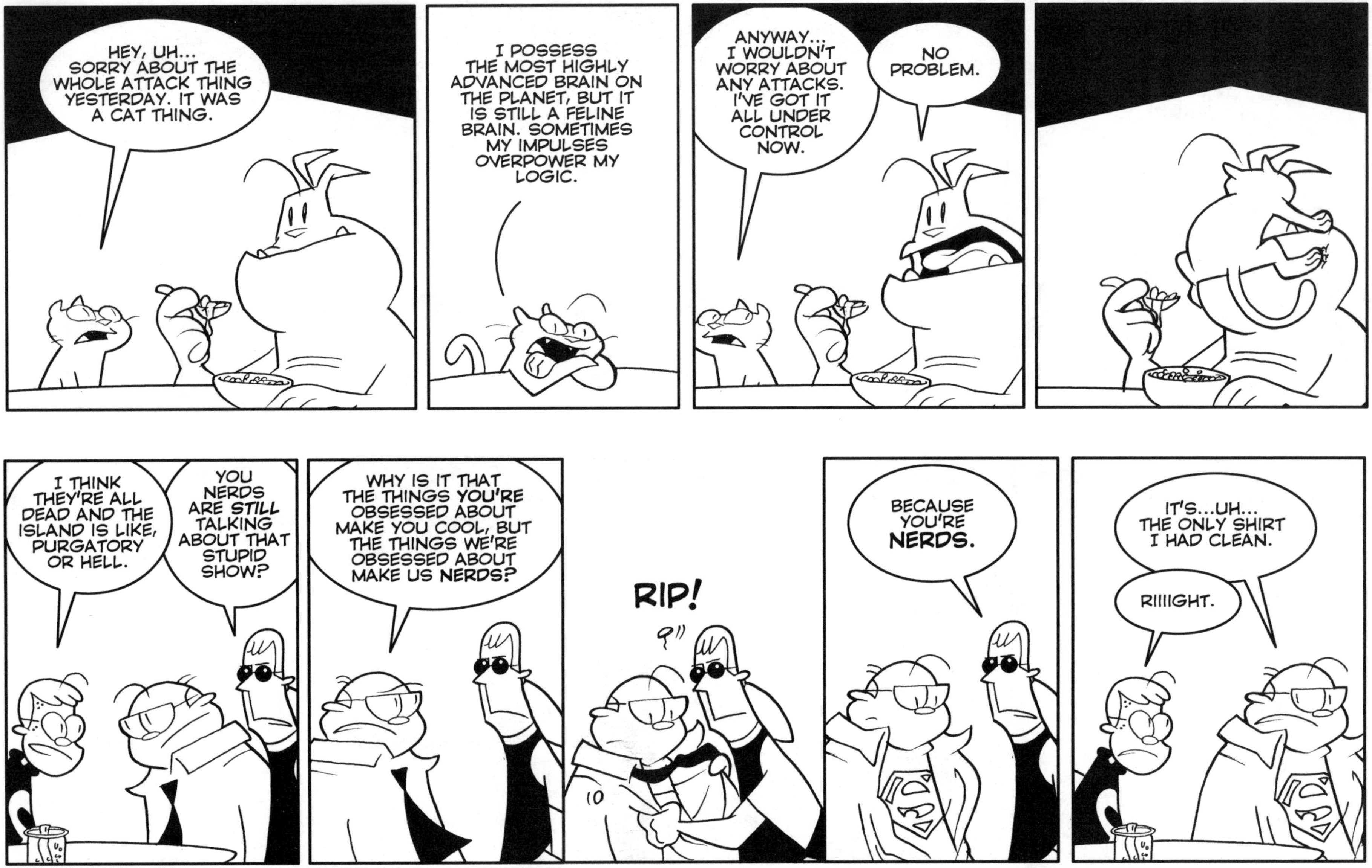

HEY, UH... SORRY ABOUT THE WHOLE ATTACK THING YESTERDAY. IT WAS A CAT THING.
I POSSESS THE MOST HIGHLY ADVANCED BRAIN ON THE PLANET, BUT IT IS STILL A FELINE BRAIN. SOMETIMES MY IMPULSES OVERPOWER MY LOGIC.
ANYWAY... I WOULDN'T WORRY ABOUT ANY ATTACKS. I'VE GOT IT ALL UNDER CONTROL NOW.
NO PROBLEM.
I THINK THEY'RE ALL DEAD AND THE ISLAND IS LIKE, PURGATORY OR HELL.
YOU NERDS ARE STILL TALKING ABOUT THAT STUPID SHOW?
WHY IS IT THAT THE THINGS YOU'RE OBSESSED ABOUT MAKE YOU COOL, BUT THE THINGS WE'RE OBSESSED ABOUT MAKE US NERDS?
RIP!
BECAUSE YOU'RE NERDS.
IT'S...UH... THE ONLY SHIRT I HAD CLEAN.
RIIIIGHT.

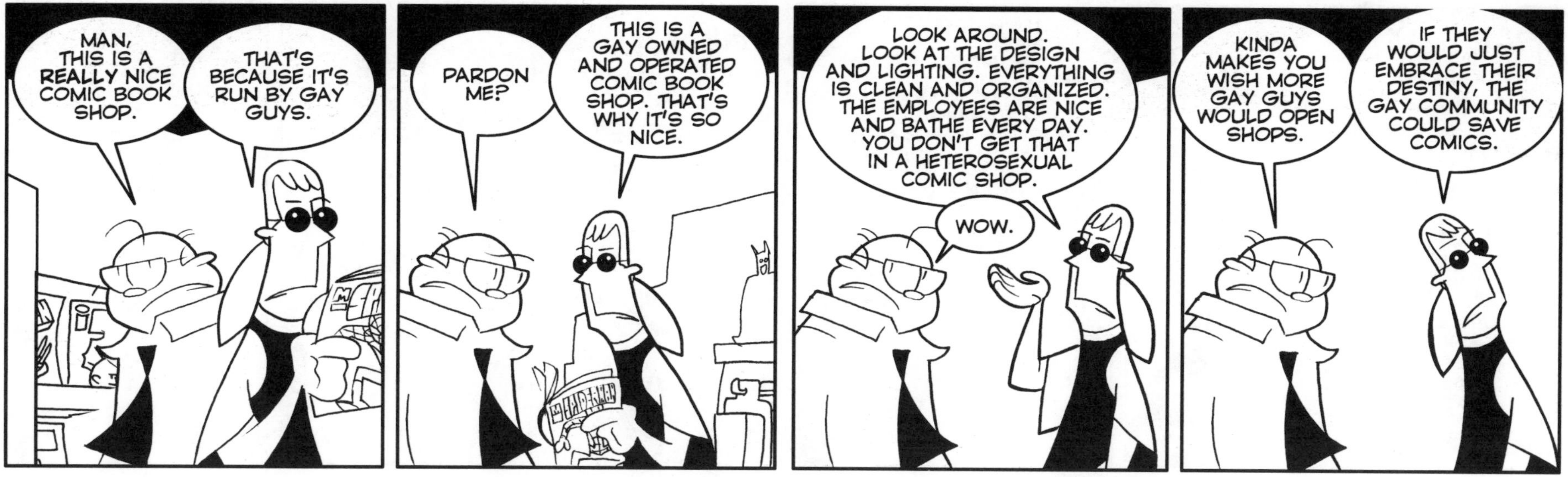
MAN, THIS IS A REALLY NICE COMIC BOOK SHOP.
THAT'S BECAUSE IT'S RUN BY GAY GUYS.
PARDON ME?
THIS IS A GAY OWNED AND OPERATED COMIC BOOK SHOP. THAT'S WHY IT'S SO NICE.
LOOK AROUND. LOOK AT THE DESIGN AND LIGHTING. EVERYTHING IS CLEAN AND ORGANIZED. THE EMPLOYEES ARE NICE AND BATHE EVERY DAY. YOU DON'T GET THAT IN A HETEROSEXUAL COMIC SHOP.
WOW.
KINDA MAKES YOU WISH MORE GAY GUYS WOULD OPEN SHOPS.
IF THEY WOULD JUST EMBRACE THEIR DESTINY, THE GAY COMMUNITY COULD SAVE COMICS.

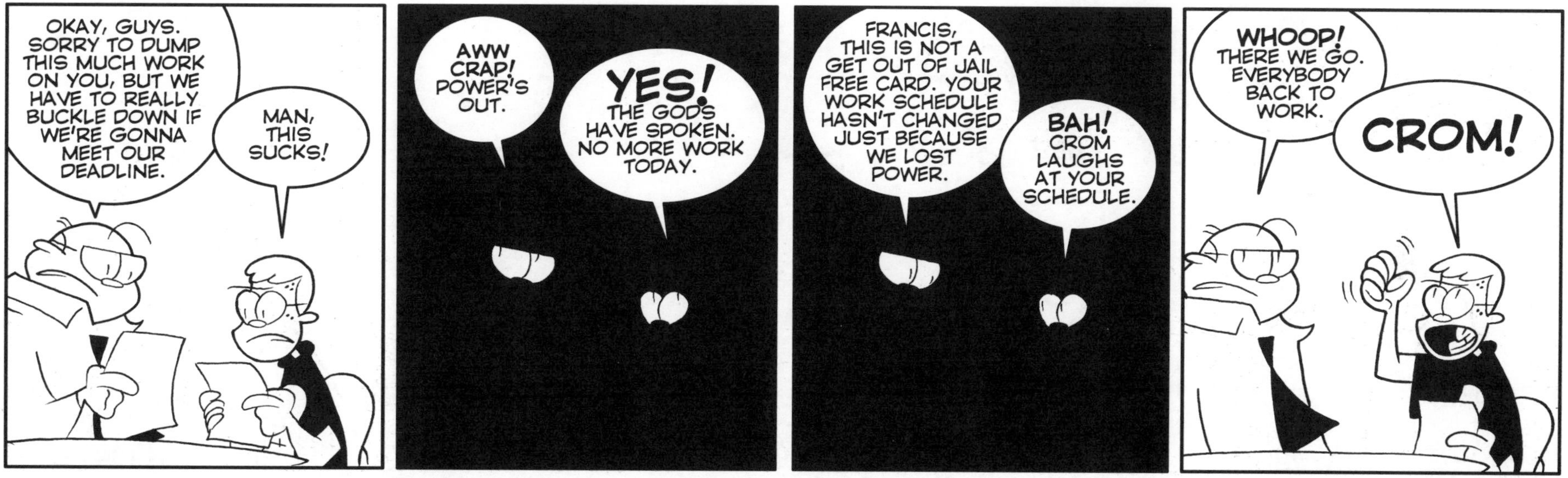
OKAY, GUYS. SORRY TO DUMP THIS MUCH WORK ON YOU, BUT WE HAVE TO REALLY BUCKLE DOWN IF WE'RE GONNA MEET OUR DEADLINE.
MAN, THIS SUCKS!
AWW CRAP! POWER'S OUT.
YES! THE GODS HAVE SPOKEN. NO MORE WORK TODAY.
FRANCIS, THIS IS NOT A GET OUT OF JAIL FREE CARD. YOUR WORK SCHEDULE HASN'T CHANGED JUST BECAUSE WE LOST POWER.
BAH! CROM LAUGHS AT YOUR SCHEDULE.
WHOOP! THERE WE GO. EVERYBODY BACK TO WORK.
CROM!

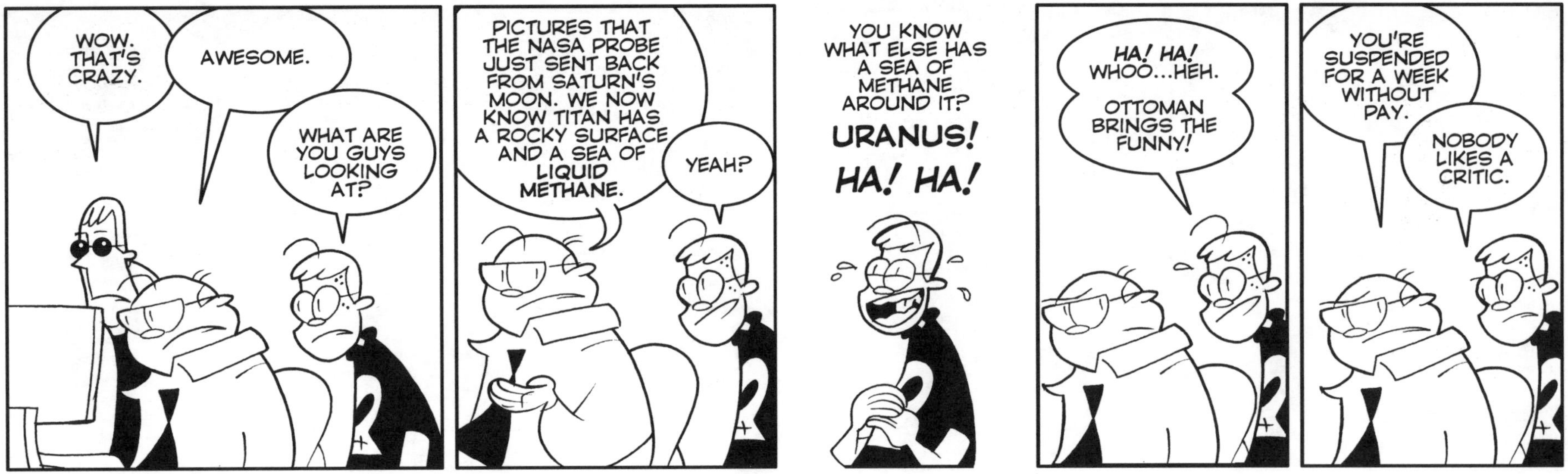
WOW. THAT'S CRAZY.
AWESOME.
WHAT ARE YOU GUYS LOOKING AT?
PICTURES THAT THE NASA PROBE JUST SENT BACK FROM SATURN'S MOON. WE NOW KNOW TITAN HAS A ROCKY SURFACE AND A SEA OF LIQUID METHANE.
YEAH?
YOU KNOW WHAT ELSE HAS A SEA OF METHANE AROUND IT?
URANUS!
HA! HA!
HA! HA! WHOO...HEH.
OTTOMAN BRINGS THE FUNNY!
YOU'RE SUSPENDED FOR A WEEK WITHOUT PAY.
NOBODY LIKES A CRITIC.

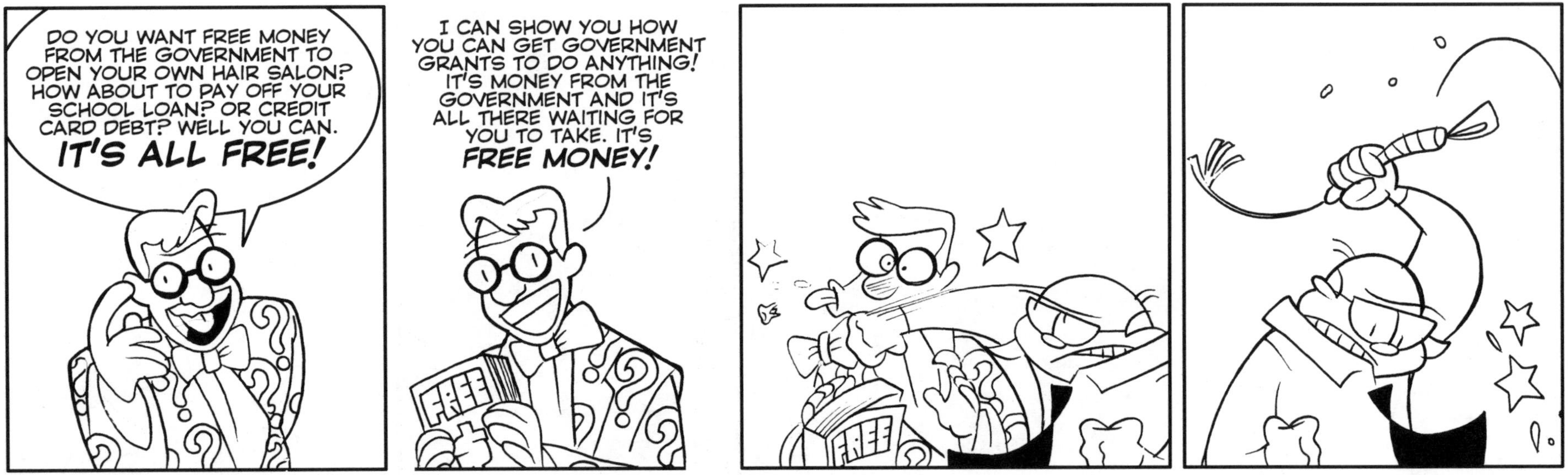
DO YOU WANT FREE MONEY FROM THE GOVERNMENT TO OPEN YOUR OWN HAIR SALON? HOW ABOUT TO PAY OFF YOUR SCHOOL LOAN? OR CREDIT CARD DEBT? WELL YOU CAN. IT'S ALL FREE!
I CAN SHOW YOU HOW YOU CAN GET GOVERNMENT GRANTS TO DO ANYTHING! IT'S MONEY FROM THE GOVERNMENT AND IT'S ALL THERE WAITING FOR YOU TO TAKE. IT'S FREE MONEY!
FREE

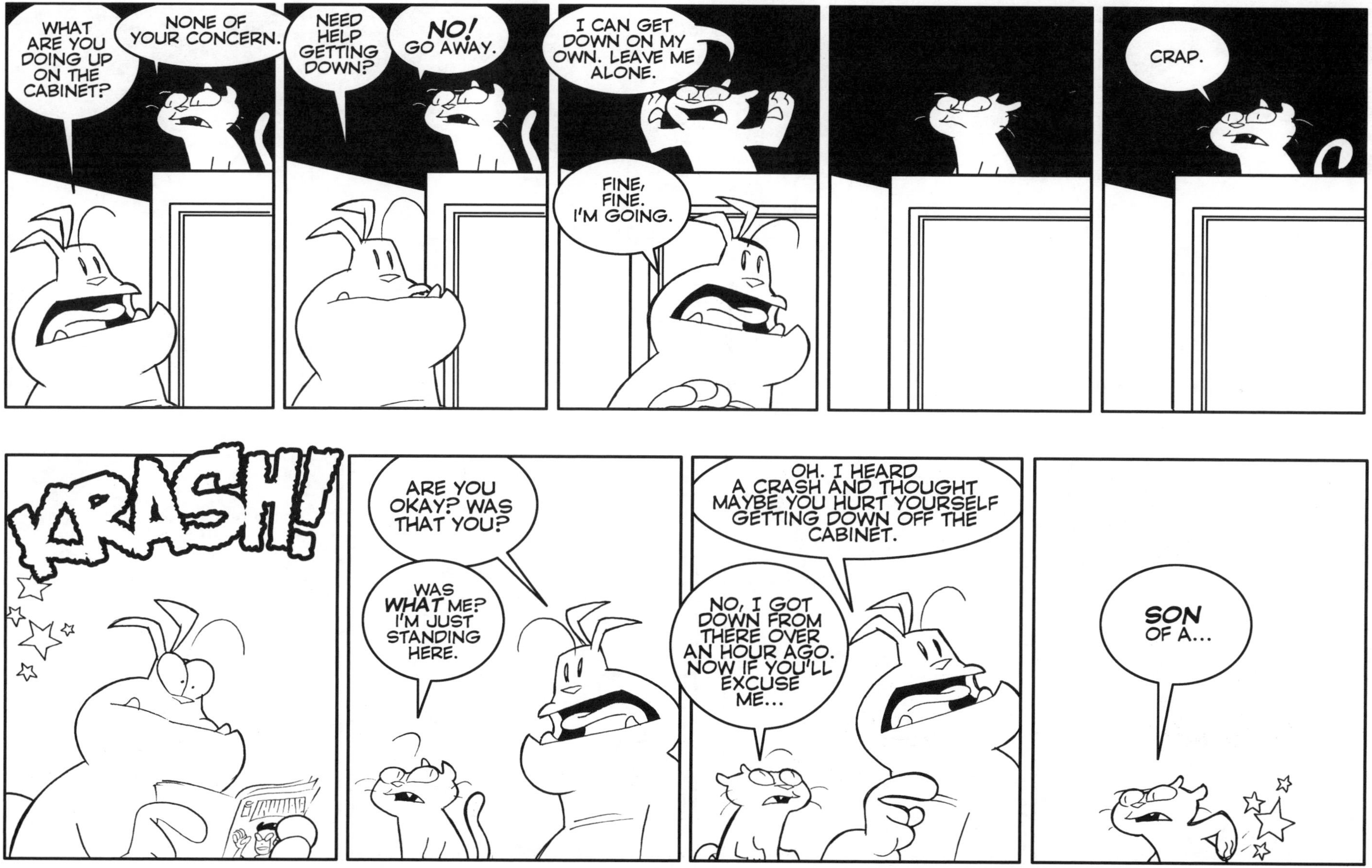
WHAT ARE YOU DOING UP ON THE CABINET?
NONE OF YOUR CONCERN.
NEED HELP GETTING DOWN?
NO! GO AWAY.
I CAN GET DOWN ON MY OWN. LEAVE ME ALONE.
FINE, FINE. I'M GOING.
CRAP.
KRASH!
ARE YOU OKAY? WAS THAT YOU?
WAS WHAT ME? I'M JUST STANDING HERE.
OH. I HEARD A CRASH AND THOUGHT MAYBE YOU HURT YOURSELF GETTING DOWN OFF THE CABINET.
NO, I GOT DOWN FROM THERE OVER AN HOUR AGO. NOW IF YOU'LL EXCUSE ME...
SON OF A...

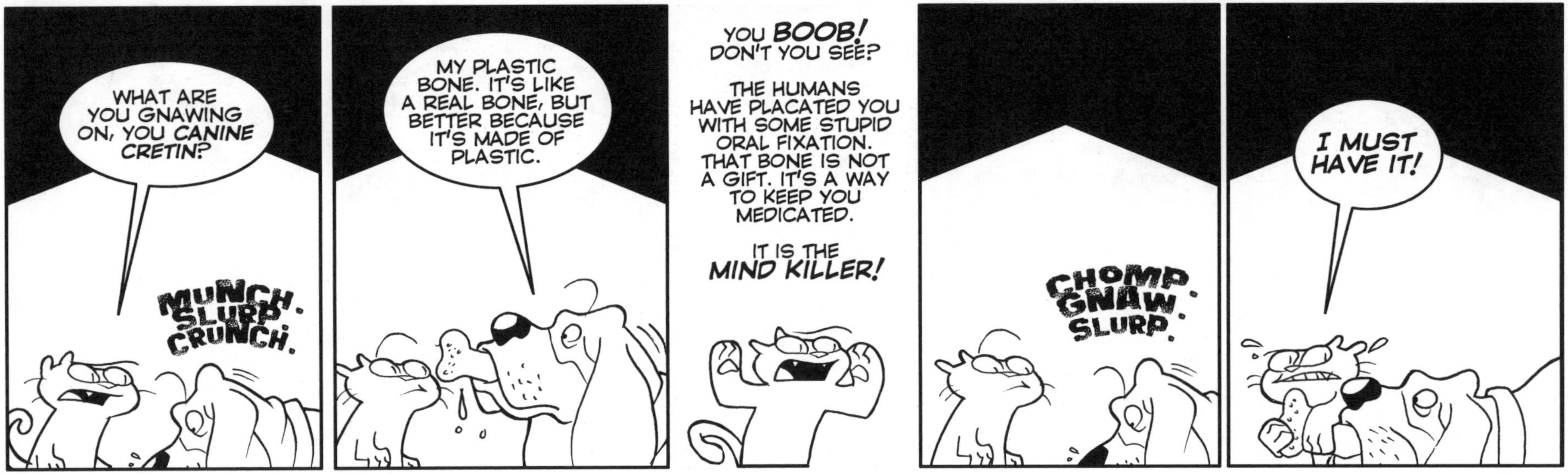
WHAT ARE YOU GNAWING ON, YOU CANINE CRETIN?
MUNCH. SLURP. CRUNCH.
MY PLASTIC BONE. IT'S LIKE A REAL BONE, BUT BETTER BECAUSE IT'S MADE OF PLASTIC.
YOU BOOB! DON'T YOU SEE?
THE HUMANS HAVE PLACATED YOU WITH SOME STUPID ORAL FIXATION. THAT BONE IS NOT A GIFT. IT'S A WAY TO KEEP YOU MEDICATED.
IT IS THE MIND KILLER!
CHOMP. GNAW. SLURP.
I MUST HAVE IT!

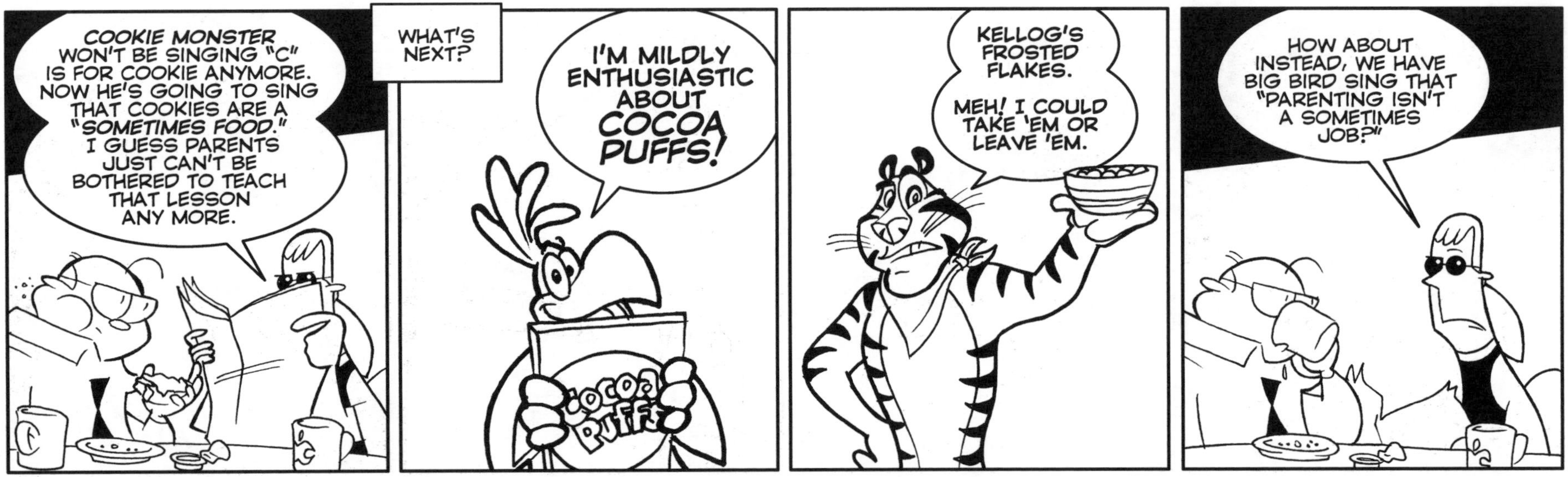
COOKIE MONSTER WON'T BE SINGING "C" IS FOR COOKIE ANYMORE. NOW HE'S GOING TO SING THAT COOKIES ARE A "SOMETIMES FOOD." I GUESS PARENTS JUST CAN'T BE BOTHERED TO TEACH THAT LESSON ANY MORE.
WHAT'S NEXT?
I'M MILDLY ENTHUSIASTIC ABOUT COCOA PUFFS!
COCOA PUFFS
KELLOG'S FROSTED FLAKES.
MEH! I COULD TAKE 'EM OR LEAVE 'EM.
HOW ABOUT INSTEAD, WE HAVE BIG BIRD SING THAT "PARENTING ISN'T A SOMETIMES JOB?"

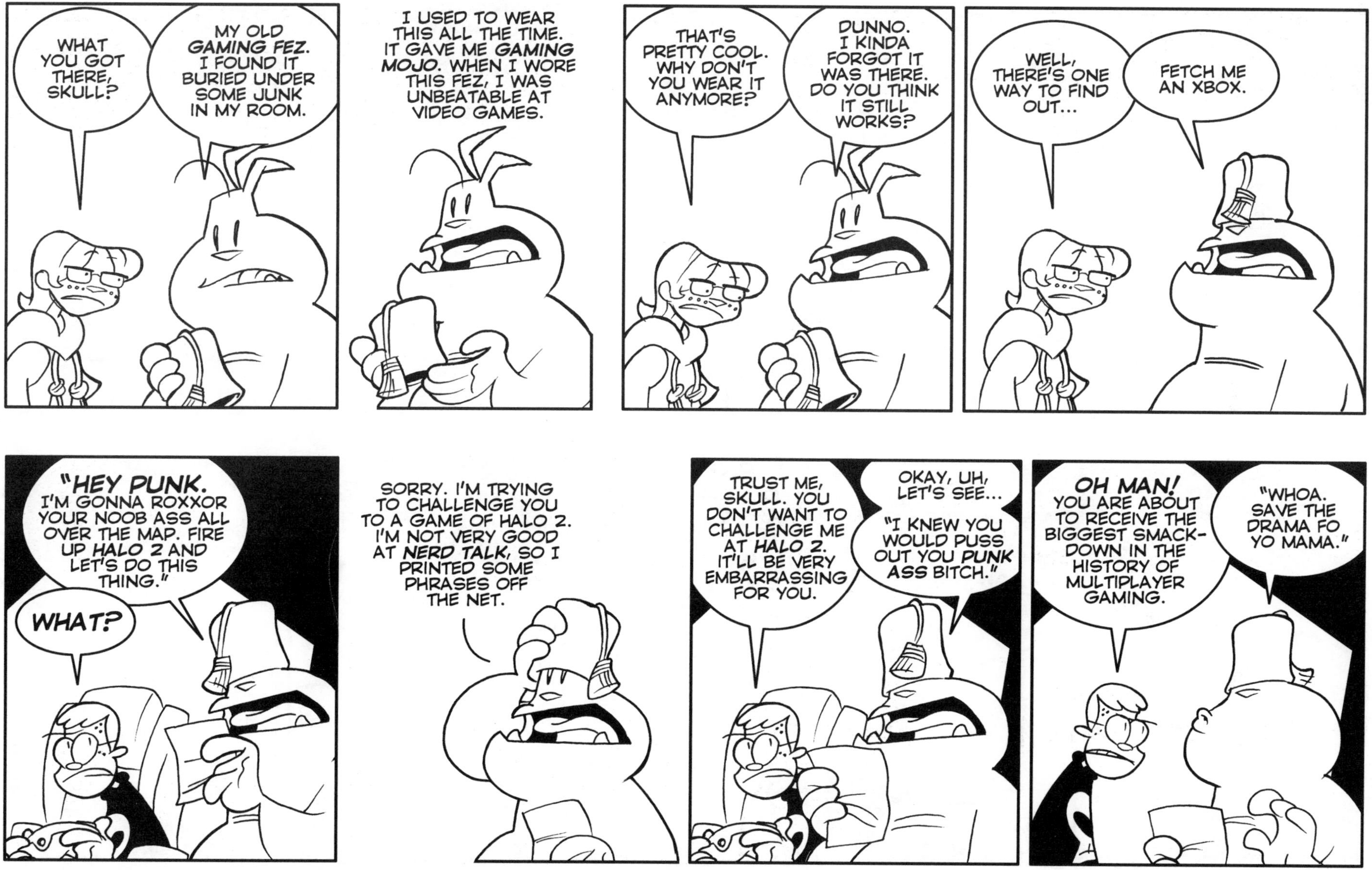
WHAT YOU GOT THERE, SKULL?
MY OLD GAMING FEZ. I FOUND IT BURIED UNDER SOME JUNK IN MY ROOM.
I USED TO WEAR THIS ALL THE TIME. IT GAVE ME GAMING MOJO. WHEN I WORE THIS FEZ, I WAS UNBEATABLE AT VIDEO GAMES.
THAT'S PRETTY COOL. WHY DON'T YOU WEAR IT ANYMORE?
DUNNO. I KINDA FORGOT IT WAS THERE. DO YOU THINK IT STILL WORKS?
WELL, THERE'S ONE WAY TO FIND OUT...
FETCH ME AN XBOX.
"HEY PUNK. I'M GONNA ROXXOR YOUR NOOB ASS ALL OVER THE MAP. FIRE UP HALO 2 AND LET'S DO THIS THING."
WHAT?
SORRY. I'M TRYING TO CHALLENGE YOU TO A GAME OF HALO 2. I'M NOT VERY GOOD AT NERD TALK, SO I PRINTED SOME PHRASES OFF THE NET.
TRUST ME, SKULL. YOU DON'T WANT TO CHALLENGE ME AT HALO 2. IT'LL BE VERY EMBARRASSING FOR YOU.
OKAY, UH, LET'S SEE...
"I KNEW YOU WOULD PUSS OUT YOU PUNK ASS BITCH."
OH MAN! YOU ARE ABOUT TO RECEIVE THE BIGGEST SMACK-DOWN IN THE HISTORY OF MULTIPLAYER GAMING.
"WHOA. SAVE THE DRAMA FO YO MAMA."

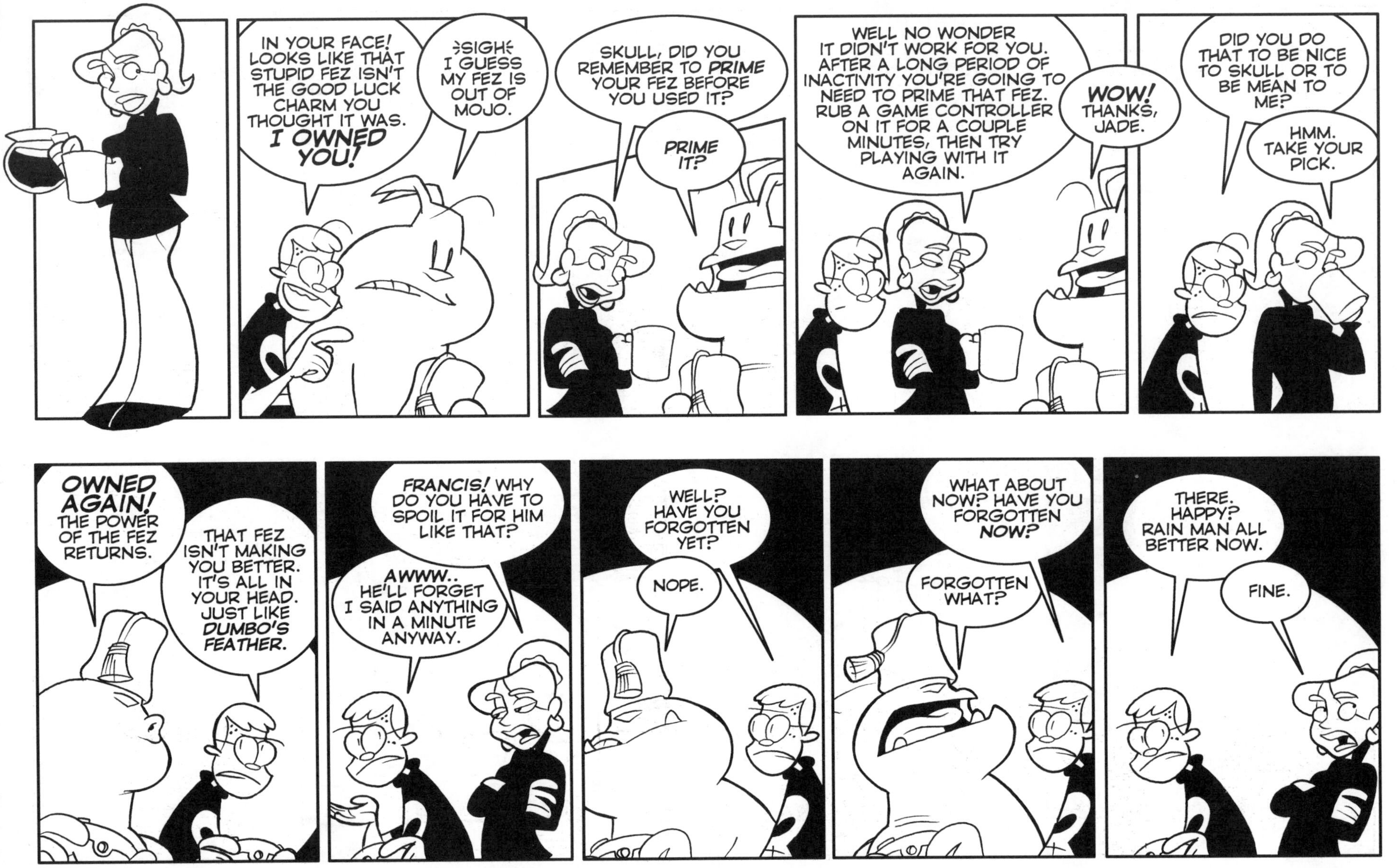
IN YOUR FACE! LOOKS LIKE THAT STUPID FEZ ISN'T THE GOOD LUCK CHARM YOU THOUGHT IT WAS. I OWNED YOU!
SIGH I GUESS MY FEZ IS OUT OF MOJO.
SKULL, DID YOU REMEMBER TO PRIME YOUR FEZ BEFORE YOU USED IT?
PRIME IT?
WELL NO WONDER IT DIDN'T WORK FOR YOU. AFTER A LONG PERIOD OF INACTIVITY YOU'RE GOING TO NEED TO PRIME THAT FEZ. RUB A GAME CONTROLLER ON IT FOR A COUPLE MINUTES, THEN TRY PLAYING WITH IT AGAIN.
WOW! THANKS, JADE.
DID YOU DO THAT TO BE NICE TO SKULL OR TO BE MEAN TO ME?
HMM. TAKE YOUR PICK.
OWNED AGAIN! THE POWER OF THE FEZ RETURNS.
THAT FEZ ISN'T MAKING YOU BETTER. IT'S ALL IN YOUR HEAD. JUST LIKE DUMBO'S FEATHER.
FRANCIS! WHY DO YOU HAVE TO SPOIL IT FOR HIM LIKE THAT?
AWWW.. HE'LL FORGET I SAID ANYTHING IN A MINUTE ANYWAY.
WELL? HAVE YOU FORGOTTEN YET?
NOPE.
WHAT ABOUT NOW? HAVE YOU FORGOTTEN NOW?
FORGOTTEN WHAT?
THERE. HAPPY? RAIN MAN ALL BETTER NOW.
FINE.

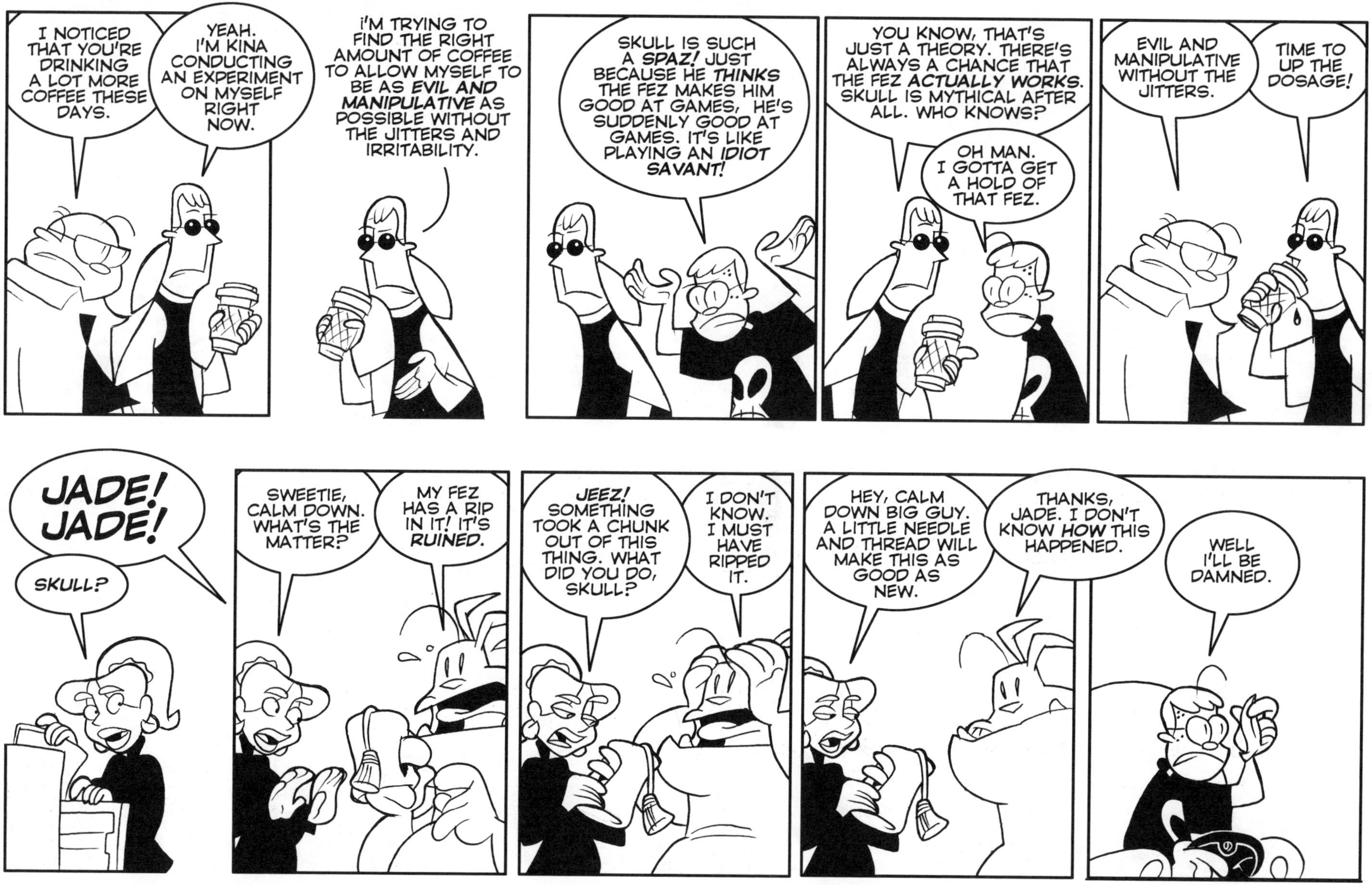

I NOTICED THAT YOU'RE DRINKING A LOT MORE COFFEE THESE DAYS.
YEAH. I'M KINA CONDUCTING AN EXPERIMENT ON MYSELF RIGHT NOW.
I'M TRYING TO FIND THE RIGHT AMOUNT OF COFFEE TO ALLOW MYSELF TO BE AS *EVIL AND MANIPULATIVE* AS POSSIBLE WITHOUT THE JITTERS AND IRRITABILITY.
SKULL IS SUCH A *SPAZ!* JUST BECAUSE HE *THINKS* THE FEZ MAKES HIM GOOD AT GAMES, HE'S SUDDENLY GOOD AT GAMES. IT'S LIKE PLAYING AN *IDIOT SAVANT!*
YOU KNOW, THAT'S JUST A THEORY. THERE'S ALWAYS A CHANCE THAT THE FEZ *ACTUALLY WORKS*. SKULL IS MYTHICAL AFTER ALL. WHO KNOWS?
OH MAN. I GOTTA GET A HOLD OF THAT FEZ.
EVIL AND MANIPULATIVE WITHOUT THE JITTERS.
TIME TO UP THE DOSAGE!
JADE! JADE!
SKULL?
SWEETIE, CALM DOWN. WHAT'S THE MATTER?
MY FEZ HAS A RIP IN IT! IT'S *RUINED*.
JEEZ! SOMETHING TOOK A CHUNK OUT OF THIS THING. WHAT DID YOU DO, SKULL?
I DON'T KNOW. I MUST HAVE RIPPED IT.
HEY, CALM DOWN BIG GUY. A LITTLE NEEDLE AND THREAD WILL MAKE THIS AS GOOD AS NEW.
THANKS, JADE. I DON'T KNOW *HOW* THIS HAPPENED.
WELL I'LL BE DAMNED.

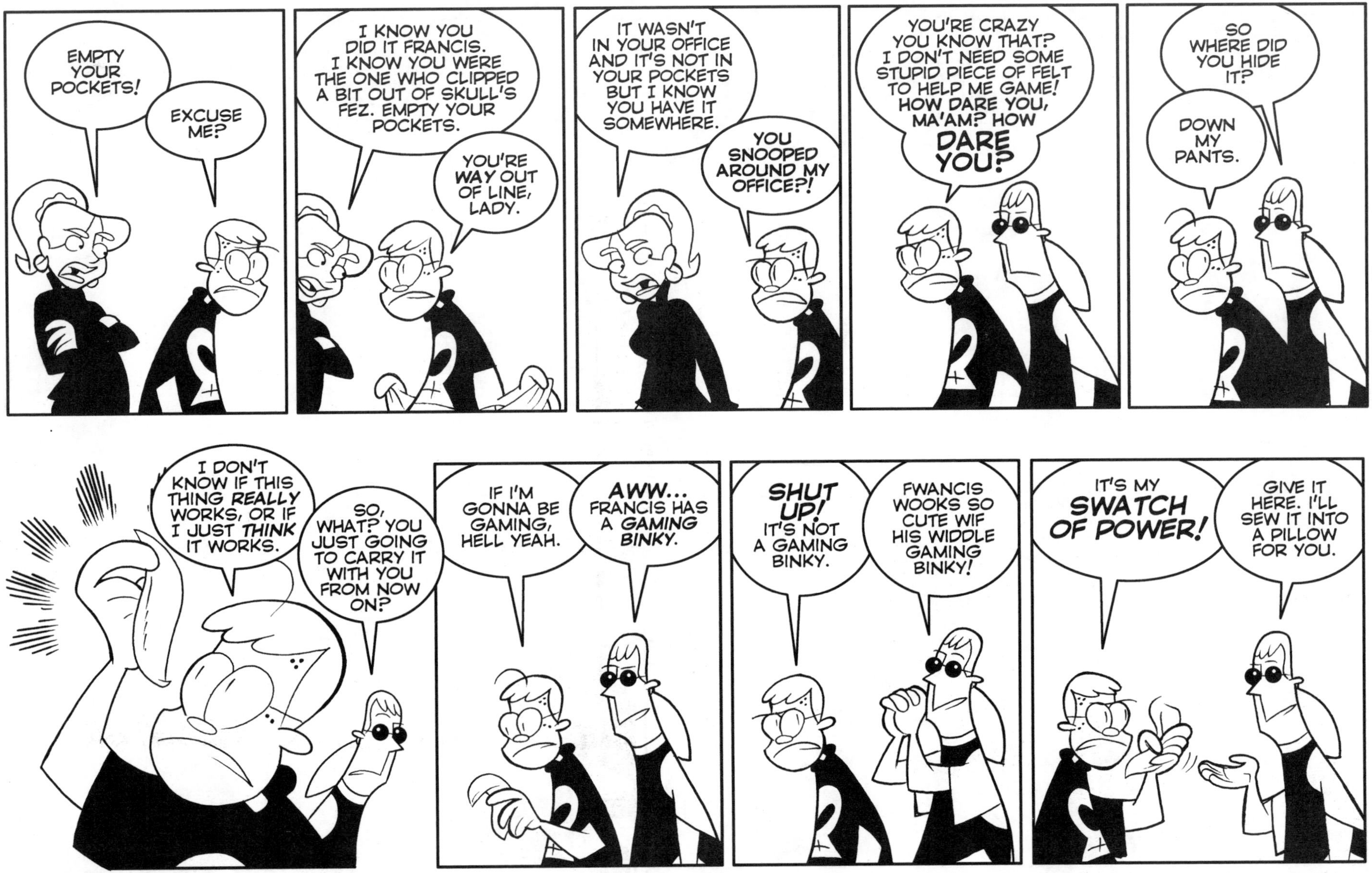
EMPTY YOUR POCKETS!
EXCUSE ME?
I KNOW YOU DID IT FRANCIS. I KNOW YOU WERE THE ONE WHO CLIPPED A BIT OUT OF SKULL'S FEZ. EMPTY YOUR POCKETS.
YOU'RE **WAY** OUT OF LINE, LADY.
IT WASN'T IN YOUR OFFICE AND IT'S NOT IN YOUR POCKETS BUT I KNOW YOU HAVE IT SOMEWHERE.
YOU SNOOPED AROUND MY OFFICE?!
YOU'RE CRAZY YOU KNOW THAT? I DON'T NEED SOME STUPID PIECE OF FELT TO HELP ME GAME! **HOW DARE YOU, MA'AM? HOW DARE YOU?**
SO WHERE DID YOU HIDE IT?
DOWN MY PANTS.
I DON'T KNOW IF THIS THING **REALLY** WORKS, OR IF I JUST **THINK** IT WORKS.
SO, WHAT? YOU JUST GOING TO CARRY IT WITH YOU FROM NOW ON?
IF I'M GONNA BE GAMING, HELL YEAH.
AWW... FRANCIS HAS A **GAMING BINKY**.
SHUT UP! IT'S NOT A GAMING BINKY.
FWANCIS WOOKS SO CUTE WIF HIS WIDDLE GAMING BINKY!
IT'S MY **SWATCH OF POWER!**
GIVE IT HERE. I'LL SEW IT INTO A PILLOW FOR YOU.

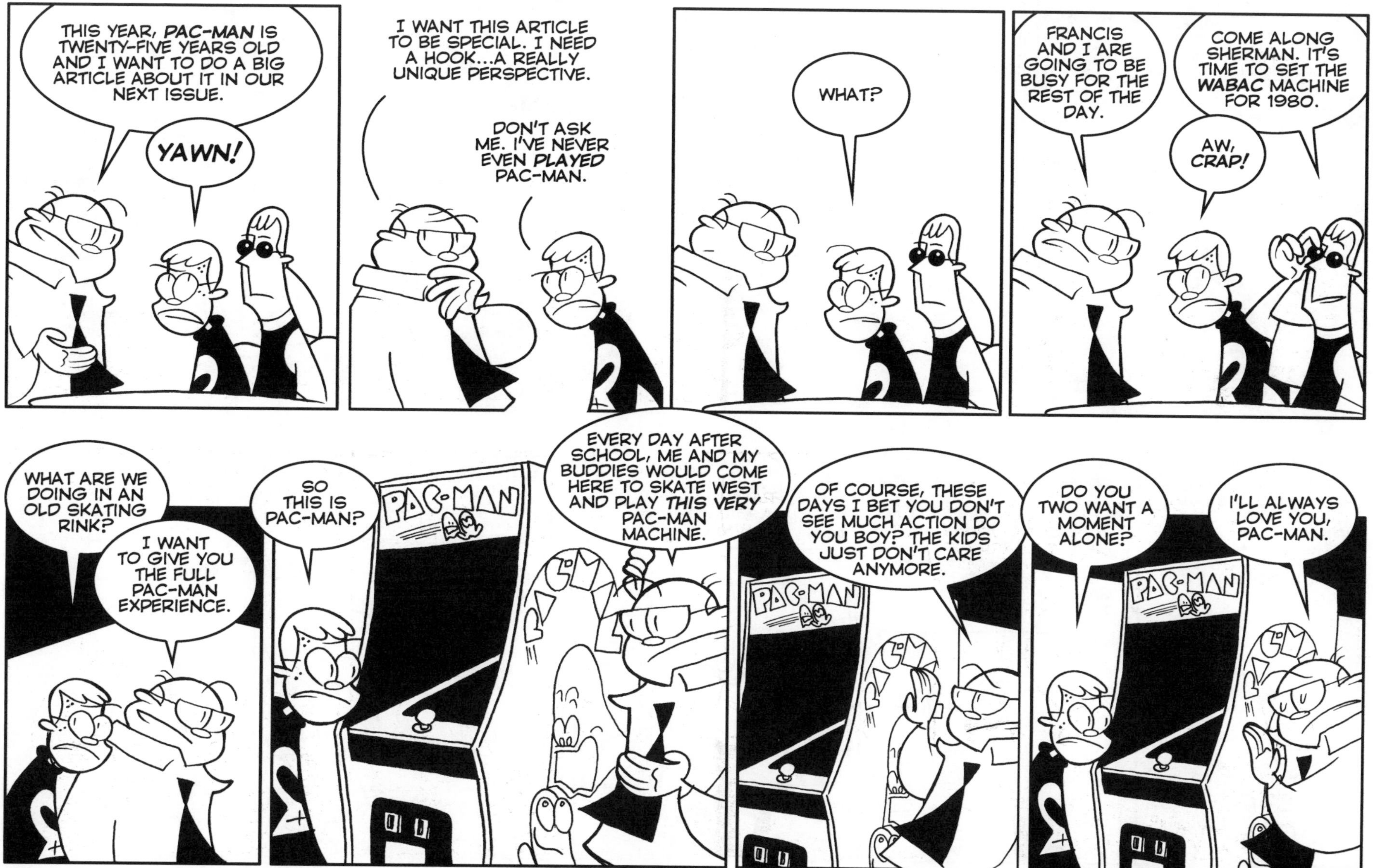
THIS YEAR, PAC-MAN IS TWENTY-FIVE YEARS OLD AND I WANT TO DO A BIG ARTICLE ABOUT IT IN OUR NEXT ISSUE.
YAWN!
I WANT THIS ARTICLE TO BE SPECIAL. I NEED A HOOK...A REALLY UNIQUE PERSPECTIVE.
DON'T ASK ME. I'VE NEVER EVEN PLAYED PAC-MAN.
WHAT?
FRANCIS AND I ARE GOING TO BE BUSY FOR THE REST OF THE DAY.
COME ALONG SHERMAN. IT'S TIME TO SET THE WABAC MACHINE FOR 1980.
AW, CRAP!
WHAT ARE WE DOING IN AN OLD SKATING RINK?
I WANT TO GIVE YOU THE FULL PAC-MAN EXPERIENCE.
SO THIS IS PAC-MAN?
PAC-MAN
EVERY DAY AFTER SCHOOL, ME AND MY BUDDIES WOULD COME HERE TO SKATE WEST AND PLAY THIS VERY PAC-MAN MACHINE.
OF COURSE, THESE DAYS I BET YOU DON'T SEE MUCH ACTION DO YOU BOY? THE KIDS JUST DON'T CARE ANYMORE.
DO YOU TWO WANT A MOMENT ALONE?
I'LL ALWAYS LOVE YOU, PAC-MAN.

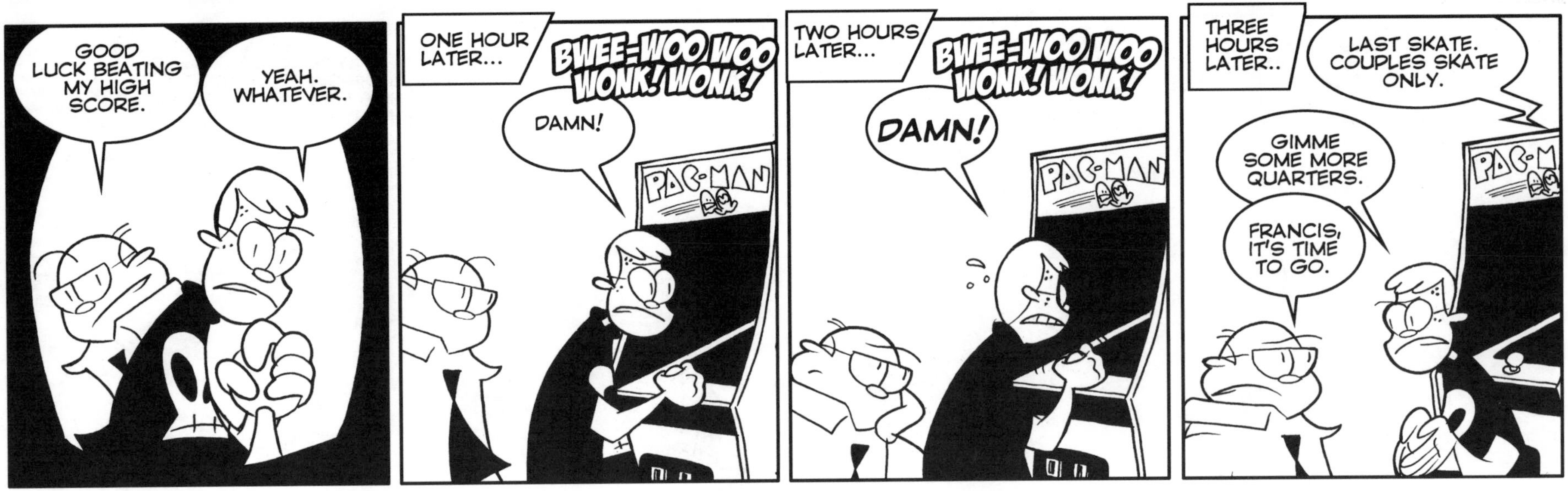
GOOD LUCK BEATING MY HIGH SCORE.
YEAH. WHATEVER.
ONE HOUR LATER...
BWEE-WOO WOO WONK! WONK!
DAMN!
PAC-MAN
TWO HOURS LATER...
BWEE-WOO WOO WONK! WONK!
DAMN!
PAC-MAN
THREE HOURS LATER..
LAST SKATE. COUPLES SKATE ONLY.
GIMME SOME MORE QUARTERS.
FRANCIS, IT'S TIME TO GO.
PAC-M

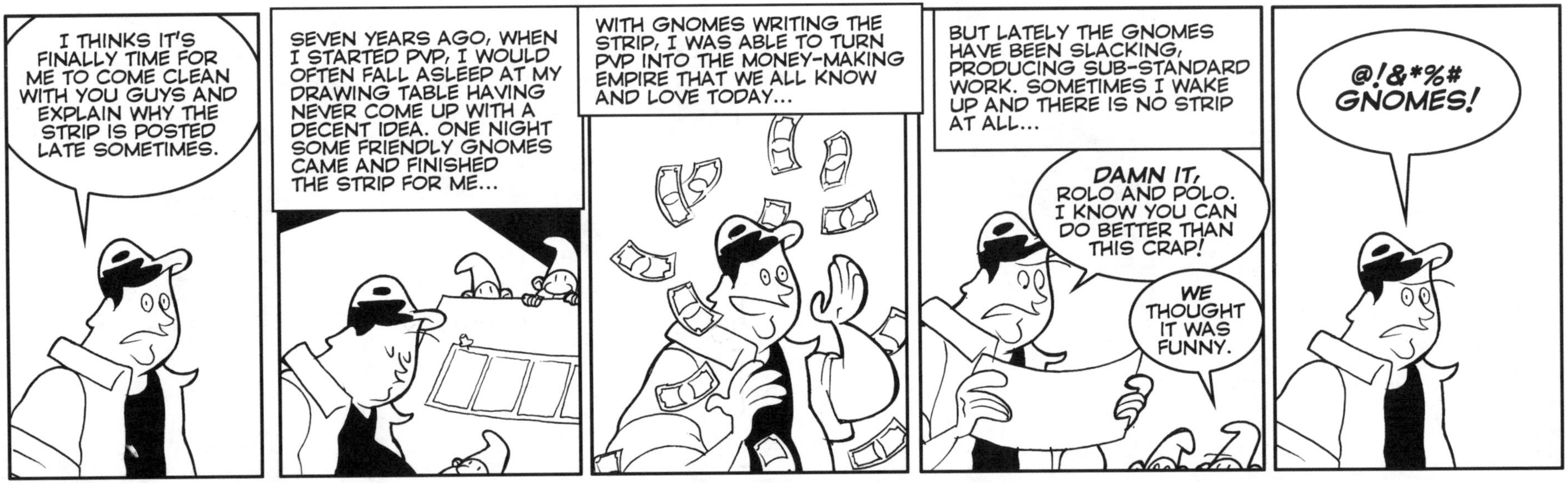
I THINKS IT'S FINALLY TIME FOR ME TO COME CLEAN WITH YOU GUYS AND EXPLAIN WHY THE STRIP IS POSTED LATE SOMETIMES.
SEVEN YEARS AGO, WHEN I STARTED PVP, I WOULD OFTEN FALL ASLEEP AT MY DRAWING TABLE HAVING NEVER COME UP WITH A DECENT IDEA. ONE NIGHT SOME FRIENDLY GNOMES CAME AND FINISHED THE STRIP FOR ME...
WITH GNOMES WRITING THE STRIP, I WAS ABLE TO TURN PVP INTO THE MONEY-MAKING EMPIRE THAT WE ALL KNOW AND LOVE TODAY...
BUT LATELY THE GNOMES HAVE BEEN SLACKING, PRODUCING SUB-STANDARD WORK. SOMETIMES I WAKE UP AND THERE IS NO STRIP AT ALL...
DAMN IT, ROLO AND POLO. I KNOW YOU CAN DO BETTER THAN THIS CRAP!
WE THOUGHT IT WAS FUNNY.
@!&*%# GNOMES!

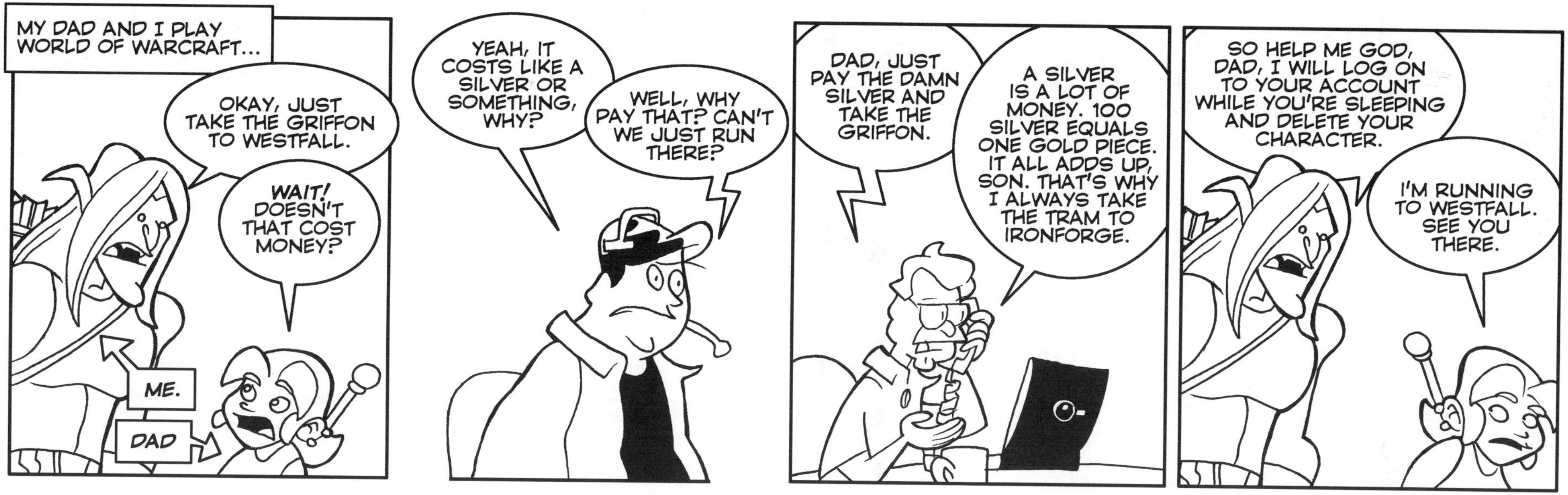
MY DAD AND I PLAY WORLD OF WARCRAFT...
OKAY, JUST TAKE THE GRIFFON TO WESTFALL.
WAIT! DOESN'T THAT COST MONEY?
ME.
DAD
YEAH, IT COSTS LIKE A SILVER OR SOMETHING, WHY?
WELL, WHY PAY THAT? CAN'T WE JUST RUN THERE?
DAD, JUST PAY THE DAMN SILVER AND TAKE THE GRIFFON.
A SILVER IS A LOT OF MONEY. 100 SILVER EQUALS ONE GOLD PIECE. IT ALL ADDS UP, SON. THAT'S WHY I ALWAYS TAKE THE TRAM TO IRONFORGE.
SO HELP ME GOD, DAD, I WILL LOG ON TO YOUR ACCOUNT WHILE YOU'RE SLEEPING AND DELETE YOUR CHARACTER.
I'M RUNNING TO WESTFALL. SEE YOU THERE.

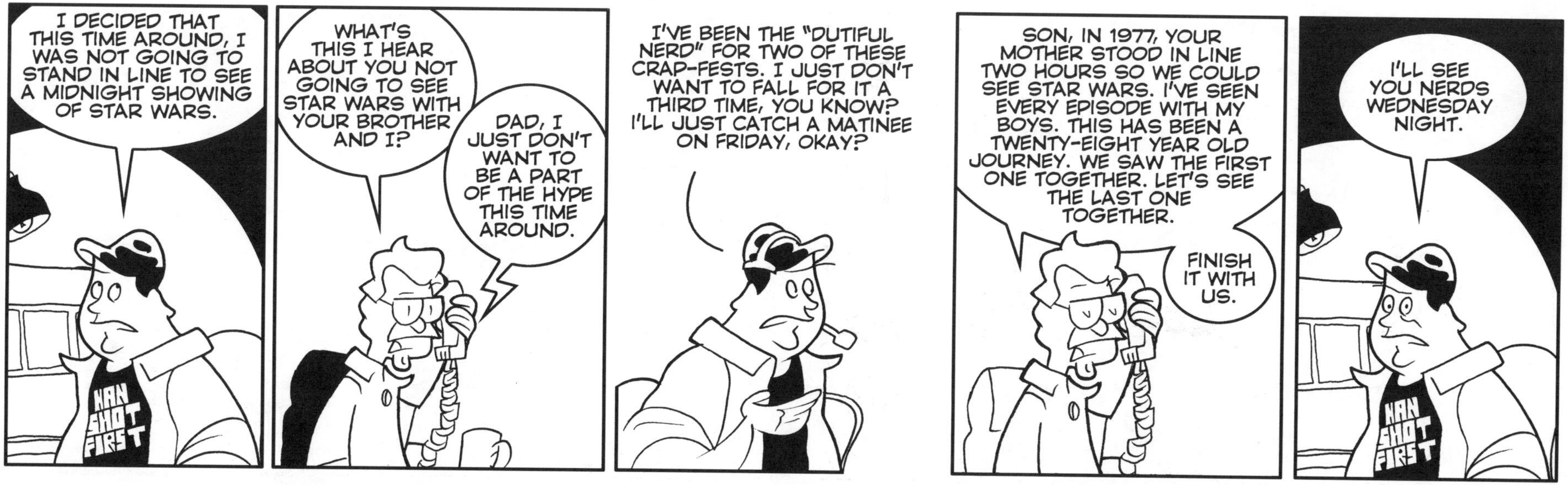
I DECIDED THAT THIS TIME AROUND, I WAS NOT GOING TO STAND IN LINE TO SEE A MIDNIGHT SHOWING OF STAR WARS.
HAN SHOT FIRST
WHAT'S THIS I HEAR ABOUT YOU NOT GOING TO SEE STAR WARS WITH YOUR BROTHER AND I?
DAD, I JUST DON'T WANT TO BE A PART OF THE HYPE THIS TIME AROUND.
I'VE BEEN THE "DUTIFUL NERD" FOR TWO OF THESE CRAP-FESTS. I JUST DON'T WANT TO FALL FOR IT A THIRD TIME, YOU KNOW? I'LL JUST CATCH A MATINEE ON FRIDAY, OKAY?
SON, IN 1977, YOUR MOTHER STOOD IN LINE TWO HOURS SO WE COULD SEE STAR WARS. I'VE SEEN EVERY EPISODE WITH MY BOYS. THIS HAS BEEN A TWENTY-EIGHT YEAR OLD JOURNEY. WE SAW THE FIRST ONE TOGETHER. LET'S SEE THE LAST ONE TOGETHER.
FINISH IT WITH US.
I'LL SEE YOU NERDS WEDNESDAY NIGHT.
HAN SHOT FIRST

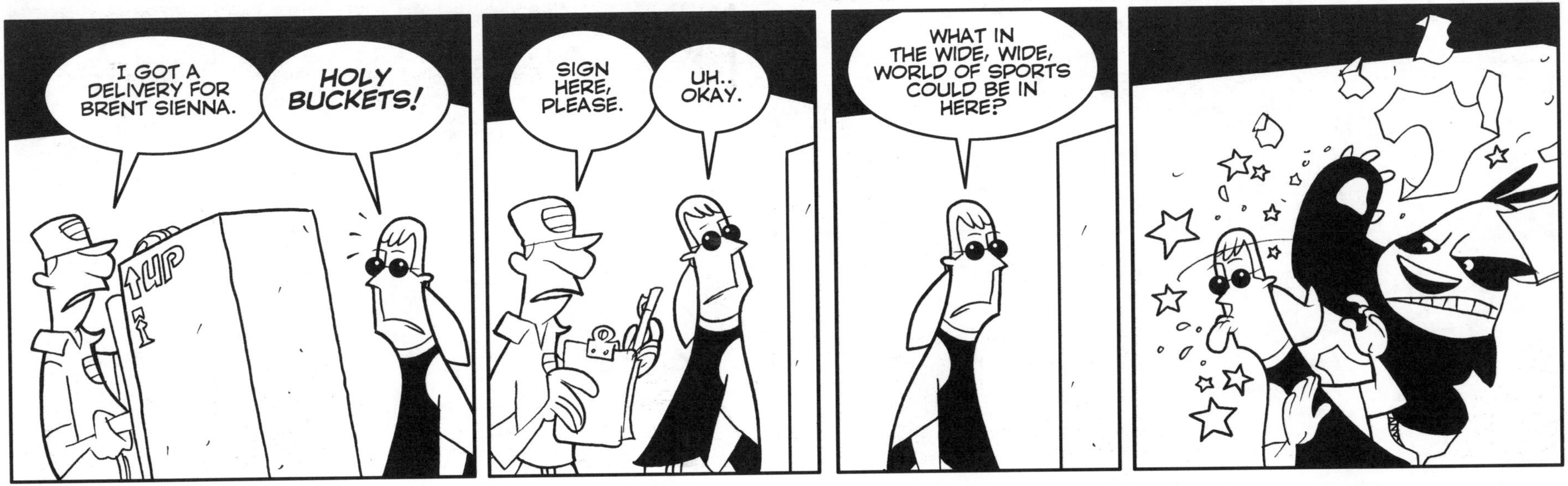
I GOT A DELIVERY FOR BRENT SIENNA.
HOLY BUCKETS!
UP
SIGN HERE, PLEASE.
UH.. OKAY.
WHAT IN THE WIDE, WIDE, WORLD OF SPORTS COULD BE IN HERE?

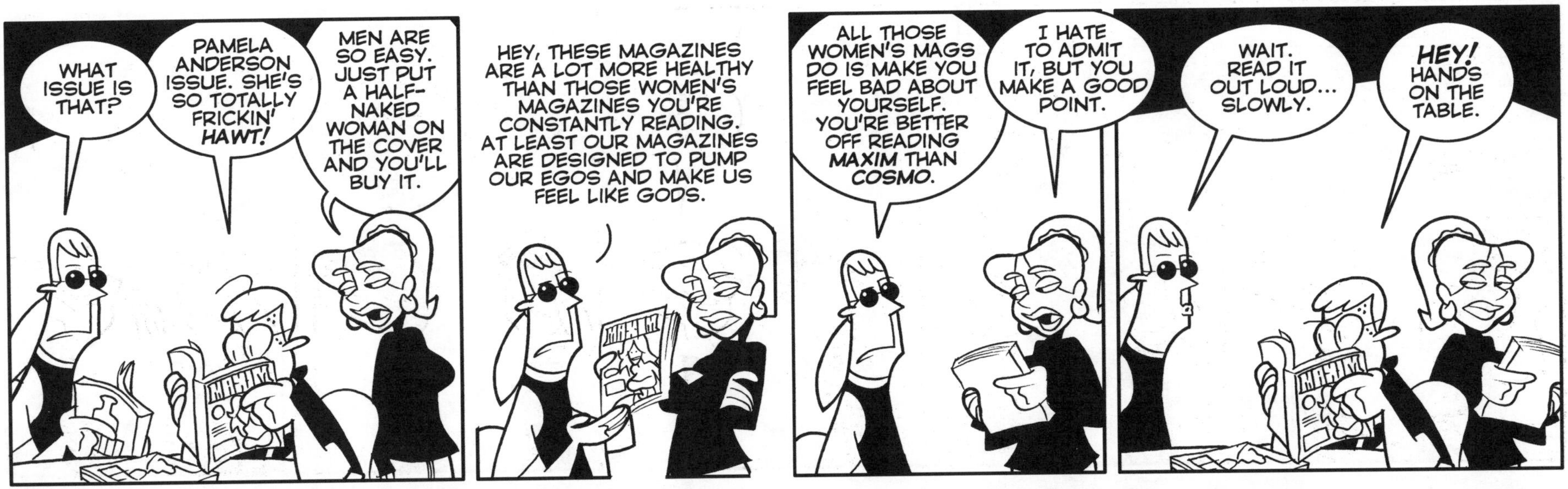
WHAT ISSUE IS THAT?
PAMELA ANDERSON ISSUE. SHE'S SO TOTALLY FRICKIN' *HAWT!*
MEN ARE SO EASY. JUST PUT A HALF-NAKED WOMAN ON THE COVER AND YOU'LL BUY IT.
MAXIM
HEY, THESE MAGAZINES ARE A LOT MORE HEALTHY THAN THOSE WOMEN'S MAGAZINES YOU'RE CONSTANTLY READING. AT LEAST OUR MAGAZINES ARE DESIGNED TO PUMP OUR EGOS AND MAKE US FEEL LIKE GODS.
MAXIM
ALL THOSE WOMEN'S MAGS DO IS MAKE YOU FEEL BAD ABOUT YOURSELF. YOU'RE BETTER OFF READING ***MAXIM*** THAN ***COSMO***.
I HATE TO ADMIT IT, BUT YOU MAKE A GOOD POINT.
WAIT. READ IT OUT LOUD... SLOWLY.
HEY! HANDS ON THE TABLE.
MAXIM

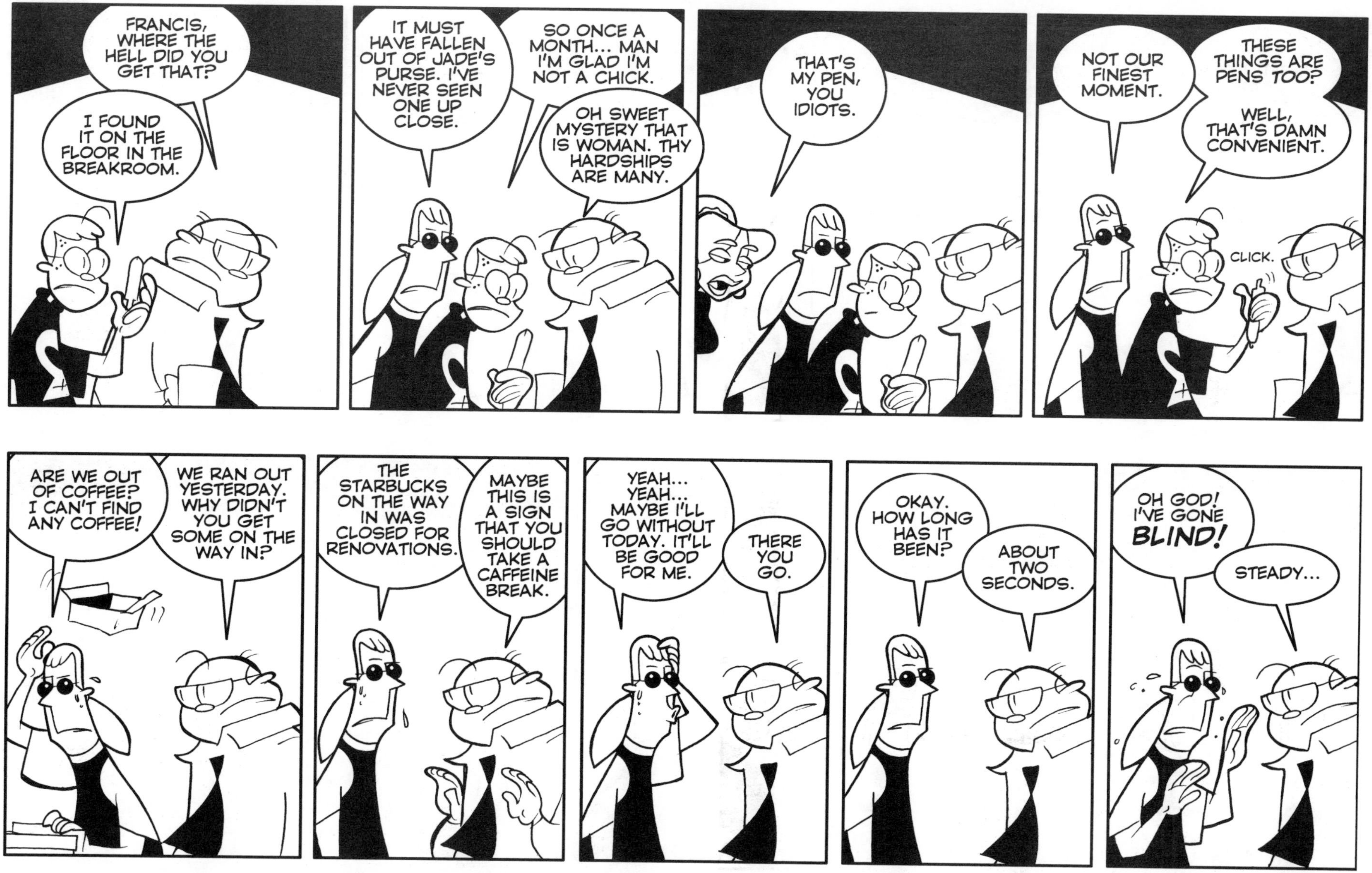
FRANCIS, WHERE THE HELL DID YOU GET THAT?
I FOUND IT ON THE FLOOR IN THE BREAKROOM.
IT MUST HAVE FALLEN OUT OF JADE'S PURSE. I'VE NEVER SEEN ONE UP CLOSE.
SO ONCE A MONTH... MAN I'M GLAD I'M NOT A CHICK.
OH SWEET MYSTERY THAT IS WOMAN. THY HARDSHIPS ARE MANY.
THAT'S MY PEN, YOU IDIOTS.
NOT OUR FINEST MOMENT.
THESE THINGS ARE PENS TOO?
WELL, THAT'S DAMN CONVENIENT.
CLICK.
ARE WE OUT OF COFFEE? I CAN'T FIND ANY COFFEE!
WE RAN OUT YESTERDAY. WHY DIDN'T YOU GET SOME ON THE WAY IN?
THE STARBUCKS ON THE WAY IN WAS CLOSED FOR RENOVATIONS.
MAYBE THIS IS A SIGN THAT YOU SHOULD TAKE A CAFFEINE BREAK.
YEAH... YEAH... MAYBE I'LL GO WITHOUT TODAY. IT'LL BE GOOD FOR ME.
THERE YOU GO.
OKAY. HOW LONG HAS IT BEEN?
ABOUT TWO SECONDS.
OH GOD! I'VE GONE BLIND!
STEADY...

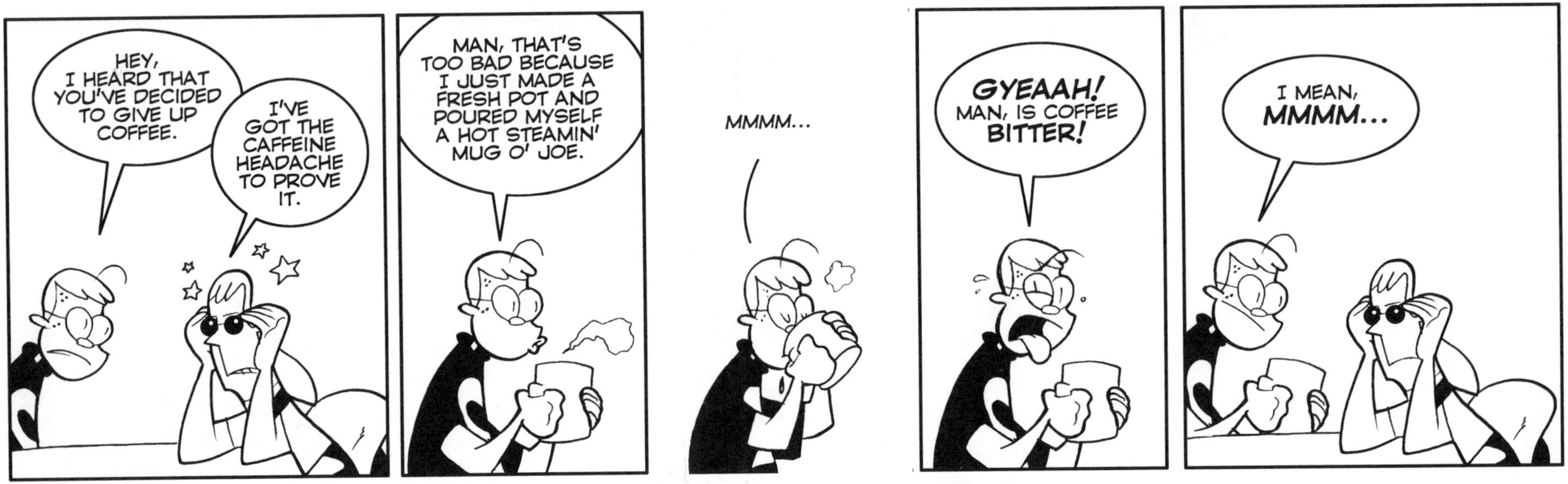
HEY, I HEARD THAT YOU'VE DECIDED TO GIVE UP COFFEE.
I'VE GOT THE CAFFEINE HEADACHE TO PROVE IT.
MAN, THAT'S TOO BAD BECAUSE I JUST MADE A FRESH POT AND POURED MYSELF A HOT STEAMIN' MUG O' JOE.
MMMM...
GYEAAH! MAN, IS COFFEE BITTER!
I MEAN, MMMM...

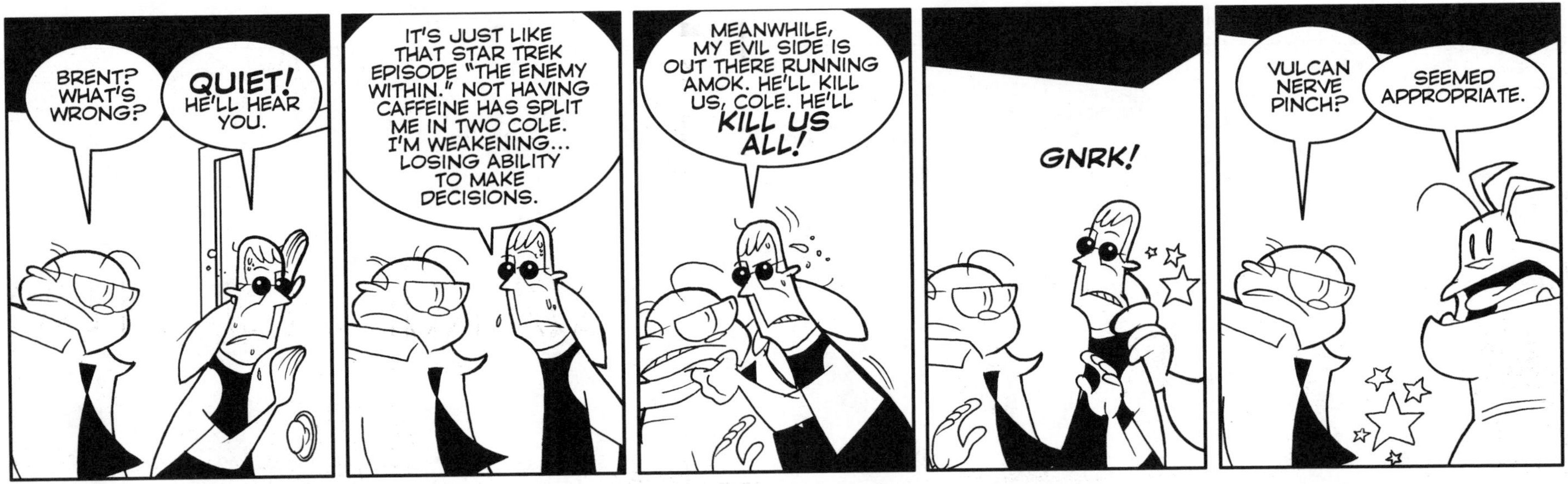
BRENT? WHAT'S WRONG?
QUIET! HE'LL HEAR YOU.
IT'S JUST LIKE THAT STAR TREK EPISODE "THE ENEMY WITHIN." NOT HAVING CAFFEINE HAS SPLIT ME IN TWO COLE. I'M WEAKENING... LOSING ABILITY TO MAKE DECISIONS.
MEANWHILE, MY EVIL SIDE IS OUT THERE RUNNING AMOK. HE'LL KILL US, COLE. HE'LL KILL US ALL!
GNRK!
VULCAN NERVE PINCH?
SEEMED APPROPRIATE.

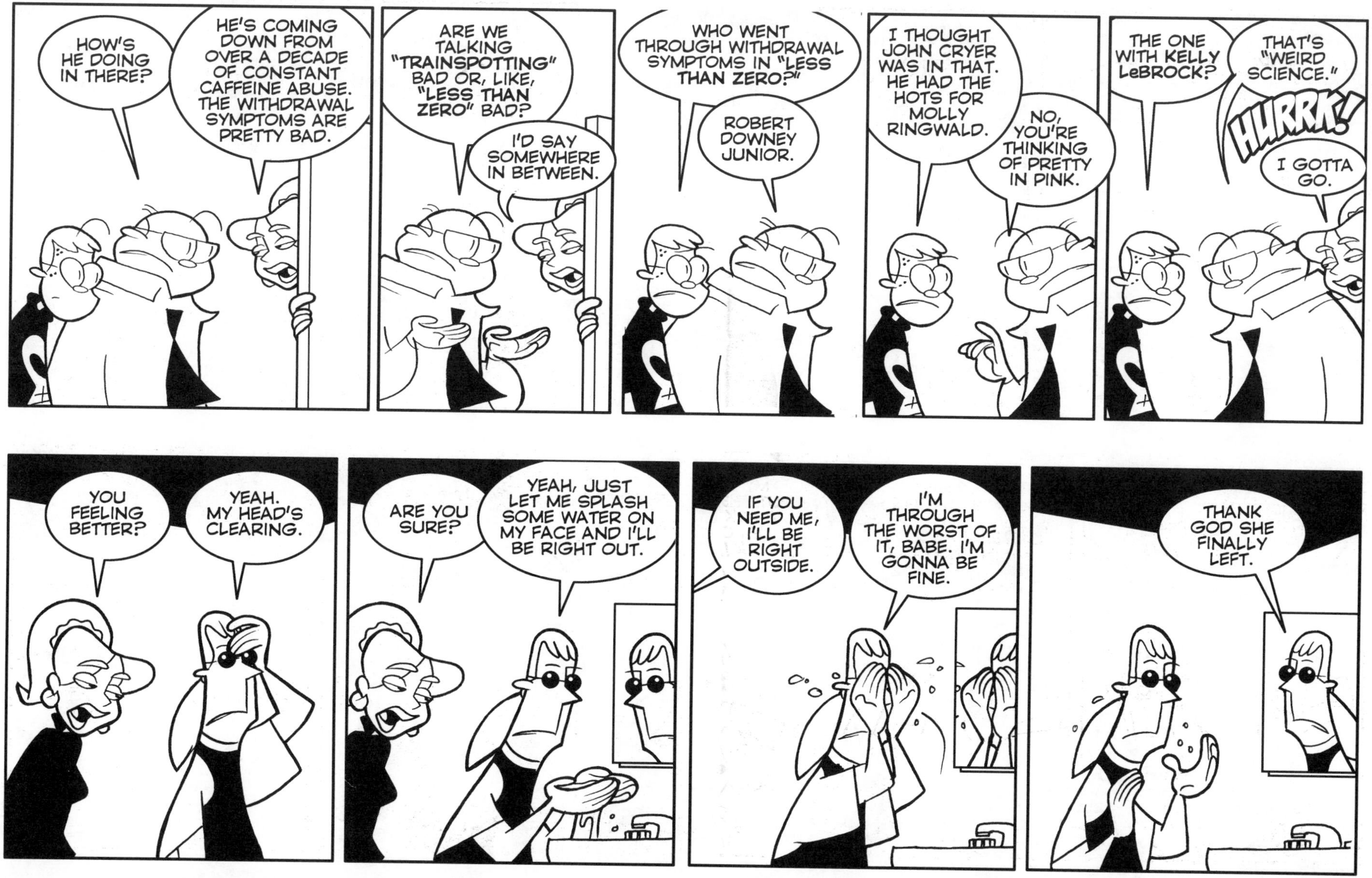
HOW'S HE DOING IN THERE?
HE'S COMING DOWN FROM OVER A DECADE OF CONSTANT CAFFEINE ABUSE. THE WITHDRAWAL SYMPTOMS ARE PRETTY BAD.
ARE WE TALKING "TRAINSPOTTING" BAD OR, LIKE, "LESS THAN ZERO" BAD?
I'D SAY SOMEWHERE IN BETWEEN.
WHO WENT THROUGH WITHDRAWAL SYMPTOMS IN "LESS THAN ZERO?"
ROBERT DOWNEY JUNIOR.
I THOUGHT JOHN CRYER WAS IN THAT. HE HAD THE HOTS FOR MOLLY RINGWALD.
NO, YOU'RE THINKING OF PRETTY IN PINK.
THE ONE WITH KELLY LeBROCK?
THAT'S "WEIRD SCIENCE."
HURRK!
I GOTTA GO.
YOU FEELING BETTER?
YEAH. MY HEAD'S CLEARING.
ARE YOU SURE?
YEAH, JUST LET ME SPLASH SOME WATER ON MY FACE AND I'LL BE RIGHT OUT.
IF YOU NEED ME, I'LL BE RIGHT OUTSIDE.
I'M THROUGH THE WORST OF IT, BABE. I'M GONNA BE FINE.
THANK GOD SHE FINALLY LEFT.

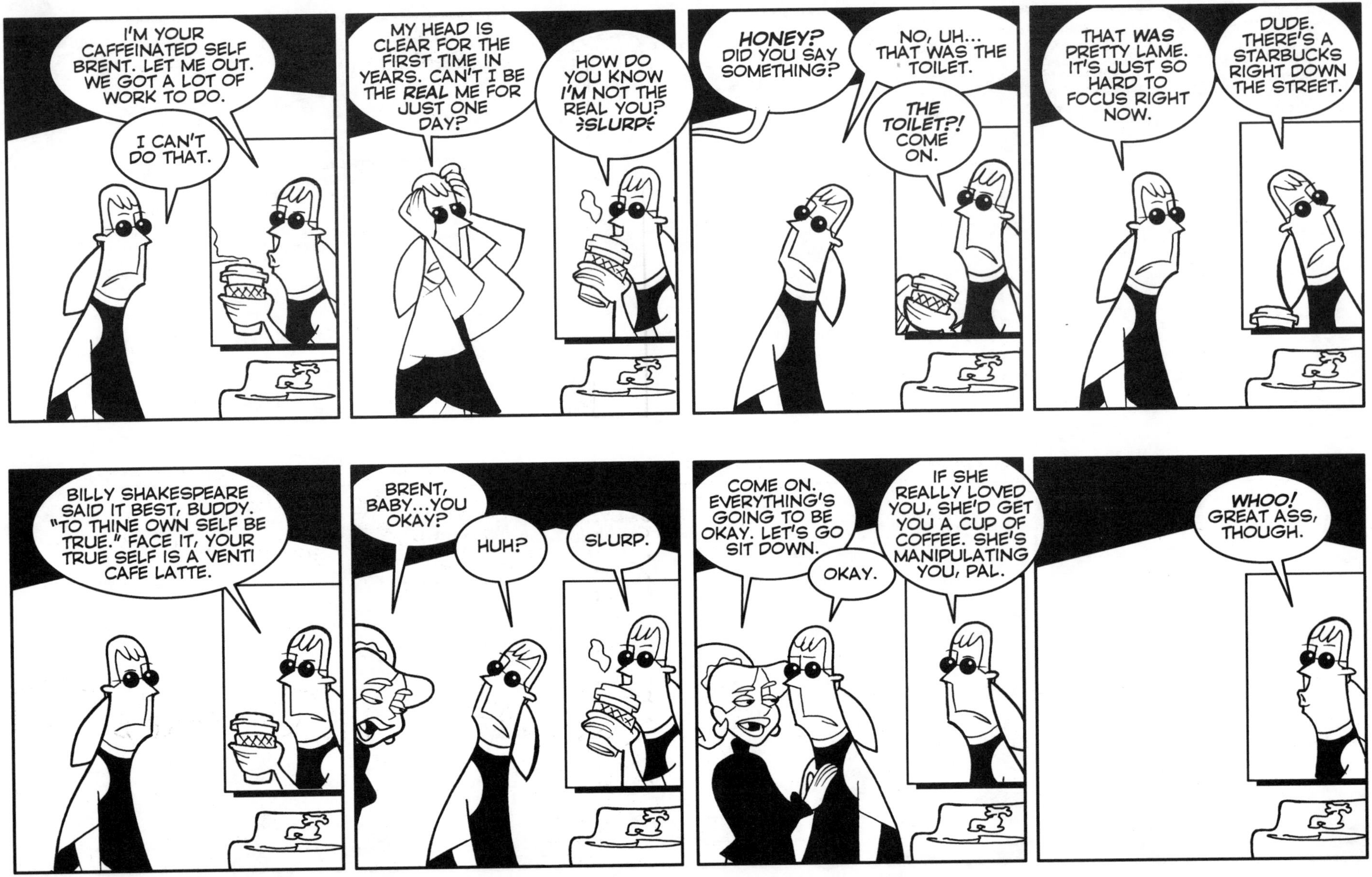
I'M YOUR CAFFEINATED SELF BRENT. LET ME OUT. WE GOT A LOT OF WORK TO DO.
I CAN'T DO THAT.
MY HEAD IS CLEAR FOR THE FIRST TIME IN YEARS. CAN'T I BE THE REAL ME FOR JUST ONE DAY?
HOW DO YOU KNOW I'M NOT THE REAL YOU? SLURP
HONEY? DID YOU SAY SOMETHING?
NO, UH... THAT WAS THE TOILET.
THE TOILET?! COME ON.
THAT WAS PRETTY LAME. IT'S JUST SO HARD TO FOCUS RIGHT NOW.
DUDE. THERE'S A STARBUCKS RIGHT DOWN THE STREET.
BILLY SHAKESPEARE SAID IT BEST, BUDDY. "TO THINE OWN SELF BE TRUE." FACE IT, YOUR TRUE SELF IS A VENTI CAFE LATTE.
BRENT, BABY...YOU OKAY?
HUH?
SLURP.
COME ON. EVERYTHING'S GOING TO BE OKAY. LET'S GO SIT DOWN.
OKAY.
IF SHE REALLY LOVED YOU, SHE'D GET YOU A CUP OF COFFEE. SHE'S MANIPULATING YOU, PAL.
WHOO! GREAT ASS, THOUGH.

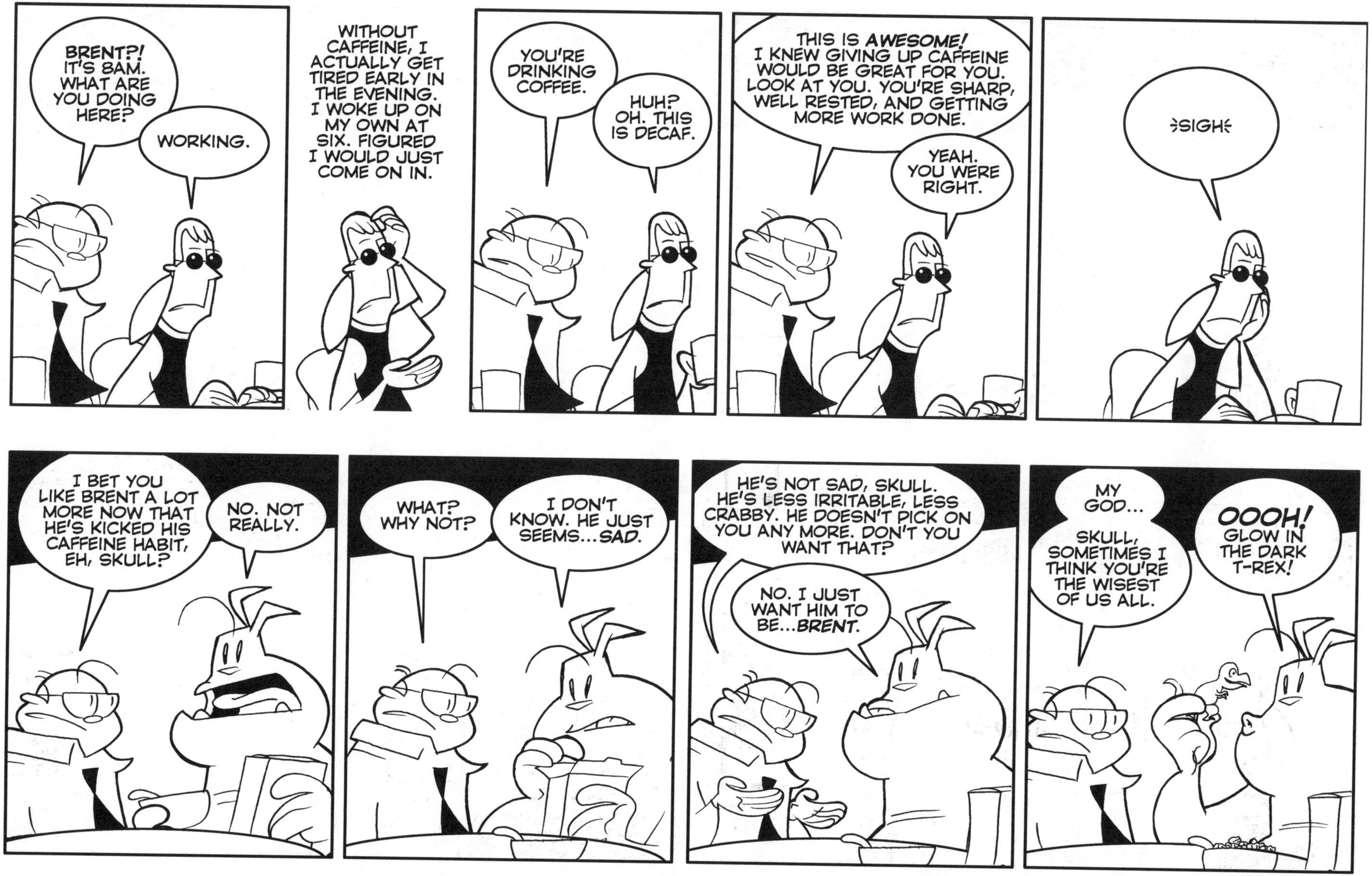
BRENT?! IT'S 8AM. WHAT ARE YOU DOING HERE?
WORKING.
WITHOUT CAFFEINE, I ACTUALLY GET TIRED EARLY IN THE EVENING. I WOKE UP ON MY OWN AT SIX. FIGURED I WOULD JUST COME ON IN.
YOU'RE DRINKING COFFEE.
HUH? OH. THIS IS DECAF.
THIS IS **AWESOME!** I KNEW GIVING UP CAFFEINE WOULD BE GREAT FOR YOU. LOOK AT YOU. YOU'RE SHARP, WELL RESTED, AND GETTING MORE WORK DONE.
YEAH. YOU WERE RIGHT.
SIGH
I BET YOU LIKE BRENT A LOT MORE NOW THAT HE'S KICKED HIS CAFFEINE HABIT, EH, SKULL?
NO. NOT REALLY.
WHAT? WHY NOT?
I DON'T KNOW. HE JUST SEEMS...**SAD.**
HE'S NOT SAD, SKULL. HE'S LESS IRRITABLE, LESS CRABBY. HE DOESN'T PICK ON YOU ANY MORE. DON'T YOU WANT THAT?
NO. I JUST WANT HIM TO BE...**BRENT.**
MY GOD...
SKULL, SOMETIMES I THINK YOU'RE THE WISEST OF US ALL.
OOOH! GLOW IN THE DARK T-REX!

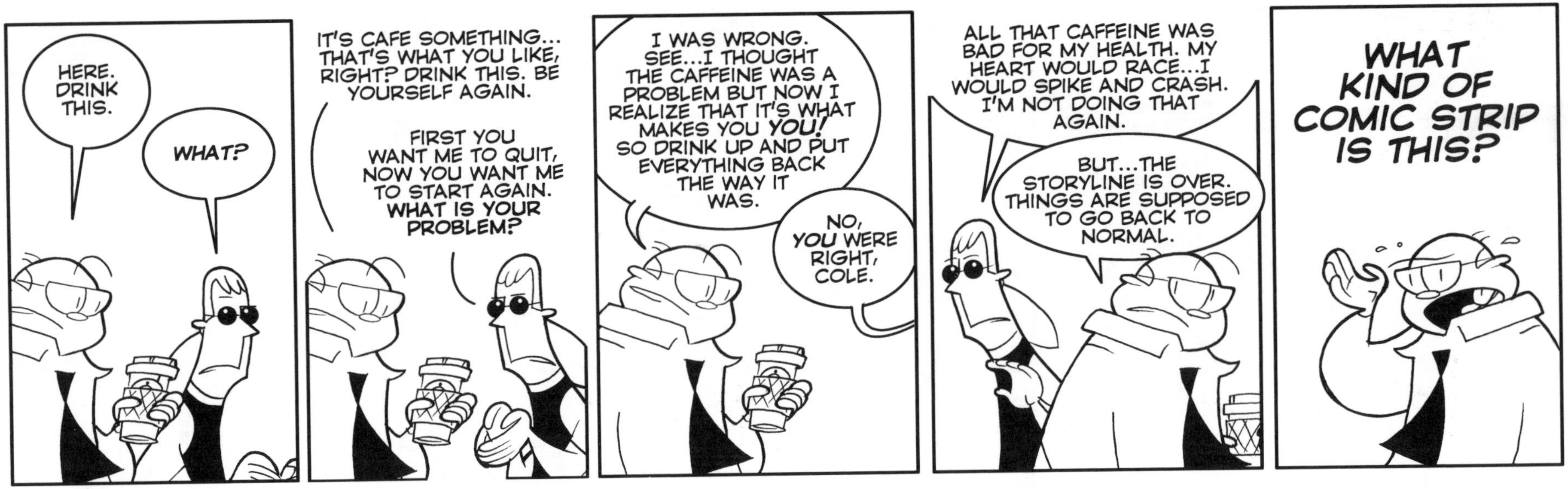
HERE. DRINK THIS.
WHAT?
IT'S CAFE SOMETHING... THAT'S WHAT YOU LIKE, RIGHT? DRINK THIS. BE YOURSELF AGAIN.
FIRST YOU WANT ME TO QUIT, NOW YOU WANT ME TO START AGAIN. **WHAT IS YOUR PROBLEM?**
I WAS WRONG. SEE...I THOUGHT THE CAFFEINE WAS A PROBLEM BUT NOW I REALIZE THAT IT'S WHAT MAKES YOU ***YOU!*** SO DRINK UP AND PUT EVERYTHING BACK THE WAY IT WAS.
NO, ***YOU*** WERE RIGHT, COLE.
ALL THAT CAFFEINE WAS BAD FOR MY HEALTH. MY HEART WOULD RACE...I WOULD SPIKE AND CRASH. I'M NOT DOING THAT AGAIN.
BUT...THE STORYLINE IS OVER. THINGS ARE SUPPOSED TO GO BACK TO NORMAL.
WHAT KIND OF COMIC STRIP IS THIS?

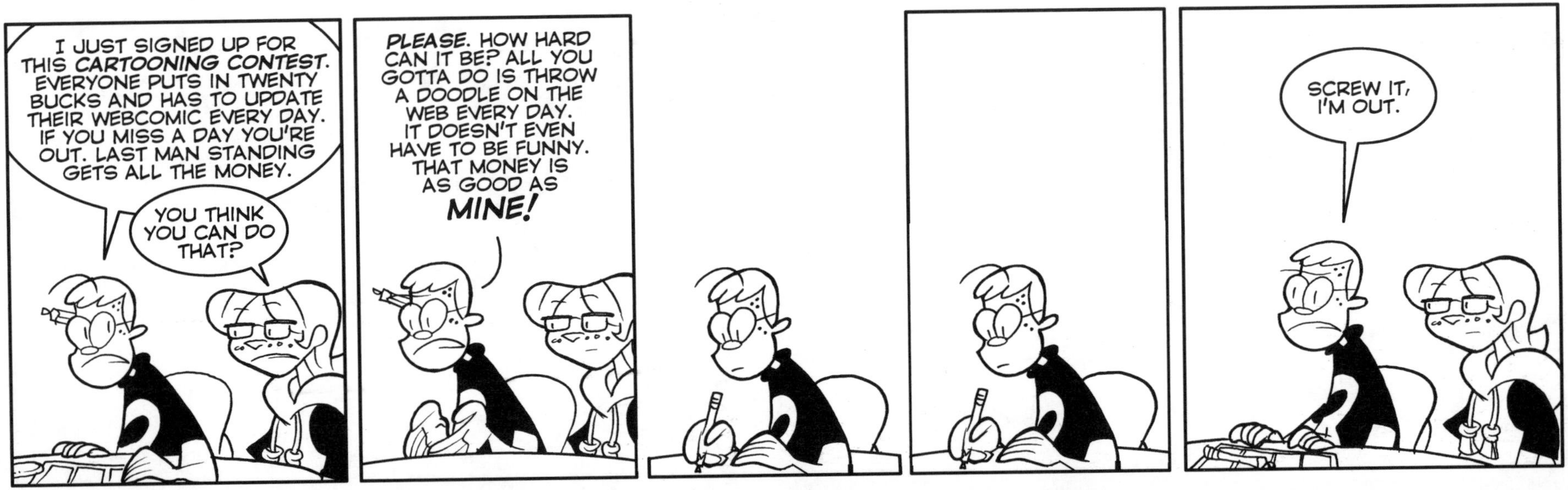
I JUST SIGNED UP FOR THIS ***CARTOONING CONTEST***. EVERYONE PUTS IN TWENTY BUCKS AND HAS TO UPDATE THEIR WEBCOMIC EVERY DAY. IF YOU MISS A DAY YOU'RE OUT. LAST MAN STANDING GETS ALL THE MONEY.
YOU THINK YOU CAN DO THAT?
PLEASE. HOW HARD CAN IT BE? ALL YOU GOTTA DO IS THROW A DOODLE ON THE WEB EVERY DAY. IT DOESN'T EVEN HAVE TO BE FUNNY. THAT MONEY IS AS GOOD AS ***MINE!***
SCREW IT, I'M OUT.

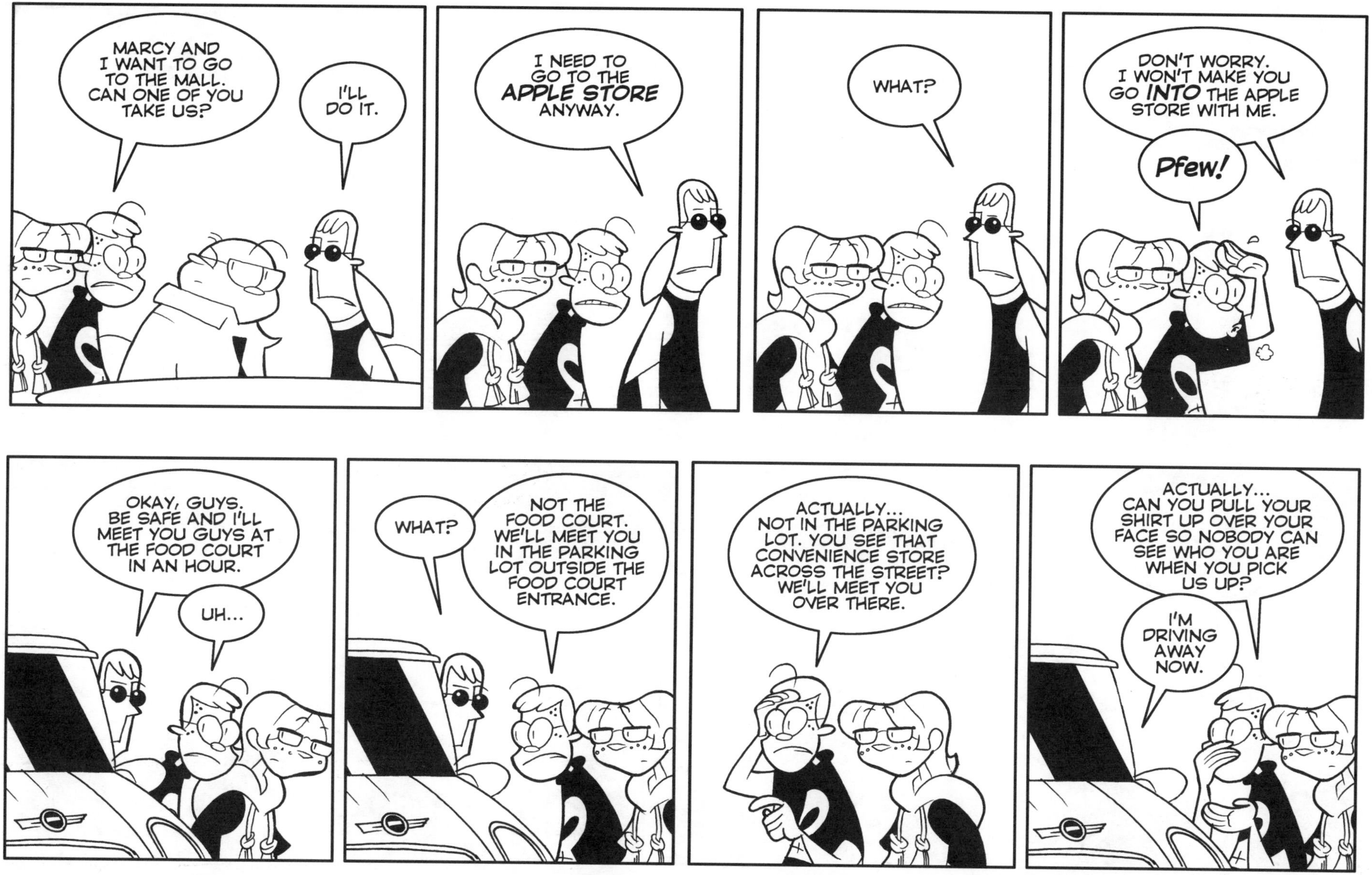
MARCY AND I WANT TO GO TO THE MALL. CAN ONE OF YOU TAKE US?
I'LL DO IT.
I NEED TO GO TO THE APPLE STORE ANYWAY.
WHAT?
DON'T WORRY. I WON'T MAKE YOU GO INTO THE APPLE STORE WITH ME.
Pfew!
OKAY, GUYS. BE SAFE AND I'LL MEET YOU GUYS AT THE FOOD COURT IN AN HOUR.
UH...
WHAT?
NOT THE FOOD COURT. WE'LL MEET YOU IN THE PARKING LOT OUTSIDE THE FOOD COURT ENTRANCE.
ACTUALLY... NOT IN THE PARKING LOT. YOU SEE THAT CONVENIENCE STORE ACROSS THE STREET? WE'LL MEET YOU OVER THERE.
ACTUALLY... CAN YOU PULL YOUR SHIRT UP OVER YOUR FACE SO NOBODY CAN SEE WHO YOU ARE WHEN YOU PICK US UP?
I'M DRIVING AWAY NOW.

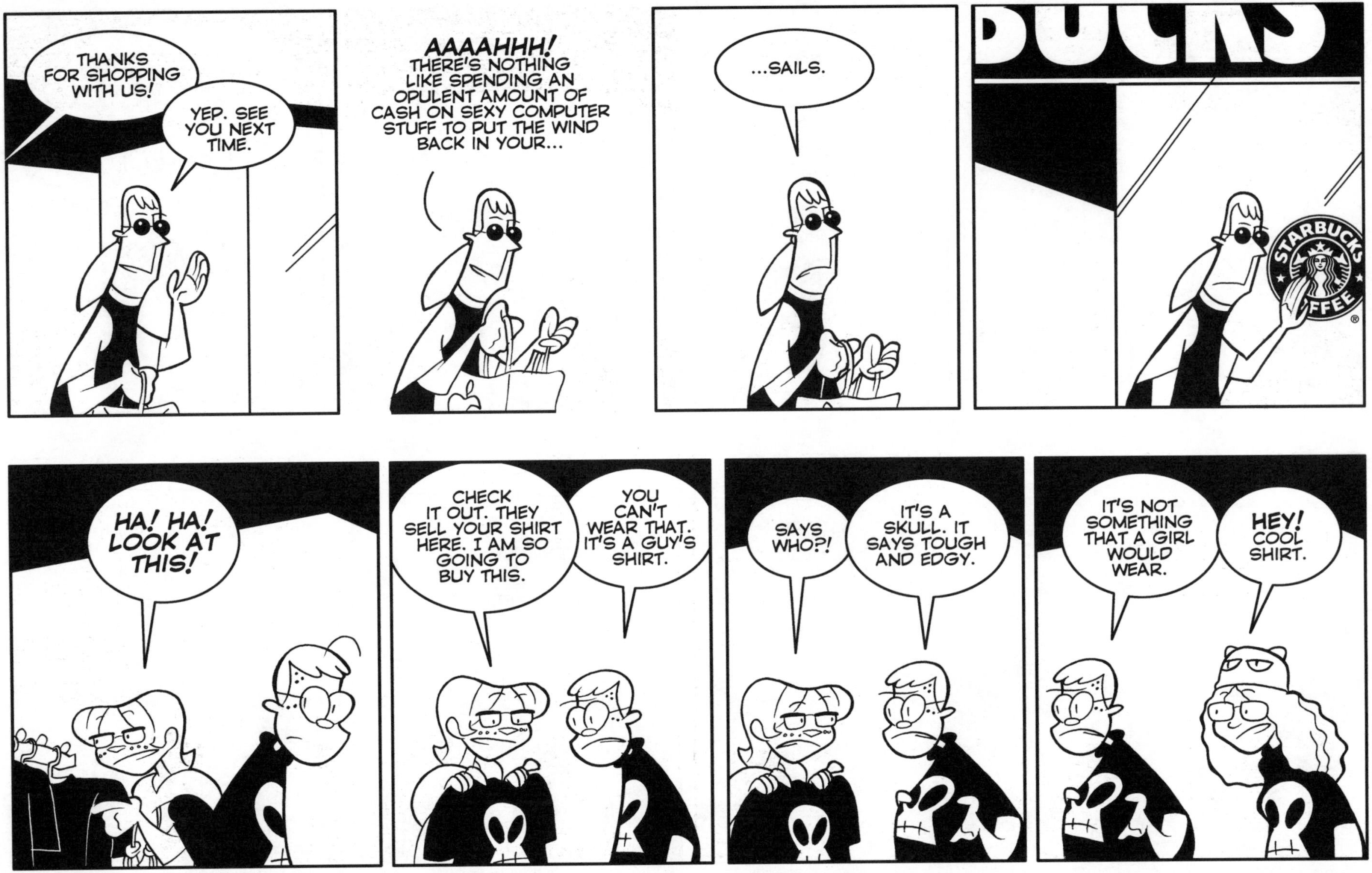

THANKS FOR SHOPPING WITH US!
YEP. SEE YOU NEXT TIME.
AAAAHHH! THERE'S NOTHING LIKE SPENDING AN OPULENT AMOUNT OF CASH ON SEXY COMPUTER STUFF TO PUT THE WIND BACK IN YOUR...
...SAILS.
BUCKS
STARBUCKS COFFEE
HA! HA! LOOK AT THIS!
CHECK IT OUT. THEY SELL YOUR SHIRT HERE. I AM SO GOING TO BUY THIS.
YOU CAN'T WEAR THAT. IT'S A GUY'S SHIRT.
SAYS WHO?!
IT'S A SKULL. IT SAYS TOUGH AND EDGY.
IT'S NOT SOMETHING THAT A GIRL WOULD WEAR.
HEY! COOL SHIRT.

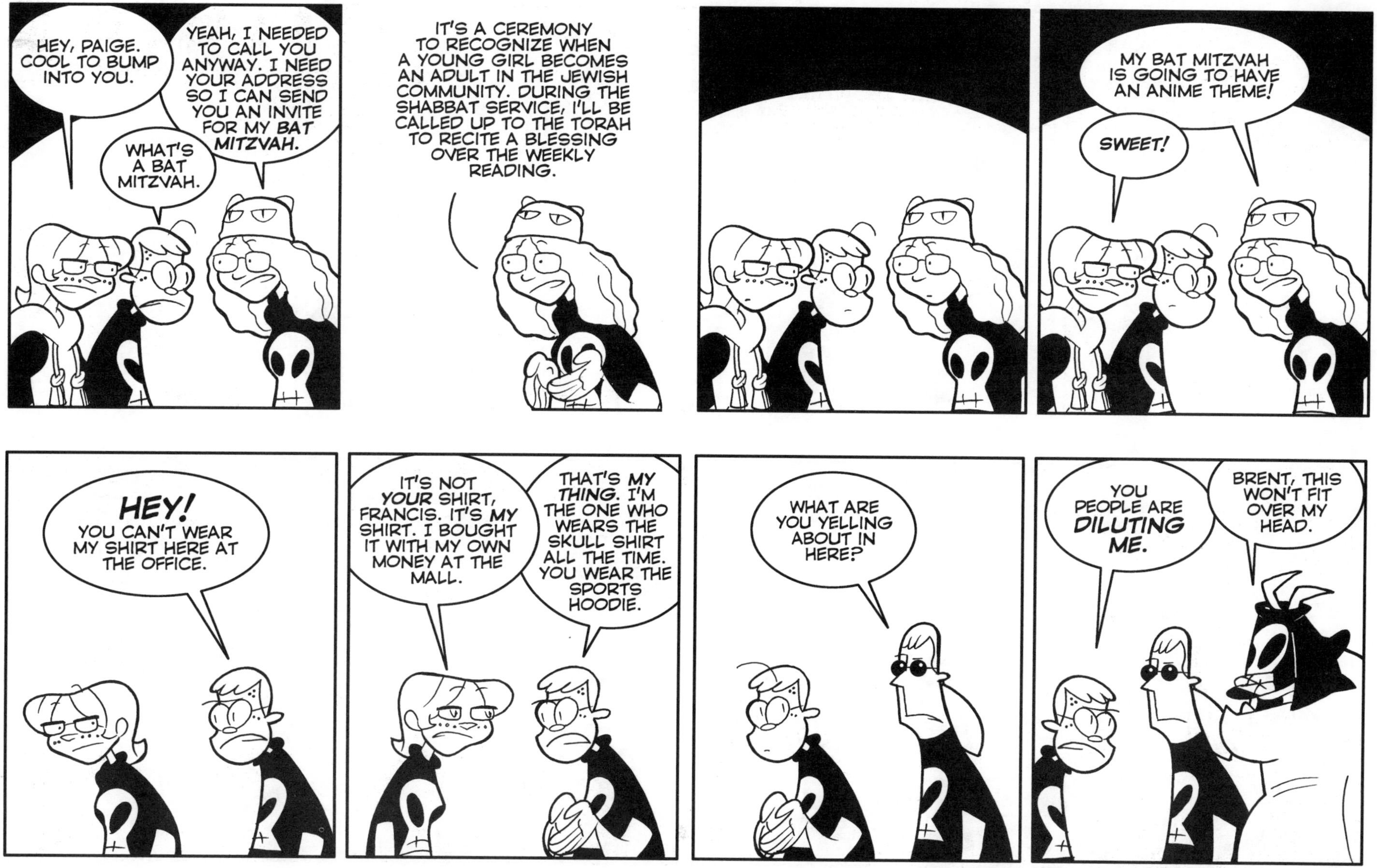
HEY, PAIGE. COOL TO BUMP INTO YOU.
WHAT'S A BAT MITZVAH.
YEAH, I NEEDED TO CALL YOU ANYWAY. I NEED YOUR ADDRESS SO I CAN SEND YOU AN INVITE FOR MY *BAT MITZVAH.*
IT'S A CEREMONY TO RECOGNIZE WHEN A YOUNG GIRL BECOMES AN ADULT IN THE JEWISH COMMUNITY. DURING THE SHABBAT SERVICE, I'LL BE CALLED UP TO THE TORAH TO RECITE A BLESSING OVER THE WEEKLY READING.
MY BAT MITZVAH IS GOING TO HAVE AN ANIME THEME!
SWEET!
HEY! YOU CAN'T WEAR MY SHIRT HERE AT THE OFFICE.
IT'S NOT ***YOUR*** SHIRT, FRANCIS. IT'S ***MY*** SHIRT. I BOUGHT IT WITH MY OWN MONEY AT THE MALL.
THAT'S ***MY THING.*** I'M THE ONE WHO WEARS THE SKULL SHIRT ALL THE TIME. YOU WEAR THE SPORTS HOODIE.
WHAT ARE YOU YELLING ABOUT IN HERE?
YOU PEOPLE ARE ***DILUTING ME.***
BRENT, THIS WON'T FIT OVER MY HEAD.

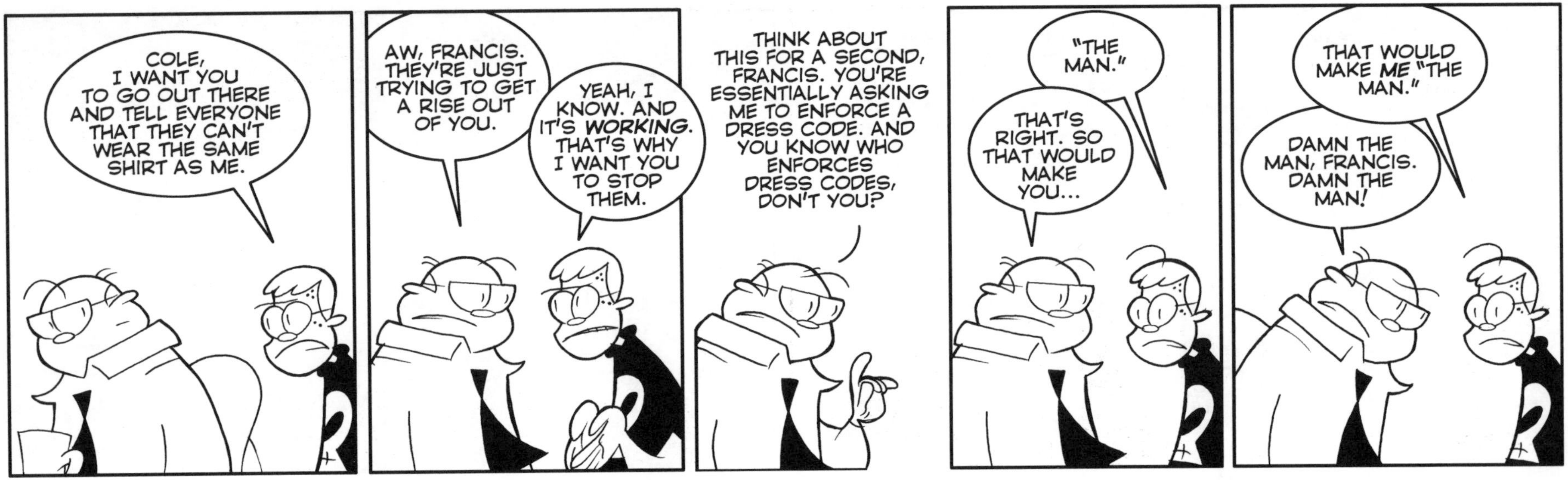
COLE, I WANT YOU TO GO OUT THERE AND TELL EVERYONE THAT THEY CAN'T WEAR THE SAME SHIRT AS ME.
AW, FRANCIS. THEY'RE JUST TRYING TO GET A RISE OUT OF YOU.
YEAH, I KNOW. AND IT'S **WORKING**. THAT'S WHY I WANT YOU TO STOP THEM.
THINK ABOUT THIS FOR A SECOND, FRANCIS. YOU'RE ESSENTIALLY ASKING ME TO ENFORCE A DRESS CODE. AND YOU KNOW WHO ENFORCES DRESS CODES, DON'T YOU?
THAT'S RIGHT. SO THAT WOULD MAKE YOU...
"THE MAN."
DAMN THE MAN, FRANCIS. DAMN THE MAN!
THAT WOULD MAKE **ME** "THE MAN."

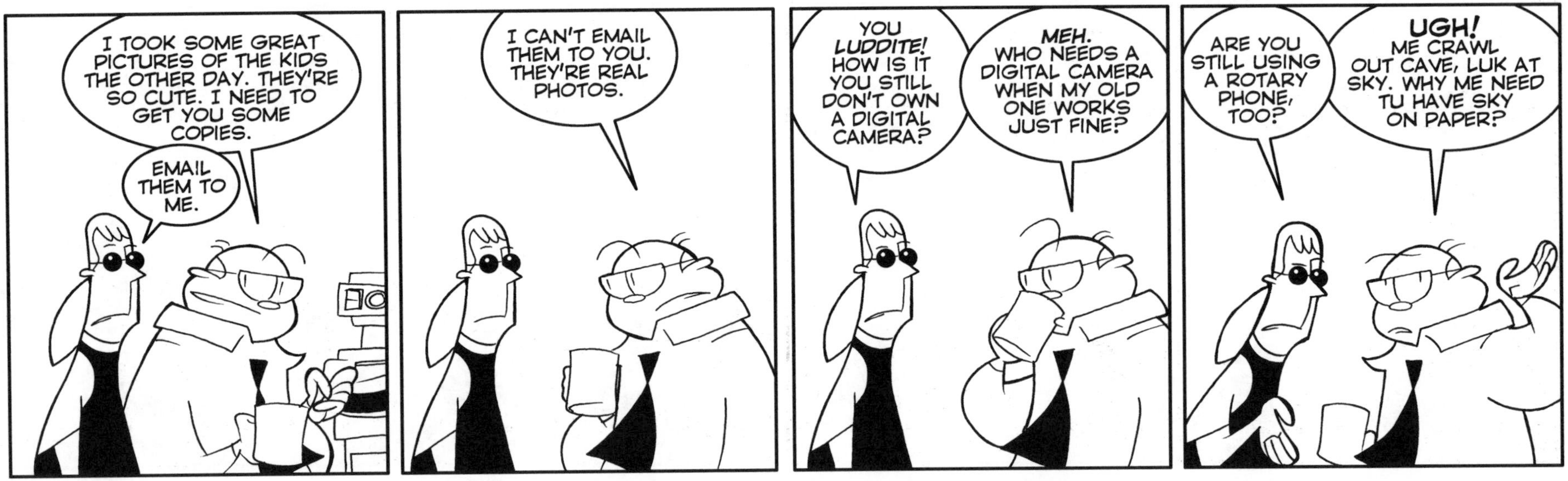
I TOOK SOME GREAT PICTURES OF THE KIDS THE OTHER DAY. THEY'RE SO CUTE. I NEED TO GET YOU SOME COPIES.
EMAIL THEM TO ME.
I CAN'T EMAIL THEM TO YOU. THEY'RE REAL PHOTOS.
YOU ***LUDDITE!*** HOW IS IT YOU STILL DON'T OWN A DIGITAL CAMERA?
MEH. WHO NEEDS A DIGITAL CAMERA WHEN MY OLD ONE WORKS JUST FINE?
ARE YOU STILL USING A ROTARY PHONE, TOO?
UGH! ME CRAWL OUT CAVE, LUK AT SKY. WHY ME NEED TU HAVE SKY ON PAPER?

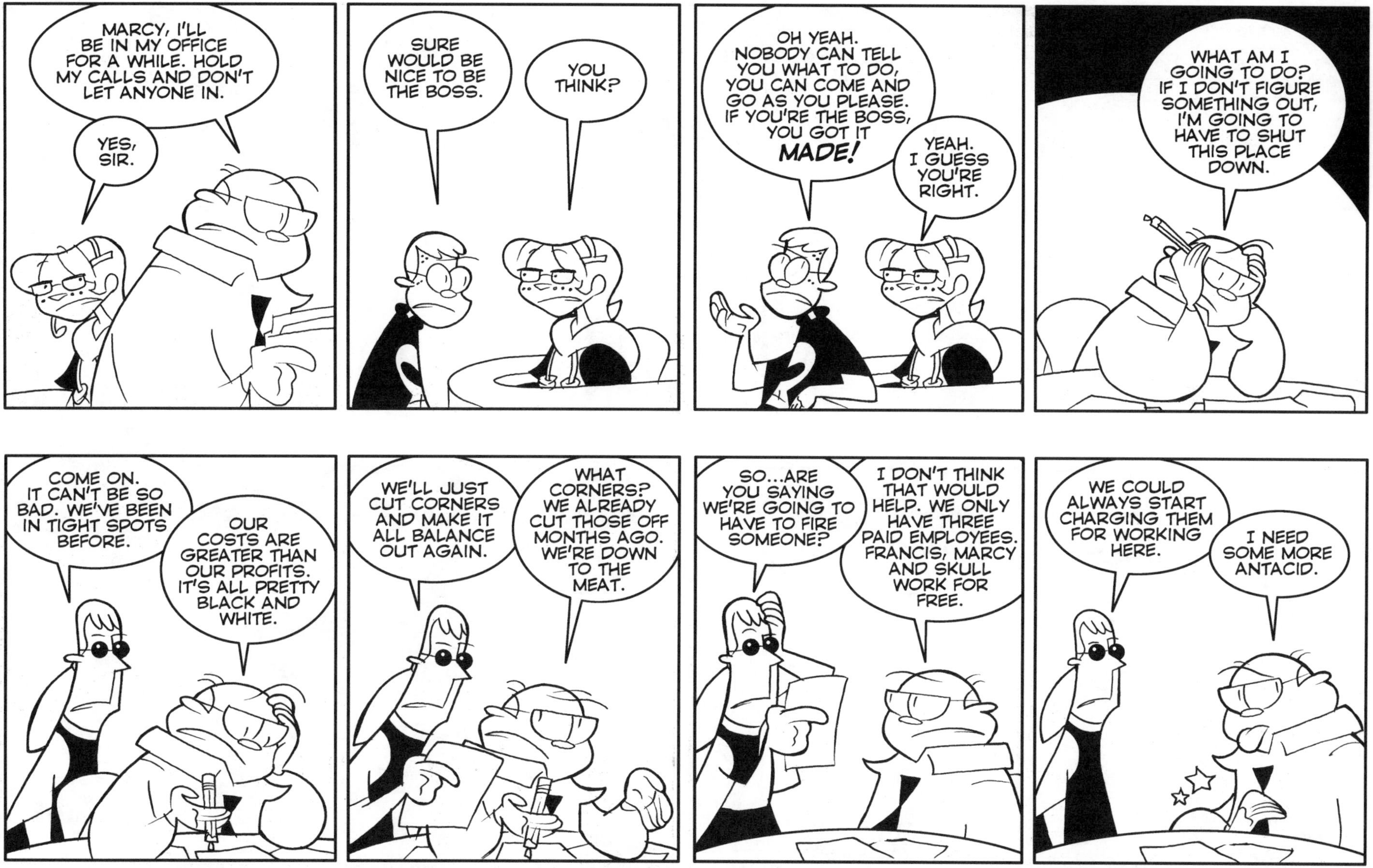

MARCY, I'LL BE IN MY OFFICE FOR A WHILE. HOLD MY CALLS AND DON'T LET ANYONE IN.
YES, SIR.
SURE WOULD BE NICE TO BE THE BOSS.
YOU THINK?
OH YEAH. NOBODY CAN TELL YOU WHAT TO DO, YOU CAN COME AND GO AS YOU PLEASE. IF YOU'RE THE BOSS, YOU GOT IT *MADE!*
YEAH. I GUESS YOU'RE RIGHT.
WHAT AM I GOING TO DO? IF I DON'T FIGURE SOMETHING OUT, I'M GOING TO HAVE TO SHUT THIS PLACE DOWN.
COME ON. IT CAN'T BE SO BAD. WE'VE BEEN IN TIGHT SPOTS BEFORE.
OUR COSTS ARE GREATER THAN OUR PROFITS. IT'S ALL PRETTY BLACK AND WHITE.
WE'LL JUST CUT CORNERS AND MAKE IT ALL BALANCE OUT AGAIN.
WHAT CORNERS? WE ALREADY CUT THOSE OFF MONTHS AGO. WE'RE DOWN TO THE MEAT.
SO...ARE YOU SAYING WE'RE GOING TO HAVE TO FIRE SOMEONE?
I DON'T THINK THAT WOULD HELP. WE ONLY HAVE THREE PAID EMPLOYEES. FRANCIS, MARCY AND SKULL WORK FOR FREE.
WE COULD ALWAYS START CHARGING THEM FOR WORKING HERE.
I NEED SOME MORE ANTACID.

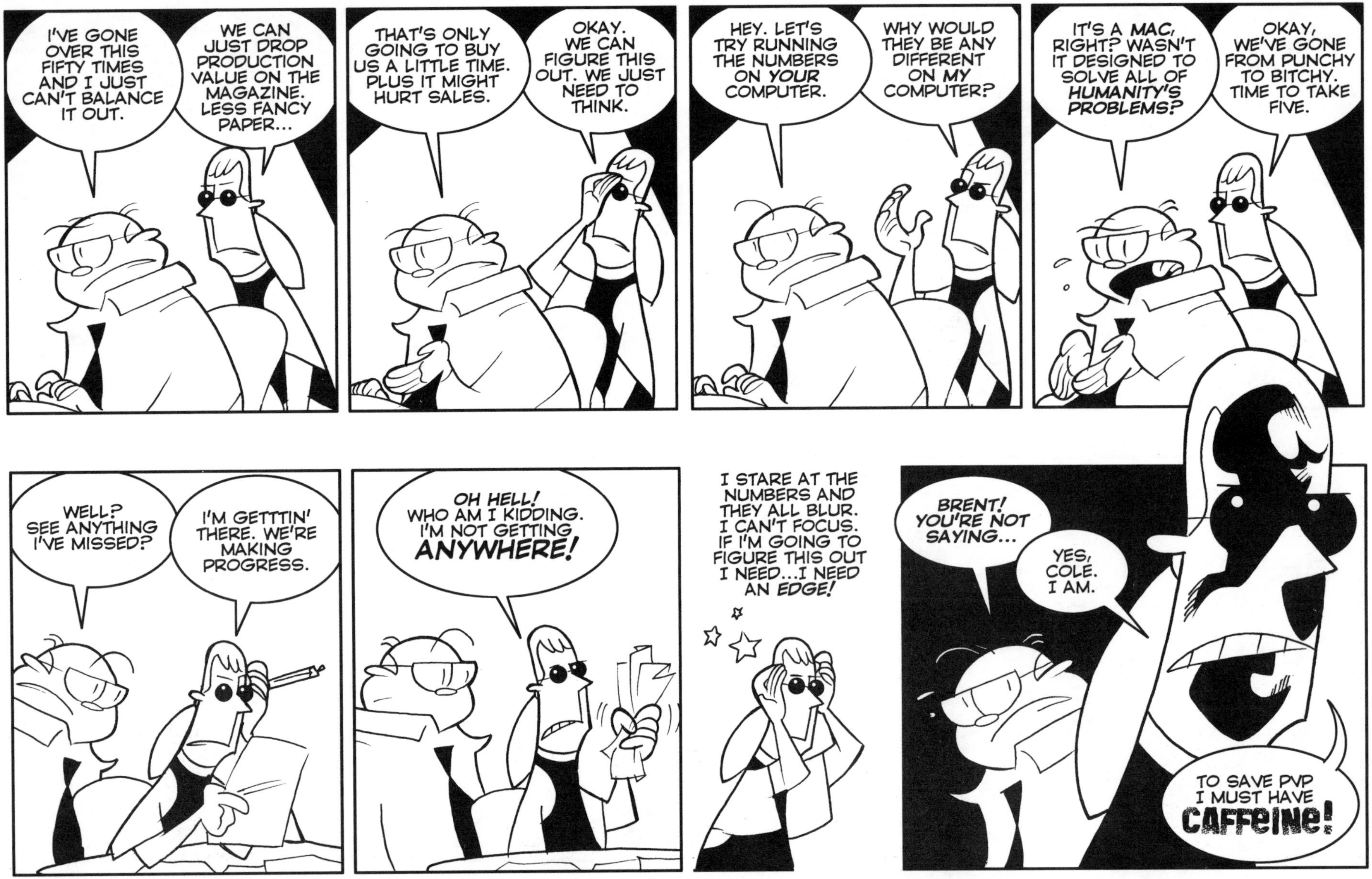
I'VE GONE OVER THIS FIFTY TIMES AND I JUST CAN'T BALANCE IT OUT.
WE CAN JUST DROP PRODUCTION VALUE ON THE MAGAZINE. LESS FANCY PAPER...
THAT'S ONLY GOING TO BUY US A LITTLE TIME. PLUS IT MIGHT HURT SALES.
OKAY. WE CAN FIGURE THIS OUT. WE JUST NEED TO THINK.
HEY. LET'S TRY RUNNING THE NUMBERS ON *YOUR* COMPUTER.
WHY WOULD THEY BE ANY DIFFERENT ON *MY* COMPUTER?
IT'S A *MAC*, RIGHT? WASN'T IT DESIGNED TO SOLVE ALL OF *HUMANITY'S PROBLEMS?*
OKAY, WE'VE GONE FROM PUNCHY TO BITCHY. TIME TO TAKE FIVE.
WELL? SEE ANYTHING I'VE MISSED?
I'M GETTTIN' THERE. WE'RE MAKING PROGRESS.
OH HELL! WHO AM I KIDDING. I'M NOT GETTING **ANYWHERE!**
I STARE AT THE NUMBERS AND THEY ALL BLUR. I CAN'T FOCUS. IF I'M GOING TO FIGURE THIS OUT I NEED...I NEED AN *EDGE!*
BRENT! YOU'RE NOT SAYING...
YES, COLE. I AM.
TO SAVE PVP I MUST HAVE **CAFFEINE!**

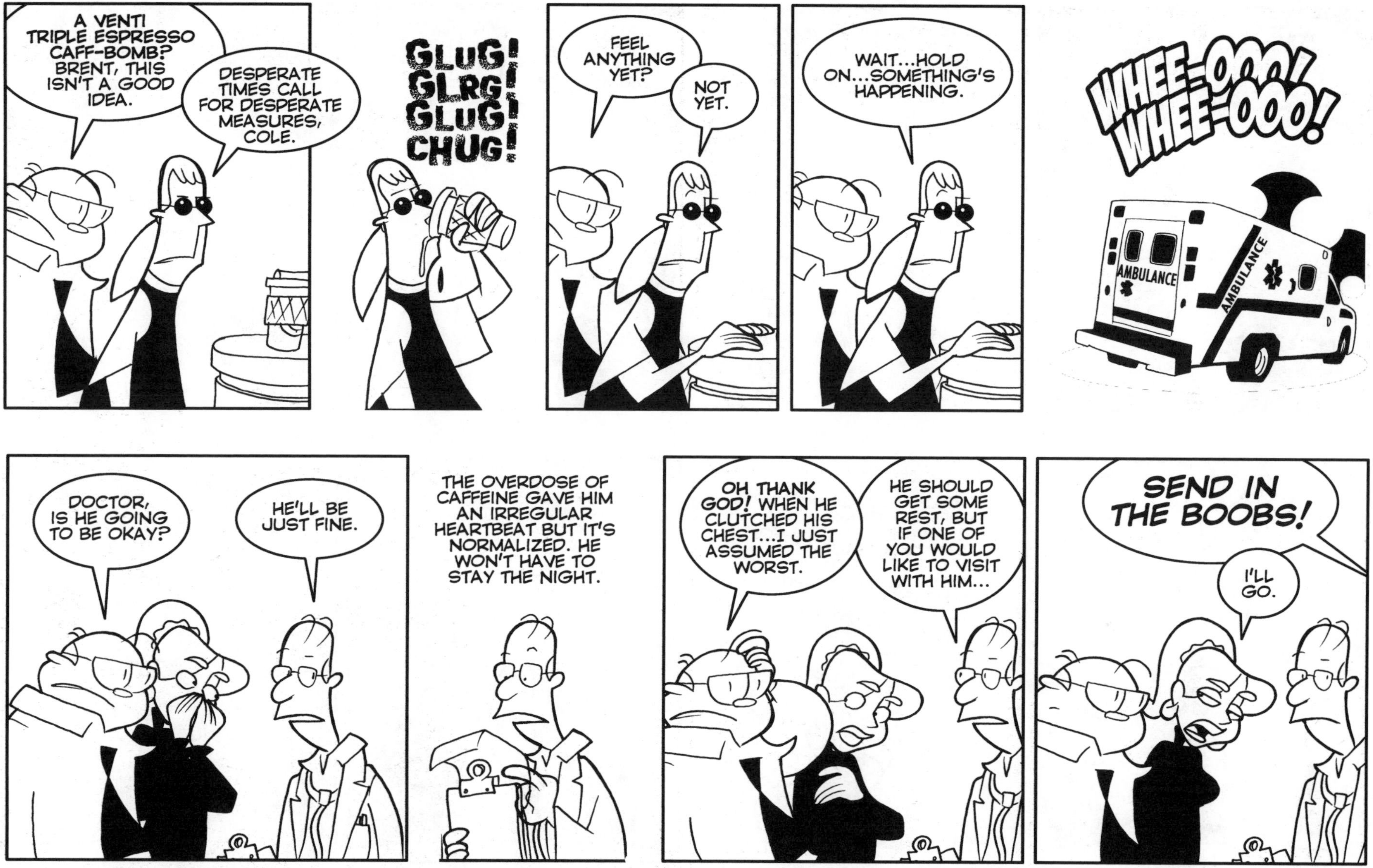
A VENTI TRIPLE ESPRESSO CAFF-BOMB? BRENT, THIS ISN'T A GOOD IDEA.
DESPERATE TIMES CALL FOR DESPERATE MEASURES, COLE.
GLUG! GLRG! GLUG! CHUG!
FEEL ANYTHING YET?
NOT YET.
WAIT...HOLD ON...SOMETHING'S HAPPENING.
WHEE-OOO! WHEE-OOO!
AMBULANCE
AMBULANCE
DOCTOR, IS HE GOING TO BE OKAY?
HE'LL BE JUST FINE.
THE OVERDOSE OF CAFFEINE GAVE HIM AN IRREGULAR HEARTBEAT BUT IT'S NORMALIZED. HE WON'T HAVE TO STAY THE NIGHT.
OH THANK GOD! WHEN HE CLUTCHED HIS CHEST...I JUST ASSUMED THE WORST.
HE SHOULD GET SOME REST, BUT IF ONE OF YOU WOULD LIKE TO VISIT WITH HIM...
SEND IN THE BOOBS!
I'LL GO.

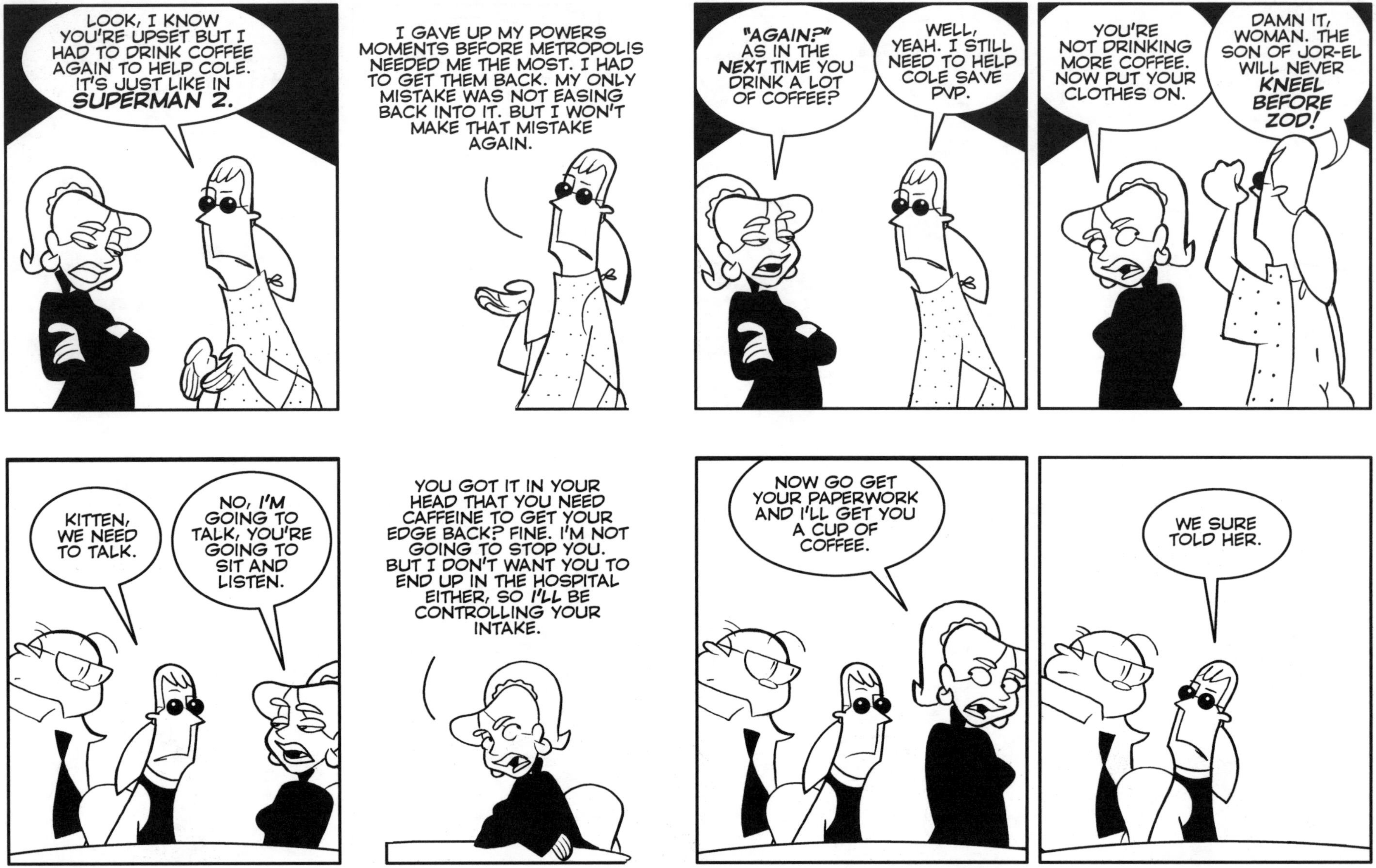

LOOK, I KNOW YOU'RE UPSET BUT I HAD TO DRINK COFFEE AGAIN TO HELP COLE. IT'S JUST LIKE IN SUPERMAN 2.
I GAVE UP MY POWERS MOMENTS BEFORE METROPOLIS NEEDED ME THE MOST. I HAD TO GET THEM BACK. MY ONLY MISTAKE WAS NOT EASING BACK INTO IT. BUT I WON'T MAKE THAT MISTAKE AGAIN.
"AGAIN?" AS IN THE NEXT TIME YOU DRINK A LOT OF COFFEE?
WELL, YEAH. I STILL NEED TO HELP COLE SAVE PVP.
YOU'RE NOT DRINKING MORE COFFEE. NOW PUT YOUR CLOTHES ON.
DAMN IT, WOMAN. THE SON OF JOR-EL WILL NEVER KNEEL BEFORE ZOD!
KITTEN, WE NEED TO TALK.
NO, I'M GOING TO TALK, YOU'RE GOING TO SIT AND LISTEN.
YOU GOT IT IN YOUR HEAD THAT YOU NEED CAFFEINE TO GET YOUR EDGE BACK? FINE. I'M NOT GOING TO STOP YOU. BUT I DON'T WANT YOU TO END UP IN THE HOSPITAL EITHER, SO I'LL BE CONTROLLING YOUR INTAKE.
NOW GO GET YOUR PAPERWORK AND I'LL GET YOU A CUP OF COFFEE.
WE SURE TOLD HER.

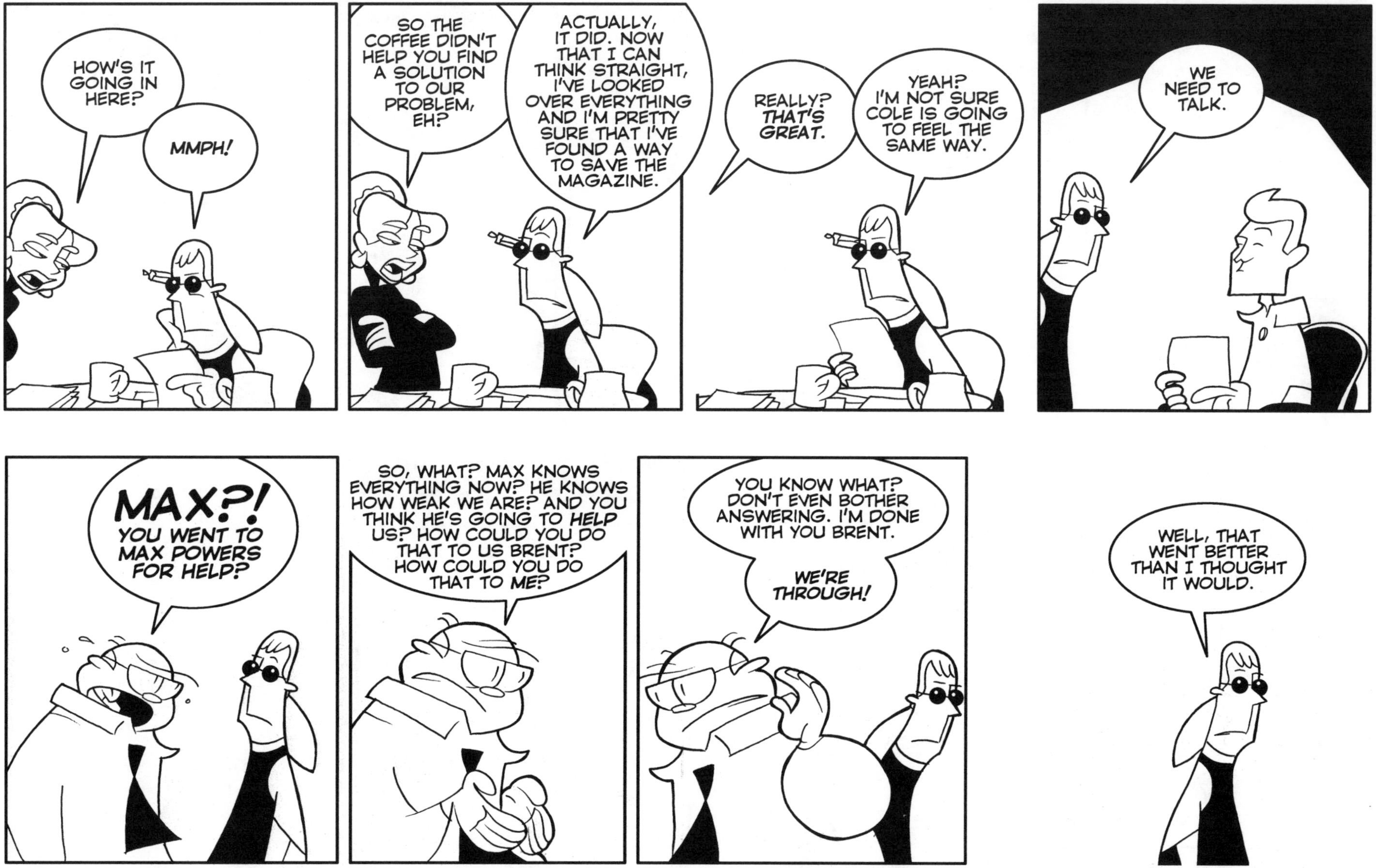
HOW'S IT GOING IN HERE?
MMPH!
SO THE COFFEE DIDN'T HELP YOU FIND A SOLUTION TO OUR PROBLEM, EH?
ACTUALLY, IT DID. NOW THAT I CAN THINK STRAIGHT, I'VE LOOKED OVER EVERYTHING AND I'M PRETTY SURE THAT I'VE FOUND A WAY TO SAVE THE MAGAZINE.
REALLY? *THAT'S GREAT.*
YEAH? I'M NOT SURE COLE IS GOING TO FEEL THE SAME WAY.
WE NEED TO TALK.
MAX?! YOU WENT TO MAX POWERS FOR HELP?
SO, WHAT? MAX KNOWS EVERYTHING NOW? HE KNOWS HOW WEAK WE ARE? AND YOU THINK HE'S GOING TO *HELP* US? HOW COULD YOU DO THAT TO US BRENT? HOW COULD YOU DO THAT TO *ME*?
YOU KNOW WHAT? DON'T EVEN BOTHER ANSWERING. I'M DONE WITH YOU BRENT.
WE'RE THROUGH!
WELL, THAT WENT BETTER THAN I THOUGHT IT WOULD.

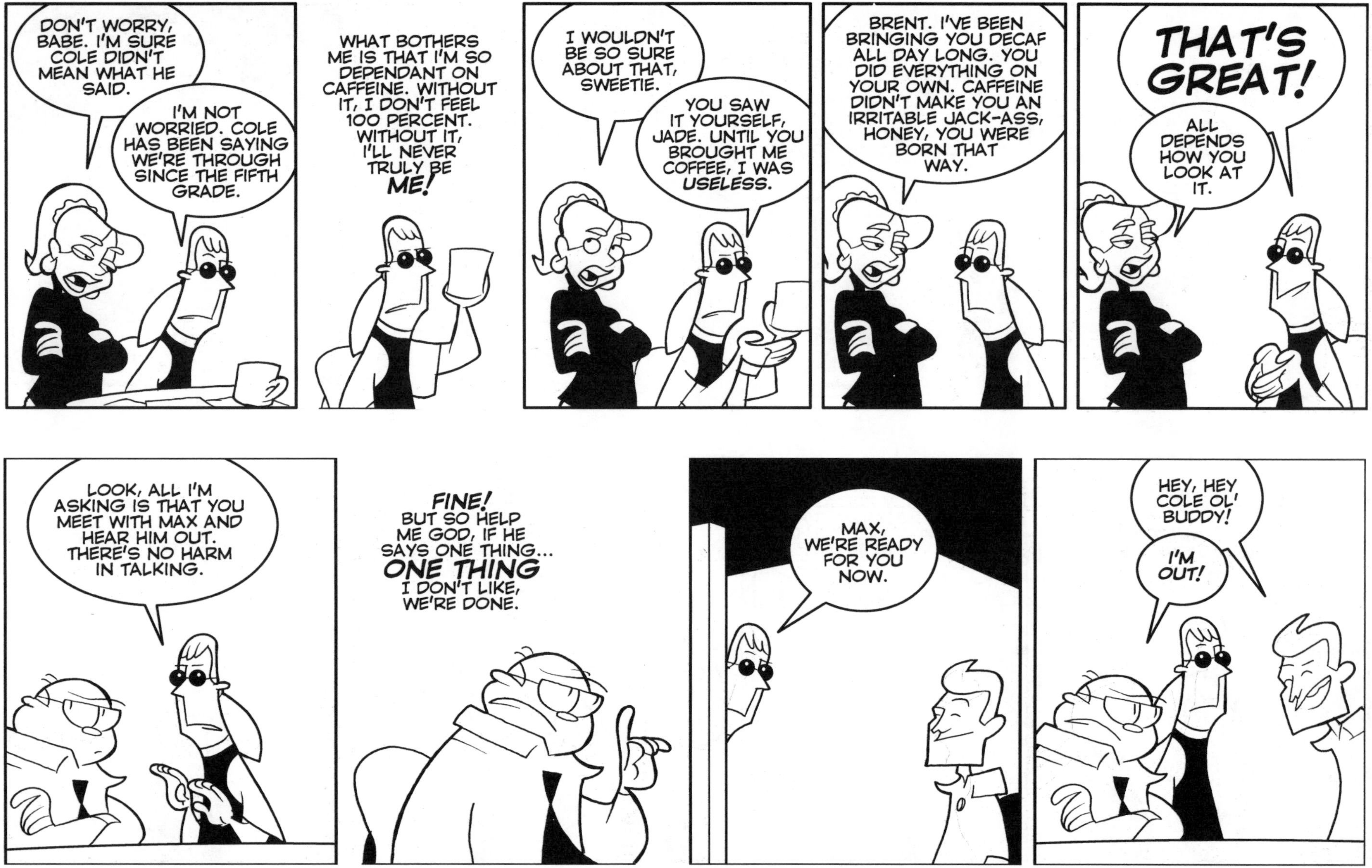
DON'T WORRY, BABE. I'M SURE COLE DIDN'T MEAN WHAT HE SAID.
I'M NOT WORRIED. COLE HAS BEEN SAYING WE'RE THROUGH SINCE THE FIFTH GRADE.
WHAT BOTHERS ME IS THAT I'M SO DEPENDANT ON CAFFEINE. WITHOUT IT, I DON'T FEEL 100 PERCENT. WITHOUT IT, I'LL NEVER TRULY BE ME!
I WOULDN'T BE SO SURE ABOUT THAT, SWEETIE.
YOU SAW IT YOURSELF, JADE. UNTIL YOU BROUGHT ME COFFEE, I WAS USELESS.
BRENT. I'VE BEEN BRINGING YOU DECAF ALL DAY LONG. YOU DID EVERYTHING ON YOUR OWN. CAFFEINE DIDN'T MAKE YOU AN IRRITABLE JACK-ASS, HONEY, YOU WERE BORN THAT WAY.
THAT'S GREAT!
ALL DEPENDS HOW YOU LOOK AT IT.
LOOK, ALL I'M ASKING IS THAT YOU MEET WITH MAX AND HEAR HIM OUT. THERE'S NO HARM IN TALKING.
FINE! BUT SO HELP ME GOD, IF HE SAYS ONE THING... ONE THING I DON'T LIKE, WE'RE DONE.
MAX, WE'RE READY FOR YOU NOW.
HEY, HEY COLE OL' BUDDY!
I'M OUT!

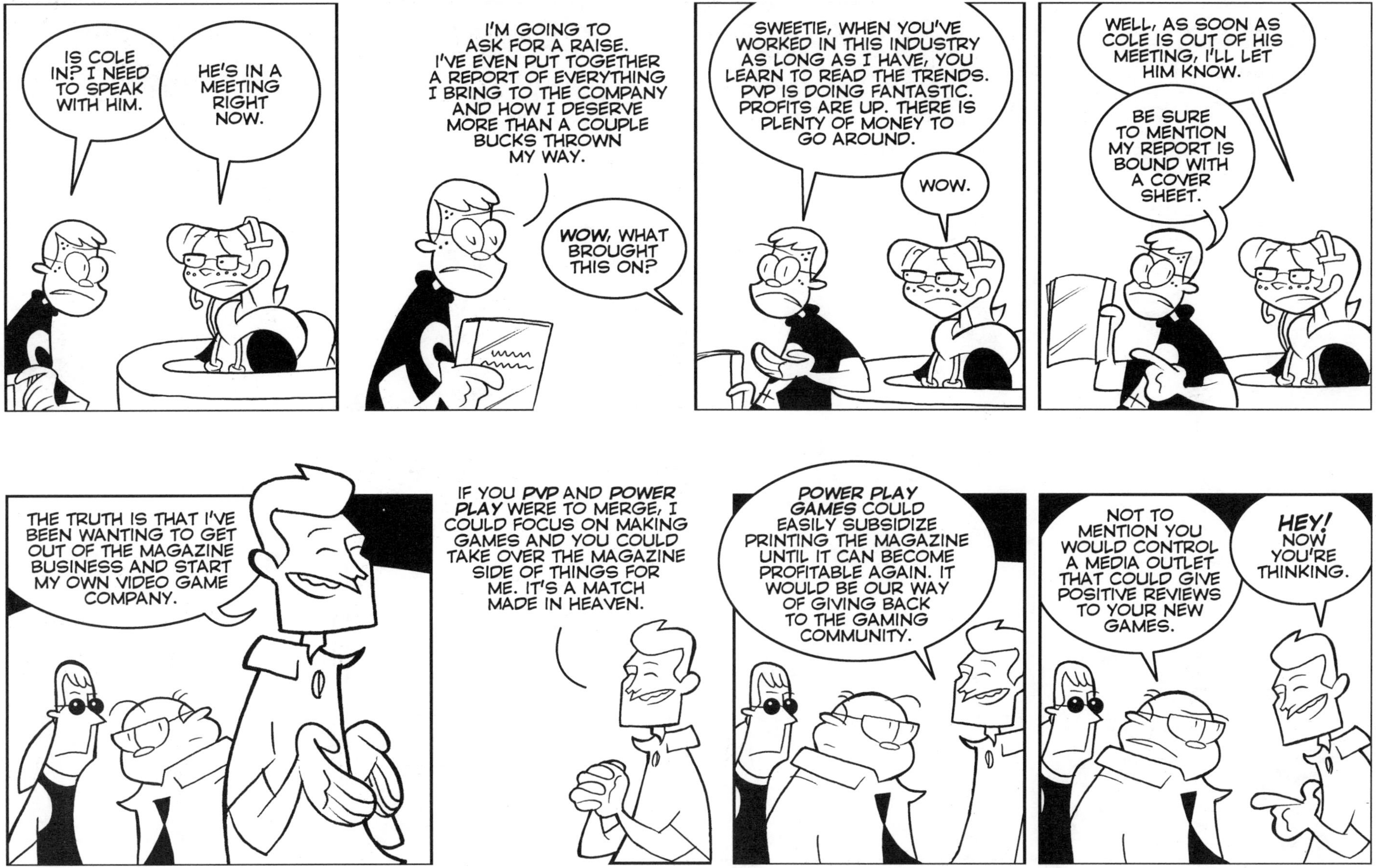
IS COLE IN? I NEED TO SPEAK WITH HIM.
HE'S IN A MEETING RIGHT NOW.
I'M GOING TO ASK FOR A RAISE. I'VE EVEN PUT TOGETHER A REPORT OF EVERYTHING I BRING TO THE COMPANY AND HOW I DESERVE MORE THAN A COUPLE BUCKS THROWN MY WAY.
WOW, WHAT BROUGHT THIS ON?
SWEETIE, WHEN YOU'VE WORKED IN THIS INDUSTRY AS LONG AS I HAVE, YOU LEARN TO READ THE TRENDS. PVP IS DOING FANTASTIC. PROFITS ARE UP. THERE IS PLENTY OF MONEY TO GO AROUND.
WOW.
WELL, AS SOON AS COLE IS OUT OF HIS MEETING, I'LL LET HIM KNOW.
BE SURE TO MENTION MY REPORT IS BOUND WITH A COVER SHEET.
THE TRUTH IS THAT I'VE BEEN WANTING TO GET OUT OF THE MAGAZINE BUSINESS AND START MY OWN VIDEO GAME COMPANY.
IF YOU PVP AND POWER PLAY WERE TO MERGE, I COULD FOCUS ON MAKING GAMES AND YOU COULD TAKE OVER THE MAGAZINE SIDE OF THINGS FOR ME. IT'S A MATCH MADE IN HEAVEN.
POWER PLAY GAMES COULD EASILY SUBSIDIZE PRINTING THE MAGAZINE UNTIL IT CAN BECOME PROFITABLE AGAIN. IT WOULD BE OUR WAY OF GIVING BACK TO THE GAMING COMMUNITY.
NOT TO MENTION YOU WOULD CONTROL A MEDIA OUTLET THAT COULD GIVE POSITIVE REVIEWS TO YOUR NEW GAMES.
HEY! NOW YOU'RE THINKING.

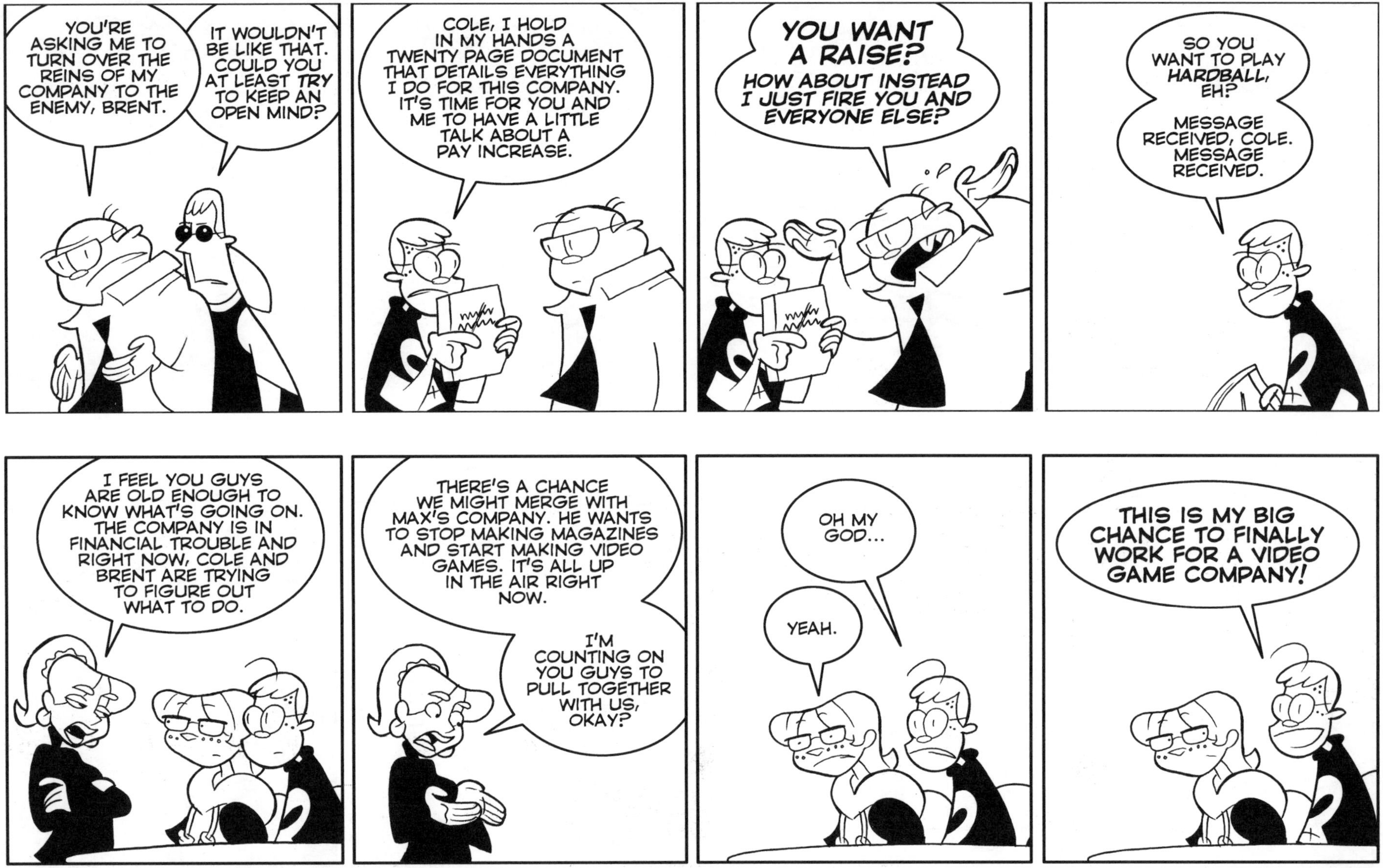
YOU'RE ASKING ME TO TURN OVER THE REINS OF MY COMPANY TO THE ENEMY, BRENT.
IT WOULDN'T BE LIKE THAT. COULD YOU AT LEAST TRY TO KEEP AN OPEN MIND?
COLE, I HOLD IN MY HANDS A TWENTY PAGE DOCUMENT THAT DETAILS EVERYTHING I DO FOR THIS COMPANY. IT'S TIME FOR YOU AND ME TO HAVE A LITTLE TALK ABOUT A PAY INCREASE.
YOU WANT A RAISE?
HOW ABOUT INSTEAD I JUST FIRE YOU AND EVERYONE ELSE?
SO YOU WANT TO PLAY HARDBALL, EH?
MESSAGE RECEIVED, COLE. MESSAGE RECEIVED.
I FEEL YOU GUYS ARE OLD ENOUGH TO KNOW WHAT'S GOING ON. THE COMPANY IS IN FINANCIAL TROUBLE AND RIGHT NOW, COLE AND BRENT ARE TRYING TO FIGURE OUT WHAT TO DO.
THERE'S A CHANCE WE MIGHT MERGE WITH MAX'S COMPANY. HE WANTS TO STOP MAKING MAGAZINES AND START MAKING VIDEO GAMES. IT'S ALL UP IN THE AIR RIGHT NOW.
I'M COUNTING ON YOU GUYS TO PULL TOGETHER WITH US, OKAY?
OH MY GOD...
YEAH.
THIS IS MY BIG CHANCE TO FINALLY WORK FOR A VIDEO GAME COMPANY!

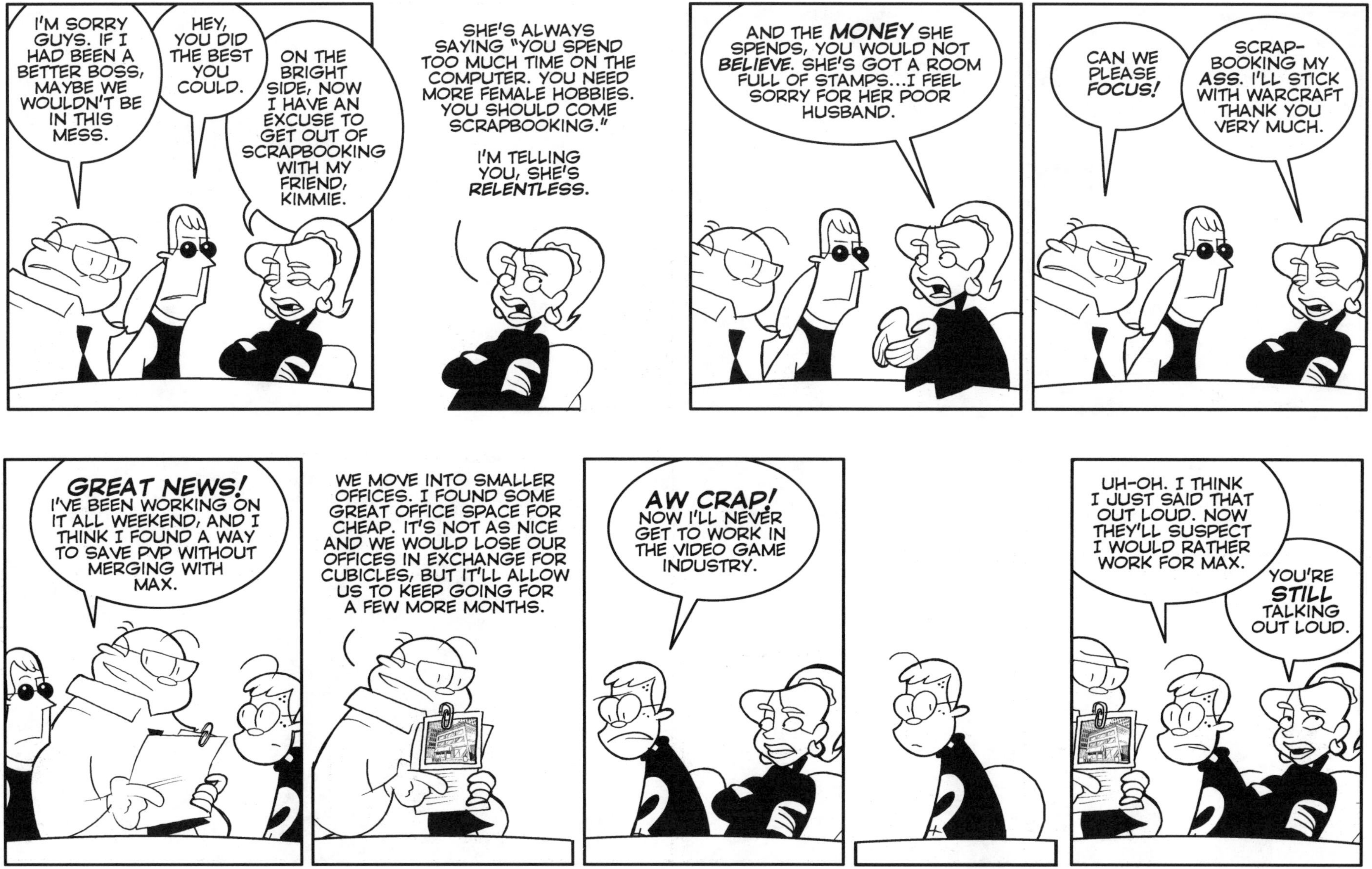
I'M SORRY GUYS. IF I HAD BEEN A BETTER BOSS, MAYBE WE WOULDN'T BE IN THIS MESS.
HEY, YOU DID THE BEST YOU COULD.
ON THE BRIGHT SIDE, NOW I HAVE AN EXCUSE TO GET OUT OF SCRAPBOOKING WITH MY FRIEND, KIMMIE.
SHE'S ALWAYS SAYING "YOU SPEND TOO MUCH TIME ON THE COMPUTER. YOU NEED MORE FEMALE HOBBIES. YOU SHOULD COME SCRAPBOOKING."
I'M TELLING YOU, SHE'S *RELENTLESS*.
AND THE ***MONEY*** SHE SPENDS, YOU WOULD NOT ***BELIEVE***. SHE'S GOT A ROOM FULL OF STAMPS...I FEEL SORRY FOR HER POOR HUSBAND.
CAN WE PLEASE *FOCUS!*
SCRAP-BOOKING MY **ASS**. I'LL STICK WITH WARCRAFT THANK YOU VERY MUCH.
GREAT NEWS! I'VE BEEN WORKING ON IT ALL WEEKEND, AND I THINK I FOUND A WAY TO SAVE PVP WITHOUT MERGING WITH MAX.
WE MOVE INTO SMALLER OFFICES. I FOUND SOME GREAT OFFICE SPACE FOR CHEAP. IT'S NOT AS NICE AND WE WOULD LOSE OUR OFFICES IN EXCHANGE FOR CUBICLES, BUT IT'LL ALLOW US TO KEEP GOING FOR A FEW MORE MONTHS.
AW CRAP! NOW I'LL NEVER GET TO WORK IN THE VIDEO GAME INDUSTRY.
UH-OH. I THINK I JUST SAID THAT OUT LOUD. NOW THEY'LL SUSPECT I WOULD RATHER WORK FOR MAX.
YOU'RE ***STILL*** TALKING OUT LOUD.

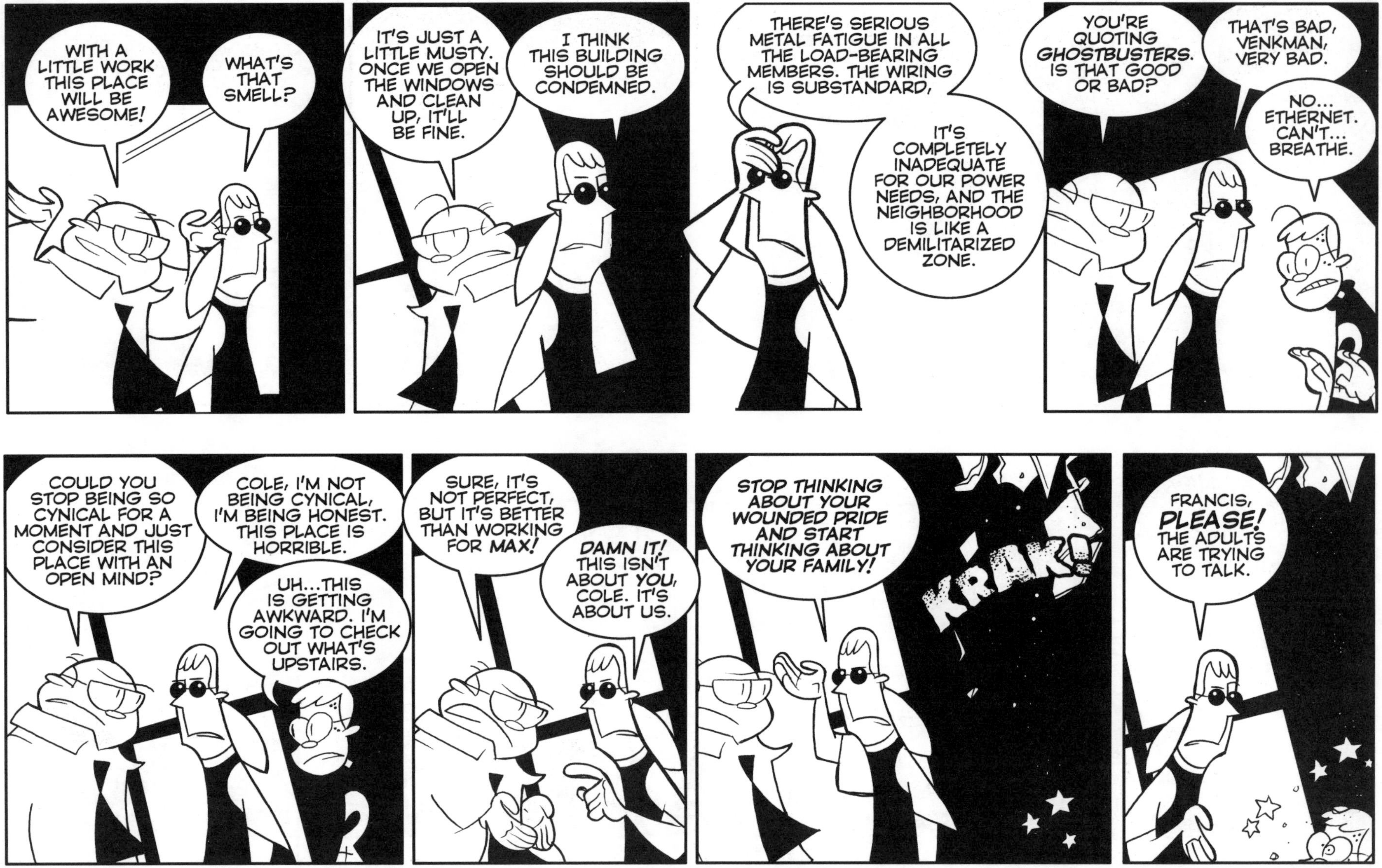
WITH A LITTLE WORK THIS PLACE WILL BE AWESOME!
WHAT'S THAT SMELL?
IT'S JUST A LITTLE MUSTY. ONCE WE OPEN THE WINDOWS AND CLEAN UP, IT'LL BE FINE.
I THINK THIS BUILDING SHOULD BE CONDEMNED.
THERE'S SERIOUS METAL FATIGUE IN ALL THE LOAD-BEARING MEMBERS. THE WIRING IS SUBSTANDARD,
IT'S COMPLETELY INADEQUATE FOR OUR POWER NEEDS, AND THE NEIGHBORHOOD IS LIKE A DEMILITARIZED ZONE.
YOU'RE QUOTING GHOSTBUSTERS. IS THAT GOOD OR BAD?
THAT'S BAD, VENKMAN, VERY BAD.
NO... ETHERNET. CAN'T... BREATHE.
COULD YOU STOP BEING SO CYNICAL FOR A MOMENT AND JUST CONSIDER THIS PLACE WITH AN OPEN MIND?
COLE, I'M NOT BEING CYNICAL, I'M BEING HONEST. THIS PLACE IS HORRIBLE.
UH...THIS IS GETTING AWKWARD. I'M GOING TO CHECK OUT WHAT'S UPSTAIRS.
SURE, IT'S NOT PERFECT, BUT IT'S BETTER THAN WORKING FOR MAX!
DAMN IT! THIS ISN'T ABOUT YOU, COLE. IT'S ABOUT US.
STOP THINKING ABOUT YOUR WOUNDED PRIDE AND START THINKING ABOUT YOUR FAMILY!
KRAK!
FRANCIS, PLEASE! THE ADULTS ARE TRYING TO TALK.

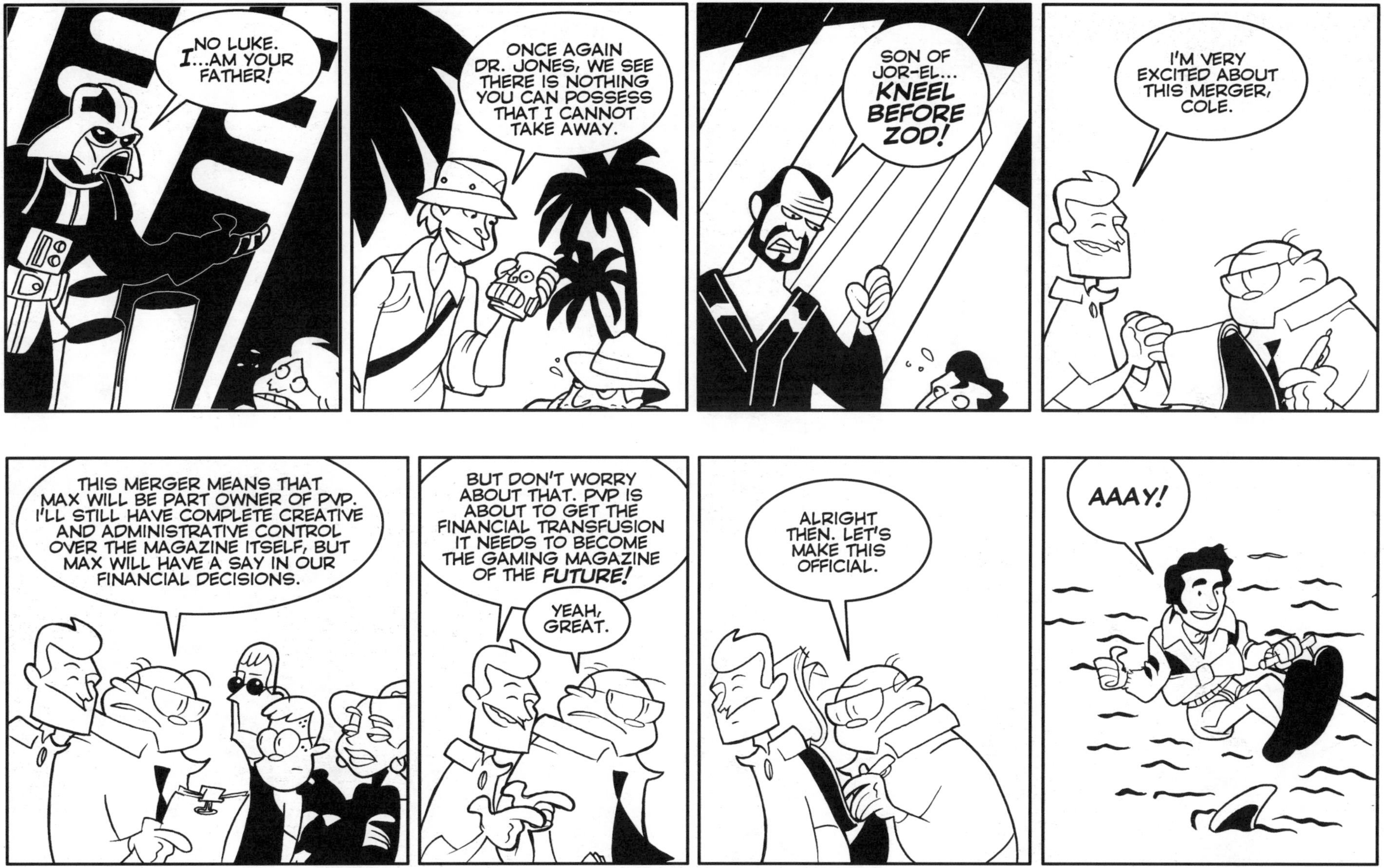
NO LUKE. I...AM YOUR FATHER!
ONCE AGAIN DR. JONES, WE SEE THERE IS NOTHING YOU CAN POSSESS THAT I CANNOT TAKE AWAY.
SON OF JOR-EL... KNEEL BEFORE ZOD!
I'M VERY EXCITED ABOUT THIS MERGER, COLE.
THIS MERGER MEANS THAT MAX WILL BE PART OWNER OF PVP. I'LL STILL HAVE COMPLETE CREATIVE AND ADMINISTRATIVE CONTROL OVER THE MAGAZINE ITSELF, BUT MAX WILL HAVE A SAY IN OUR FINANCIAL DECISIONS.
BUT DON'T WORRY ABOUT THAT. PVP IS ABOUT TO GET THE FINANCIAL TRANSFUSION IT NEEDS TO BECOME THE GAMING MAGAZINE OF THE FUTURE!
YEAH, GREAT.
ALRIGHT THEN. LET'S MAKE THIS OFFICIAL.
AAAY!

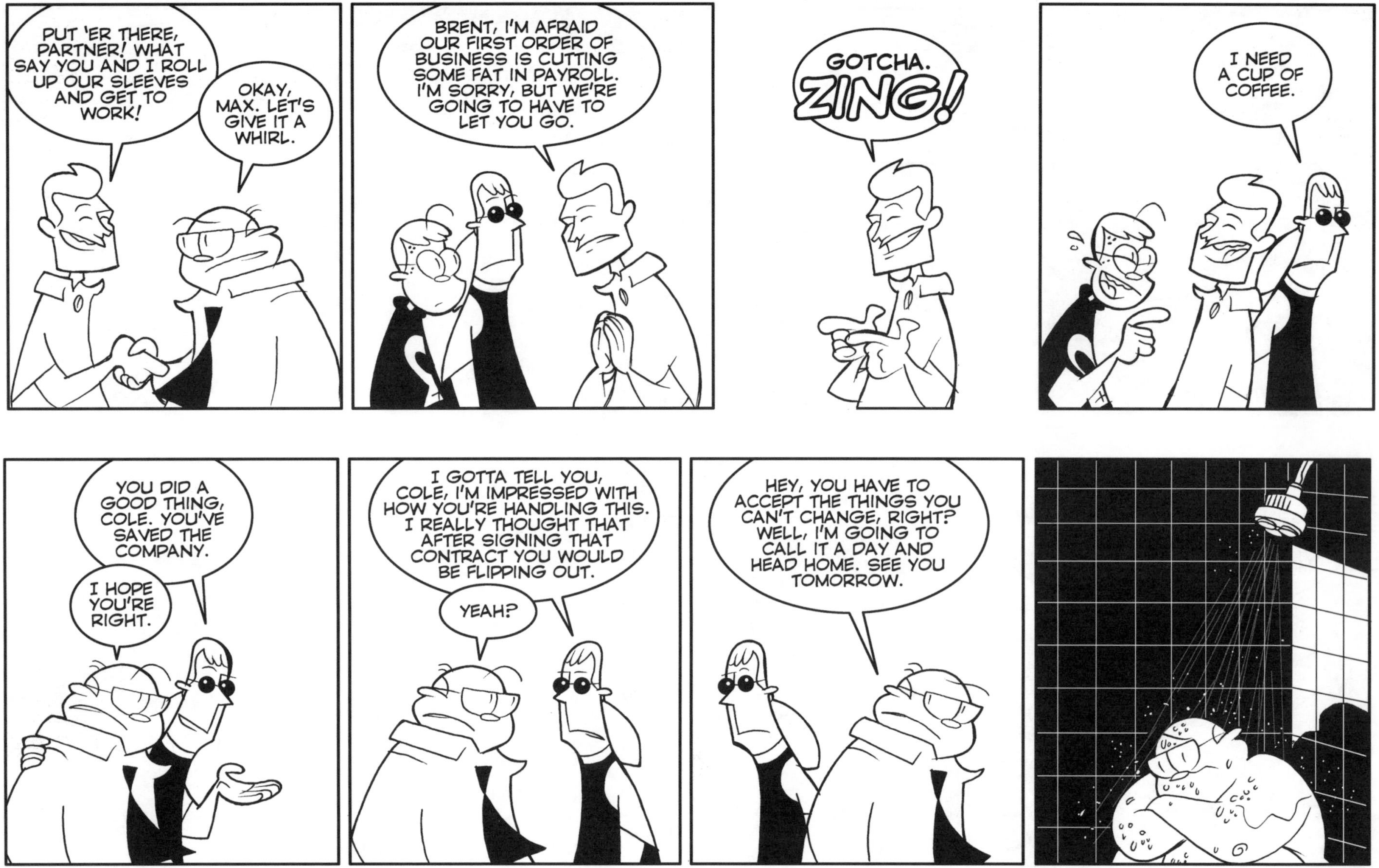
PUT 'ER THERE, PARTNER! WHAT SAY YOU AND I ROLL UP OUR SLEEVES AND GET TO WORK!
OKAY, MAX. LET'S GIVE IT A WHIRL.
BRENT, I'M AFRAID OUR FIRST ORDER OF BUSINESS IS CUTTING SOME FAT IN PAYROLL. I'M SORRY, BUT WE'RE GOING TO HAVE TO LET YOU GO.
GOTCHA. ZING!
I NEED A CUP OF COFFEE.
YOU DID A GOOD THING, COLE. YOU'VE SAVED THE COMPANY.
I HOPE YOU'RE RIGHT.
I GOTTA TELL YOU, COLE, I'M IMPRESSED WITH HOW YOU'RE HANDLING THIS. I REALLY THOUGHT THAT AFTER SIGNING THAT CONTRACT YOU WOULD BE FLIPPING OUT.
YEAH?
HEY, YOU HAVE TO ACCEPT THE THINGS YOU CAN'T CHANGE, RIGHT? WELL, I'M GOING TO CALL IT A DAY AND HEAD HOME. SEE YOU TOMORROW.

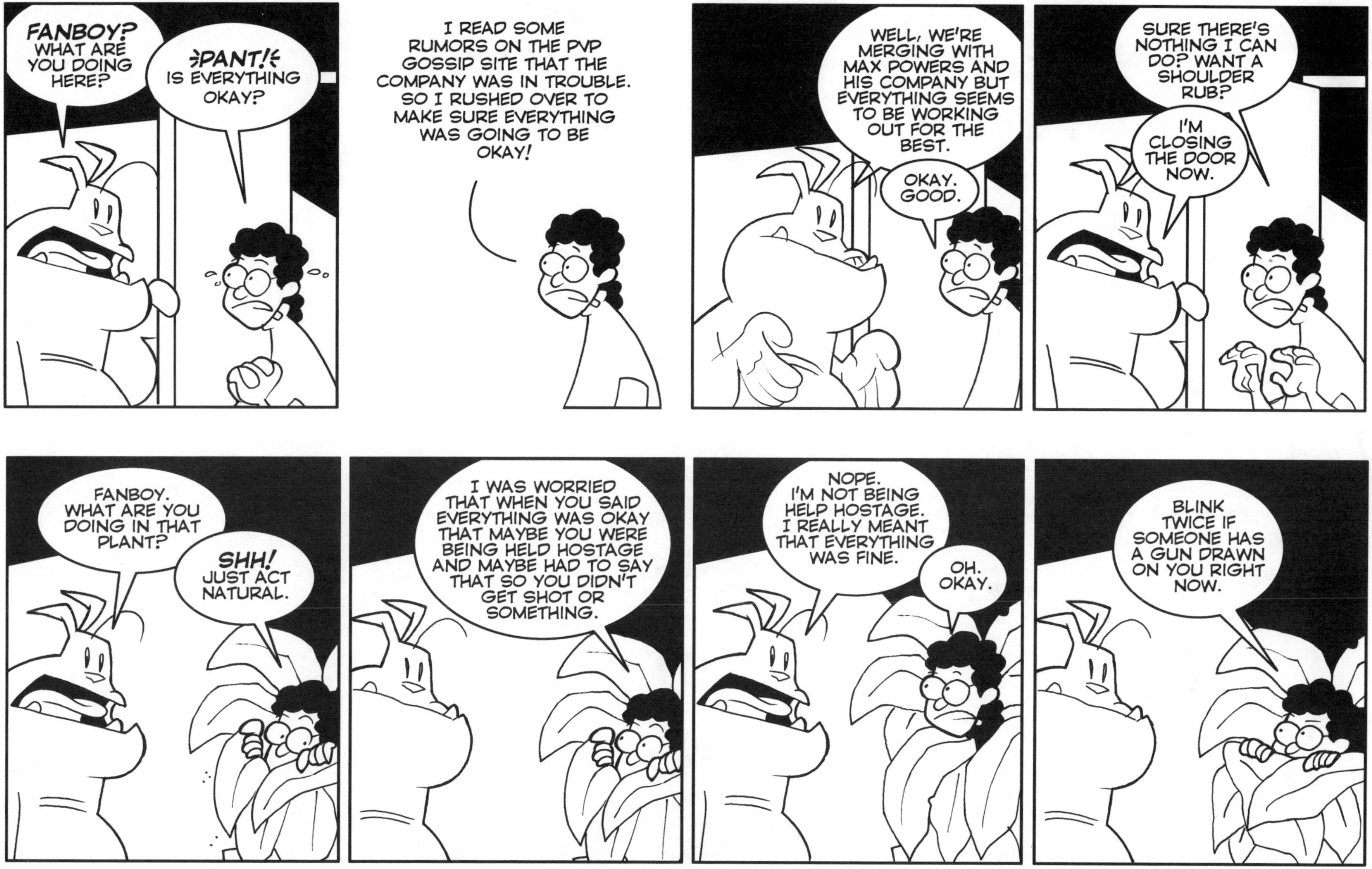
FANBOY? WHAT ARE YOU DOING HERE?
PANT! IS EVERYTHING OKAY?
I READ SOME RUMORS ON THE PVP GOSSIP SITE THAT THE COMPANY WAS IN TROUBLE. SO I RUSHED OVER TO MAKE SURE EVERYTHING WAS GOING TO BE OKAY!
WELL, WE'RE MERGING WITH MAX POWERS AND HIS COMPANY BUT EVERYTHING SEEMS TO BE WORKING OUT FOR THE BEST.
OKAY. GOOD.
SURE THERE'S NOTHING I CAN DO? WANT A SHOULDER RUB?
I'M CLOSING THE DOOR NOW.
FANBOY. WHAT ARE YOU DOING IN THAT PLANT?
SHH! JUST ACT NATURAL.
I WAS WORRIED THAT WHEN YOU SAID EVERYTHING WAS OKAY THAT MAYBE YOU WERE BEING HELD HOSTAGE AND MAYBE HAD TO SAY THAT SO YOU DIDN'T GET SHOT OR SOMETHING.
NOPE. I'M NOT BEING HELP HOSTAGE. I REALLY MEANT THAT EVERYTHING WAS FINE.
OH. OKAY.
BLINK TWICE IF SOMEONE HAS A GUN DRAWN ON YOU RIGHT NOW.

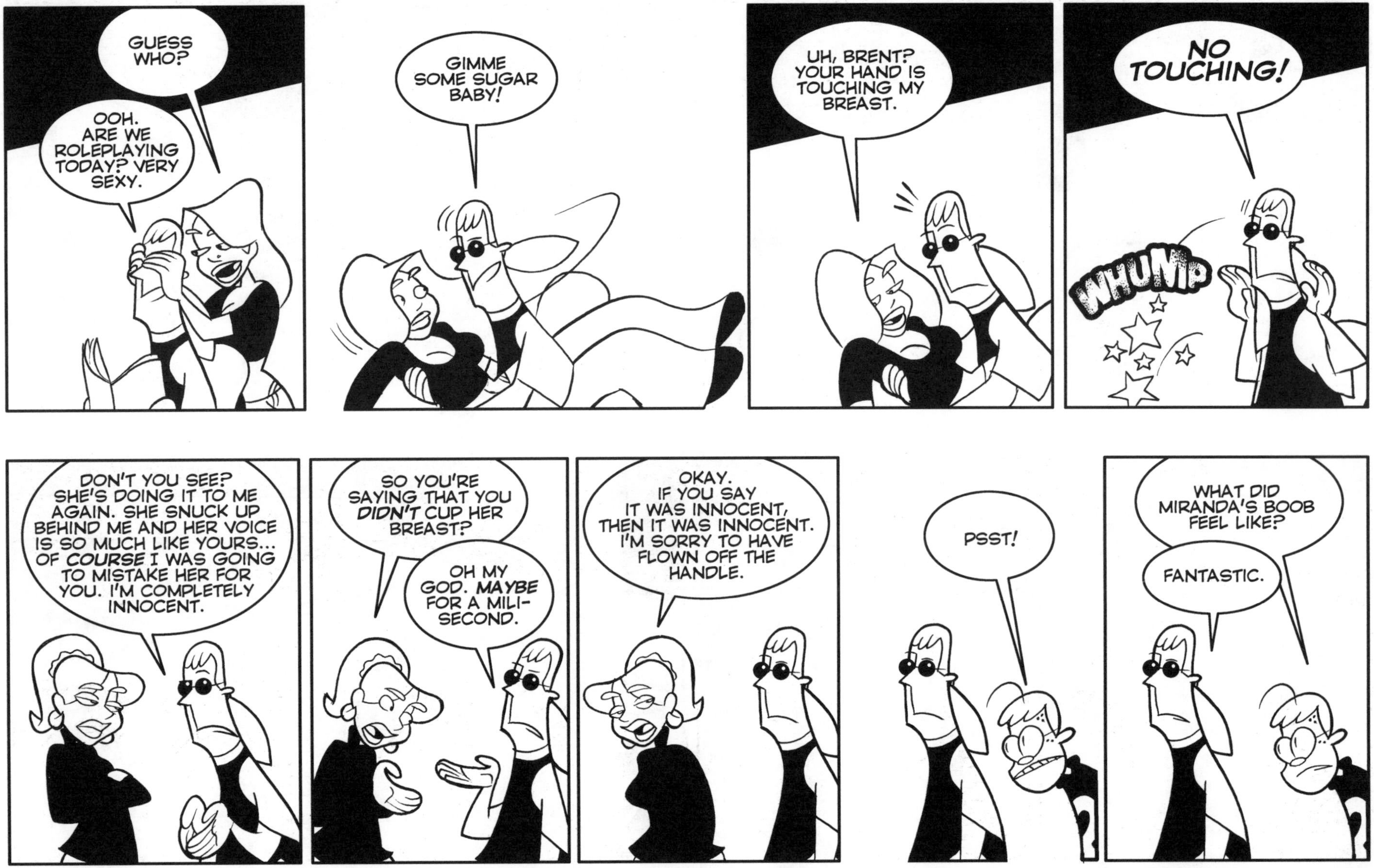
GUESS WHO?
OOH. ARE WE ROLEPLAYING TODAY? VERY SEXY.
GIMME SOME SUGAR BABY!
UH, BRENT? YOUR HAND IS TOUCHING MY BREAST.
NO TOUCHING!
WHUMP
DON'T YOU SEE? SHE'S DOING IT TO ME AGAIN. SHE SNUCK UP BEHIND ME AND HER VOICE IS SO MUCH LIKE YOURS... OF *COURSE* I WAS GOING TO MISTAKE HER FOR YOU. I'M COMPLETELY INNOCENT.
SO YOU'RE SAYING THAT YOU *DIDN'T* CUP HER BREAST?
OH MY GOD. *MAYBE* FOR A MILI-SECOND.
OKAY. IF YOU SAY IT WAS INNOCENT, THEN IT WAS INNOCENT. I'M SORRY TO HAVE FLOWN OFF THE HANDLE.
PSST!
WHAT DID MIRANDA'S BOOB FEEL LIKE?
FANTASTIC.

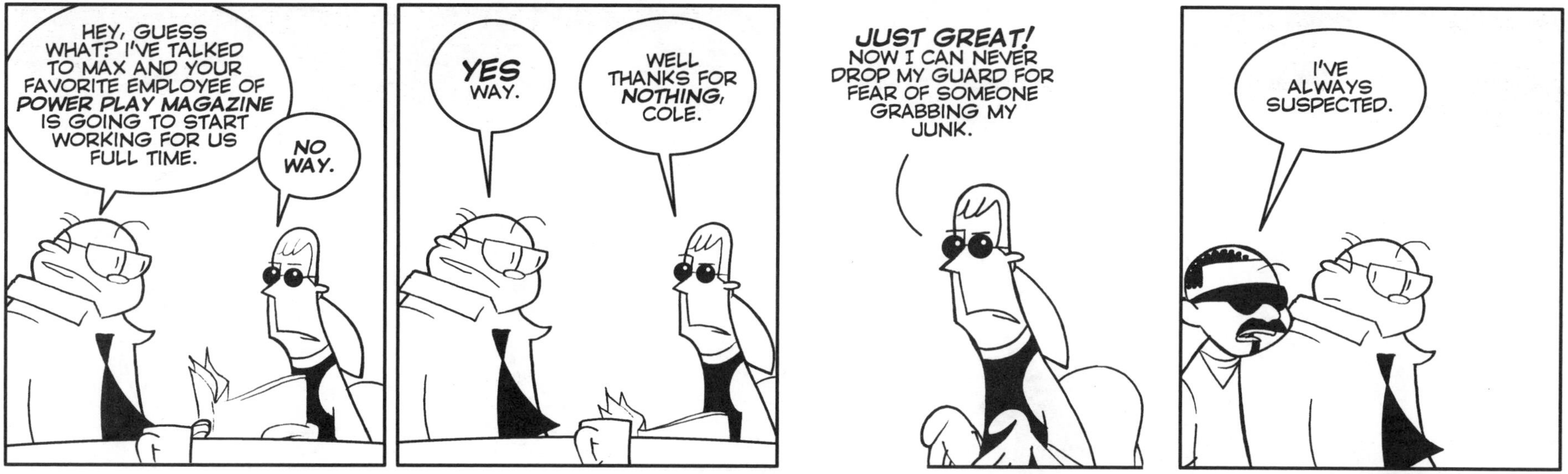

HEY, GUESS WHAT? I'VE TALKED TO MAX AND YOUR FAVORITE EMPLOYEE OF POWER PLAY MAGAZINE IS GOING TO START WORKING FOR US FULL TIME.
NO WAY.
YES WAY.
WELL THANKS FOR NOTHING, COLE.
JUST GREAT! NOW I CAN NEVER DROP MY GUARD FOR FEAR OF SOMEONE GRABBING MY JUNK.
I'VE ALWAYS SUSPECTED.

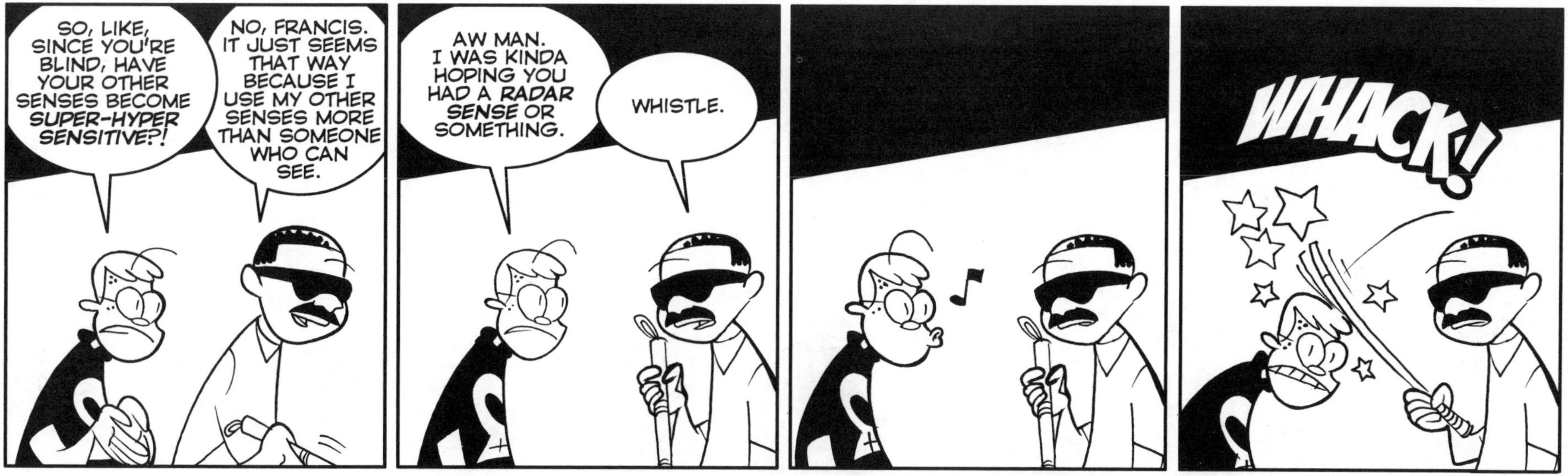

SO, LIKE, SINCE YOU'RE BLIND, HAVE YOUR OTHER SENSES BECOME SUPER-HYPER SENSITIVE?!
NO, FRANCIS. IT JUST SEEMS THAT WAY BECAUSE I USE MY OTHER SENSES MORE THAN SOMEONE WHO CAN SEE.
AW MAN. I WAS KINDA HOPING YOU HAD A RADAR SENSE OR SOMETHING.
WHISTLE.
WHACK!

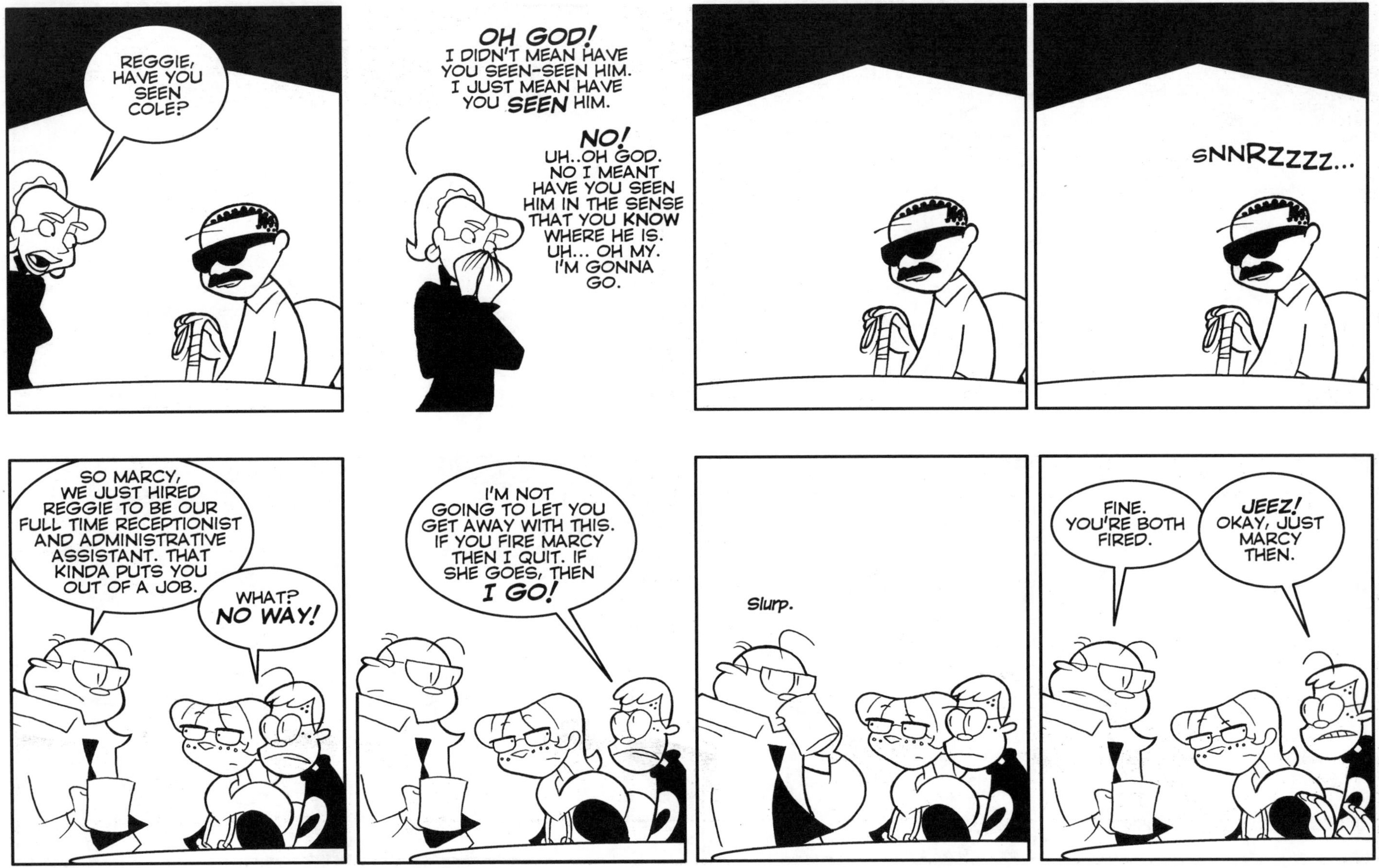
REGGIE, HAVE YOU SEEN COLE?
OH GOD! I DIDN'T MEAN HAVE YOU SEEN-SEEN HIM. I JUST MEAN HAVE YOU SEEN HIM.
NO! UH..OH GOD. NO I MEANT HAVE YOU SEEN HIM IN THE SENSE THAT YOU KNOW WHERE HE IS. UH... OH MY. I'M GONNA GO.
SNNRZZZZ...
SO MARCY, WE JUST HIRED REGGIE TO BE OUR FULL TIME RECEPTIONIST AND ADMINISTRATIVE ASSISTANT. THAT KINDA PUTS YOU OUT OF A JOB.
WHAT? NO WAY!
I'M NOT GOING TO LET YOU GET AWAY WITH THIS. IF YOU FIRE MARCY THEN I QUIT. IF SHE GOES, THEN I GO!
Slurp.
FINE. YOU'RE BOTH FIRED.
JEEZ! OKAY, JUST MARCY THEN.

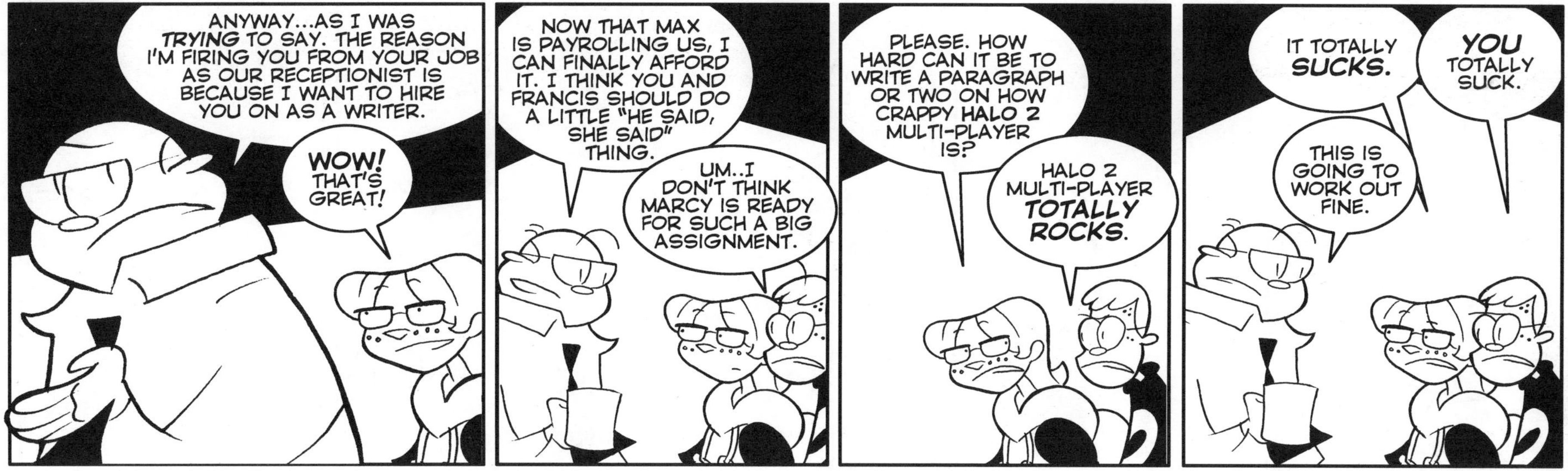
ANYWAY...AS I WAS TRYING TO SAY. THE REASON I'M FIRING YOU FROM YOUR JOB AS OUR RECEPTIONIST IS BECAUSE I WANT TO HIRE YOU ON AS A WRITER.
WOW! THAT'S GREAT!
NOW THAT MAX IS PAYROLLING US, I CAN FINALLY AFFORD IT. I THINK YOU AND FRANCIS SHOULD DO A LITTLE "HE SAID, SHE SAID" THING.
UM..I DON'T THINK MARCY IS READY FOR SUCH A BIG ASSIGNMENT.
PLEASE. HOW HARD CAN IT BE TO WRITE A PARAGRAPH OR TWO ON HOW CRAPPY HALO 2 MULTI-PLAYER IS?
HALO 2 MULTI-PLAYER TOTALLY ROCKS.
IT TOTALLY SUCKS.
YOU TOTALLY SUCK.
THIS IS GOING TO WORK OUT FINE.
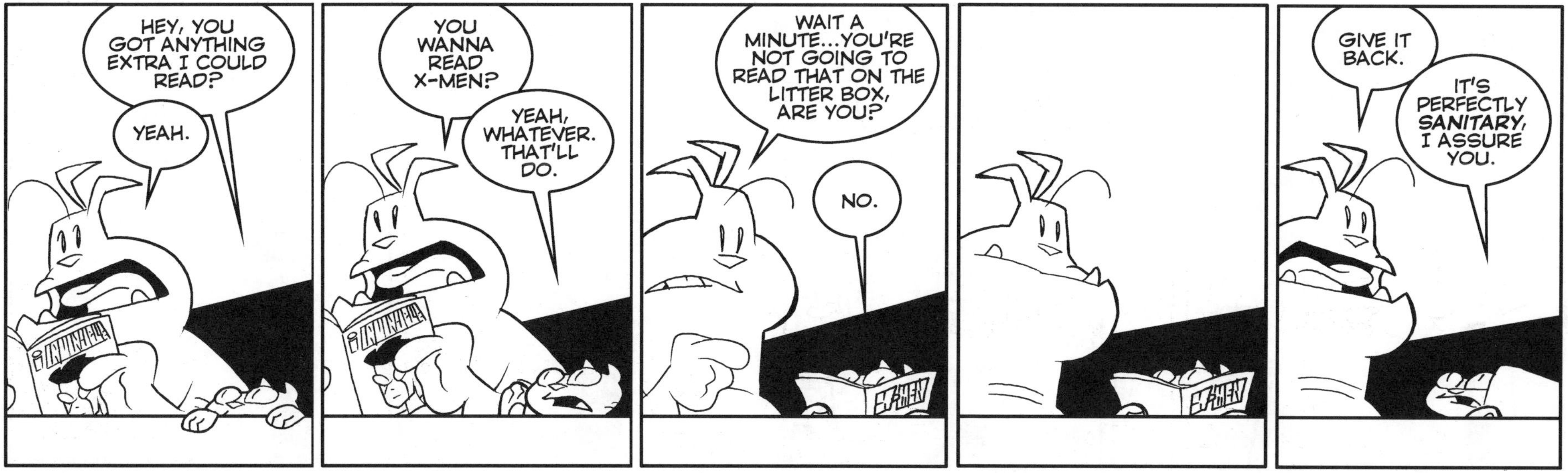
HEY, YOU GOT ANYTHING EXTRA I COULD READ?
YEAH.
YOU WANNA READ X-MEN?
YEAH, WHATEVER. THAT'LL DO.
WAIT A MINUTE...YOU'RE NOT GOING TO READ THAT ON THE LITTER BOX, ARE YOU?
NO.
GIVE IT BACK.
IT'S PERFECTLY SANITARY, I ASSURE YOU.

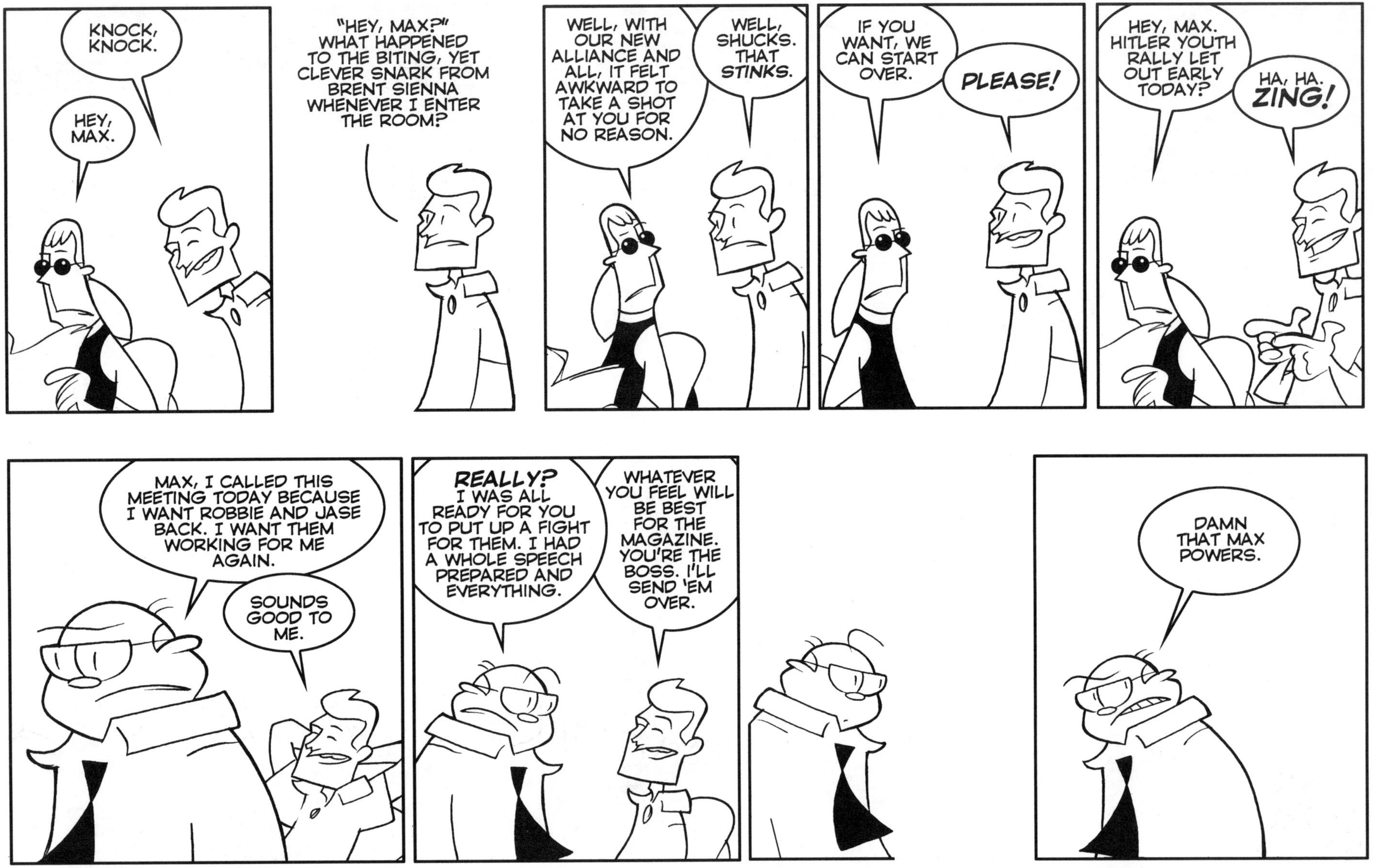
KNOCK, KNOCK.
HEY, MAX.
"HEY, MAX?" WHAT HAPPENED TO THE BITING, YET CLEVER SNARK FROM BRENT SIENNA WHENEVER I ENTER THE ROOM?
WELL, WITH OUR NEW ALLIANCE AND ALL, IT FELT AWKWARD TO TAKE A SHOT AT YOU FOR NO REASON.
WELL, SHUCKS. THAT *STINKS*.
IF YOU WANT, WE CAN START OVER.
PLEASE!
HEY, MAX. HITLER YOUTH RALLY LET OUT EARLY TODAY?
HA, HA. **ZING!**
MAX, I CALLED THIS MEETING TODAY BECAUSE I WANT ROBBIE AND JASE BACK. I WANT THEM WORKING FOR ME AGAIN.
SOUNDS GOOD TO ME.
REALLY? I WAS ALL READY FOR YOU TO PUT UP A FIGHT FOR THEM. I HAD A WHOLE SPEECH PREPARED AND EVERYTHING.
WHATEVER YOU FEEL WILL BE BEST FOR THE MAGAZINE. YOU'RE THE BOSS. I'LL SEND 'EM OVER.
DAMN THAT MAX POWERS.

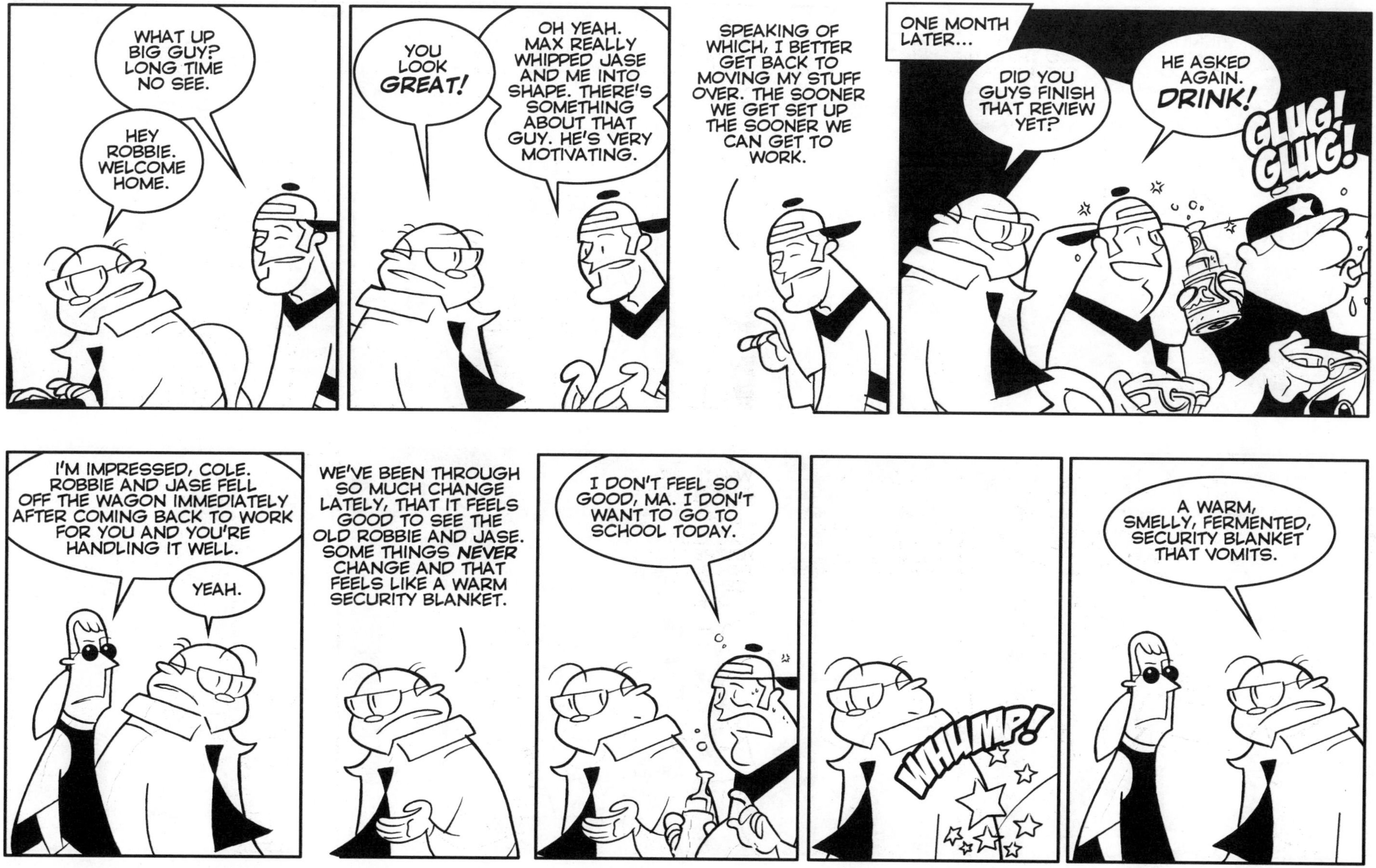
WHAT UP BIG GUY? LONG TIME NO SEE.
HEY ROBBIE. WELCOME HOME.
YOU LOOK GREAT!
OH YEAH. MAX REALLY WHIPPED JASE AND ME INTO SHAPE. THERE'S SOMETHING ABOUT THAT GUY. HE'S VERY MOTIVATING.
SPEAKING OF WHICH, I BETTER GET BACK TO MOVING MY STUFF OVER. THE SOONER WE GET SET UP THE SOONER WE CAN GET TO WORK.
ONE MONTH LATER...
DID YOU GUYS FINISH THAT REVIEW YET?
HE ASKED AGAIN. DRINK!
GLUG! GLUG!
I'M IMPRESSED, COLE. ROBBIE AND JASE FELL OFF THE WAGON IMMEDIATELY AFTER COMING BACK TO WORK FOR YOU AND YOU'RE HANDLING IT WELL.
YEAH.
WE'VE BEEN THROUGH SO MUCH CHANGE LATELY, THAT IT FEELS GOOD TO SEE THE OLD ROBBIE AND JASE. SOME THINGS NEVER CHANGE AND THAT FEELS LIKE A WARM SECURITY BLANKET.
I DON'T FEEL SO GOOD, MA. I DON'T WANT TO GO TO SCHOOL TODAY.
WHUMP!
A WARM, SMELLY, FERMENTED, SECURITY BLANKET THAT VOMITS.

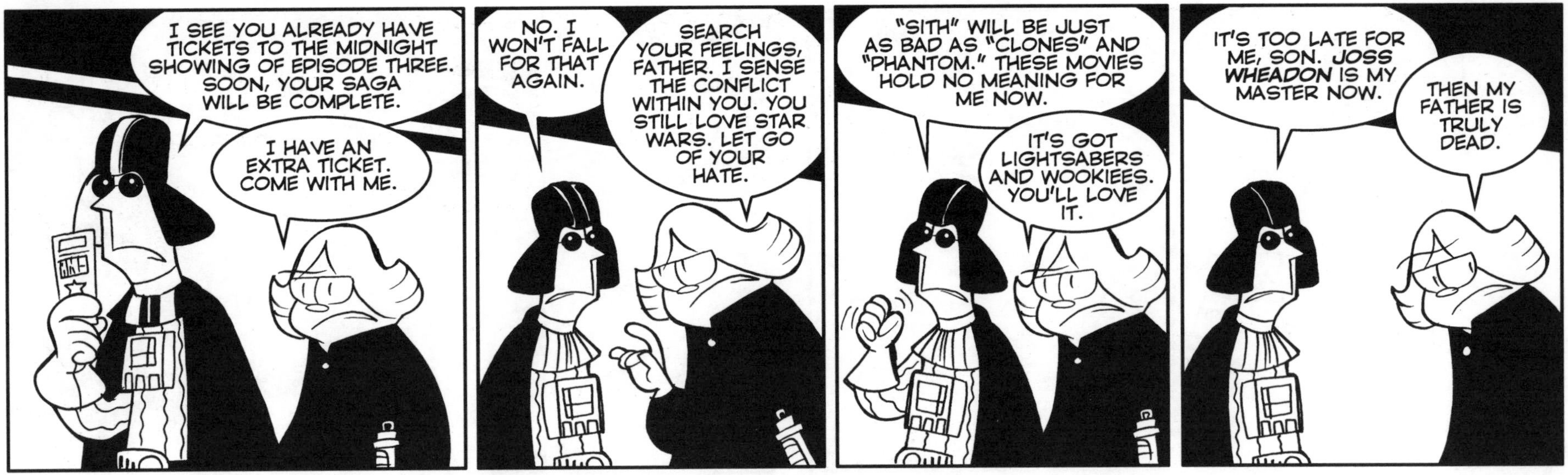
I SEE YOU ALREADY HAVE TICKETS TO THE MIDNIGHT SHOWING OF EPISODE THREE. SOON, YOUR SAGA WILL BE COMPLETE.
I HAVE AN EXTRA TICKET. COME WITH ME.
NO. I WON'T FALL FOR THAT AGAIN.
SEARCH YOUR FEELINGS, FATHER. I SENSE THE CONFLICT WITHIN YOU. YOU STILL LOVE STAR WARS. LET GO OF YOUR HATE.
"SITH" WILL BE JUST AS BAD AS "CLONES" AND "PHANTOM." THESE MOVIES HOLD NO MEANING FOR ME NOW.
IT'S GOT LIGHTSABERS AND WOOKIEES. YOU'LL LOVE IT.
IT'S TOO LATE FOR ME, SON. JOSS WHEADON IS MY MASTER NOW.
THEN MY FATHER IS TRULY DEAD.

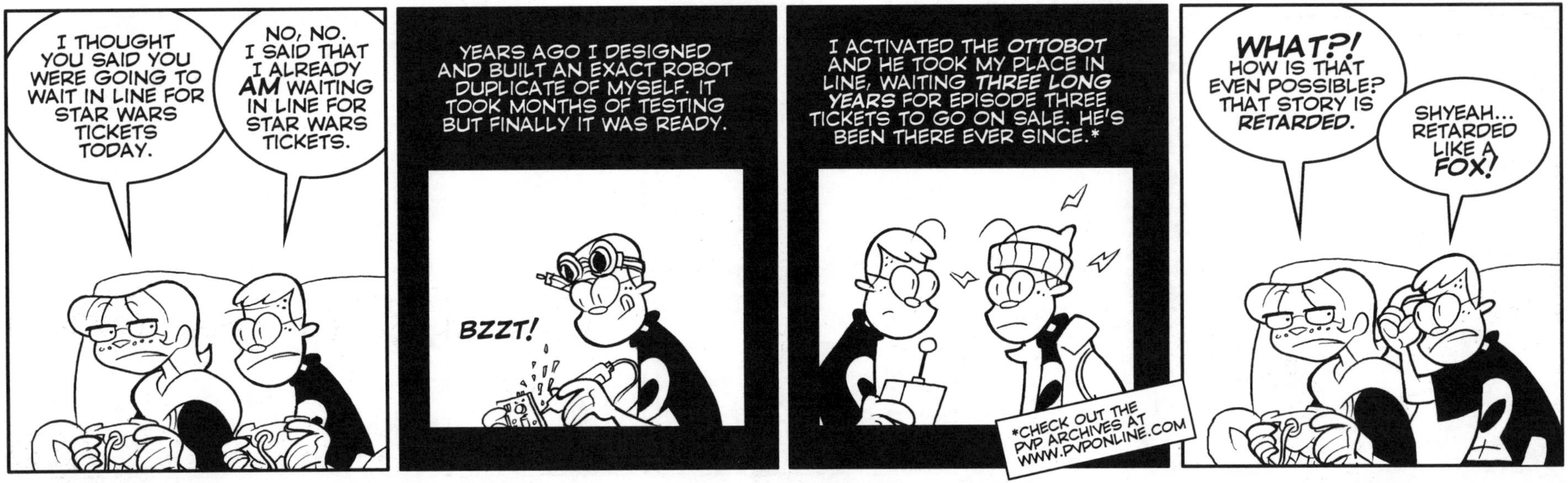
I THOUGHT YOU SAID YOU WERE GOING TO WAIT IN LINE FOR STAR WARS TICKETS TODAY.
NO, NO. I SAID THAT I ALREADY AM WAITING IN LINE FOR STAR WARS TICKETS.
YEARS AGO I DESIGNED AND BUILT AN EXACT ROBOT DUPLICATE OF MYSELF. IT TOOK MONTHS OF TESTING BUT FINALLY IT WAS READY.
BZZT!
I ACTIVATED THE OTTOBOT AND HE TOOK MY PLACE IN LINE, WAITING THREE LONG YEARS FOR EPISODE THREE TICKETS TO GO ON SALE. HE'S BEEN THERE EVER SINCE.*
*CHECK OUT THE PVP ARCHIVES AT WWW.PVPONLINE.COM
WHAT?! HOW IS THAT EVEN POSSIBLE? THAT STORY IS RETARDED.
SHYEAH... RETARDED LIKE A FOX!

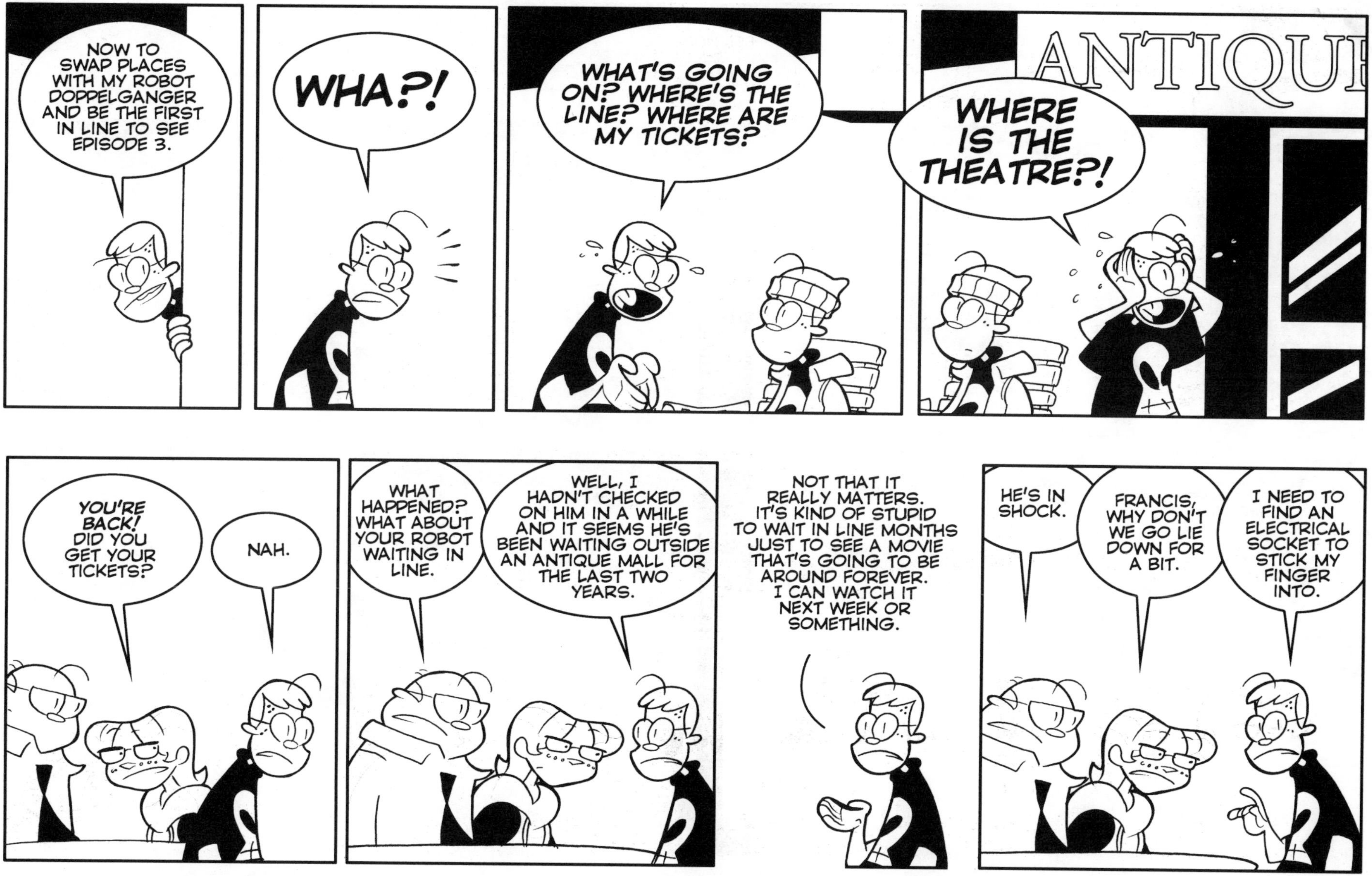
NOW TO SWAP PLACES WITH MY ROBOT DOPPELGANGER AND BE THE FIRST IN LINE TO SEE EPISODE 3.
WHA?!
WHAT'S GOING ON? WHERE'S THE LINE? WHERE ARE MY TICKETS?
WHERE IS THE THEATRE?!
ANTIQUE
YOU'RE BACK! DID YOU GET YOUR TICKETS?
NAH.
WHAT HAPPENED? WHAT ABOUT YOUR ROBOT WAITING IN LINE.
WELL, I HADN'T CHECKED ON HIM IN A WHILE AND IT SEEMS HE'S BEEN WAITING OUTSIDE AN ANTIQUE MALL FOR THE LAST TWO YEARS.
NOT THAT IT REALLY MATTERS. IT'S KIND OF STUPID TO WAIT IN LINE MONTHS JUST TO SEE A MOVIE THAT'S GOING TO BE AROUND FOREVER. I CAN WATCH IT NEXT WEEK OR SOMETHING.
HE'S IN SHOCK.
FRANCIS, WHY DON'T WE GO LIE DOWN FOR A BIT.
I NEED TO FIND AN ELECTRICAL SOCKET TO STICK MY FINGER INTO.

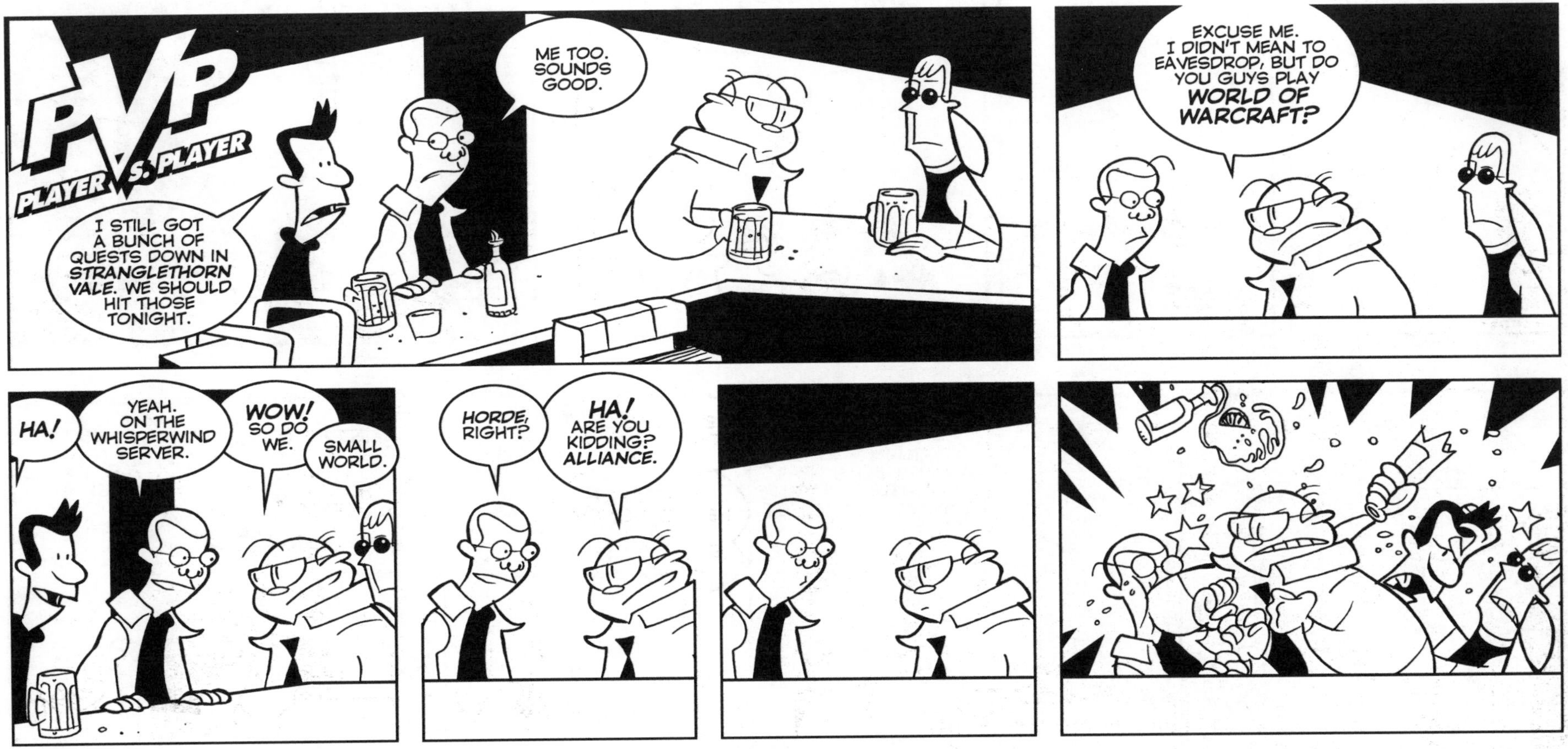
PVP
PLAYER VS. PLAYER
I STILL GOT A BUNCH OF QUESTS DOWN IN STRANGLETHORN VALE. WE SHOULD HIT THOSE TONIGHT.
ME TOO. SOUNDS GOOD.
EXCUSE ME. I DIDN'T MEAN TO EAVESDROP, BUT DO YOU GUYS PLAY WORLD OF WARCRAFT?
HA!
YEAH. ON THE WHISPERWIND SERVER.
WOW! SO DO WE.
SMALL WORLD.
HORDE, RIGHT?
HA! ARE YOU KIDDING? ALLIANCE.

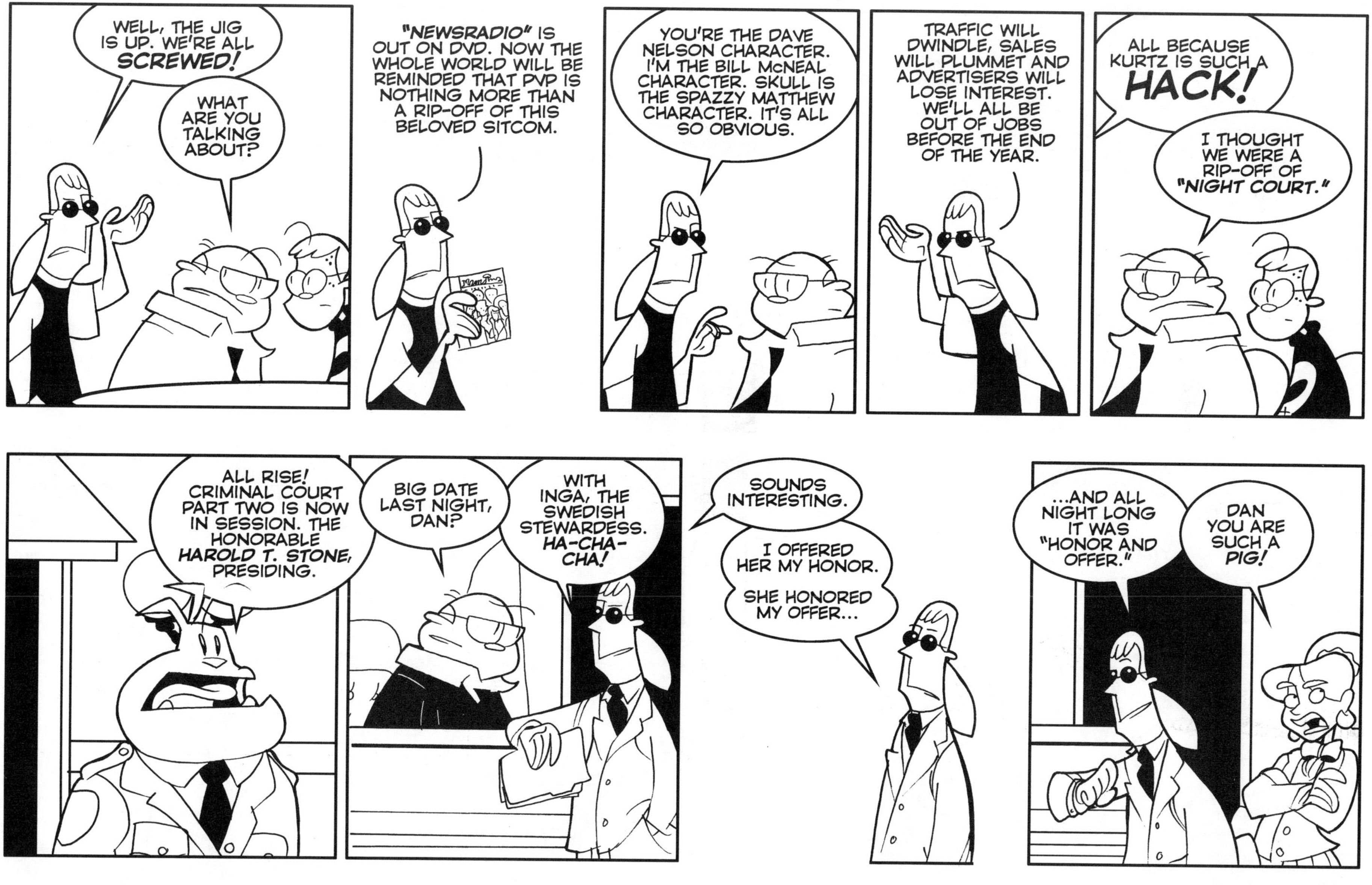
WELL, THE JIG IS UP. WE'RE ALL **SCREWED!**
WHAT ARE YOU TALKING ABOUT?
"**NEWSRADIO**" IS OUT ON DVD. NOW THE WHOLE WORLD WILL BE REMINDED THAT PVP IS NOTHING MORE THAN A RIP-OFF OF THIS BELOVED SITCOM.
YOU'RE THE DAVE NELSON CHARACTER. I'M THE BILL McNEAL CHARACTER. SKULL IS THE SPAZZY MATTHEW CHARACTER. IT'S ALL SO OBVIOUS.
TRAFFIC WILL DWINDLE, SALES WILL PLUMMET AND ADVERTISERS WILL LOSE INTEREST. WE'LL ALL BE OUT OF JOBS BEFORE THE END OF THE YEAR.
ALL BECAUSE KURTZ IS SUCH A **HACK!**
I THOUGHT WE WERE A RIP-OFF OF "**NIGHT COURT.**"
ALL RISE! CRIMINAL COURT PART TWO IS NOW IN SESSION. THE HONORABLE ***HAROLD T. STONE,*** PRESIDING.
BIG DATE LAST NIGHT, DAN?
WITH INGA, THE SWEDISH STEWARDESS. ***HA-CHA-CHA!***
SOUNDS INTERESTING.
I OFFERED HER MY HONOR.
SHE HONORED MY OFFER...
...AND ALL NIGHT LONG IT WAS "HONOR AND OFFER."
DAN YOU ARE SUCH A ***PIG!***

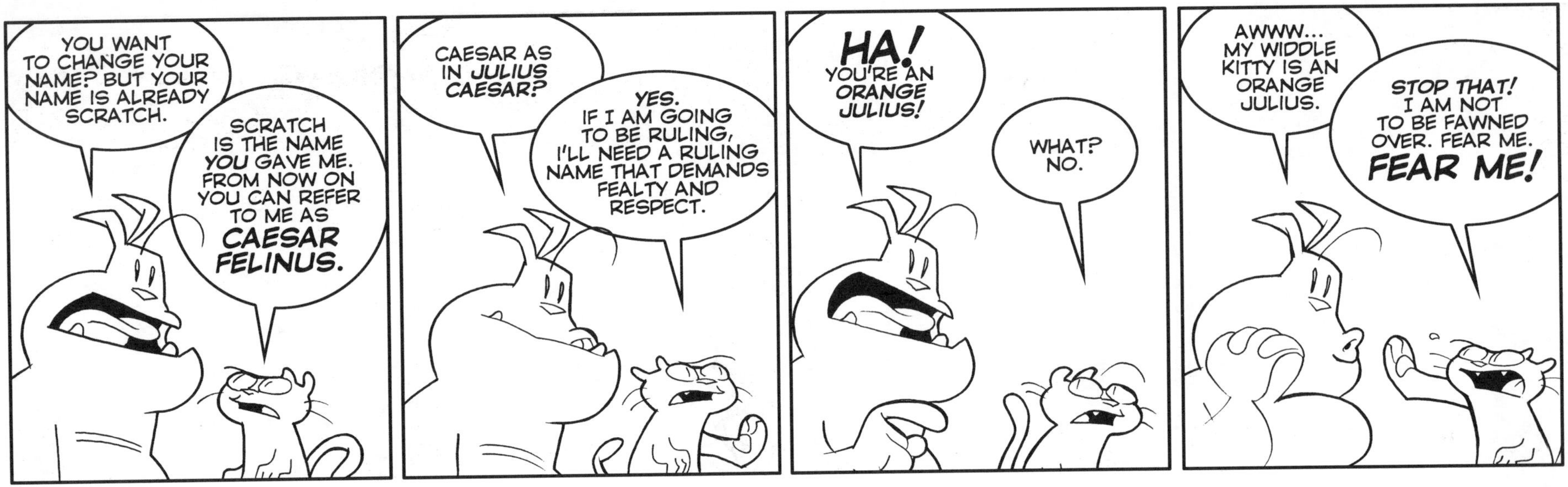
YOU WANT TO CHANGE YOUR NAME? BUT YOUR NAME IS ALREADY SCRATCH.
SCRATCH IS THE NAME YOU GAVE ME. FROM NOW ON YOU CAN REFER TO ME AS CAESAR FELINUS.
CAESAR AS IN JULIUS CAESAR?
YES. IF I AM GOING TO BE RULING, I'LL NEED A RULING NAME THAT DEMANDS FEALTY AND RESPECT.
HA! YOU'RE AN ORANGE JULIUS!
WHAT? NO.
AWWW... MY WIDDLE KITTY IS AN ORANGE JULIUS.
STOP THAT! I AM NOT TO BE FAWNED OVER. FEAR ME. FEAR ME!

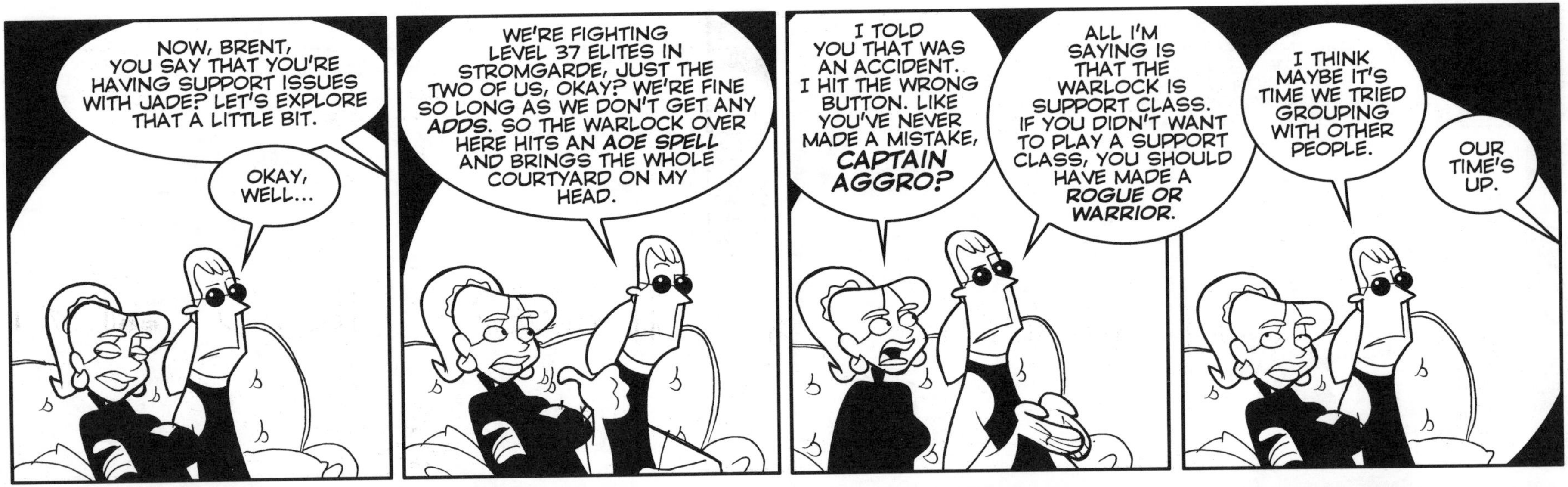
NOW, BRENT, YOU SAY THAT YOU'RE HAVING SUPPORT ISSUES WITH JADE? LET'S EXPLORE THAT A LITTLE BIT.
OKAY, WELL...
WE'RE FIGHTING LEVEL 37 ELITES IN STROMGARDE, JUST THE TWO OF US, OKAY? WE'RE FINE SO LONG AS WE DON'T GET ANY ADDS. SO THE WARLOCK OVER HERE HITS AN AOE SPELL AND BRINGS THE WHOLE COURTYARD ON MY HEAD.
I TOLD YOU THAT WAS AN ACCIDENT. I HIT THE WRONG BUTTON. LIKE YOU'VE NEVER MADE A MISTAKE, CAPTAIN AGGRO?
ALL I'M SAYING IS THAT THE WARLOCK IS SUPPORT CLASS. IF YOU DIDN'T WANT TO PLAY A SUPPORT CLASS, YOU SHOULD HAVE MADE A ROGUE OR WARRIOR.
I THINK MAYBE IT'S TIME WE TRIED GROUPING WITH OTHER PEOPLE.
OUR TIME'S UP.

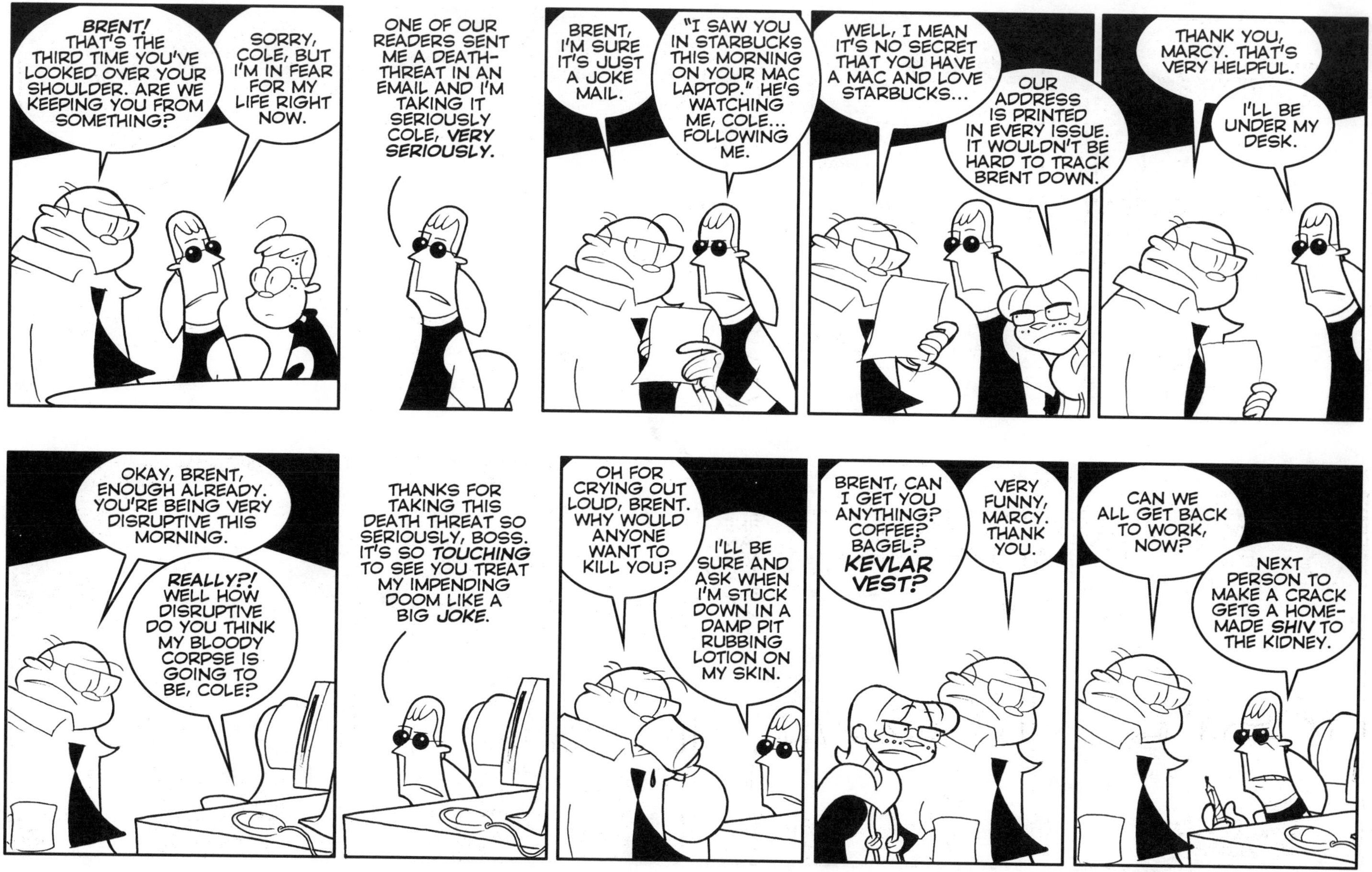
BRENT! THAT'S THE THIRD TIME YOU'VE LOOKED OVER YOUR SHOULDER. ARE WE KEEPING YOU FROM SOMETHING?
SORRY, COLE, BUT I'M IN FEAR FOR MY LIFE RIGHT NOW.
ONE OF OUR READERS SENT ME A DEATH-THREAT IN AN EMAIL AND I'M TAKING IT SERIOUSLY COLE, VERY SERIOUSLY.
BRENT, I'M SURE IT'S JUST A JOKE MAIL.
"I SAW YOU IN STARBUCKS THIS MORNING ON YOUR MAC LAPTOP." HE'S WATCHING ME, COLE... FOLLOWING ME.
WELL, I MEAN IT'S NO SECRET THAT YOU HAVE A MAC AND LOVE STARBUCKS...
OUR ADDRESS IS PRINTED IN EVERY ISSUE. IT WOULDN'T BE HARD TO TRACK BRENT DOWN.
THANK YOU, MARCY. THAT'S VERY HELPFUL.
I'LL BE UNDER MY DESK.
OKAY, BRENT, ENOUGH ALREADY. YOU'RE BEING VERY DISRUPTIVE THIS MORNING.
REALLY?! WELL HOW DISRUPTIVE DO YOU THINK MY BLOODY CORPSE IS GOING TO BE, COLE?
THANKS FOR TAKING THIS DEATH THREAT SO SERIOUSLY, BOSS. IT'S SO TOUCHING TO SEE YOU TREAT MY IMPENDING DOOM LIKE A BIG JOKE.
OH FOR CRYING OUT LOUD, BRENT. WHY WOULD ANYONE WANT TO KILL YOU?
I'LL BE SURE AND ASK WHEN I'M STUCK DOWN IN A DAMP PIT RUBBING LOTION ON MY SKIN.
BRENT, CAN I GET YOU ANYTHING? COFFEE? BAGEL? KEVLAR VEST?
VERY FUNNY, MARCY. THANK YOU.
CAN WE ALL GET BACK TO WORK, NOW?
NEXT PERSON TO MAKE A CRACK GETS A HOME-MADE SHIV TO THE KIDNEY.

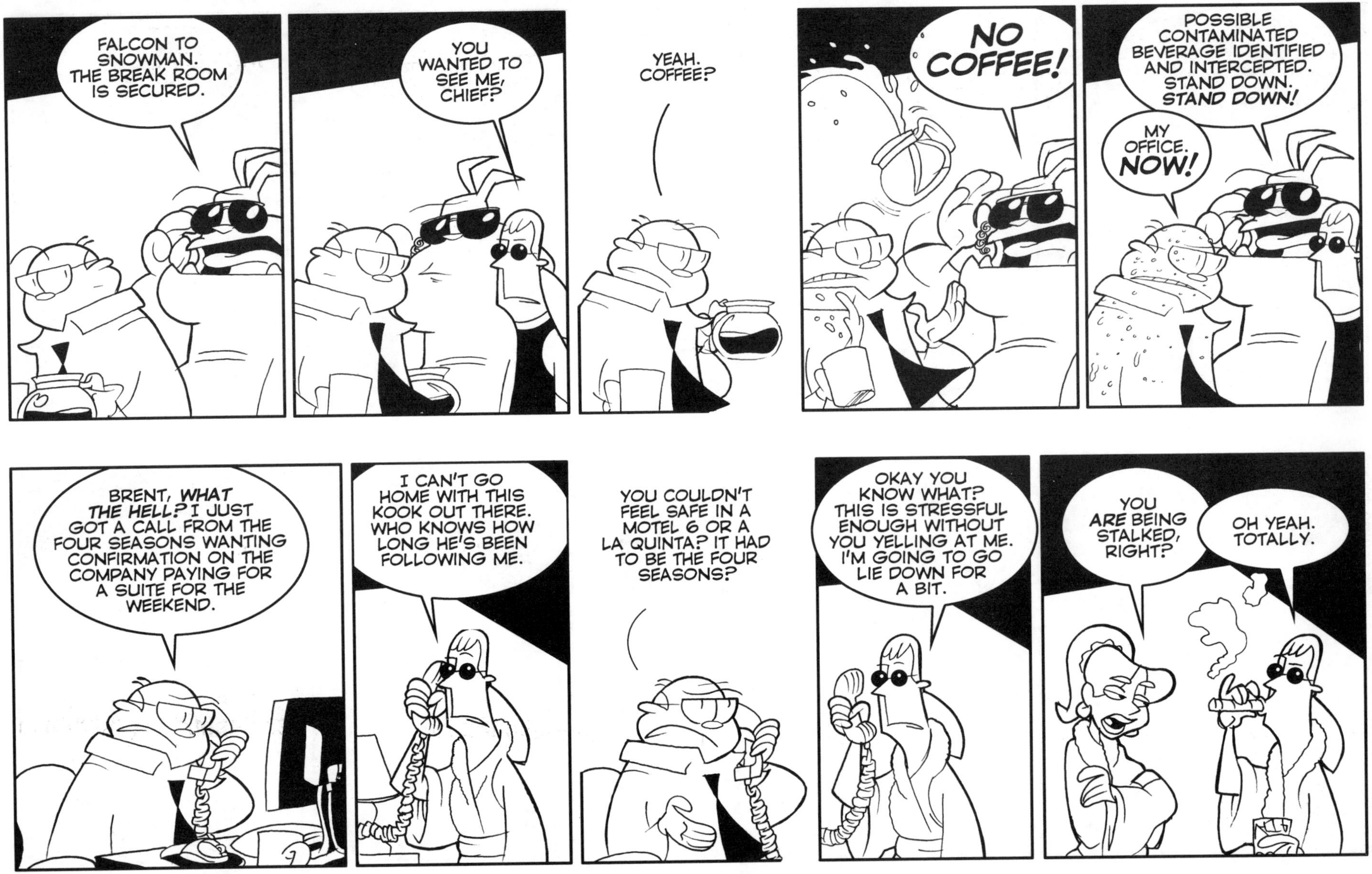

FALCON TO SNOWMAN. THE BREAK ROOM IS SECURED.
YOU WANTED TO SEE ME, CHIEF?
YEAH. COFFEE?
NO COFFEE!
POSSIBLE CONTAMINATED BEVERAGE IDENTIFIED AND INTERCEPTED. STAND DOWN. STAND DOWN!
MY OFFICE. NOW!
BRENT, WHAT THE HELL? I JUST GOT A CALL FROM THE FOUR SEASONS WANTING CONFIRMATION ON THE COMPANY PAYING FOR A SUITE FOR THE WEEKEND.
I CAN'T GO HOME WITH THIS KOOK OUT THERE. WHO KNOWS HOW LONG HE'S BEEN FOLLOWING ME.
YOU COULDN'T FEEL SAFE IN A MOTEL 6 OR A LA QUINTA? IT HAD TO BE THE FOUR SEASONS?
OKAY YOU KNOW WHAT? THIS IS STRESSFUL ENOUGH WITHOUT YOU YELLING AT ME. I'M GOING TO GO LIE DOWN FOR A BIT.
YOU ARE BEING STALKED, RIGHT?
OH YEAH. TOTALLY.

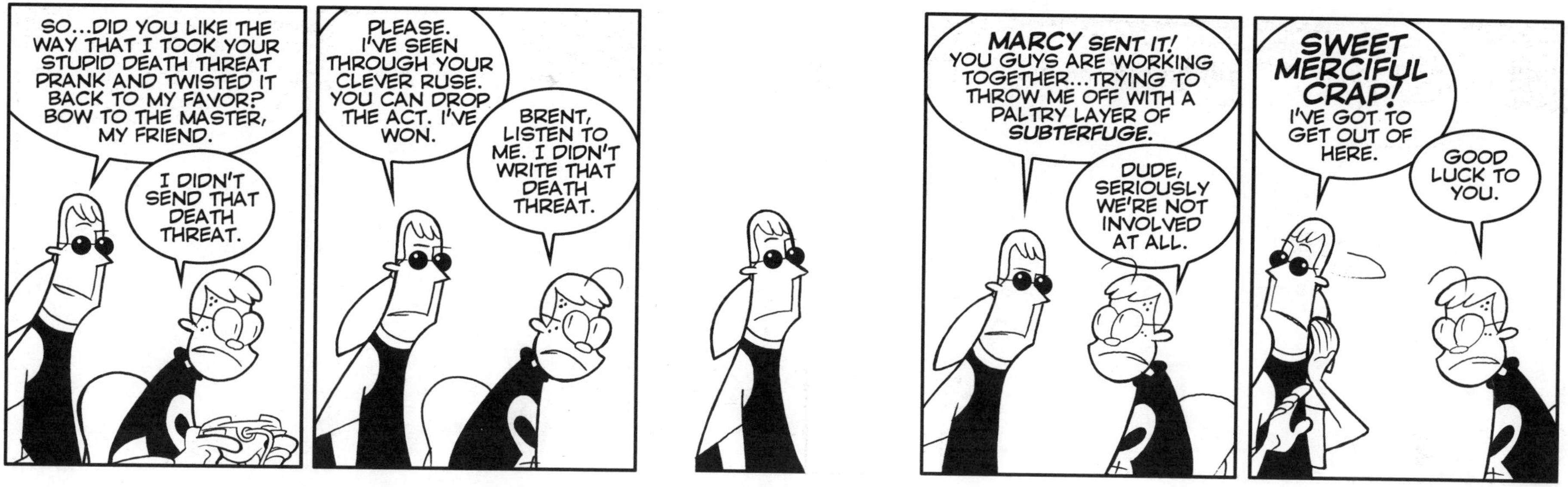
SO...DID YOU LIKE THE WAY THAT I TOOK YOUR STUPID DEATH THREAT PRANK AND TWISTED IT BACK TO MY FAVOR? BOW TO THE MASTER, MY FRIEND.
I DIDN'T SEND THAT DEATH THREAT.
PLEASE. I'VE SEEN THROUGH YOUR CLEVER RUSE. YOU CAN DROP THE ACT. I'VE WON.
BRENT, LISTEN TO ME. I DIDN'T WRITE THAT DEATH THREAT.
MARCY SENT IT! YOU GUYS ARE WORKING TOGETHER...TRYING TO THROW ME OFF WITH A PALTRY LAYER OF SUBTERFUGE.
DUDE, SERIOUSLY WE'RE NOT INVOLVED AT ALL.
SWEET MERCIFUL CRAP! I'VE GOT TO GET OUT OF HERE.
GOOD LUCK TO YOU.

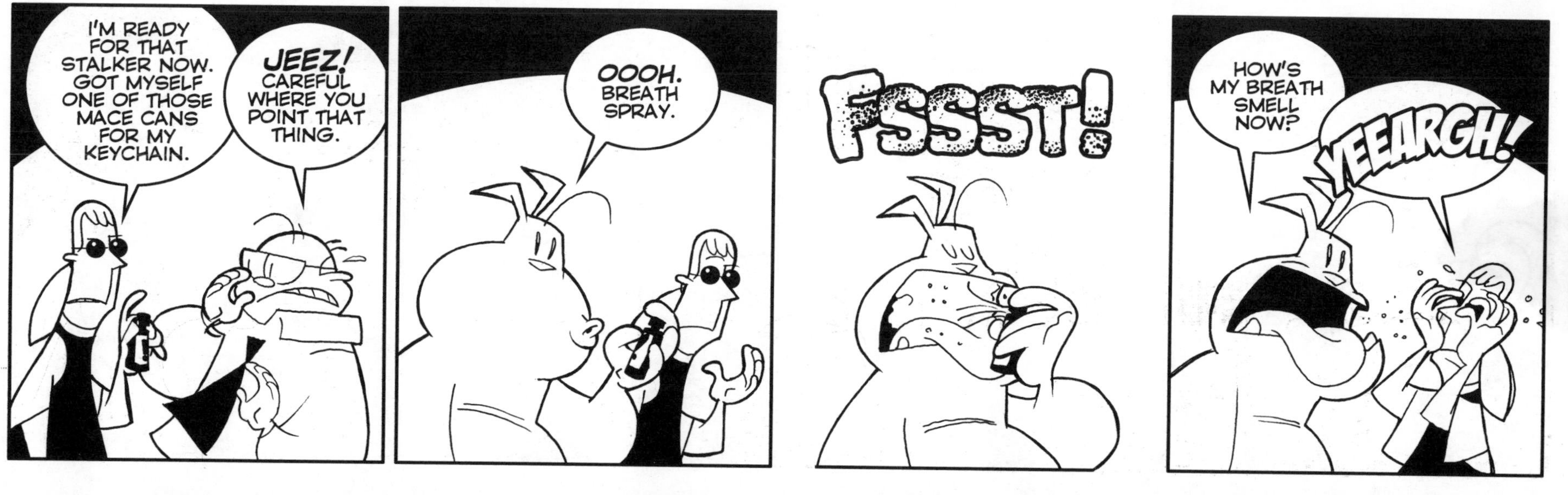
I'M READY FOR THAT STALKER NOW. GOT MYSELF ONE OF THOSE MACE CANS FOR MY KEYCHAIN.
JEEZ! CAREFUL WHERE YOU POINT THAT THING.
OOOH. BREATH SPRAY.
FSSST!
HOW'S MY BREATH SMELL NOW?
YEEARGH!

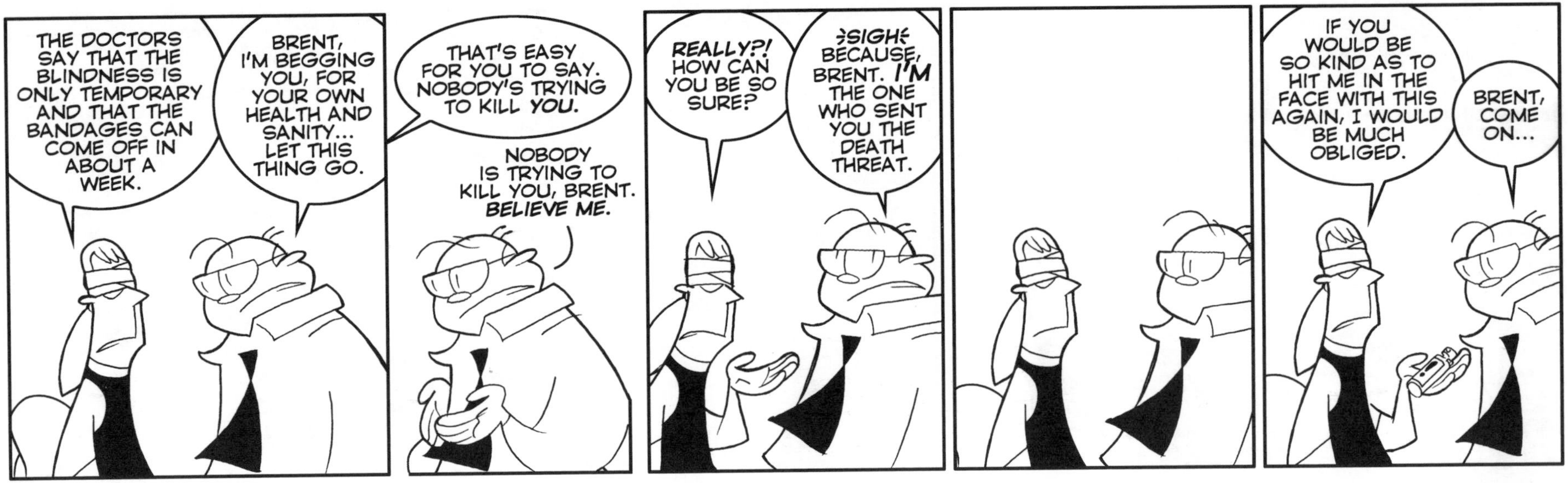
THE DOCTORS SAY THAT THE BLINDNESS IS ONLY TEMPORARY AND THAT THE BANDAGES CAN COME OFF IN ABOUT A WEEK.
BRENT, I'M BEGGING YOU, FOR YOUR OWN HEALTH AND SANITY... LET THIS THING GO.
THAT'S EASY FOR YOU TO SAY. NOBODY'S TRYING TO KILL YOU.
NOBODY IS TRYING TO KILL YOU, BRENT. BELIEVE ME.
REALLY?! HOW CAN YOU BE SO SURE?
SIGH BECAUSE, BRENT. I'M THE ONE WHO SENT YOU THE DEATH THREAT.
IF YOU WOULD BE SO KIND AS TO HIT ME IN THE FACE WITH THIS AGAIN, I WOULD BE MUCH OBLIGED.
BRENT, COME ON...

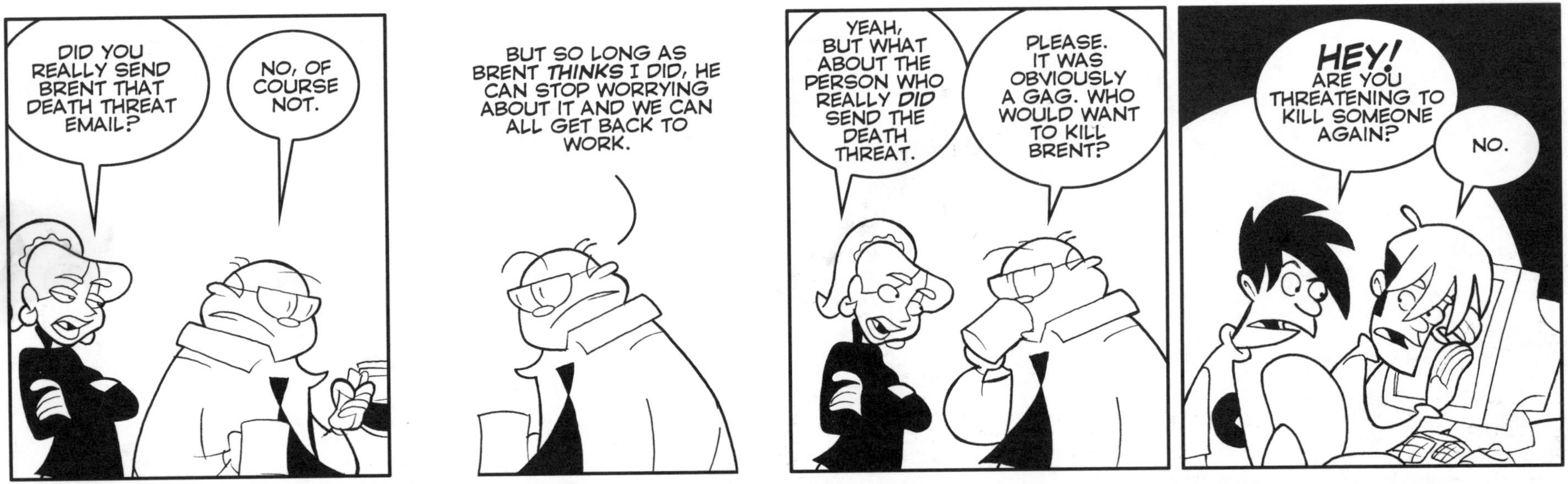
DID YOU REALLY SEND BRENT THAT DEATH THREAT EMAIL?
NO, OF COURSE NOT.
BUT SO LONG AS BRENT THINKS I DID, HE CAN STOP WORRYING ABOUT IT AND WE CAN ALL GET BACK TO WORK.
YEAH, BUT WHAT ABOUT THE PERSON WHO REALLY DID SEND THE DEATH THREAT.
PLEASE. IT WAS OBVIOUSLY A GAG. WHO WOULD WANT TO KILL BRENT?
HEY! ARE YOU THREATENING TO KILL SOMEONE AGAIN?
NO.

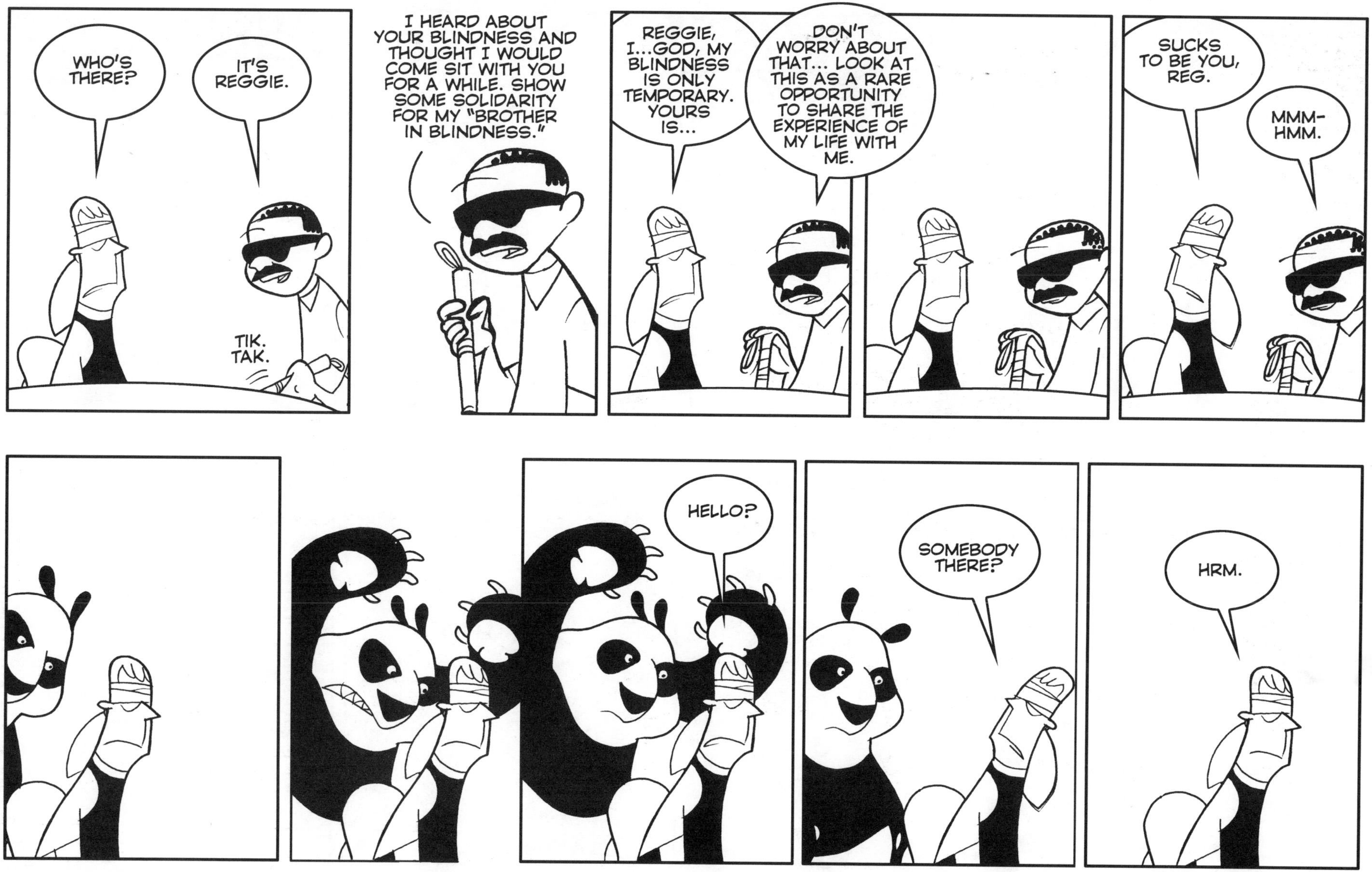
WHO'S THERE?
IT'S REGGIE.
TIK. TAK.
I HEARD ABOUT YOUR BLINDNESS AND THOUGHT I WOULD COME SIT WITH YOU FOR A WHILE. SHOW SOME SOLIDARITY FOR MY "BROTHER IN BLINDNESS."
REGGIE, I...GOD, MY BLINDNESS IS ONLY TEMPORARY. YOURS IS...
DON'T WORRY ABOUT THAT... LOOK AT THIS AS A RARE OPPORTUNITY TO SHARE THE EXPERIENCE OF MY LIFE WITH ME.
SUCKS TO BE YOU, REG.
MMM-HMM.
HELLO?
SOMEBODY THERE?
HRM.

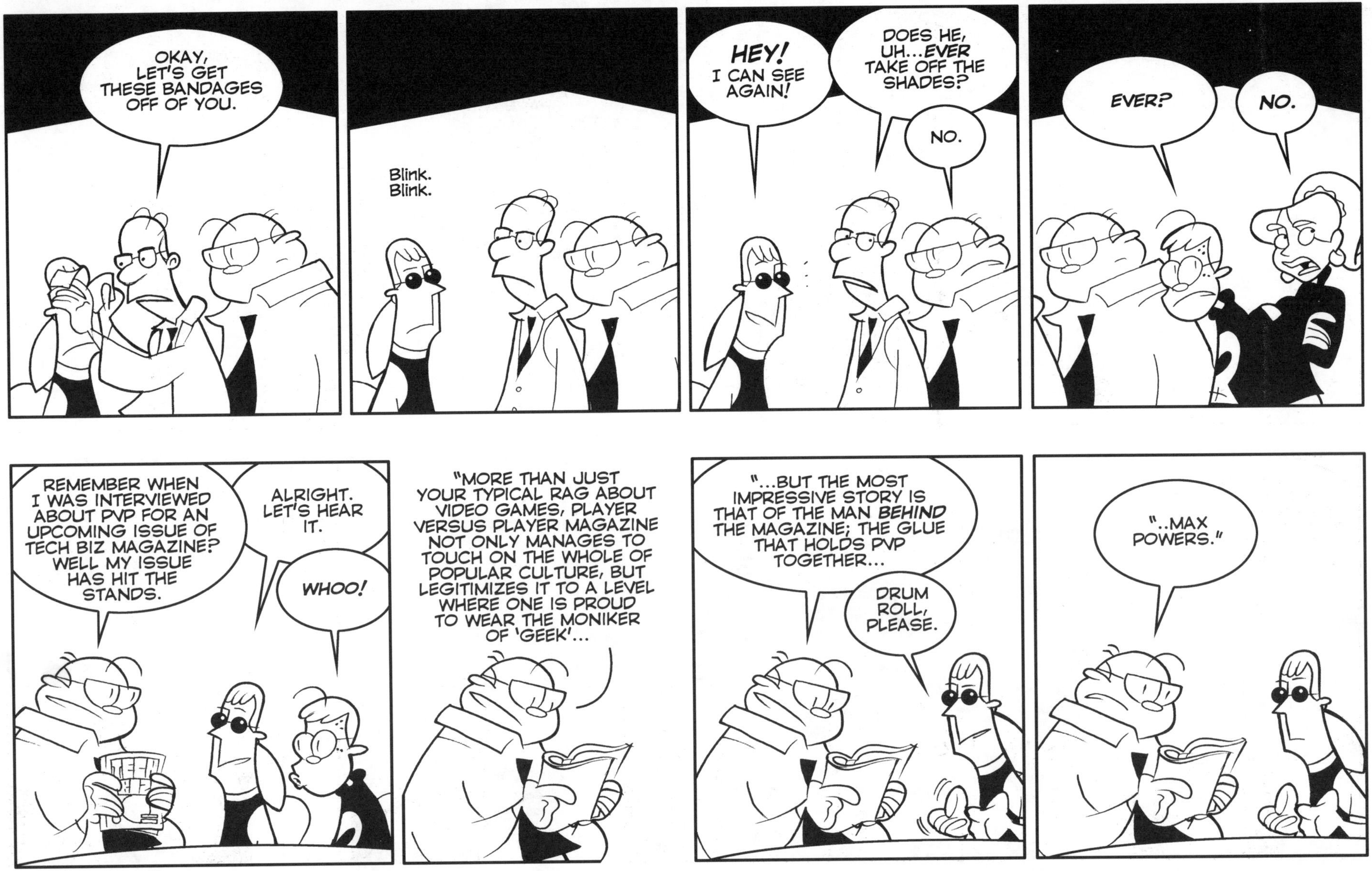
OKAY, LET'S GET THESE BANDAGES OFF OF YOU.
Blink. Blink.
HEY! I CAN SEE AGAIN!
DOES HE, UH...EVER TAKE OFF THE SHADES?
NO.
EVER?
NO.
REMEMBER WHEN I WAS INTERVIEWED ABOUT PVP FOR AN UPCOMING ISSUE OF TECH BIZ MAGAZINE? WELL MY ISSUE HAS HIT THE STANDS.
ALRIGHT. LET'S HEAR IT.
WHOO!
"MORE THAN JUST YOUR TYPICAL RAG ABOUT VIDEO GAMES, PLAYER VERSUS PLAYER MAGAZINE NOT ONLY MANAGES TO TOUCH ON THE WHOLE OF POPULAR CULTURE, BUT LEGITIMIZES IT TO A LEVEL WHERE ONE IS PROUD TO WEAR THE MONIKER OF 'GEEK'...
"...BUT THE MOST IMPRESSIVE STORY IS THAT OF THE MAN BEHIND THE MAGAZINE; THE GLUE THAT HOLDS PVP TOGETHER...
DRUM ROLL, PLEASE.
"..MAX POWERS."

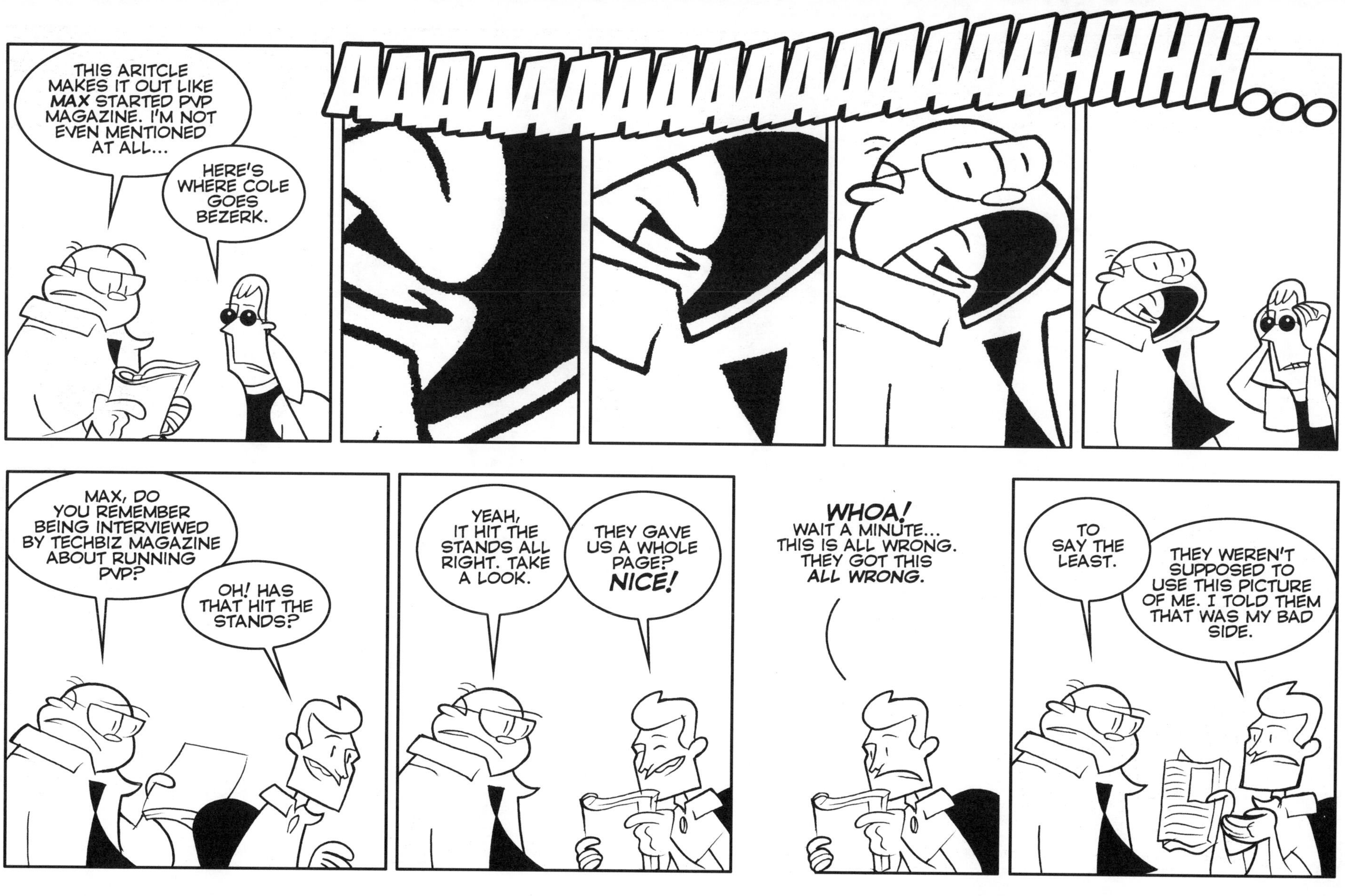

THIS ARITCLE MAKES IT OUT LIKE **MAX** STARTED PVP MAGAZINE. I'M NOT EVEN MENTIONED AT ALL...
HERE'S WHERE COLE GOES BEZERK.
AAAAAAAAAAAAAAAAAHHHH...
MAX, DO YOU REMEMBER BEING INTERVIEWED BY TECHBIZ MAGAZINE ABOUT RUNNING PVP?
OH! HAS THAT HIT THE STANDS?
YEAH, IT HIT THE STANDS ALL RIGHT. TAKE A LOOK.
THEY GAVE US A WHOLE PAGE? ***NICE!***
WHOA! WAIT A MINUTE... THIS IS ALL WRONG. THEY GOT THIS ***ALL WRONG***.
TO SAY THE LEAST.
THEY WEREN'T SUPPOSED TO USE THIS PICTURE OF ME. I TOLD THEM THAT WAS MY BAD SIDE.

COVER GALLERY

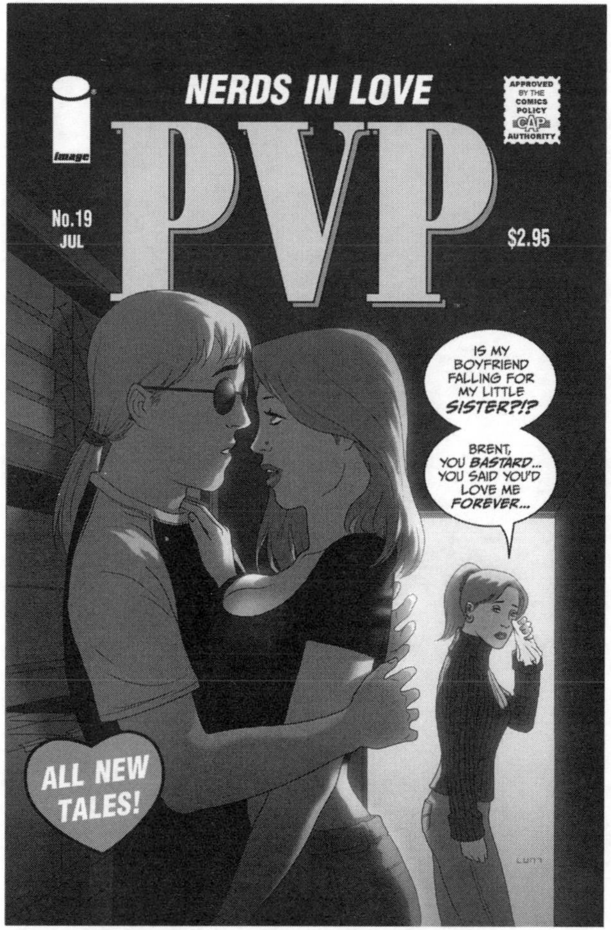
NERDS IN LOVE
APPROVED BY THE COMICS POLICY CAP AUTHORITY
PVP
No.19
JUL
$2.95
IS MY BOYFRIEND FALLING FOR MY LITTLE SISTER?!?
BRENT, YOU BASTARD... YOU SAID YOU'D LOVE ME FOREVER...
ALL NEW TALES!

PvP 19 cover by the Luna Bros.

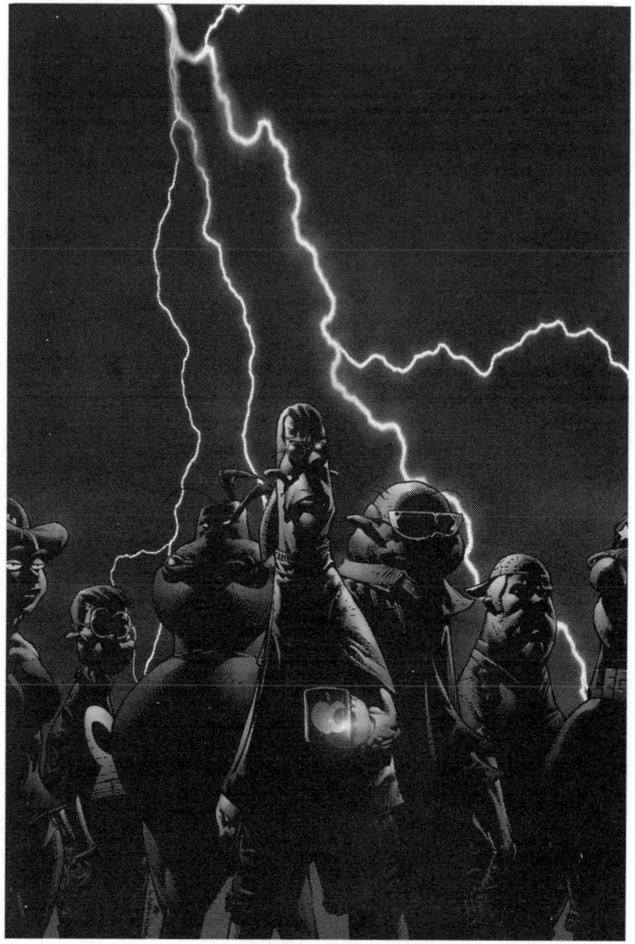

PvP 20 cover by David Finch.

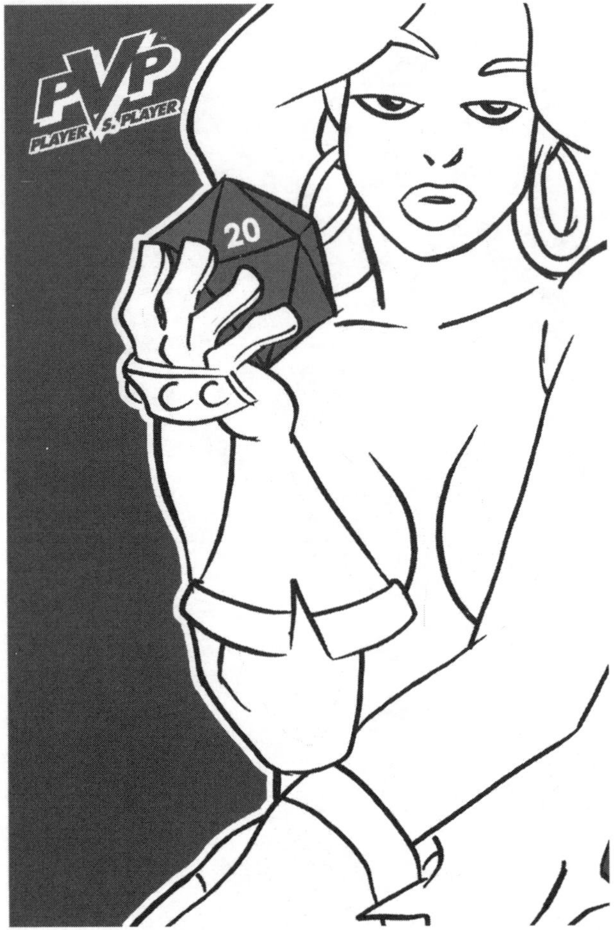
PVP
PLAYER VS. PLAYER
20

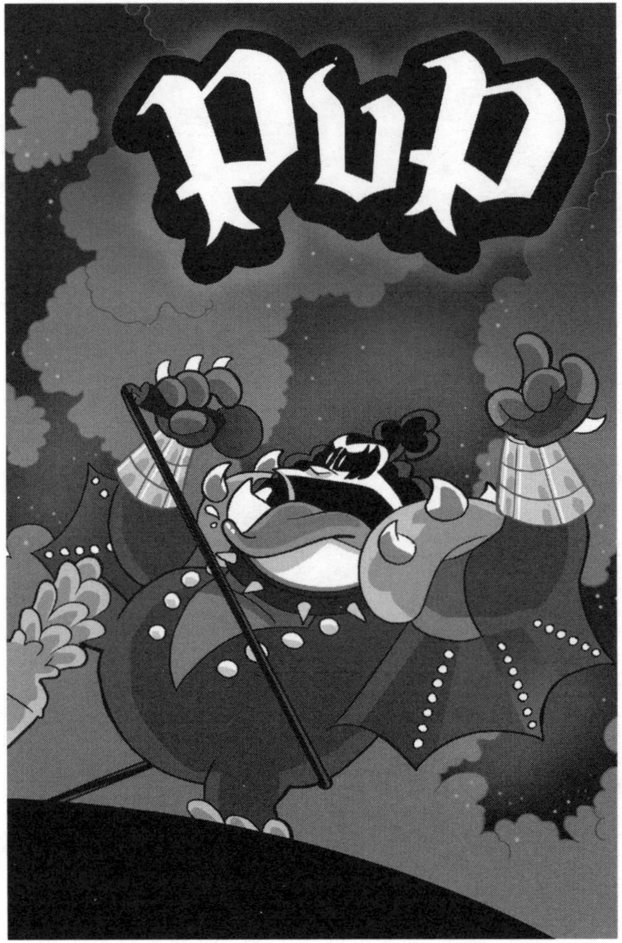
PvP

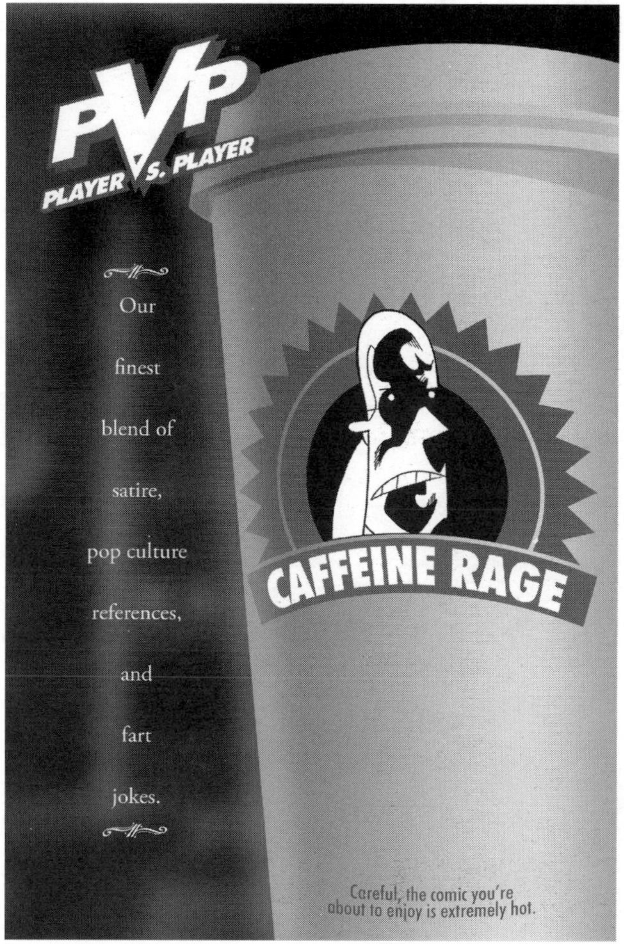
PVP
PLAYER VS. PLAYER
Our finest blend of satire, pop culture references, and fart jokes.
CAFFEINE RAGE
Careful, the comic you're about to enjoy is extremely hot.

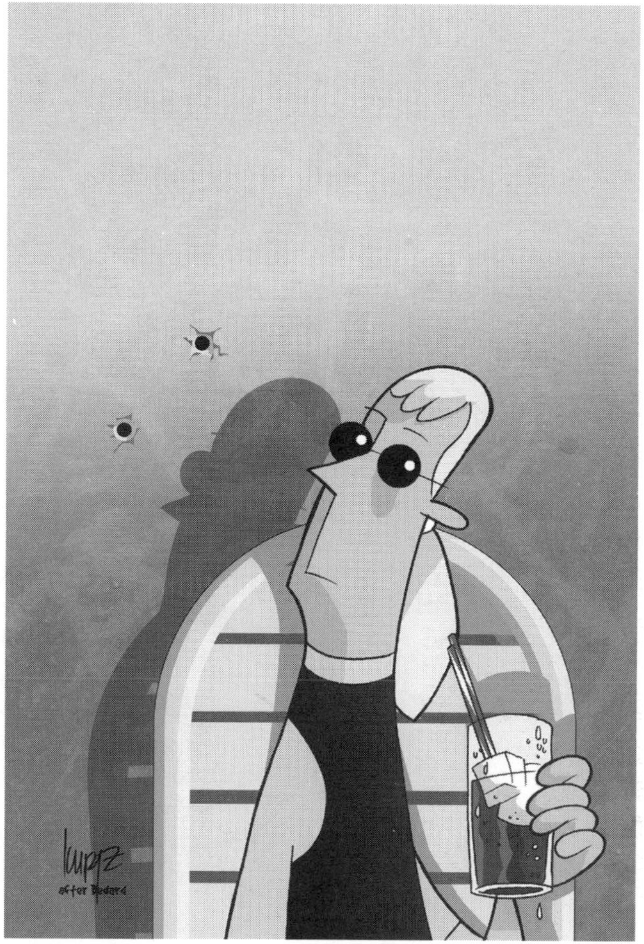

· SKETCH COVER ·

David Finch provided a sketch-variant cover for PvP 20.

·UNUSED COVER·

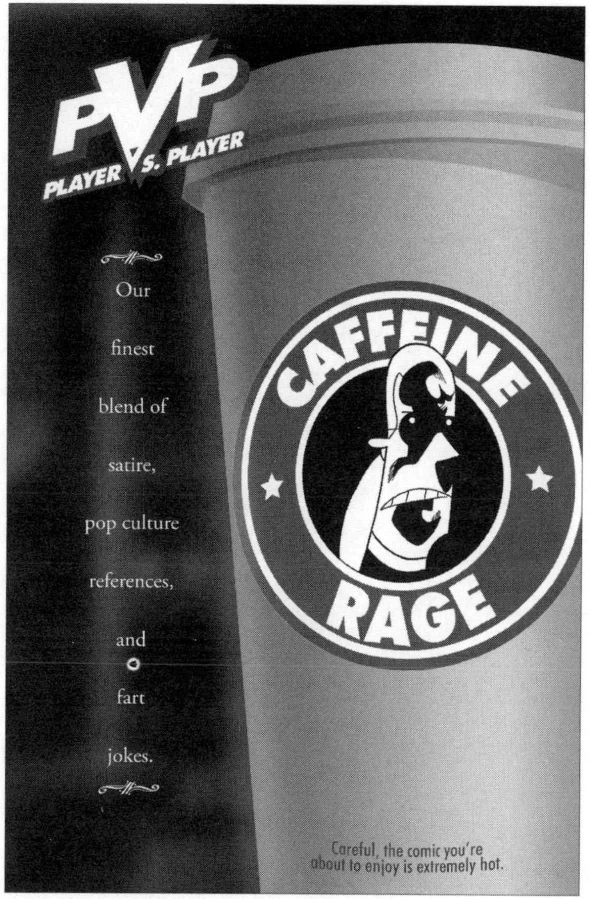
PVP
PLAYER VS. PLAYER
Our
finest
blend of
satire,
pop culture
references,
and
fart
jokes.
CAFFEINE
RAGE
Careful, the comic you're
about to enjoy is extremely hot.

The logo on the original cover looked too much like the Starbucks logo and I feared I would be visited by the trademark police. So I changed it.

·UNUSED COVER·

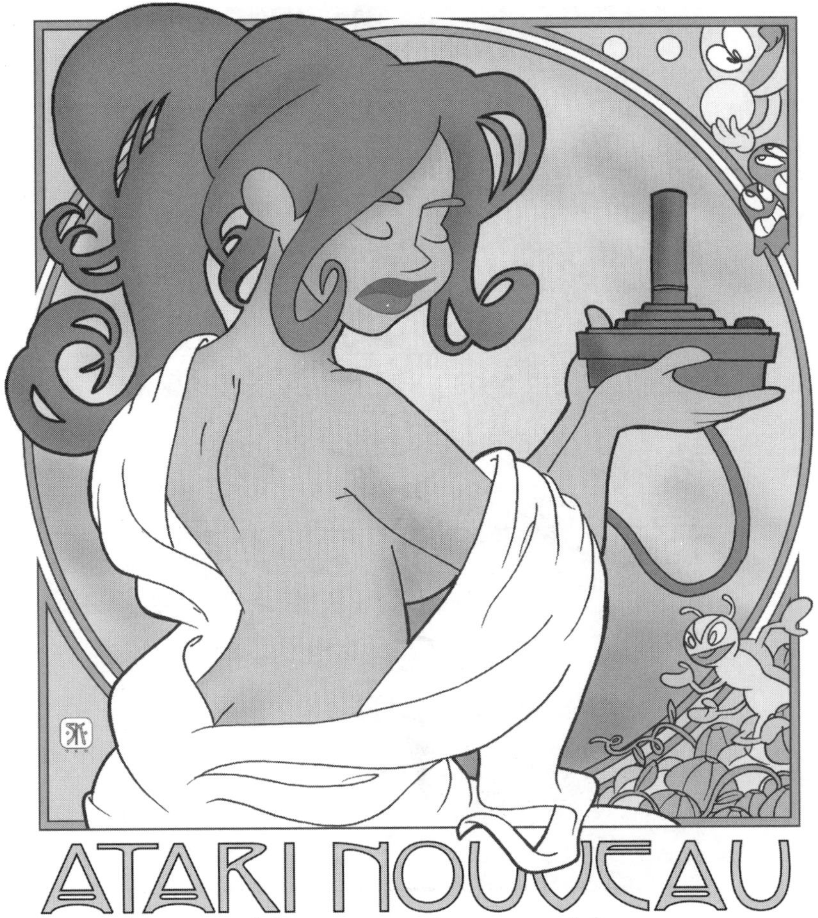
ATARI NOUVEAU

I was worried this concept wasn't strong enough for a cover so I never used it.

· EISNER UPSET ·

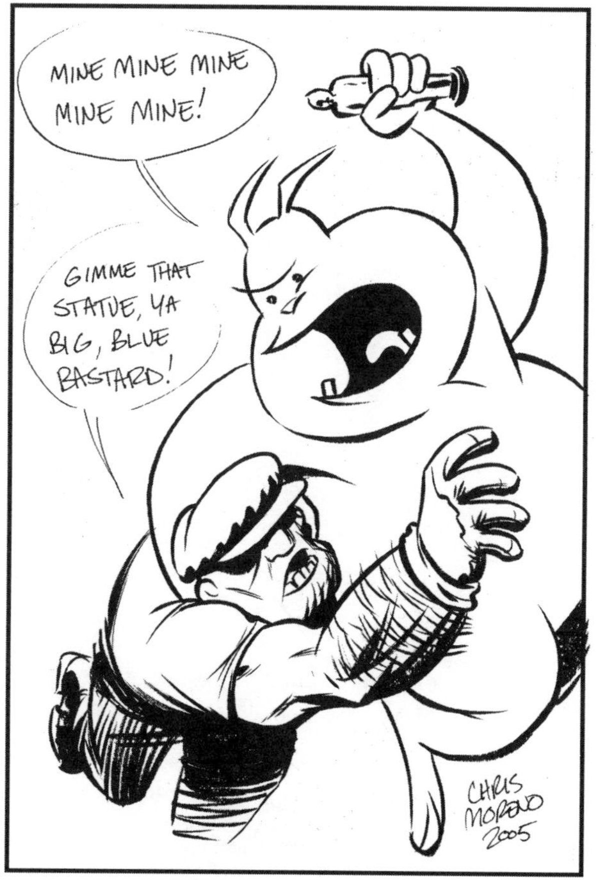
MINE MINE MINE
MINE MINE!
GIMME THAT STATUE, YA BIG, BLUE BASTARD!
CHRIS MORENO 2005

Chris Moreno drew this for me in San Diego the day after I failed to win the Eisner award for Best Writer/Artist - Humor.

· ABOUT THE AUTHOR ·

Scott Kurtz has been creating comic strips since he was
in the fourth grade. In 1998, his comic strip PvP appeared on the
web for the first time with a couple hundred readers. Today
the strip is read by over 200,000 people daily and
collected each month by Image Comics.

Scott currently resides in suburban North Texas with his
wife Angela, his basset hound Kirby, and Tiffany, the cat
he refuses to admit he likes.

Other books by Scott Kurtz
PvP: The Dork Ages
PvP: At Large
PvP: Reloaded
PvP: Rides Again
Truth, Justin and the American Way
Captain Amazing

CHECK
OUT MORE
GREAT BOOKS
FROM SCOTT
KURTZ!

PVP, VOLUME 1:
PVP AT LARGE
ISBN# 978-1-58240-374-8
$11.99

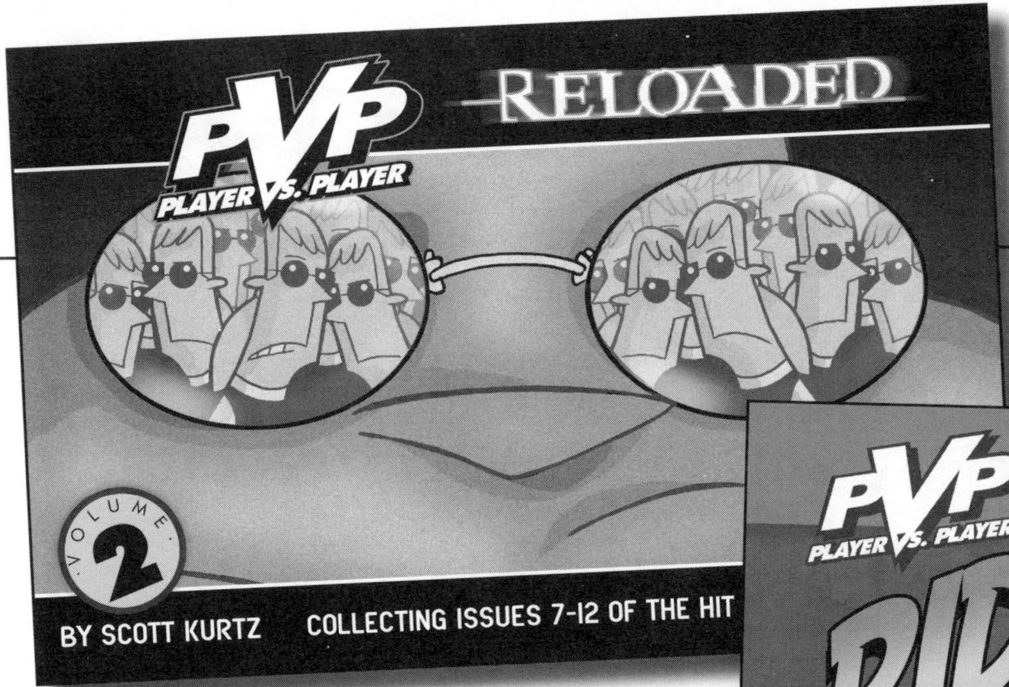
PVP
PLAYER VS. PLAYER
RELOADED
VOLUME 2
BY SCOTT KURTZ
COLLECTING ISSUES 7-12 OF THE HIT

PVP, VOLUME 2:
PVP RELOADED
ISBN# 978-1-58240-433-2
$11.95

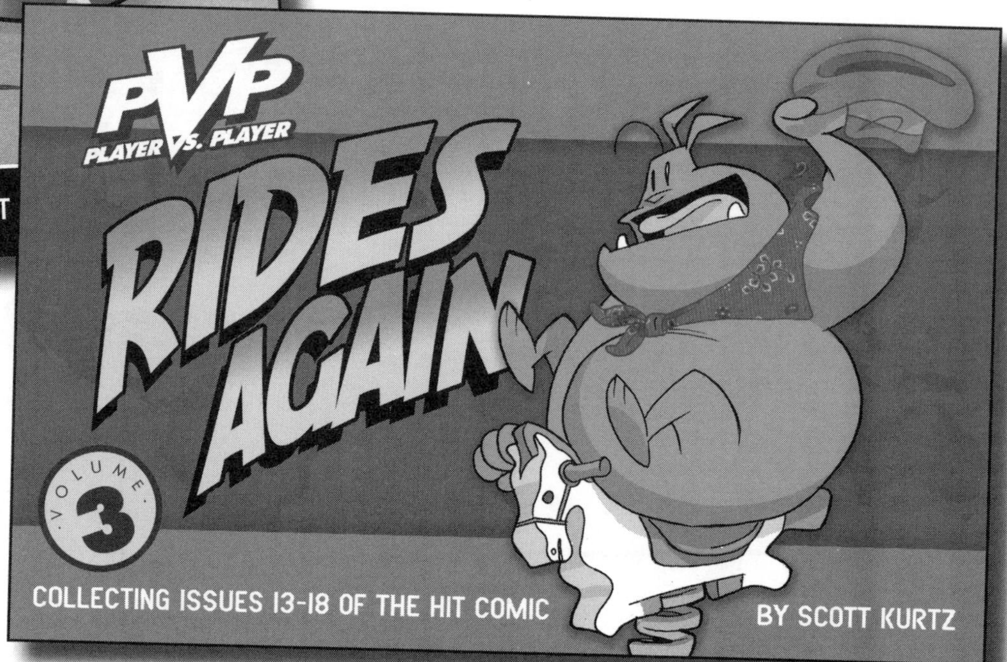
PVP
PLAYER VS. PLAYER
RIDES AGAIN
VOLUME 3
COLLECTING ISSUES 13-18 OF THE HIT COMIC
BY SCOTT KURTZ

PVP RIDES AGAIN
ISBN# 978-1-58240-553-7
$11.99